Maritime Interception and the Law of Naval Operations

Martin Fink

Maritime Interception and the Law of Naval Operations

A Study of Legal Bases and Legal Regimes in Maritime Interception Operations

ASSER PRESS

Springer

Martin Fink
Royal Netherlands Navy
The Hague
The Netherlands

ISBN 978-94-6265-248-4 ISBN 978-94-6265-249-1 (eBook)
https://doi.org/10.1007/978-94-6265-249-1

Library of Congress Control Number: 2018941214

Published by T.M.C. ASSER PRESS, The Hague, The Netherlands www.asserpress.nl
Produced and distributed for T.M.C. ASSER PRESS by Springer-Verlag Berlin Heidelberg

Printed on acid-free paper

This T.M.C. ASSER PRESS imprint is published by the registered company Springer-Verlag GmbH, DE part of Springer Nature
The registered company address is: Heidelberger Platz 3, 14197 Berlin, Germany

Acknowledgements

This study on maritime interception operations and international law is the result of my doctoral thesis, which I finished in 2016 at the University of Amsterdam. That thesis could not have been finished without the guidance and patience of my supervisor professor Terry Gill. I was privileged that I was given the opportunity to learn from him and study the international law of military operations under his wings.

As a legal officer in the Royal Netherlands Navy, the Navy provided me with the much wanted and needed experience to understand the real world of military operations. But it also gave me a reason and a basis for my academic explorations. I was lucky enough that the Royal Netherlands Navy allowed me to spend time overseas on military operations and in the academic arena, a combination that has been the fruitful soil for this book.

Looking back at the process of ultimately finishing this study, two additional reasons have made it possible. The first is that I simply enjoyed writing this book. As a labor of solace, giving me some satisfaction when adventures were too far beyond the horizon for me to see them. Second, and much more important, I was given the opportunity and time to actually write it. Because Emilie, throughout all the stages of the process, was there to command our ship, even more so when our ship grew out to become a fleet of one heavy cruiser surrounded by many small destroyers, who all wanted to sail their own course. And if writing my thesis was not enough, I extended her ordeal even more by putting her through the production of a more publishable version. And again, her patience and tight command of our fleet has pulled us through safely.

Acknowledgements

Contents

Abbreviations

AAV	Approach and assist visits
AFOR	Allied Force
AJIL	American Journal of International Law
AMISOM	African Union Mission in Somalia
AMO	Area of maritime operations
AMS	Allied maritime strategy
API	First Additional Protocol to the Geneva Convention (1977)
APII	Second Additional Protocol to the Geneva Convention (1977)
ASEAN	Association of Southeast Asian Nations
ATP	Allied tactical publication
BSA	Bilateral shipboarding agreements
BWC	Biological Weapons Convention
BYBIL	British Yearbook of International Law
CA 3	Common Article 3 of the Geneva Conventions
CENTCOM	Central Command
Chap.	Chapter
CHS	Convention on the High Seas
CJA	Council joint action
CMF	Combined maritime forces
CPA	Coalition provisional authority
CPERS	Captured persons
CTF	Combined taskforce
CWC	Chemical Weapons Convention
CYIL	Canadian Yearbook of International Law
DILS	Defense Institute of Legal Studies
DPH	Direct participation in hostilities
ECA	Effective control over an area
ECHR	European Convention on Human Rights
ECJ	European Court of Justice

ECOMOG	ECOWAS monitoring group
ECOWAS	Economic Community of West African States
ECtHR	European Court for Human Rights
EEZ	Exclusive Economic Zone
EJIL	European Journal of International Law
E-MIO	Expanded maritime interception operations
EU	European Union
EUMSS	European Union maritime security strategy
EUNAVFOR	European Union naval force
GC (I-IV)	Geneva Convention (1949) (I-IV)
GIA	Governor's Island Agreement
GMO	Grondslagen van het maritiem optreden (fundaments of naval operations)
GWOT	Global war on terror
HC	Hague Convention
Hr. Ms.	Hare Majesteits (Her Majesty)
HRC	Human Rights Council
HSC	High Seas Convention (1958)
ICC	International Criminal Court
ICCPR	International Convention on Civil and Political Rights
ICJ	International Court of Justice
ICTY	International Criminal Tribunal for the former Yugoslavia
IDF	Israel Defense Forces
IHL	International humanitarian law
IHRL	International human rights law
IHT	International Herald Tribune
ILC	International Law Commission
ILMO	International law of military operations
ILS	International law studies
IRRC	International Review of the Red Cross
IRTC	Internationally recognized transit corridor
ISAF	International Security and Assistance Force
ITLOS	International Tribunal for the Law of the Sea
IUU	Illegal, Unreported, Unregulated
IYIL	Israel Yearbook of International Law
LAF	Lebanese Armed Forces
LD	London Declaration
LEDET	Law enforcement detachments
LIO	Leadership interdiction operation
LJIL	Leiden Journal of International Law
LOAC	Law of armed conflict
MDA	Maritime domain awareness
MEO	Maritime embargo operation
MEZ	Maritime exclusion zone
MIF	Maritime interception force

MIO	Maritime interception operation
MNF-I	Multinational Force Iraq
MRT	Militair Rechtelijk Tijdschrift (Netherlands Military Law Journal)
MSA	Maritime security awareness
MSO	Maritime security operations
MTF UNIFIL	Maritime Task Force United Nations Interim Force in Lebanon
NAC	North Atlantic Council
NATO	North Atlantic Treaty Organization
NFZ	No fly zone
NGS	Naval gunfire support
NILR	Netherlands International Law Review
NJB	Nederlands Juristenblad
NLMARFOR	Netherlands maritime force
NLR	Naval Law Review
NMIOTC	NATO maritime interdiction operations training center
NNN	Non NATO Nations
NPT	Non-proliferation treaty
NWCR	Naval War College Review
NYIL	Netherlands Yearbook of International Law
OAE	Operation Active Endeavour
OAP	Operation Allied Protector (I)/Provider (II)
OCD	Operation Change Direction
OCL	Operation Cast Lead
ODIL	Ocean Development and International Law
OEF	Operation Enduring Freedom
OIF	Operation Iraqi Freedom
OOD	Operation Odyssey Dawn
OOS	Operation Ocean Shield
OSG	Operation Sea Guardian
OUP	Operation Unified Protector
PCA	Permanent Court of Arbitration
PICJ	Permanent Court of International Justice
PSI	Proliferation Security Initiative
PSO	Peace support operations
PW	Prisoners of war
Rhib	Rigid hull inflatable boats
RNLN	Royal Netherlands Navy
ROE	Rules of engagement
SAA	State agent authority
SACEUR	Supreme Allied Commander Europe
SC Res.	Security Council Resolution
SFIR	Stabilization Force Iraq
SHADE	Shared awareness and deconfliction (-meeting)

SNMG	Standing NATO maritime group
SRM	San Remo Manual
STANAVFORMED	Standing Naval Forces Mediterranean
STROGOPS	Strait of Gibraltar Operations
SUA	Convention on the suppression of unlawful acts at sea
TFG	Transitional federal government
UK	United Kingdom
UN	United Nations
UNBEF	United Nations blockading and escorting force
UNCLOS	United Nations Convention on the Law of the Sea
UNFICYP	United Nations Force in Cyprus
UNGA	United Nations General Assembly
UNIFIL	United Nations Interim Force in Lebanon
UNMIH	United Nations Mission in Haiti
UNSC	United Nations Security Council
UNSG	United Nations Secretary-General
US	United States of America
USS	United States Ship
VJIL	Virginia Journal of International Law
VPD	Vessel protection detachment
WEU	West European Union
WFP	World Food Program
WMD	Weapons of mass destruction
YIHL	Yearbook of International Humanitarian Law
YILC	Yearbook of the International Law Commission
Zr. Ms.	Zijne Majesteits (His Majesty)

Part I
General Aspects of Maritime Interception Operations

Chapter 1
Introduction: Maritime Interception and the Law of Naval Operations

There is no mystery about the war at sea, though like all science and art it can be obscured by skillful elaboration.
—Carlyon Bellairs (1871–1955), Commander Royal Navy

Contents

1.1 Introduction

In 2006, on board the Netherlands warship *Hr. Ms. De Zeven Provinciën* operating in Operation *Enduring Freedom*,[1] a USCENTCOM[2] unclassified slide came to my attention containing a matrix with a number of legal bases for the different maritime interception operations that were being conducted by US naval forces around the Arabian Peninsula. Glancing over this matrix, my first thoughts were that it must be a challenge for warship-commanders to separate all those legal bases and authorities and apply them correctly to the situations they could potentially encounter at sea. At that moment, *Hr. Ms. De Zeven Provinciën* was operating in the Indian Ocean, in Taskforce 150. The legal environment at the time in the seas around the Arabian

[1] Bellairs 1919, p. 41.
[2] United States Central Command.

M. Fink, *Maritime Interception and the Law of Naval Operations*,
https://doi.org/10.1007/978-94-6265-249-1_1

Peninsula was a complex situation. A multitude of military operations were and had been conducted in these seas that had either a maritime dimension or were primarily a naval operation. Many of the conflicts with a maritime dimension in the Middle East, Near East and Northern Africa come together in these seas; from counter-piracy operations off the coast of Somalia and the Gulf of Aden, to the search for terrorists as a result of the attacks on the United States on 11 September 2001. The Persian Gulf and the Red Sea have been a constant theatre for naval operations ever since the start of the Iraq-Iran War in 1980, with periodically changing legal frameworks constantly adapting to the political situation of conflicts in the region. In the Persian Gulf, over the last twenty five years warships of many different States have been tasked with a diverse range of operations, ranging from convoy operations to support the freedom of navigation, enforcing UN-mandated embargos, and executing the belligerent right of visit and search during the situations of armed conflict. In recent years, so-called maritime security operations have been added to this list. All this naval activity urges to a study of legal frameworks applicable to maritime interception operations, having the words of Mark Janis in the back of my mind: 'States may use their navies to demonstrate and enforce their perception of the proper law of the sea. If such naval operations are consistent, effective and accepted, customary international law of the sea may develop. But if such naval operations are inconsistent, ineffective, or resisted, chaos may result.'[3]

During the last decades, naval operations that have become known as 'maritime interception operations' (MIO) have grown to become a well-established operational activity for navies around the world. As Craig Allen notes, MIO are: '[A] familiar element in the daily routine of units assigned to the maritime component of combined and joint forces commands in some theaters'.[4] Allen's comes from a US perspective, but his observation can be applied to many other navies. Maritime interception operations have firmly established themselves as one of the roles for navies and have found its way into the maritime doctrines of States and international organizations. The establishment of a NATO Centre of Excellence for maritime interception operations (NMIOTC)[5] in Crete, Greece, in 2004[6] for the purpose of training and education on all aspects of MIO, from tactics to doctrine, is one example that shows the increased attention and importance to MIO.

Next to being a well-accepted role for naval forces, the challenges that naval forces are confronted with while conducting MIO have evolved. In particular, maritime interception operations face the challenge of operating in an environment in which the legal character of the conflict may not be clear. Also, next to

---

[3] Janis 1976, p. 75.

[4] Allen 2007, p. 1.

[5] NATO maritime interdiction operations training center. See their homepage at: www.nmiotc.nato.int.

[6] Roberts 2009, p. 10.

non-international armed conflicts, the emergence of a focus on human beings poses new practical and legal challenges for maritime interception operations. Whereas the early MIO were focused on goods, today individuals can also be the subject of MIO. This grown importance of persons as part of the focus in MIO surfaces other legal issues, such as the applicability of human rights law and detention and handling of persons at sea.

The legal aspects connected to maritime interception operations are manifold and will expand the more one considers maritime interception operations in a broader context. In the widest sense, MIO are not a stand-alone activity at sea, but involve activities both in the stage before and after the actual interception at sea. Examples of legal efforts in the phase before are the establishment of legal frameworks to form partnerships or mutual cooperation, collecting and exchanging information between States and organizations and adopting domestic laws that enable States through their naval forces to act, to confiscate goods sanctioned by the UN, or to enable a court of law to adjudicate a prize case. All of these activities are connected to the actual boarding operation at sea. The counter-piracy operations off the coast of Somalia have highlighted that the aftermath of interception operations is equally important to succeed in effectively combating piracy at sea. This is a phase that is now more commonly known as the 'legal finish'. Many legal questions exist in this phase, such as what to do with persons and goods once they are intercepted at sea and how they could be transferred to a court of law. Counter-piracy operations also firmly established the importance of international human rights law to maritime interception operations. Counter-piracy operations have underlined the need to view MIO not solely as a naval activity, but as an activity that needs an interagency approach with the involvement and cooperation of other governmental agencies, such as the departments of Justice and Foreign Affairs. As Brian Wilson mentions, 'The governance challenge is ensuring the existence of a process to acquire and validate information and align efforts across multiple agencies – or even nations. Effectively countering transnational criminal activities on the high seas imposes greater demand for integration.'[7] The core legal issues *at sea,* however, revolve around the notion that maritime interception operations include the boarding of foreign-flagged vessels and a possible subsequent capture of ships, goods and detention of persons. As Chap. 3 will underline, the term MIO has evolved in such a manner that it has moved away from the view that MIO has a distinct legal framework of its own. Instead, as MIO are nowadays conducted as part of international armed conflicts, during counter-piracy operations or anti-terrorism operations and to implement UN mandates, today maritime interception operations can be based on different legal frameworks.

[7] Wilson 2016, p. 154.

1.2 Purpose of the Study

This study examines the scope and content of the international law applicable to maritime interception operations. The general aim is to provide a structural analysis of law and practice of maritime interception operations. This study views the law applicable to maritime interception from a broad perspective of international law rather than the more usual point of view that is based solely on the legal possibilities to board foreign-flagged vessels available within the law of the sea.[8] In my opinion, this approach better connects with the current day threats in the maritime dimension and the legal discussions that emerge from those threats. Consequently, however, the study will primarily provide a broad overview rather than a very detailed legal analysis of certain specific aspects of maritime interception. Additionally, this broad approach to the law applicable to maritime interception allows for a study of how different legal frameworks interrelate within the context of such naval operations. Maritime interception, therefore, are discussed within the scope of general international law that applies to naval operations as a whole. This is, however, limited to a number of limitations mentioned in the following paragraphs. The first is that maritime interception operations will be analysed within the limits of international peace and security. The second is that the study is limited to naval operations outside the territorial sovereignty of a State or its functional jurisdiction in coastal areas that possess sovereign rights. Third and last is that this study focuses on contemporary naval operations.

1.2.1 Naval Operations and International Peace and Security

What law applies to maritime interception can be analysed from different angles of international law. Douglas Guilfoyle's study on *Shipping interdiction and the law of the sea* (2009) has focused on interception from primarily a law enforcement perspective. Guilfoyle has used the term 'maritime policing' to cover a number of subjects that deal with interception on the high seas, such as violence against shipping, piracy, smuggling, counter-proliferation, and human food security, all of which are 'matters of State security interest'.[9] Natalie Klein's study *Maritime security and the law of the sea* (2011) has taken the notion of maritime security as the central matter, in which maritime interception operations play a significant role to enhance maritime security.[10] Another study that needs mentioning in this context

[8] Arguably, the term 'law of the sea' includes both peacetime and wartime international law that applies at sea. Today, it seems to be more occupied with peacetime law of the sea rather than to include also the law applicable during time of war or conflict.

[9] Guilfoyle 2009, p. 24.

[10] Klein 2011, p. 9.

is the study by Efthymios Papastravridis, *The Interception of Vessels on the High Seas* (2013). He has taken a more general and theoretical approach to maritime interception, centralizing the area of the high seas from which interception operations are considered. Apart from these three monographs, other studies exist that analyse aspects of the laws applicable to maritime interception from a specific topic, such as the interception of weapons of mass destruction, piracy, armed conflict or UN-mandated embargo operations. This study focuses in particular on naval operations undertaken by a State in support of international peace and security. The first part of this focus includes the term 'naval operations'. This term is used to focus on operations conducted by the military at sea. The term 'naval operations' is more limited than the term 'maritime operations', excluding operations that are executed by State organs outside the military. 'Naval' refers to the use of military forces and assets at sea, whereas 'maritime' encompasses also non-military operations at sea by a State, such as coastguard operations or maritime police operations to deal with illegal fishing or customs issues.[11] 'Maritime' is a broader term that encompasses all activities of a State in relation to the sea.

The second part of the focus is 'international peace and security'. What constitutes international peace and security, or a threat or breach thereof, is determined by the UN Security Council (UNSC) and is not pre-defined. It is, however, interpreted in an extensive manner, not just to include breaches of the prohibition of the use of force in international relations, but also to include serious and widespread violations of human rights or criminal acts that have large effects on the security interests of States.[12] In the last decade, the UNSC has determined that acts of terrorism[13] constitutes a threat to international peace and security,[14] and has taken a similar approach with regard to piracy.[15] As a result of the scope of what the UNSC determines as threats or breaches of international peace and security, naval

---

[11] Although it is understood that in some States coastguard vessels can belong to the armed forces and may even by deployed expeditionary to theatres of conflict.

[12] Blokker 2005, p. 13.

[13] SC Res. 1368 (2001) notes the following:

> 1. Unequivocally condemns in the strongest terms the horrifying terrorist attacks which took place on 11 September 2001 in New York, Washington, D.C. and Pennsylvania and regards such acts, like any act of international terrorism, as a threat to international peace and security;
>
> See also SC Res. 2249 (2015) adopted by the Council after the "Paris 2" terrorist attacks in Paris on 18 November 2015.

[14] Some operations, such as the maritime security operations that are conducted under CTF 152, include a mandate to act against drug trafficking. It is, however, not an activity that has been determined by the UNSC as a breach of international peace and security.

[15] Although the piracy resolutions state that action is taken under Chapter VII of the UN Charter, the UNSC did not explicitly determine piracy to constitute a threat to international peace and security. The first resolution on piracy, SC Res. 1816 (2008) notes the following:

> Determining that the incidents of piracy and armed robbery against vessels in the territorial waters of Somalia and the high seas off the coast of Somalia exacerbate the situation in

operations have also moved into the realm of operations that can be characterized as law enforcement operations. A law enforcement task for naval forces is by itself not a new phenomenon as, for example, acting against piracy has already been a task for warships for centuries. And outside the scope of international peace and security naval forces are deployed to intercept illegal activities of drug smuggling or illegal fishing patrols. A Netherlands warship acting against piracy in the North Sea would be labelled as maritime policing, while that same warship deployed in Operation *Atalanta* in the Gulf of Aden would perform its task within the context of international peace and security because the Security Council has determined the situation in Somalia as a threat to peace and security of which piracy is an aggravating factor.[16] Apart from the approach that the UNSC defines international peace and security, the focus on international peace and security in this study is viewed in the more general sense to mean subjects that may fall within the scope of international peace and security. Typically, what belongs to the spectrum of upholding or restoring international peace and security are maritime interception operations conducted during peace support operations and armed conflicts (Fig. 1.1).

1.2.2 Operations Outside the Territorial Sovereignty of a State

The second limitation is a geographical one. This study only considers activities of warships outside the territorial sovereignty of a State. This excludes, therefore, a State's internal and territorial waters. In other words, the study will focus on naval operations on the high seas and the zones to which the regime of the high seas is made applicable. Article 86 of the *United Nations Convention on the Law of the Sea* (UNCLOS)[17] states that the high seas are those parts of sea that are not included in the exclusive economic zone, the territorial sea, the internal waters of a State, or in the archipelagic waters of an archipelagic State. UNCLOS furthermore states that a number of rules of the high seas,[18] which include the freedoms of the high seas and acting against piracy, are also applicable in the Exclusive Economic Zone (EEZ) of a coastal State under the limiting condition of due regard.[19] The essence of this

Somalia which continues to constitute a threat to international peace and security in the region, Acting under Chapter VII of the Charter of the United Nations.

[16] With regard to types of counter-piracy operations, Zheng has noted two types of international cooperation between States on the issue of piracy: the Malacca way, which relates to cooperation between coastal States, and the Somali way, which relates to the cooperation between flag States. Zheng 2012, p. 304.

[17] *United Nations Convention on the Law of the Sea*, Montego Bay 10 December 1982.

[18] Articles 88–115 UNCLOS.

[19] Article 58(2) UNCLOS.

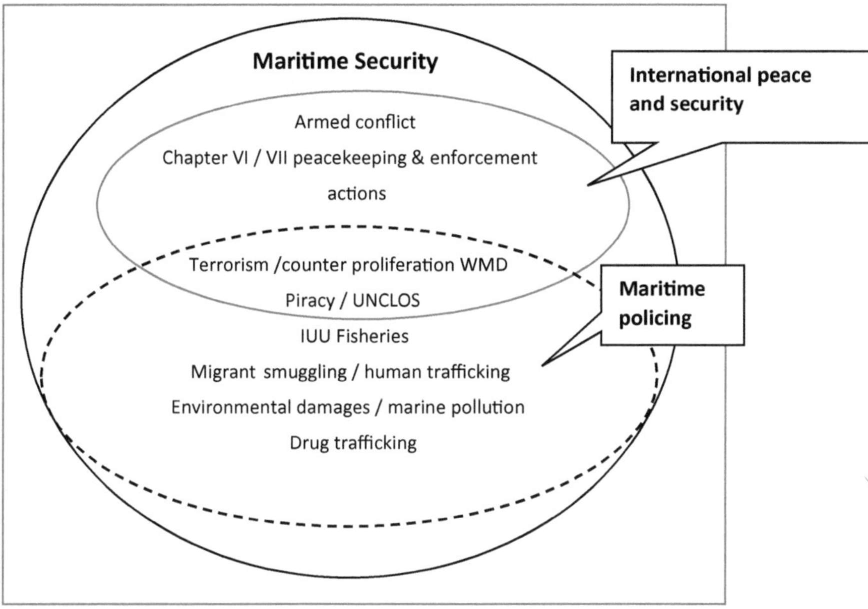

Fig. 1.1 Spectrums of maritime security, maritime policing and international peace and security (*Source* M. Fink)

geographical limitation in this study is that it will not take a coastal State's approach and will not consider how coastal States can conduct interception operations in their own territory.[20] I will not, therefore, include the seaward stretch of the jurisdiction of a State and the legal frameworks applicable in the maritime zones where coastal States have either complete or functional jurisdiction over maritime zones.

1.2.3 Contemporary Naval Operations

The third delineation is a temporal one. Maritime interception operations are a current issue of which its historical roots could probably be traced back all the way to Roman or Greek naval history and its laws. Even Julius Caesar experienced his share of piracy in the Mediterranean Sea.[21] 'There was never a time when piracy was not practiced, nor may it cease as long as the nature of mankind remains the

[20] For example, an interception operation that is conducted outside territorial waters based on the right of hot pursuit. See Article 111 UNCLOS.

[21] Plutarch 1925, p. 2; Suetonius 1957, p. 10; Goldsworthy 2006, pp. 75–78.

same', wrote the prophetical Roman consul Cassius Dio.[22] Centuries later, in the 16th century,[23] the Knights of St. John were engaged to rid the Mediterranean of Barbarossa's corsairs.[24] Clearly, we must also not forget the interception of the Portuguese vessel *Santa Catharina* in 1603 as a result of which Hugo de Groot took up his pen defining the fundamentals of the law of the sea for centuries to come, the boarding and subsequent burning of the *Caroline* in 1837 that resulted in the famous *Caroline-criteria* for anticipatory self-defence, the hand-to-hand fighting between the boarding party of *HMS Cossack* and the defenders of the German auxiliary vessel *Altmark* in 1940 in Norwegian territorial waters, or the Greek tanker *Joanna V* that ignored the orders to divert after being boarded by the UK warship *HMS Berwick* in 1966 during the Rhodesia crisis, in which the UNSC for the first time used its enforcement powers to authorize a maritime interception operation, to name just a few maritime interceptions that helped develop international law. However, as Chap. 3 will elaborate on, the 'modern' use of the term MIO was introduced and accepted after the Cold War, during the Iraq-Kuwait crisis in 1990. Logically, since then the term has also spurred authors to look back into history to look for comparable naval operations in the past, such as the operations during the Korean War (1950–1953), the Algerian crisis (1954), the India-Pakistan conflict (1974), the Cuban crisis (1961), and the Beira Patrol (1968–1975).[25] This study will draw a temporal line by starting to follow the path that MIO has taken since the 1990 Iraq-Kuwait crisis to the present day.[26] A few situations that occurred earlier and which cannot be left out of a proper analysis of MIO will be given attention.

1.3 What Are Maritime Interception Operations?

Although the term MIO is a well-accepted term, there is no internationally and generally accepted definition of MIO. Obviously, definitions exist in national military manuals or other documents that originate from governments, but there is no internationally and generally recognized definition. There is not even agreement on what the acronym should stand for. Some refer to *interception* operations while

---

[22] MacCartney 1925, p. 177. The *Lex Gabina*, promulgated in 67 BC gave Cneius Pompei the possibility to build a large fleet to destroy the piracy threat in the Mediterranean Sea. See on the *Lex Gabina*, Appendix E of Ormerod 1924.

[23] It is noted here that there is a legal difference between pirates and corsairs (or privateers). The latter, as opposed to the first, are commissioned by a State to raid on the State's enemy. The Declaration of Paris (1856) declared for the signatories that 'privateering is and remains abolished'.

[24] Bradford 1972, Chap. 18.

[25] Robertson 1991, pp. 289–299.

[26] This study was concluded in 2016.

others refer to *interdiction* operations.[27] Nuances may also exist between these terms, one of which is that 'interception' is viewed as being the limited activity to stop a vessel, whereas 'interdiction' has a wider interpretation to include all kinds of interference over a foreign-flagged vessel.[28] The choice of using either one of them may also be subject to what is commonly used within the particular field of law. Maritime interception is, for example, commonly used in the issue of refugees at sea. Be that as it may, both terms are usually used in an intermixed manner for the purpose of expressing generally the same thing.[29]

To define what MIO are, it is important to note from the outset, as Heintschel von Heinegg has very rightly noted, that MIO should be considered an operational term of art which encompasses a certain activity at sea.[30] It is not a legal term. This means that the term does not come with a legal framework of its own. In the early days, when MIO were synonymous with maritime embargo operations conducted within the legal basis of the UN collective security system, it was understandable to consider this legal basis as a particular feature connected to MIO. But as Chap. 3 will underline, the term MIO is now used in a much broader sense. The Royal Netherlands Navy most recent definition on MIO dates from 2014 and considers that the aim of MIO is to stop certain categories of goods or individuals that are in or pass through a certain sea area.[31] In 2005, NATO's main publication on MIO, *Allied Tactical Publication* (ATP) 71, defined MIO as: 'A maritime interdiction operation (MIO) encompasses seaborne enforcement measures to intercept the movement of certain types of designated items into or out of a nation or specific area'.[32] The Dutch definition submits that MIO can also include the interception of

---

[27] To name a few examples of several States and international organizations: NATO refers to maritime interdiction operations. The EU appears to use maritime interception, mostly in the context of the refugees at sea issues. The Netherlands Maritime Doctrine (Grondslagen van Maritiem Optreden, GMO) uses maritime interdiction operations. The UK refers in its *British Maritime Doctrine* (BR 1806, 3rd ed 2004) to the NATO doctrines and thus refers to interdiction rather than interception.

[28] A view that is for instance held by Commander (US Navy JAG) Smart, who states in her paper (Smart 2015, footnote 4) that:

> Maritime interception operations (as opposed to maritime interdiction operations) are a form or subset of interdiction used for sanction enforcement that are military or legal in nature, and serve both political and military purposes. Like the broader category of maritime interdiction operations, the political objective is to compel a country or group to conform to the objectives of the initiating body, while the military objective focuses on establishing a barrier that is selective, allowing only authorized goods or persons to enter or exit.

[29] Papastavridis 2013, pp. 60–61; Carr 2002, p. 3.

[30] Heintschel von Heinegg 2015, p. 375.

[31] GMO 2014, p. 385. *In Dutch:* Een maritieme interdictie operatie (MIO) is een operatie die wordt uitgevoerd om het transport van bepaalde goederen of personen door of in een bepaald zeegebied te voorkomen.

[32] NATO ATP 71 2005, p. 1-1. At: http://www.navedu.navy.mi.th/stg/databasestory/data/laukniyom/ship-active/big-country-ship/United-States/ATP/ATP_71.pdf.

persons. This is in fact one of the important developments in conducting MIO. Interestingly, having understood this development, NATO has included persons in its MIO-definition when it updated its MIO-publication in 2013. The definition in current version of ATP 71 now reads: 'An operation conducted to enforce prohibition on the movement of specified persons or materials within a defined geographic area'.[33] Several definitions exist in US-documents on MIO. The US-doctrine on *Command and Control in Maritime Operations* (2013) understands MIO to be 'efforts to monitor, query, and board merchant vessels in international waters to enforce sanctions against other nations such as those in support of United Nations Security Council resolutions (UNSCRs) and/or prevent the transport of restricted goods'.[34] Another US publication, Joint Publication (3-03) on interdiction operations defines MIO in a number of ways, essentially, that its purpose is to interdict goods or persons prohibited by a lawful sanction.[35] This may be done on the basis of a UN resolution, through the use of belligerent visit and search and, according to the US-doctrine, pursuant the right of self-defence.[36] As such, apart from the understanding that MIO can now include the interception of both goods *and* persons, this last remark also points out that different legal bases can apply to MIO.[37]

Some authors reserve the term MIO for naval operations that are governed by the law of naval warfare.[38] Heintschel von Heinegg makes a clear distinction between naval operations that are conducted in the context of the law of naval warfare, and MIO to which the legal regime of the law of armed conflict is not applicable: 'It is important to note that MIO are naval operations which are not governed by the law of naval warfare'.[39] 'MIO', he continues, 'are measures used in times of peace or of crisis only'. He does not appear to disagree, however, that interception operations based on the law of naval warfare and interceptions outside this framework may not be distinguishable from each other on the practical operational level. Others use it in a broader sense, to include both warfare and law enforcement operations.[40]

---

[33] NATO ATP 71 2013, p. 1-1.

[34] US DoD, Joint Publication 3-32, p. xiv.

[35] US DoD, Joint Publication 3-03, pp. 1–8.

[36] US DoD, Joint Publication 3-03, p. II-5.

[37] The EU, another actor within the realm of international peace and security, uses the term maritime interception. Although no definition appears to exist, maritime interception within the EU is primarily focused on trafficking of persons by sea, such as refugees, but also on pirates.

[38] E.g. Allen. He notes that MIO in US-doctrine only applies to situations outside armed conflict (Allen 2014), but also seems to generalize the term to a broader scope, as he uses the term 'peacetime MIO', to exclude MIO that are conducted under the law of naval warfare. The word "peacetime" is in fact redundant if there was absolute consistency that the term MIO is only used outside armed conflict.

[39] Heintschel von Heinegg 2015, p. 376.

[40] Guilfoyle 2015, n. 44.

The distinction to reserve the term MIO solely for situations outside armed conflict is attractive in terms of its clarity. It is also understandable from the perspective of the historical evolution of the term. Arguments to define the scope of MIO in a different way, however, also exist. A broader view is that as an ultimate consequence of MIO being an operational term of art, this operational art of MIO can also be -and is- used in situations of armed conflict. Secondly, MIO undertaken, within the context of Chapter VII of the UN Charter within an *all necessary means*-mandate could also rise to a level of hostilities against another State where the law of naval warfare may become applicable. Some States argued during Operation *Enduring Freedom* that the law of naval warfare applied, to which the term MIO by that time had expanded into. Furthermore, in military practice the term MIO is now used in the widest sense, including peace, crisis *and* armed conflict circumstances, in which an interception operation could take place. This broad use of the term is, for instance, also underlined in the 2013 Netherlands Maritime Doctrine that states that MIO can be conducted in a number of situations, ranging from armed conflict to illegal smuggling of drugs.[41] It is also underlined in the above-mentioned US-description of MIO. Operationally, a broad view also makes sense, because MIO are an operational tool consisting of a certain activity that tactically does not differ much in how it is performed in armed conflict, crisis or peacetime circumstances. There is merit, therefore, not to focus on a legal divide in which the line of separation is whether or not the law of naval warfare applies, but to take the operational point of view as the starting point. This will lead to include that MIO can also be conducted within the context of the law of naval warfare, which is ultimately the consequence of defining MIO as a term of operational art, rather than legal term. As a last, not wholly legal, argument but which should not to be completely ignored, is that MIO in 'every day speak' within the naval, defence and security organizations is simply used to define an activity in which the core is to board another vessel for certain purposes. In this context, although admitting that this has been different during the early stages of MIO, military definitions of MIO today do not limit its application to be applied only outside armed conflict. This study will take the broad view. As will be elaborated upon in Chap. 2, maritime interception operations should not be mis-characterized as being similar to maritime security operations (MSO). This term *is* generally accepted to be reserved for naval operations that are outside armed conflict. To sum up, for the purpose of this book, MIO will be defined as: naval operations that include the boarding, search and seizure of goods and the detention of persons on a foreign-flagged vessel, outside the sovereign jurisdiction of a State.

[41] GMO 2014, p. 342.

1.4 Maritime Interception Operations and the Right of Visit

Because the essence of maritime interception operations by warships involves the stopping of goods and persons at sea on foreign-flagged vessels, there may be something to say for replacing the broadly taken title of *Maritime interception and the law of naval operations* by 'The right of visit by warships on the high seas'. Much of the literature concerning maritime interception operations approaches MIO from a right of visit perspective. The laws applicable to maritime interception and the right of visit are, however, not completely interchangeable. The different manifestations of the right of visit only partly consider the question concerning legal bases and regimes for maritime interception operations. Whereas a classic right of visit approach could touch upon, for instance, the right of self-defence as a legal basis, and international the law of the sea or the law of naval warfare as applicable legal frameworks, it will not necessarily consider other possible applicable legal bases and regimes, such as *ad hoc* consent as a basis or international human rights law as a regime. Although one would logically start by finding the legal framework for MIO within the laws that regulate activities at sea, centralizing maritime interception operations rather than centralizing one specific body of law allows to analyse the applicable law to maritime interception operations through more legal frameworks that might possible regulate MIO. Exchanging the law applicable to MIO for the right of visit, therefore, does not grasp the complete scope of the law that could apply to it.

The law of naval operations with regard to maritime interception is still more limited to what is nowadays by some authors described as 'international law of maritime security'. Kraska and Pedrozo define international maritime security law as: 'legal authorities to counter traditional and conventional threats, as well as irregular and asymmetric dangers against the territorial integrity or political independence of flag, port, coastal and land-locked States'.[42] The scope of the law of naval operations with regard to maritime interception is more limited. It firstly does not focus on legal authorities that coastal States may have in their maritime zones, but approaches the law from the perspective of State authorities that warships can execute outside the sovereign territory of a State. It, for example, excludes the legal possibilities that States may have to enhance their port security. Secondly, in this study the law of maritime interception in naval operations is limited to issues within the context of international peace and security. Maritime *safety*, which is obviously an intimate 'dancing-partner' with *security* in the sense that it aims to minimize danger in the maritime environment, and which is part of the broader maritime security law, is not dealt with in this book.[43]

---

[42] Kraska and Pedrozo 2013, p. 6.

[43] Aspects of maritime safety are those subjects that deal for instance with construction or equipment of the vessel, the labour conditions under which the crews operate, the manner in which way cargo is being shipped and navigational aspects of sailing a vessel. Maritime safety and

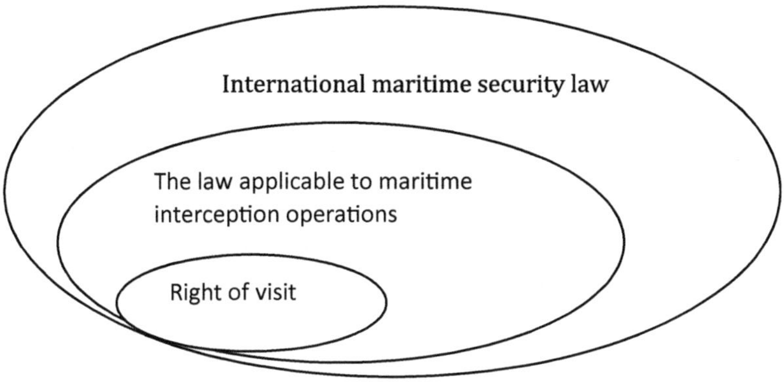

Fig. 1.2 Relationship between the right of visit, the law applicable to maritime interception operations and international maritime security law (*Source* M. Fink)

A separate law of maritime interception operations does not exist. Maritime interception operations are subject to the various rules of international law and not a separate category of its own. While on the one hand, as Guilfoyle suggests, 'There may be a law that is generally applicable to how interdictions are conducted and to the consequences of wrongfully conducted interdictions before national tribunals,'[44] on the other hand, the challenges of these various rules applied specifically to maritime interception may, however, surface a certain uniqueness as to how these rules interrelate. There is, therefore, merit in bringing together the various rules and areas of international law from the perspective of the law applicable to maritime interception operations (Fig. 1.2).

One remark is to be made with regard to the term used in the title of this book, namely *The law of naval operations*. In the last decade the subject of international law applicable to military operations has earned a place of its own within the international legal arena. It comes even with its own acronym: ILMO, International Law of Military Operations. This way of dividing international law does not come so much from the idea that the international law of military operations is a separate legal framework with new or different law, but it underlines the understanding that the legal environment of military operations must be seen as having to apply a number of legal frameworks in a special context. During military operations different legal frameworks come together, raising discussion on how these frameworks interrelate and should be applied in particular situations. One of the consequences of a complete melting away of the division between war and peace, the use of military means outside the context of armed conflict and the expanding scope of application of certain legal frameworks, such as human rights law, urge for a more

security have the common objective of ensuring minimizing all possible dangers for vessel and crew. Maritime safety approaches that objective by trying to minimize accidents, whereas maritime security seeks to minimize the intentional damage or harm to vessel and crews.

[44] Guilfoyle 2009, p. 344.

comprehensive view towards applicable law during military operations. It is by far not enough to look at military operations solely through the lens of the law of armed conflict. As Gill and Fleck mention, in their explanation on what ILMO stands for, 'the international law of military operations comprises of all areas of public international law which relate to subjects such as legal bases, legal regimes, command and control, deployment of forces and the status of forces abroad.'[45] In the same sense, the term *The law of naval operations* is not a separate legal framework of its own, but can be considered to be a subset of the international law of military operations that applies to military operations conducted at sea.

1.5 Structure

The issue of maritime interception operations and its applicable law is analysed by exploring two main and familiar themes of international law in the context of military operations. The first theme (explored in Part II) is the legal bases in international law to conduct MIO. The legal basis in this context refers to the legal authority to conduct maritime interception operations. The sub-question of this Part is what legal bases exist and what challenges emerge from applying these legal bases to MIO? The second theme relates to the legal regimes applicable to MIO. The legal regime refers to the bodies of international law that regulate actions taken during interception operations. For instance the application of force while boarding a vessel or the right to detain a person on board. This theme, which is central to Part III, is touched upon through three specific activities during a MIO, namely the right of visit, the application of force and detention. The two themes, legal bases and regimes, considered in Parts II and III are the main body of the analysis. Added to this are a general part (Part I) and conclusions (Part IV). More in detail these four Parts consist of the following chapters:

Part I consists of a general introduction and contains a brief sketch of the context in which naval operations take place (Chap. 2). It furthermore addresses contemporary maritime interception operations by means of a short history of the evolution of the term MIO in four strands (Chap. 3). This chapter will also introduce significant naval operations and incidents that occurred in which MIO has formed a part of the operation.[46] Chapter 4 will consider the two fundamental ground-rules of the international law of the sea as a legal point of departure that are central to the law applicable to maritime interception operations.

Part II consists of four chapters (Chaps. 5–8) and will study the different legal bases for maritime interception operations. These legal bases for MIO are a combination of the generally accepted exceptions on the use of armed force and the notion of general international law where States can allow other States to conduct activities within their own area of jurisdiction, either by *ad hoc consent* or consent

[45] Gill and Fleck 2015, p. 3.

[46] A shortlist of vessels and naval operations is provided in Annex A and Annex B respectively.

through international agreements. Part II will therefore analyse four legal bases: the collective security system, self-defence, (*ad hoc*) consent and international agreements.

Part III will discuss the legal regimes applicable during maritime interception operations. International human rights law and the law of armed conflict will play a central role in this part. The legal regimes will be touched upon through the lens of three particular subjects: the right of visit (Chap. 9), the application of force (Chap. 10) and detention at sea (Chap. 11). Lastly, Part IV (Chap. 12) will consist of concluding remarks.

References

Allen C (2007) A Primer on the non-proliferation regime for maritime security operation forces. Naval Law Review 54 pp. 1–28

Allen CH (2014) International law for seagoing officers, 6th edn. Naval Institute Press, Annapolis, Maryland

Bellairs C (1919) The battle of Jutland. The sowing and the reaping. Hodder & Stoughton, London

Blokker N (2005) The Security Council and the use of force – one recent practice. In: Blokker N, Schrijver N (eds) The Security Council and the use of force. Theory and reality - A need for a change. Martinus Nijhoff Publishers, Leiden/Boston, pp. 1–30

BR 1806 (2004) British Maritime Doctrine, 3rd edn. The Stationary Office, Norwich

Bradford E (1972) The Shield and the Sword. The Knights of St John. Penguin Classic, London

Carr A (2002) Maritime interdiction operations in support of the counter-terrorism war. Naval War College paper

Gill T, Fleck D (2015) Concept and sources of the international law on military operations. In: Gill T, Fleck D (eds) The Handbook of the International Law of Military Operations, 2nd edn. Oxford University Press, New York

Goldsworthy A (2006) Caesar. Life of a colossus. Yale University Press, New Haven/London

Guilfoyle D (2009) Shipping interdiction and the law of the sea. Cambridge University Press, New York

Guilfoyle D (2015) The use of force against pirates. In: Weller M (ed) The Oxford Handbook of the Use of Force in International Law. Oxford University Press, New York, pp. 1057–1076

Heintschel von Heinegg W (2015) Maritime interception/interdiction operations. In: Gill T, Fleck D (eds) The Handbook of the International Law of Military Operations, 2nd edn. Oxford University Press, New York, pp. 375–393

Janis M (1976) Sea power and the law of the sea. Lexington Books, Massachusetts/Toronto

Klein N (2011) Maritime Security and the Law of the Sea. Oxford University Press, New York

Kraska J, Pedrozo P (2013) International Maritime Security Law. Martinus Nijhof Publishers, Leiden/Boston

Koninklijke Marine (2014) Grondslagen van het Maritieme Optreden. www.defensie.nl/downloads/publicaties/2014/02/13/grondslagen-van-het-maritieme-optreden-nederlandse-maritiemmilitaire-doctrine. Accessed 6 January 2018

MacCartney A (1925) Shepard, Sea power in ancient history. William Heinemann LTD, London

NATO Allied Tactical Publication (ATP) 71 (2013) Allied maritime interdiction operations

NATO Allied Tactical Publication (ATP) 71 (2005) Allied maritime interdiction operations. www.navedu.navy.mi.th/stg/databasestory/data/laukniyom/ship-active/big-country-ship/United-States/ATP/ATP_71.pdf. Accessed 12 February 2017

Ormerod H (1924) Piracy in the ancient world. An essay in Mediterranean history. Hodder & Stoughton Ltd., London

Papastavridis E (2013) The interception of vessels on the high seas. Hart Publishing, Oxford/Portland, OR

Plutarch (1925) Levensbeschrijvingen van Alexander (den Groote) en Cajus (Julius) Caesar (transl. Mendes da Costa M). Wereldbibliotheek, Amsterdam

Roberts G (2009) Hostis Humani Generis: The threat of WMD terrorism and how NATO is facing the ultimate threat. Defence Against Terrorism Review 2:1 pp. 1–13

Robertson H (1991) Interdiction of Iraqi Maritime Commerce in the 1990–1991 Persian Gulf conflict. Ocean Development and International Law 22 pp. 289–299

Suetonius (1957) The twelve Caesars (transl. Graves R). Penguin Books Inc., Baltimore

Smart S (2015) Maritime interdiction operations. In: Corn G, VanLandingham R, Reeves S, McChrystal S (eds) U.S. Military Operations: Law, Policy, and Practice. Oxford University Press, New York, pp. 730–777

US DoD, Joint publication 3-32, 7 August 2013

US DoD, Joint Publication 3-03, Joint Interdiction, 14 October 2011

Wilson B (2016) The complex nature of today's maritime security issues. Why whole-of-government frameworks matter. In: Krause J, Bruns S (eds) Routledge Handbook on naval strategy and security. Taylor & Francis Group, London/New York, pp. 153–165

Zheng H (2012) Confidence building measures and non-traditional security. In: Dutton P, Ross R Tunsjo O (eds) Twenty-First century seapower. Cooperation and conflict at sea. Taylor & Francis Group London/New York, pp. 298–314

Chapter 2
Some Introductory Remarks on Naval Operations

Contents

Abstract This chapter briefly touches upon the context and conduct of maritime interception operations. The evolution of the role of naval forces has facilitated the emergence of the use of maritime interception operations as an important and effective role for naval forces in current naval operations. MIO are also performed in a dimension that has certain specific features that impact upon the manner in which way maritime interceptions are conducted. A brief remark is also made regarding particular technical terms that emerged during the conduct of maritime interception operations.

Keywords Maritime security · naval peacekeeping · maritime geography · maritime interception operations terminology · maritime rules of engagement · maritime coalition operations

2.1 Introduction

To understand the law applicable to maritime interception operations, one must grasp to a certain extent the context and environment in which maritime interception operations take place. This chapter focuses on this context and environment by means of three perspectives: an evolutionary, a geographical and a practical

M. Fink, *Maritime Interception and the Law of Naval Operations*,
https://doi.org/10.1007/978-94-6265-249-1_2

perspective. The first perspective points at the evolution of the use of maritime power,[1] and more specifically, how States use naval forces to pursue their national and international objectives. The second perspective underlines the uniqueness of the maritime dimension and its effects on maritime interception operations. The third perspective places a few remarks on practical naval conduct and terminology that has emerged as standard conduct and terminology for maritime interception operations.

2.2 Evolution of the Role of Naval Forces

Up until the end of the Cold War there had been a general idea that the primary focus for naval forces was on the naval fleet of the opponent, in support of a national defence role. For Western navies it meant a deep interest in the Russian fleet during the period of the Cold War. As Staley notes, this focus was also one of the reasons why the UN did not make much use of naval forces during the Cold War.[2] It is not, however, that the UN did not use naval forces at all. Naval efforts under the UN flag (albeit under US operational command) during the Korean War is one example. The international security context of the 1990s after the Cold War moved the focus towards cooperation between navies, outside the perspective of a national defence role.[3] In particular, this new security reality pushed the view forward that naval forces could also be used to play a role in implementing international UN mandates and act within the realm of international peacekeeping, referred to by some as 'naval peacekeeping'.[4] This kind of support in peace support operations provided new meaning for the use of naval forces after the Cold War. Seeking to find further purpose, next to this shift, it was viewed that naval forces could also play a role in so-called *constabulary tasks*.[5] This meant that naval forces could play a role in what is generally considered as non-military policing tasks in support of minimizing criminal acts at sea, such as drug trafficking, illegal fisheries activities, illegal immigrants or marine pollution. In terms of actual practical activities naval peacekeeping overlapped with constabulary operations. Naval peacekeeping and constabulary operations were both at the low end of the use of

---

[1] Maritime power in NATO is defined as military, political and economic power exerted through the use of the sea, and exercised by sea, air and land resources. See AJP 3.1., April 2004, para 1010. It describes a State's ability to implement its interests at sea through the use of political, economic and military activities in order to pursue national objectives. The UK Maritime Doctrine uses words of a similar kind: 'The ability to project power at sea and from the sea to influence the behaviour of people or the course of events'. See JDP 0-10, August 2011, p. V.

[2] Staley 1992, p. 13.

[3] Benbow 1999, pp. 107–125; Pugh et al. 1994, pp. 10–31.

[4] Pugh and Gregory 1998; Carvalho de Oliviera 2012, pp. 48–61.

[5] Booth 1985, p. 192; Pugh and Gregory 1998, pp. 74–101.

force spectrum. The beginning of the New World Order therefore introduced navies to both peacekeeping and maritime policing next to their national defence role.

Ten years later, and by the time the attacks on the United States in September 2001 had occurred, naval forces had firmly established a role in supporting UN peace support operations from the sea, which they conducted from Iraq to the former Yugoslavia to Haiti. States now also more generally accepted a role for naval forces in constabulary tasks, but as maritime strategist Geoffrey Till noted, constabulary operations were '…regarded something that navies could do when nothing more important was occupying their attention'.[6] The 9/11 attacks and the subsequent focus of fighting maritime terrorism through enhancing maritime security, pushed towards a view for a larger role for naval forces in maritime security, a term without a clear definition but with an ever growing content. Constabulary operations now developed from a peacetime 'nothing else to do' task to one of the important main tasks that navies are called upon to conduct. The notion of maritime security is not at all new, but its scope is first of all not well defined, and secondly, has expanded in recent years to encompass more and more issues that are considered a threat to the security interests of States. Natalie Klein has aptly noted that maritime security is usually not defined by defining the term itself, but by stating what can threaten maritime security.[7] Illustratively, the UN Secretary-General, in his 2008 *Report on Oceans and the Law of the Sea,* did exactly that and identified a number of threats that can generally be perceived as threatening maritime security.[8] It lists issues such as piracy, armed robbery against ships, terrorist acts, intentional and unlawful damage to the marine environment, illegal dumping and the discharge of pollutants from vessels, and depletion of natural resources, such as by illegal fishing. Although maritime security seems to focus on law enforcement orientated issues, it is not, however, limited to such matters. It includes the whole range of security matters of a State. This could include also armed conflict. The wide context of maritime security, in which conducting MIO plays an important role to operationalize its enhancement, includes

[6] Till 2013, p. 305.

[7] Klein 2011, p. 9.

[8] UN Doc A/63/63, 10 March 2008. Paragraph 131 reads:

> 39. There is no universally accepted definition of the term "maritime security". Much like the concept of "national security", it may differ in meaning, depending on the context and the users. At its narrowest conception, maritime security involves protection from direct threats to the territorial integrity of a State, such as an armed attack from a military vessel. Most definitions also usually include security from crimes at sea, such as piracy, armed robbery against ships, and terrorist acts. However, intentional and unlawful damage to the marine environment, including from illegal dumping and the discharge of pollutants from vessels, and depletion of natural resources, such as from IUU fishing, can also threaten the interests of States, particularly coastal States. Various approaches have been taken to maritime security, depending on the State's perspective of the interests that may be threatened, either directly or indirectly, by activities in the oceans and seas.

a growing number of security threats that threaten both the exclusive and inclusive good order of the oceans.[9] Because of the globalization in which, using Geoffrey Till's words again, 'everything is connected to everything',[10] it urges cooperation between States. Against this background, the legal means of international agreements have become more opportune, as every State has an interest to enhance maritime security for its own good.

International security organizations such as NATO started to embrace the notion of maritime security, strengthening the view that countering these threats is also a military, naval, task. The so-called maritime security operations (MSO) conducted as an operational result of this focus have also changed, or rather, broadened the purpose of boarding operations; from stopping and searching for prohibited goods, to include boardings that are conducted to gather information in order to support thwarting possible threats against issues of maritime security. Commodore (UK Navy) Neil Brown has defined MSO very broadly as 'commonly used to describe the full range of naval operations outside of international armed conflict, including those which include an exercise of rights under Article 110 of the United Nations Convention on the Law of the Sea (UNCLOS)'.[11] Important is that this view underlines the point that MSO are conducted *outside* the situation of armed conflict.

Using naval forces as a means to police the seas also lead to tactical level practices such as 'friendly approaches' or 'approach and assist visits' by warships that may include stepping onto another vessel to communicate with the fellow seafarer. Such activities have become part of standing operating procedures within MSO. Navies, therefore, have started to 'police the sea' by means of engaging with the maritime community. The general view is that policing the seas, or, in more military terms, enhancing maritime situational awareness (MSA),[12] as one author states: 'adds to warning time', and offers opportunities, 'to engage adversaries well before they can cause harm (…)'.[13] Enhancing MSA is viewed as the basis for successfully countering maritime threats at sea.[14] The wide context of maritime security and the acceptance that naval forces have a role to play in enhancing maritime security opens the door more widely to the idea that naval forces should play an active role within the realm of law enforcement. Law enforcement, as Nils Melzer states, 'refers to the exercise by state agents of police powers.'[15] In the naval context this would, for instance, occur when naval forces act against piracy. The

---

[9] Maintaining exclusive good order of the oceans relates to issues that could affect the public order of the State, such as illegal immigrants and drug-trafficking. Maintaining the inclusive good order relates to securing the common use and richness of the oceans. Examples are counter-piracy, or illegal fisheries or marine pollution.

[10] Till 2013, p. 283.

[11] Brown 2015, pp. 69–82.

[12] Maritime Security Awareness (MSA) is the term used by NATO. The US use the term Maritime Domain Awareness (MDA).

[13] Krajewski 2008, p. 219.

[14] Nimmich and Goward 2007, pp. 57–65.

[15] Melzer 2010, p. 34.

focus on enhancing maritime security in the first decade of the 21st century was also translated into newly adopted national and international maritime strategies. Two important naval powers—the US and (the collective of States in) NATO—conceptualized the role for naval forces in maritime security in their maritime strategies. The US released its *National Strategy for Maritime Security* (NSMS) in 2005,[16] while NATO adopted its new *Alliance Maritime Strategy* (AMS) in January 2011. Both maritime strategies in the first place strongly underline the notion of maritime security and list a number of threats to maritime security.[17] NATO, for the first time added maritime security as a role its naval forces could play. Also, in March 2014, the European Commission and the High Representative of the European Union for Foreign Affairs and Security Policy adopted a Joint Communication as a pre-step towards an EU maritime strategy, titled: 'For an open and secure global maritime domain: elements for a European Union maritime security strategy.'[18] The EU document is not a maritime strategy which centers on the role of naval forces in enhancing maritime security, but centers on issues of maritime security itself, in which naval forces within an EU context might play a role.[19] The EU Maritime Security Operations concept provides an option on how maritime forces can contribute to maritime security. All documents, however, start from the classic idea that the importance of maritime security is supported by the fundamental view that the freedom of the sea remains of the utmost importance for the security interests of States. Baroness Catherine Ashton stated to the Joint Communication that: 'The security and well-being of Europeans greatly depend on open and safe seas. It is therefore necessary for the EU to deal with maritime threats and challenges.'[20] This was later repeated when the EU Maritime Security Strategy (EUMSS) was adopted in June 2015:[21]

> The Sea is a valuable source of growth and prosperity for the European Union and its citizens. The EU depends on open, protected and secure seas and oceans for economic development, free trade, transport, energy security, tourism and good status of the marine environment.[22]

---

[16] At: http://georgewbush-whitehouse.archives.gov/homeland/maritime-security.html.

[17] The NSMS (2005) mentions Nation-State threats, terrorist threats, transnational criminal and piracy threats, environmental destruction and illegal seaborne immigration.

[18] EU Council. JOIN (2014) 9 final, Brussels, 6 March 2014. *Joint communication to the European Parliament and the Council for an open and secure global maritime domain: elements for a European Union maritime security strategy.*

[19] It mentions for instance (at page 7) that the EU should plan, on a regular basis, 'EU-flagged' maritime exercises with third countries in the context of a common security and defence policy operation or EU exercise, in order to improve the visibility of the EU in the global maritime domain.

[20] Press release, European Commission, 'Towards an EU-integrated approach to global maritime security', Brussels 6 March 2014.

[21] Council of the European Union. EU Maritime Strategy, 11205/14, Brussels, 24 June 2014.

[22] Interestingly enough, the EU has taken a different approach on how to describe the term maritime security in the sense that the term is more defined as an end state:

The freedom of the sea is ensured by protecting it against a wide range of possible threats in which naval forces would have a role to counter them at sea. In the AMS, NATO identified that: 'The maintenance of the freedom of navigation, sea-based trade routes, critical infrastructure, energy flows, protection of marine resources and environmental safety are all in Allies' security interests.'[23] But apart from describing the maritime security environment, the AMS does not detail what exactly maritime security for NATO means and simply states that it may act against security threats arising in the maritime environment. Derived from NATO's actual maritime operations, next to Article 5 and non-Article 5 peace support operations, international terrorism, piracy and refugee operations are the only issues that NATO has currently expanded to in terms of enhancing maritime security.

In sum, naval forces are expected to operate in many different contexts: Within the context of a national defence and warfighting role, in the context of supporting the maintenance of international peace and security, and in the context of maintaining good order of the oceans. Some even see the role for naval forces even more expanded to include support in humanitarian operations,[24] to support other States with the effects of natural disasters, like earthquakes and help rebuilding a State after a devastating storm.[25] It is submitted here that the relationship between maritime security and maritime interception operations is that maritime interception operations are the practical means to support the enhancement of maritime security.

2.3 Maritime Geography

Naval operations take place in a geographical area that is often called 'the global commons'.[26] As Chap. 4 will underline, the global commons in legal terms signifies primarily that no one owns it, that all States are equally authorized to use it and its resources and all have a responsibility to ensure those freedoms. The maritime environment has a number of characteristics that also have an effect on naval operations. Five are mentioned here.

First, States can operate their naval forces in the commons without the need for a legal basis to deploy its forces at sea. This allows, for instance, for early deployment of military assets as contingency positioning into or close to a theatre of conflict

Maritime security is understood as a state of affairs of the global maritime domain, in which international law and national law are enforced, freedom of navigation is guaranteed and citizens, infrastructure, transport, the environment and marine resources are protected.

[23] AMS, para 5.

[24] The Netherlands maritime doctrine categorizes these tasks as maritime assistance operations.

[25] Wirtz 2009, pp. 1–13.

[26] See e.g. Windsor-Smith 2009.

even though the UNSC has not (yet) mandated any military enforcement measures. Those assets can still be tasked with roles, such as monitoring measures that are taken by the UNSC short of military enforcement measures. Their presence in the area may have an influence on the political course of the conflict. The situation with regard to Libya in early 2011 can serve as an example where States first massed their fleets off the coast of Libya to support national non-combatant evacuation operations and at the same time pre-staged their forces in view of growing tension and subsequent action by the UNSC. Naval forces were on station to immediately start enforcement action against Libya when the UNSC authorized States to do so. Further back in history, NATO launched *Maritime Monitor* to monitor the implementation of UN sanctions without the existence of an explicit enforcement mandate, but to support the UN in its efforts to deal with the conflict.

Second, operating in the global commons means that naval operations will occur in areas where other States' vessels have a freedom to navigate and make use of the ocean as they wish. Most of that use is economy-related. Naval operations can on the one hand support these activities by protecting the sea lanes of communication and by taking away the threats of criminal activity at sea, but it can also hamper the economy when, for instance, embargo operations or the existence of armed conflict allows interference with foreign-flagged merchant vessels. The point to note is that maritime interception operations include the military application of force that is generally not directly against the military opponent. Instead, MIO include mostly the stopping of merchant vessels, for instance to check their neutral status, whether an embargo is being breached, to keep vessels in or outside a targeted State, or to arrest criminals at sea. Maritime interception may be part of a military campaign which can also consist of naval forces that both conduct hostilities and perform interception operations, but its addressee is primarily non-military. To put it in the terminology of the law of armed conflict, MIO will deal mainly with civilians.

Operating in the global commons means, thirdly, that there is a possibility that navies could take up the task of policing the high seas. Basically, maritime security operations that are conducted by standing multinational fleets, such as Combined Maritime Forces (CMF) or NATO's Standing NATO maritime groups (SNMG), to enhance maritime security at sea in general, are typically actions that would be considered as policing the seas. Although MSO, or policing the high seas to use the latter term, may be at the political-strategic level the way forward, conceptually, it does not sit well with the basic framework upon which the international law of the sea is built. This issue will be touched upon in Chap. 4. Be that as it may, maritime security on an operational level is viewed to be largely based on two legs. One leg is the increase of awareness of what happens at sea. The second leg is to take action against threats. In both legs maritime interception operations play a role. In the first, by means of approaches of warships to other vessels to gather and exchange information adds to the maritime awareness. In the second, MIO are used to actually act against the threat.

A fourth point to note on the maritime geography and maritime interception operations is that naval operations with different legal bases and regimes may overlap each other in one geographical area. For example, when Operation *Iraqi*

Freedom (OIF) started in 2003, US forces were allowed to board suspect vessels as far away as the Mediterranean Sea, quite some distance away from the operational theatre in the Persian Gulf. At the same time, NATO's Operation *Active Endeavour* was also operating in the Mediterranean Sea, but different authorities were given to the participating warships. States can assign their warships to different ongoing operations in one area, which will lead to the complexity that warships from the same State operating in the same area, could theoretically have a different legal basis and authorities under which they perform their task. Or one warship could be assigned to take part in more operations in one area. It is quite understandable, therefore, that merchant vessels that are stopped will also have a challenge to understand what the actual legal scope of the boarding could be.

The fifth and last point to note is that it appears that the different applicable frameworks of international law are also viewed as a toolbox. In this view international law provides choices to a commander. If a vessel, for example, cannot be boarded because there is no reasonable suspicion that it has breached a UN embargo, if opportune, it may switch to the legal basis of statelessness or use *ad hoc* consent as the basis to board the same vessel. While the legal toolbox is a welcome instrument for a warship commander, the danger may be that the toolbox is used in a too creative manner in which a legal basis might be misused to achieve something else than what it is meant for. Creative use of legal bases might, theoretically, increase where the parameters of a visit are not detailed, such as *ad hoc* consent or statelessness as a ground for boarding a vessel.

2.4 Some Operational Points on MIO

Certain operational points connected to maritime interception operations are the third issue that need highlighting in this introductory chapter. Three in particular are mentioned here: maritime coalition operations, boarding operations and maritime rules of engagement.

2.4.1 Maritime Coalition Operations

Maritime interception operations in the context of international peace and security are generally conducted as a multinational effort by a coalition of States. In terms of command structure, multinational operations can either be performed as a 'loose' coalition of individual States that form a coalition in a specific conflict, usually operationally led by a leading State, or under the command structure of an international organization, such as the UN, NATO or the EU. The choice of command structure will firstly have an effect on the way in which authorities are given to the participating warships, and can secondly have an effect on the actual authorities itself. This is because of the fact that different organizations will work from their own political and legal perspective and will interpret and fulfill an authorizing mandate against the background of that perspective.[27] For example, authorities for warships operating in the counter-piracy operations in the EU or NATO differ, although the overall UNCLOS and additional UNSC mandate are the same for both organizations. States participating in multinational operations may also, in their own procedural manner, differ within the coalition on authority given to warships. This makes it difficult to determine exactly what kind of authorities participating warships within a certain operation may have. It is, therefore, not automatically said that one can take as a point of departure that all participating warships in one operation will have the same authorities.[28] How much it differs, depends also on the way the commanding organization allows for any differences in authorities. During the coalition Operation *Enduring Freedom* the authorities—or rules of engagement (ROE)—differed between participating States.[29] As such, the legal regime used for boarding operations in OEF is rather diffuse. Lastly, different operations can be conducted based on one legal basis. For example, SC Res. 1973 (2011) with regard to Libya prompted the coalition operation *Odyssey Dawn*, the NATO operation *Unified Protector* (OUP) and individual operations conducted by States. Where MIO are conducted in the context of law enforcement, maritime interception also asks for 'coalitions' in a number of others ways. As underlined above, in the first place there is the view that enhancing maritime security in a globalized world means working together between States and organizations that have a specific focus on areas that coincide with issues of maritime security. On an operational level, it also needs coalitions between the military and other relevant government agencies, as the aftermath of an interception at sea is of equal importance as the interception itself for the success of the overall mission.

2.4.2 Boarding Operations

Warships' crews are trained to perform a number of roles, one of which is to perform boarding operations. Usually the boarding team will either consist of the warship's crew that is appointed a secondary task in the boarding team, or additional personnel will be attached to the warship's crew to perform the boarding operations. The latter will be opportune when situations occur in which the boardings are the primary task within the operation and the use of the original warship's crew will put a strain on operating the warship itself, or when there is a chance that greater coercion and a higher level of force is needed to board a vessel

[27] See on the coalition challenges of ROE Stephens 2006, pp. 17–27.

[28] To overcome the multitude of authorities, multinational commanders are usually forced to make all kinds of matrices in which States are asked to define their authorities or caveats for a specific operation.

[29] Houben 2007, pp. 82–85.

for which specifically trained personnel may be needed.[30] For example, in cases of opposed boardings and in situations where personnel with specific legal authorities is needed which are not invested in military personnel. Military personnel may have authority to board a vessel when the boarding is based on a UN resolution, but may not have authority when the boarding is part of stopping a criminal act at sea. With regard to the US naval forces, Ivan Luke, for instance, explains that the US Coast Guard has statutory law enforcement authority, whereas the US Navy does not.[31]

The boarding of another vessel can be done in a number of ways, but is generally done by sending a boarding team either on small boats (Rhibs)[32] to the target vessel, or inserting the boarding team by helicopter onto the deck of the vessel to be boarded. The boarding team itself will generally consist of a security (or guard) team, a search team and a bridge team. The first team deals with force protection, the second with inspecting the vessel and the third with staying in contact with the master and exerting control over the vessel. The organization of the boarding team, however, also depends on the actual circumstances of the case, such as available personnel and whether the situation might be threatening, or is a routine friendly-approach boarding.

2.4.3 Maritime Rules of Engagement

In current naval operations, it is unusual if the authorities of the warships' crews during an operation are not laid down in so-called rules of engagement (ROE). ROE regulate the use of force during military operations in its broadest sense and are based on a combination of legal, political and operational factors that need to be considered for a particular military campaign.[33] Force can either be the actual use of weapons, but also the threatening or de-escalating positioning of warships relative to the opponent or a State, the detention or seizure of persons and goods, or the boarding of foreign-flagged vessels. There are some typical ROE that are used in the maritime dimension. In very general terms, for instance, to stop another vessel a warship can use warnings, graduated use of force against the vessel, boarding the vessel and subsequently seizing the vessel, goods and or persons and ultimately sailing the vessel to a port. In this context, typical maritime ROE are rules on

[30] A Dutch ship boarding team will generally be trained to the level of conducting non-cooperative boardings.

[31] Luke 2013, pp. 11–26.

[32] Rigid hull inflatable boats.

[33] See elaborately on ROE Boddens Hosang 2017.

positioning,[34] warning(s) (shots), (non-)disabling fire, boarding and diversion.[35] With regard to boarding ROE, from a tactical perspective boarding operations can be divided into three levels. They can either be unopposed, non-cooperative or opposed.[36] These levels relate to the level of physical cooperation a boarding team can expect from the master and crew of the target vessel. In a un-opposed situation the master of the vessel will cooperate with the boarding party in all aspects of the boarding process. In a non-cooperative situation the master neither complies nor obeys given orders. This may result in passive resistance, such as not stopping the vessel or not answering the warship's orders. In an opposed situation, it is expected that the master or others on board will actively oppose the boarding, which may include the use of force against the boarding party.[37] The Israeli boarding of the *Mavi Marmara*, for instance, is exemplary of a boarding that was clearly opposed by a number of persons on board the target vessel.

The level of physical cooperation of the master must be separated from the legal basis to board a vessel, which is usually expressed in terms of either consensual or non-consensual boarding. A consensual boarding exists where the flag State has consented to the boarding of its vessel.[38] When taking these legal and operational circumstances together, a boarding can, for example, be consensual but opposed in the situation where the flag State has consented to the boarding but the master actively refuses to be boarded. This occurred for instance during the *MV Light* incident.[39] The issue of consent does not appear in cases where a legal basis exists that allows the boarding of a foreign-flagged vessel, such as in cases where the UNSC has explicitly authorized the inspection of vessels, the belligerent right of visit applies, or where a treaty has authorized a boarding. In such cases, the ROE will only have to refer to the physical part of the boarding.

Diversion relates to an activity to divert a vessel off its original course, for instance to divert it away from a maritime area that is restricted by a UN mandate, or where diversion of the vessel is needed to send it in-port for further inspection. In many situations, diversion may be the better alternative to boarding and inspection at sea. For one reason, within the context of UN-mandated embargo operations, because, and apart from the many practical challenges that arise with boarding and

---

[34] Positioning of naval vessels relates either to the geographical positioning of a warship, or the positioning of a warship in relation to other vessels in the maritime area.

[35] Diversion relates to authority to divert a vessel off its original course, for instance to divert it from an area that is restricted by a UN mandate or where diversion of the vessel is needed to send it in-port for further inspection.

[36] Houben 2008, p. 32.

[37] Papastavridis 2013, p. 67. The terminology is now a quite established part of naval (NATO) doctrine. Before, the terminology differed and the term (non-)compliant was also used. During the NATO and EU embargo operations in the Adriatic Sea and at the beginning of Operation *Active Endeavour* the term compliant instead of consensual appears. In any case, the term compliant also refers to the physical levels of force that may be expected against the boarding party.

[38] But see discussion on this point in Chap. 7.

[39] See Chap. 3 on this incident.

inspection,[40] the mandate could also be successfully upheld when ships with suspicious cargo do not arrive at the port of the State under sanctions.

Disabling and non-disabling fire relates to the activity of using actual force against a ship by means of the use of weapons. This ROE authority aims at coercing the vessel to stop and obey the apprehending warships' orders and is usually meant as another gradual step in a warning cycle against a vessel. Non-disabling will allow firing into parts of the ship that are not essential for navigational purposes. Disabling fire allows for aiming at parts of the vessel that will impact on operating the vessel without endangering its seaworthiness. For instance, firing at the engine of a small boat. What part of the vessel can be targeted obviously depends on factors such as the type of available weapons, the type of targeted vessel and the whereabouts of the people on board the vessel.

Depending on the command structure and the national political and legal guidelines warship commanders receive from their capitals, it is possible that naval forces in one and the same multinational operation may have different ROE. It must also be understood that, as mentioned earlier, ROE are not a legal regime, but a result of policy, legal and operational factors. Because of this combination of factors that weigh into the ROE, they may be more restrictive due to political or operational reasons than what is allowed on an extant legal regime. For example, a reason why a boarding may not be authorized even though there are legal grounds available, may be a lack of available specialized forces that can perform an opposed boarding in a possibly volatile environment. What is, therefore, important to note is that although the authorities (ROE) that warship commanders get issued to do their mission are a good indicator of the applicable law, it may not be the same as reflecting the law itself.

References

Benbow T (1999) Maritime Power in the 1990–91 Gulf War and the Conflict in the Former Yugoslavia. In: Dorman A, Lawrence Smith M, Uttley M (eds) The changing face of maritime power. Macmillan Press Ltd, London, pp. 107–125

Boddens Hosang J (2017) Rules of Engagement. Rules on the use of force as linchpin or the international law of military operations. Dissertation, University of Amsterdam, Amsterdam

Booth K (1985) Law, force and diplomacy at sea. George Allen and Unwin, London/Boston/Sydney

Brown N (2015) Jurisdictional Problems Relating to Non-Flag State Boarding of Suspect Ships in International Waters: A Practitioner's Observations. In: Ringbom R (ed) Jurisdiction over Ships. Brill, Dordrecht, pp. 69–82

Carvalho de Oliviera G (2012) Naval peacekeeping and piracy: Time for a critical debate. International Peacekeeping, 19:1 pp. 48–61

European Commission (2014) Towards an EU integrated approach to global maritime security. Press release 6 March 2014.

[40] Such as having to understand whether paperwork may or may not be falsified. This was one of the challenges during the Red Sea interception operations of the MIF. See Pokrant 1999, pp. 189–192.

EU Council (2014) EU Maritime Strategy, 11205/14, Brussels, 24 June 2014
EU Council (2014) JOIN (2014) 9 final, Brussels, 6 March 2014
Houben M (2007) Making Waves and Building Bridges: Dutch Experiences in the Arabian Sea. RUSI Defence System, June 2007, pp. 82–85
Houben M (2008) Food for Life. De inzet van Hr. Ms. Evertsen ter ondersteuning van het VN Wereldvoedsel programma. Working Paper Maritiem optreden nr. 1, Maritieme Doctrine en Tactieken Centrum, Den Helder
Klein N (2011) Maritime security and the law of the sea. Oxford University Press, New York
Krajewski J (2008) Out of Sight, Out of Mind? A Case for Long Range Identification and Tracking of Vessels on the High Seas. Naval Law Review 56, pp. 219–250
Luke I (2013) Naval operations in peacetime. Not just "warfare lite". Naval War College Review 66-2:11–26
Melzer N (2010) Conceptual distinction and overlaps between law enforcement and the conduct of hostilities. In: Gill T, Fleck D (eds) The Handbook of International Law of Military Operations. Oxford University Press, New York, pp. 33–50
NATO (2004) AJP 3.1. Allied Joint Maritime Operations, April 2004
Nimmich J, Goward N (2007) Maritime Domain Awareness: The Key to Maritime Security. In: Carsten M (ed) International Law Studies 83 Naval War College, Newport RI, pp. 57–65
Papastavridis E (2013) The interception of vessels on the high seas. Hart Publishing, Oxford/ Portland, OR
Pokrant M (1999) Desert Shield at Sea. What the Navy Really Did. Greenwood Press, Westport, Connecticut/London
Pugh M, Ginifer J, Grove E (1994) Sea power, security and peacekeeping after the Cold War. In: Pugh M (ed) Maritime security and peacekeeping. A framework for United Nations operations. Manchester University Press, Manchester/New York
Pugh M, Gregory F (1998) Maritime constabulary roles for non-military security. In: Pugh M (ed) Maritime security and peacekeeping. A framework for United Nations operations. Manchester University Press, Manchester/New York
Staley R (1992) The Wave of the Future: The United Nations and naval peacekeeping. International Peace Academy, Occasional Paper series, Boulder, CO/London
Stephens D (2006) Coalition warfare – challenges and opportunities. International Yearbook of Human Rights 36, pp. 17–27
Till G (2013) Seapower. A guide for the twenty-first century. Routledge, London/New York
United Kingdom Ministry of Defence (2011) JDP 0-10 (British Maritime Doctrine), August 2011
United Nations, A/63/63, 10 March 2008
United States (2005) National Strategy for Maritime Security, 2005
Windsor-Smith B (2009) Securing the commons. Towards NATO's new maritime strategy. Research paper, NATO Defense College, Rome
Wirtz J (2009) Introduction. In: Wirtz J, Larsen J (eds) Naval Peacekeeping and humanitarian operations. Stability from the sea. Routledge, London/New York, pp. 1–13

Chapter 3
A Short History of Maritime Interception Operations

There is no point in getting into the semantics; what matters is that the oil is being stopped.
—Alleged quote by former US President George Bush Sr.

Contents

Abstract The evolution of the use of the term maritime interception operations (MIO) can largely be sketched along the lines of four strands. These four strands are: enforcing economic sanctions imposed by the UN Security Council, the use of MIO immediately after the 11 September attacks, the wider use of MIO against terrorism at sea in the context of enhancing maritime security, and counter-piracy operations. Instead of a term with distinct legal connotation, this chapter argues that the use of the

M. Fink, *Maritime Interception and the Law of Naval Operations*,
https://doi.org/10.1007/978-94-6265-249-1_3

term MIO has evolved into a term of operational art that is now used to describe an operational activity at sea.

Keywords History of MIO · Maritime embargo operations · piracy · maritime security operations · Enduring Freedom · Active Endeavour · UN sanctions enforcement at sea

3.1 Introduction

Different authors suggest that it may have been[1] US Secretary of State James A. Baker[2] that coined the term interception operations in its modern understanding during the early stages of the Iraq-Kuwait conflict in 1990.[3] Apparently he did so, according to Pokrant, to avoid 'the words 'blockade' or 'quarantine', because under international law those terms can be interpreted as acts of war, which were viewed to be inappropriate terminology at the time when the New World Order was trying to do away with the Cold War.[4] Whether Baker, or one of his legal or political advisors, is the actual founding father of the term interception operations may not be precisely traceable in history.[5] But what matters, however, is that the term stuck and has since become an accepted and much used acronym in naval operations: MIO.

During the Iraq-Kuwait conflict and the conflicts that followed shortly after Iraq in the Former Yugoslavia and the crisis in Haiti, maritime interception operations emerged as one of the means that the UNSC resorted to in order to restore international peace and security. Today, the term MIO is not solely reserved for naval operations that aim to enforce economic sanctions at sea adopted by the UNSC, as it has been the view for quite some years. On the contrary, its use in recent history shows an evolution that has significantly widened the use of the term. MIO transformed in different forms and shapes, for instance in the form of counter-piracy operations off the coast of Somalia, as part of a friendly approach during maritime security operations, or as part of UN-mandated military operations in the Mediterranean Sea against Libya. Naval strategist Milan Vego has noted that apart from UN-mandated economic enforcement measures 'MIOs can also be applied by a major naval power or group of powers to prevent maritime terrorism or illicit trafficking in narcotics, humans, and weapons'.[6] In an even broader view, the term MIO has also been used in naval operations that

[1] Olson 1993, p. 3.

[2] US Secretary of State between 1989 and 1992.

[3] E.g. Freedman and Karsh 1993, pp. 144–145; Peace 1991, p. 561.

[4] Pokrant 1999, p. 29; Morabito 1991, p. 307.

[5] Pokrant mentions that General Colin Powell (then Chairman of the Joint Chiefs of Staff) in August 1990 first issued orders for the Maritime *quarantine* force to begin operations, but soon after issued new orders which replaced the words quarantine with 'interception' and the name of the operation to Maritime Interception Force. See Pokrant 1999, p. 29.

[6] Vego 2008, p. 11.

based boarding operations on the law of naval warfare. In fact, during the very first use of the term in the 1990 Iraq-Kuwait crisis, it was this belligerent authority the US-led coalition applied under the mask of MIO, which ultimately transformed into UN-mandated maritime embargo operations.

The evolution of the use of the term MIO can largely be sketched along the lines of four strands. First is the continued use by the UN Security Council of maritime embargo operations to enforce economic sanctions at sea. The second and third strands start with the changed security situation after 9/11. As a reaction to the terrorist attacks on the Twin Towers in the United States, a number of States undertook to deploy warships to interdict terrorists that would make use of the sea. The event of 9/11 also proved to be the start of several initiatives that shifted the use of naval forces more and more to naval activities under the umbrella of an expanded view of the notion of maritime security. This expansion is the third strand. The fourth strand of evolution started when the UNSC adopted SC Resolution 1816 (2008), which signaled the beginning of an active engagement of the Council and its member States in the fight against piracy and the protection of international trade in the Gulf of Aden and the Somali basin. These four strands are not alternative in the sense that one meaning of the term MIO has taken over from the other. Instead, the four strands of evolution have broadened the different ways in which way the term MIO is now used. This chapter introduces these four strands, the naval operations conducted in the context of these strands, and the relevant incidents that occurred in relation to them.

3.2 Strand 1: Enforcing UN Sanctions at Sea

The number of sanctions imposed by the UNSC significantly increased from two—Southern Rhodesia (1966–1979) and South Africa (1977)—[7]during the Cold War to fourteen immediately after the Cold War, rising to a total of 27 in 2010.[8] Since the aftermath of the Cold War, the UNSC has continued to utilize the means of sanctions on a regular basis. Only a limited number of measures taken through sanctions have also included a naval enforcement dimension at sea. Already during the Cold War, naval forces were used as a means to enforce the UN sanctions. During the Southern Rhodesia crisis the UNSC in resolution 216 (1965) condemned Ian Smith's unilateral declaration of independence of Southern Rhodesia. After the *Joanna V* incident,[9] the UNSC authorized the former colonial power, Great Britain, through subsequent resolutions to take action and interdict oil tankers

[7] Gowland-Debbas 2004, pp. 3–31.

[8] Charron 2011, pp. 5–6.

[9] O'Connell mentions that the Greek tanker *Joanna V* was boarded by the UK warship *HMS Berwick* on 4 April 1966, after which it refused to divert from sailing to the port of Beira without the UK being able to do anything about it. After this incident, the UNSC took measures that involved the authority to arrest the *Joanna V* upon departure and authority to stop vessels breaching the embargo when sailing into Beira. O'Connell 1975, pp. 174–175.

sailing into the port of Beira. This was the start of the so-called *Beira Patrol*, which lasted until 1975.[10] The decision back then by the UNSC to authorize a State to stop oil tankers, is often seen as enforcing UN sanctions through a maritime embargo operation *avant la lettre*. After the Cold War, the UNSC started to use the naval dimension more frequently as an asset to enforce UN sanctions. The sanctions that had a maritime dimension and came immediately after the end of the Cold War included Iraq, the Former Yugoslavia, Haiti and Sierra Leone. Since the start of the 21st century, the UNSC has resorted twice to the use of naval forces as a means to enforce UN sanctions: Lebanon (2006) and Libya (2011). Including the Beira Patrol, seven naval operations have therefore taken place in order to enforce economic measures at sea.

3.2.1 Iraq (1990–2003)

The Iraqi invasion of Kuwait started on 2 August 1990, at 01:00hrs.[11] The UNSC responded quickly that same day with the adoption of SC Res. 660 (1990). In line with Article 39 of the UN Charter the UNSC determined that the Iraqi invasion was a breach of international peace and security and demanded an immediate withdrawal of Iraqi forces. At that stage, no mention was made of Article 51 of the UN Charter. The affirmation that the situation was indeed considered a situation of self-defence followed four days later, on August 6, when the Council adopted SC Res. 661 (1990).[12] In addition, the UNSC also imposed a trade embargo on the import into the territories of all member nations of all the commodities and products originating in Iraq or Kuwait.[13] Assisting Kuwait, the US and UK started maritime interception operations on 16 August 1990. The Chinese freighter *Heng Chung Hai* was the first vessel boarded by *USS England* and released again after inspection.[14] With both the UN and individual States acting at the same time, discussions started on the legal basis with regard to the ongoing maritime interception operations. On August 25, the UNSC adopted SC Res. 665 (1990). After this resolution it was generally recognized that the UNSC indeed had authorized seaborne enforcement of the earlier adopted UN sanctions. Between 16 and 25 August, US naval assets diverted two vessels, of which one was boarded.[15] States that had deployed their

---

[10] Mobley 2002, pp. 64–84.

[11] Freedman and Karsh 1993, p. 67.

[12] The preamble of SC Resolution 661(1990) notes:

> Affirming the inherent right of individual or collective self-defence, response to the armed attack by Iraq against Kuwait, in accordance with article 51 of the Charter.

[13] SC Res. 661, para 2(a).

[14] Pokrant 1999, p. 32.

[15] Robertson 1991, p. 295. Marolda and Schneller mention only the boarding of the Chinese freighter *Heng Chung Hai*. Marolda and Schneller 1998, p. 86.

warships to the Persian Gulf and other parts of the seas around the Arabian Peninsula now started to enforce UN-mandated economic sanctions against Iraq in a multinational coalition operation. The participating warships that enforced the UN sanctions were dubbed to be part of the *Maritime Interception Force* (MIF). The inspection area for the MIF ran from the Persian Gulf to the Indian Ocean and from the Northern Red Sea to the Gulf of Aqaba, but was after some time limited to the Persian Gulf and the Indian Ocean.[16] The MIF lasted for thirteen years when the UNSC adopted SC Res. 1483 in 2003 that was taken in light of the new situation in Iraq. In March 2003, military forces of the US-led coalition had entered Iraq to oust Saddam Hussain from its reign and to search for weapons of mass destruction.

3.2.2 The Former Yugoslavia (1992–1996)

The breakup of the Former Yugoslavia in the beginning of the 1990s continued breathing life into the maritime interception model that was set up by the MIF. While Yugoslavia was falling apart, in 1991, the UNSC adopted SC Res. 713 (1991) under Article 41, establishing an arms embargo. The adoption of SC Res. 757 (1992) in May 1992, which put Yugoslavia under a general export embargo of ‘all commodities and products originating from the Federal Republic of Yugoslavia (Serbia and Montenegro),[17] prompted both NATO and WEU into examining the question whether the organizations could support the UN decisions by means of maritime peacekeeping operations. For NATO, this became a landmark question because it meant that NATO would be extending its purpose from its primary role as a collective self-defence organization to so-called ‘out of area’ operations. NATO ultimately defined its additional role to collective self-defence during the Oslo Summit in June 1992, in which it stated in its final communiqué:[18] ‘…we are prepared to support, on a case-by-case basis in accordance with our own procedures, *peacekeeping activities* [emphasis MDF] under the responsibility of the CSCE,[19] including by making available Alliance’s resources and expertise.’[20]

On 16 July 1992, NATO launched its first ‘out of area’, or non-Article 5 operation: Operation *Maritime Monitor*. It was also the first real naval *operation* NATO ever started.[21] Alongside NATO, the WEU launched Operation *Sharp Vigilance*. After the adoption of SC Res. 787 in November 1992, in which the

[16] Graham-Brown states that the MIF stopped inspections in the Gulf of Aqaba in 1994 when Lloyds in Jordan started land-based inspections of cargo bound for Iraq. Graham-Brown 1999, p. 96 n. 43.

[17] SC Res. 757 (1992), para 4a.

[18] See on the development that led to this decision Bono 2003, Chapter 2.

[19] Conference on Security and Cooperation in Europe. In 1995 the CSCE transformed into the (nowadays known as) OSCE (Organization for Security and Co-operation in Europe).

[20] Ministerial Meeting of the North Atlantic Council in Oslo, 4 June 1992, para 11.

[21] Ruiz Palmer 2016, p. 371.

UNSC explicitly authorized naval enforcement of an arms embargo at sea, NATO and the WEU changed their operational names into *Maritime Guard* and *Sharp Fence*. After the adoption of SC Res. 820 in 1993, both operations were combined into one: Operation *Sharp Guard*. This operation was suspended in June 1996 and terminated on 1 October 1996, after the adoption of SC Res. 1074 (1996). The resolution ended, after five years, all sanctions against the Former Yugoslavia. During *Sharp Guard*, in 1994, the *Lido II* incident occurred:

> The *Lido II* incident involved a Maltese-flagged vessel that in April 1994 left Tunisia to sail for Croatia, with mainly petrol products as its cargo. After a first inspection by the NATO/WEU forces while entering the Adriatic Sea it proceeded on its way to Croatia. The *Lido II* however changed course to the Albanian port of Durazzo while repeating requests for assistance as the vessel started to take water into the engine room (which later turned out to be untrue). The master then changed course again towards Montenegro, which was off limits due to SC Res. 820. While the *Lido II* sailed in the direction of Montenegro, Serbian patrol boats came out to meet the *Lido II*. Dutch forces from *Hr. Ms. Van Kinsbergen* who were also on scene were inserted by helicopter to take control of the vessel before it entered the territorial waters of Montenegro. The *Lido II* was seized and towed to Brindisi, Italy, to be dealt with by the Italian authorities.[22]

Although NATO and the EU were to get even more military involved in the crises in the Balkan region, which included Kosovo from 1999 onwards, after 1996 no MIO were conducted as part of those military operations in the Adriatic Sea. During Operation *Allied Force* (AFOR) with regard to Kosovo, naval forces were part of the operation. Despite SACEUR's wish to establish a belligerent blockade to cut off oil shipments to Serbia, the deployed naval forces did not fulfill such a role.[23] According to Diego Ruiz Palmer during the MIO conducted off the coast of the Former Yugoslavia, 'NATO forces, in cooperation with those of the Western European Union, challenged over 74,000 ships, boarded and inspected at sea nearly 6,000 and diverted for inspection in port nearly 1,500.'[24]

---

[22] See on this incident (in Dutch) *Grondslagen van het maritiem optreden* 2013.

[23] Stigler 2008, pp. 183–192. According to Ryan, who comments on the reasons why ultimately the decision was made not to use belligerent blockades, firstly the NATO nations did not want to publicly recognize Operation Allied Force as an international armed conflict (let alone a war), which led to a reluctance to use belligerent rights. Second, he mentions a rather strange argument that; 'even if participating NATO States were willing to recognize the Kosovo operation as an international armed conflict, Great Britain (as previously discussed relating to the Iran -Iraq Tanker War) refuses to recognize "visit and search" as a viable belligerent right existing independent of Article 51 of the U.N. Charter.' And thirdly, he mentions that NATO nations did not want to create more trouble with opposing states, such as Russia, China, and India, especially in the event that vessels of those states were to be visited. Ryan 2000, p. 15.

[24] Ruiz Palmer 2007. At: www.nato.int/docu/review/2007/issue4/english/analysis4.html. In more detail, a NATO factsheet mentions that during this operation 5.951 vessels were boarded and inspected and 1.480 vessels were diverted and inspected in port. 74.192 vessels were challenged. At: www.nato.int/ifor/general/shrp-grd.htm.

3.2.3 *Haiti (1993–1996)*

While the world was closely watching the Balkan crises develop, on the other side of the world general Raoul Cedras, commander of the Haitian Armed Forces, staged a coup against president Jean-Bertrand Aristide. In September 1991, Cedras forced Aristide to flee. The coup would lead to a five year struggle to return to a democratically elected government. During this period, the UNSC also authorized maritime embargo operations in support of its efforts to reinstate the ousted president, who was in exile in Venezuela. Pressure was put on Cedras with the imposition of economic sanctions by the Organization of American States (OAS), which was later followed by sanctions adopted by the UNSC in SC Res. 841 (1993). This resolution embargoed oil, weapons and petroleum. Diplomatic negotiations led to the so-called *Governors Island Agreement* (GIA) that aimed at returning Aristide to the presidency.[25] The agreement also stated that when a new prime minister was installed, the imposed sanctions against Haiti would be lifted. On 27 August 1993, the UN lifted the sanctions through SC Res. 861(1993) and not much later approved the United Nations Mission in Haiti (UNMIH) through SC Res. 867 (1993). Economic sanctions were reinstated[26] after an incident that threatened US soldiers coming into Haiti, which occurred only a few days after the incident in Somalia where US soldiers lost their lives in Mogadishu.[27] The reinstated sanctions in SC Res. 873 were bolstered when the UNSC also adopted a maritime embargo operation through SC Res. 875 (1993) and 917 (1994). A multinational but primarily US-led[28] force authorized by SC Res. 940 was mounted that would execute Operation *Uphold Democracy* to remove the *de facto* regime and reinstate Aristide. When Cedras finally left Haiti in September 1994, the multinational force (MNF) handed its tasks over to UNMIH. This UN mission ended its operations in 1996, after held elections were observed to be free and fair.

3.2.4 *Sierra Leone (1997–2010)*[29]

In 1991 civil war started in Sierra Leone. In general terms, the development in Sierra Leone initially followed the same pattern as the situation in Haiti. The elected president, Ahmed Tejan Kabbah, was overthrown by Johnny Paul Koroma in May 1997, who established the *Armed Forces Revolutionary Council* (AFRC). The

[25] Malone 1998, p. 87.

[26] SC Res. 873 (1993).

[27] The incident involved the prevention of the physical landing of troops on board the *USS Harlan County* while threatening that Haiti would become another Somalia.

[28] Kreps 2007, pp. 449–474.

[29] Cortright and Lopez 2000, pp. 167–181; Adebajo and Keen 2007, pp. 246–273; Hirsch 2004, pp. 521–536.

regional organization ECOWAS reacted to this coup by adopting economic sanctions against Sierra Leone, trying to restore the elected president. It also prepared for military action in the event this scheme of coercion would fail.[30] The sanctions imposed by ECOWAS and the subsequent deployment of the Economic Community of West African States Military Observer Group (ECOMOG) were followed by UN-decisions. In October 1997, the UNSC adopted sanctions in SC Res. 1132 (1997). These sanctions implemented an oil and arms embargo and also a travel-ban on members of the AFRC and their families. Paragraph 8 of the resolution requested ECOMOG to halt all inward maritime shipping to Sierra Leone in order to implement the sanctions. In 1997, the *Conakry Agreement* was reached that aimed to reinstall the president. When the agreement was not honoured by the AFRC, ECOMOG intervened and ousted the Junta in October 1998. ECOMOG operations included enforcing the sanctions of SC Res. 1132, although they apparently lacked capabilities to effectively enforce a maritime embargo operation.[31] Finally, in 1998 Kabbah was reinstated as president of Sierra Leone. A year later, however, the country fell back into conflict, during which time sanctions against Sierra Leone were not lifted. When the government ultimately re-established control over its territory in 2010, the UNSC adopted SC Res. 1940 (2010) that ended the sanctions against Sierra Leone.

3.2.5 Lebanon (2006–Present)

The maritime embargo operations off the coast of Lebanon came into being after the war of 2006, between Israel and Hezbollah. Israel's military operations (operation *Change Direction*) against Hezbollah in Lebanon started after an incident in which Hezbollah kidnapped two Israeli soldiers. A naval blockade was also part of Israel's operations.[32] When, on 11 August 2006, the UNSC adopted SC Res. 1701 (2006) Israel refused to end the blockade until alternative measures were undertaken to ensure that Hezbollah was not receiving any arms from outside Lebanon. Based on SC Res. 1701 and in coordination with Lebanon, the UN expanded the long-standing and land-based UNIFIL operation, which already existed since 1978, with a maritime dimension: Maritime Taskforce UNIFIL (MTF UNIFIL). It was the first time that a maritime operation came under command and control of the UN. The MTF UNIFIL supports the Lebanese authorities in policing its maritime borders for illegal weapons coming into Lebanon.[33] The mission aims to be concluded when Lebanon has sufficient capabilities to control its maritime borders. As of

[30] Hirsch 2004, p. 525.

[31] See on this S/1997/895.

[32] In 2006, the UN Human Rights Council installed a commission of inquiry to scrutinize the Israeli operations, including the blockade. See the report at: A/HRC/3/2, 23 November 2006.

[33] Fink 2008.

2016, the MTF UNIFIL is still ongoing. In a press release from February 2015, the UN stated that, 'Since the start of its operations on 15 October 2006, MTF has hailed around 63,000 ships and referred almost 6,000 suspicious vessels to the Lebanese authorities for further inspection.'[34]

3.2.6 Libya (2011–Present)

The most recent maritime embargo operation that the UNSC authorized is part of a chapter in the tumultuous developments in Northern Africa, where the people of Egypt, Tunisia and Libya rose against their leaders, a development commonly known as the Arab Spring. In the uprising against the Libyan leader Qaddafi, the UNSC decided in February 2011 to impose economic sanctions against Qaddafi by adopting SC Res. 1971. An arms embargo, an asset freeze and a travel ban were imposed by the UNSC to force Qaddafi to stop using violence against the Libyan population. After Qaddafi used fighter jets to stop the uprising, the international community's call for a no fly zone (NFZ) became louder. A few weeks later, on 17 March 2011, the UNSC adopted SC Res. 1973 (2011), which authorized the use of force to protect the civilian population and also authorized the enforcement of the imposed sanctions at sea. SC Res. 1973 formed the basis for two military operations: Operation *Odyssey Dawn* (OOD) and the NATO-led force *Unified Protector* (OUP). Part of the latter operation consisted of a maritime arms embargo operation off the coast of Libya.[35] NATO's factsheet mentions on the embargo operation's *modus operandi*:

> 8 Allies (Belgium, Canada, Greece, Italy, Netherlands, Spain, Turkey, and United Kingdom) are providing 18 ships and submarines to monitor and enforce the arms embargo mandated by the UN. They are supported by surveillance planes and fighter jets as required. The Task Force's ships enforcing the arms embargo will remain in international waters and will not enter Libyan territorial waters. While NATO cannot block all routes into the country, it has cut off the quickest, easiest and straightest route to Libya.
>
> NATO ships will use surveillance to verify the activity of shipping in the region, separating out legitimate commercial and private traffic from suspicious vessels that warrant closer inspection. Suspicious traffic will be hailed by radio, and if they cannot give satisfactory information about their cargoes, the NATO ships are authorized to intercept them. As a last resort, the Task Force is empowered to use force.

---

[34] UNIFIL website, 'UNIFIL Maritime Task Force transfer of authority', 26 February 2015. At: http://unifil.unmissions.org/Default.aspx?tabid=11552&ctl=Details&mid=15105&ItemID=24484&language=en-US.

[35] Fink 2011, pp. 237–260.

> If weapons or mercenaries are found, the vessel and its crew will be escorted to a secure port where international and national authorities will take charge. Suspected aircraft can be intercepted and escorted to an airport designated by NATO.[36]

The NATO operation ended eight months later, shortly after the death of Qaddafi on 20 October 2011, after the Council stopped the authorization to use force with regard to the situation in Libya in SC Res. 2016 (2011). NATO published that 2.862 vessels had been diverted and 293 vessels had been boarded. Eleven ships were denied entry into Libyan ports, as they posed a risk to the civilian population.[37]

The end of NATO's operations in 2011, however, did not prove to be the start of a calm process of rebuilding the State. In March 2014, about three years after the conflict and with Libya going through an internal struggle with local militias fighting against the Libyan government and holding oil ports while attempting to sell the oil at sea, the UNSC adopted another resolution, SC Res. 2146 (2014), that authorized inspecting vessels on the high seas, when designated by the Sanctions Committee. The UN resolution was adopted a few days after US Navy Seals operating from *USS Roosevelt* had stopped and boarded the *Morning Glory* in international waters in the vicinity of Cyprus. The vessel was said to be stateless and tried to sell crude oil with a tanker that was stolen earlier.[38] The vessel was escorted back to the Libyan port of Es Sidra.

3.3 Strand 2: The September 11 Attacks

The September 11, 2001 attacks on the Twin Towers in the United States expanded the scope of using maritime interception into new waters. MIO became an important means in the fight against terrorism at sea. While in the ten years before the attack MIO grew out to be firmly connected to the UN collective security system, during the naval operations that followed the 9/11 attacks a definite step was taken away from the view that maritime interception operations were only related to maritime economic enforcement operations mandated by the UN. MIO were was now applied in a wider scope. Not only did the scope of application widen from UN sanctions to terrorism, but it also widened from goods to persons.

The military reaction to the terrorist attacks resulted into two naval operations that started almost immediately after 11 September: Operation *Enduring Freedom*

---

[36] NATO Factsheet (no date), Operation UNIFIED PROTECTOR NATO Arms Embargo against Libya. At: www.nato.int/nato_static/assets/pdf/pdf_2011_03/unified-protector-arms-embargo-factsheet.pdf.

[37] NATO Factsheet (October 2011), Operation UNIFIED PROTECTOR NATO-led Arms Embargo against Libya. At: http://www.nato.int/nato_static/assets/pdf/pdf_2011_10/20111005_111005-factsheet_arms_embargo.pdf.

[38] *US Department of Defense*, press release, no. NR-126-14; March 17, 2014, DoD Statement on Boarding of Commercial Tanker Morning Glory. At http://www.defense.gov/Releases/Release.aspx?ReleaseID=16582.

(OEF) and Operation *Active Endeavour* (OAE). Both were predominantly interception operations. In the first phase of OEF, however, naval forces were also supporting combat operations in Afghanistan from the sea. The aim of both maritime interception operations was not to enforce economic measures imposed by the UNSC, but rather to locate suspected terrorists along with their supporting networks and to deny them the use of the sea. The subsequent focus on weapons of mass destruction and Iraq that followed after September 11 led to a third military operation that included a maritime dimension. The perceived threat of WMD in the hands of terrorists moved the attention back to Iraq, which led to the military invasion of the Iraq, on 20 March 2003: Operation *Iraqi Freedom* (OIF).

3.3.1 Operation Enduring Freedom

Even though Afghanistan does not have a coastline or a navy, the military campaign against the Taliban and Al Qaida in Afghanistan still had a maritime dimension. On 7 October 2001, naval forces of a coalition of States[39] started interception operations in the seas around the Arabian Peninsula. The operation aimed at deterring, denying and disrupting the movement of terrorists, and also supported the war in Afghanistan from the sea with strike and close air support operations.[40] With regard to the first aspect of the operation, the US coined the term *Leadership Interdiction Operations* (LIO) for the search for terrorists at sea. Tactically, LIO are similar to MIO but with a different objective: persons instead of goods. The area in which the searches were undertaken was the waters between Pakistan and the Horn of Africa. Although the *Enduring Freedom* mission was firstly connected to military operations in relation to Afghanistan, it has over the years developed into an overarching title for different military efforts against terrorism, all of which may have different legal backgrounds.

3.3.2 Operation Active Endeavour

NATO's involvement in Afghanistan since 2003 did not include a maritime dimension.[41] There has never been a naval component within the ISAF operation.[42] That is, however, not to say that NATO did not do anything at sea as a reaction to 9/11.

[39] Schneller mentions that the order of battle on 7 October was a total of 48 coalition warships: 23 US, 20 British, 2 French and 1 Australian. Schneller 2008, pp. 193–207.

[40] Schneller 2008, p. 196.

[41] NATO deployed the International Security and Assistance Force (ISAF).

[42] Warships from several NATO States did, however, apparently support ISAF with aircraft carriers in the Arabian Sea, from where NATO aircraft would take off to provide air support in Afghanistan. See Ruiz Palmer 2016, pp. 371–372. But the ISAF operation never had a naval component command to command a naval force under the ISAF operation.

It started Operation *Active Endeavour* (OAE). The operation was mounted by NATO on 26 October 2001 aiming '*to help deter, defend, disrupt and protect against terrorism*'.[43] The operation was unique in the sense that NATO for the first time ever invoked its cornerstone-article, Article 5 of the NATO-Treaty.[44] Launching OAE was one of the eight measures NATO took to support the US in its activities against terrorism.[45] The Standing NATO Maritime Group (SNMG, back then named STANAVFORMED)[46] was assigned to patrol the Eastern Mediterranean Sea. In 2003, NATO expanded OAE into the Strait of Gibraltar in order to protect merchant shipping passing through the strait. The escort operations through the strait of Gibraltar (STROGOPS) were suspended in 2004, and were kept dormant ever since. In 2004, operations expanded to encompass the whole Mediterranean Sea.[47] Apart from the development in 2004 to include also non-NATO nations in OAE (which created another purpose to the operation, as a vehicle for regional military cooperation) a second significant change in 2009 moved the operation from a platform based operation to a network-based operation.[48] With that the focus of operations moved away from 'grey hulls' patrolling the seas to building networks between States and relevant organizations, and interlinking data to enhance maritime situational awareness at sea. Ultimately, by the end of 2016 NATO decided to terminate OAE and transform the existing operation in Operation *Sea Guardian* (OSG). The transformation from OAE to OSG meant a shift from supporting counter-terrorism operations to enhancing maritime security. NATO's Maritime Command in Northwood (UK) that commanded OAE on an operational level stated that more than 100.000 vessels were hailed and 155 vessels boarded during the course of the operation.[49] No major interception incidents have however been highlighted in the public realm since the existence of OAE, which can be attributed to the efforts of this operation.

3.3.3 Operation Iraqi Freedom

On board the *USS Abraham Lincoln,* on 1 May 2003, US President George Bush announced that major combat operations against the Iraqi Armed Forces were over.[50] Although the renewed focus on Iraq in relation to the possible existence of

[43] http://www.nato.int/cps/ar/natolive/topics_7932.htm.

[44] NATO *press release* 124, 12 September 2011. www.nato.int/docu/pr/2001/p01-124e.htm.

[45] See on these measures Gordon 2001–2002, pp. 1–18.

[46] Standing Naval Force Mediterranean.

[47] *NATO Briefing paper, Active Endeavour*, July 2006.

[48] http://www.nato.int/cps/en/natolive/topics_7932.htm.

[49] http://www.mc.nato.int/ops/Pages/OAE.aspx.

[50] Bergen 2011, p. 172.

weapons of mass destruction and the legal basis for the invasion of Iraq in 2003 was hotly debated, it is clear that Operation *Iraqi Freedom* (OIF) that commenced in March 2003 was undertaken within the legal context of the law of armed conflict. Whereas the US prepared for prize taking during OIF, warships of the UK appear not to have been involved in any interception of vessels.[51] After major combat ended, the US and UK became occupying powers in Iraq, the so-called *coalition provisional authority*, CPA, which was supported by other States. On 28 June 2004, the head of the CPA, Paul Bremer III, handed back the sovereignty to Iraq after the adoption of SC Res. 1546 (2004). Even though the occupation of Iraq was over, the military presence of the coalition in Iraq lasted until 2012. Unable to obtain sufficient legal guarantees against possible criminal prosecution of foreign service-members in Iraq, the US, UK and NATO forces left Iraq just before the first of January 2012.[52]

3.3.4 Multiple MIO

It is interesting to note that at one stage in 2003 multiple maritime interceptions operations with different legal bases were conducted simultaneously in the Persian Gulf and Arabian Sea region, carried out by warships of different States. During Operation *Iraqi Freedom* the UN sanctions imposed against Iraq were still operative and enforced by the MIF.[53] At the same time interceptions by OEF took place in other maritime areas around the Arabian Peninsula in the context of military operations with regard to Afghanistan. Different legal bases for MIO existed therefore in roughly the same operational area. Since 2002[54] all naval operations were coordinated from the US/UK-led naval headquarters in Bahrain, the

[51] See Brown 2010, p. 133. Brown states that: 'During the international armed conflict in 2003, while it was determined by coalition partners that their naval forces could as a matter of law have exercised belligerent rights of visit and search against enemy and (in certain circumstances) neutral vessels, this never occurred'.

[52] Fink 2012, pp. 261–264.

[53] Although SC Res. 1483 ended the economic embargo that was a result of the Iraq-Kuwait invasion, arguably, it did not lift the embargo for arms-related material. In the post-conflict situation it appears that still a ground for MIO against Iraq was left. Paragraph 10 of SC Res. 1483 (2003) reads:

> Decides that, with the exception of prohibitions related to the sale or supply to Iraq of arms and related materiel other than those arms and related materiel required by the Authority to serve the purposes of this and other related resolutions, all prohibitions related to trade with Iraq and the provision of financial or economic resources to Iraq established by resolution 661 (1990) and subsequent relevant resolutions, including resolution 778 (1992) of 2 October 1992, shall no longer apply;

[54] Before 2002 the headquarters was primarily a US naval headquarters.

Combined Forces Maritime Component Command (CFMCC), tasked to coordinate all the naval operations around the Arabian Peninsula. The forces commanded by this headquarters were split in several different taskforces to keep a clear enough separation of the different mandates that were coordinated by the headquarters.[55] One can imagine, however, the challenges of multiple MIO in the same area and coordinated by one headquarters. In his paper, Crist relates to the following incident:

> A boarding action was undertaken by a Canadian warship that boarded a vessel within the OEF-context, after which the vessel was released. The commander of the warship was asked, however, to board again to search for Iraqi agents. The Canadians declined a second boarding of the same vessel because Canada did not take part in OIF.[56]

The existence of multiple and simultaneously ongoing maritime interception operations prompted States to politically decide to follow different paths in the manner in which way they gave authority to their warships participating in these operations. An Australian military legal advisor, participating in both the MIF and OIF relates that, although the Iraq War of 2003 opened up to the legal regime of the law of armed conflict, Australian warships continued utilizing the UN MIO regime, rather than switching to belligerent rights.[57] She states:

> The coalition forces could have used the traditional laws of naval warfare as just outlined, or the long-standing and long-practised Security Council resolution regime. It was the latter legal framework that was utilised. Given that for the previous 13 years, the MIO forces had been using the sanctions resolutions regime — and importantly, that the neutral or friendly shipping in the Gulf was also familiar with the mechanisms of that regime — it was appropriate that those resolutions, rather than naval warfare, continued to be utilized.[58]

In that same respect, Commodore Neil Brown, head of the UK Navy Legal Services, mentions that:

> …the United Kingdom decided to rely solely upon the UN Security Council resolutions that permitted the use of all necessary means to stop and search all inward and outward shipping, and to seize any goods breaking the comprehensive sanctions against Iraq. US naval forces, on the other hand, sought in addition to establish the necessary mechanisms to be able to exercise the belligerent rights of visit and search.[59]

---

[55] Throughout the years, the headquarters had to make several changes to its organizational structure to accommodate all the different mandates and politics that comes with it that occurred in the area around the Arabian Peninsula. Currently, the naval headquarters in Bahrain has separate US (NAVCENT), UK (UKMCC) and coalition headquarters, the Combined Maritime Forces (CMF). The latter exists of TF 150, 151 and 152. A detailed description (in Dutch) of the history of the naval headquarters is given by Kuijper and Both 2010, pp. 600–617.

[56] Crist 2008, p. 210.

[57] See also Commodore (Australian Navy) David Letts, who appears to imply that although a number of legal bases could have been used during the Iraq War, Australia settled with UNCLOS authorities only. Letts 2005.

[58] Campbell 2009, p. 264. The Netherlands stopped participating in the MIF in 2000, before the 9/11 attacks. It then started to participate in OEF.

[59] Brown 2010, p. 133.

Be that as it may, by this time the term MIO had evolved beyond the meaning connected to UN-mandated maritime embargo operations. It had by now become an operational term of art in which the operational action of boarding operations of foreign-flagged vessels was meant, irrespective of its legal basis or purpose.

3.4 Strand 3: Enhancing Maritime Security

The third strand of evolution in MIO is the expansion of MIO beyond Al Qaida, the Taliban and its supporters to various maritime threats of terrorism in general. Many military initiatives have started since the so-called *Global War on Terror* (GWOT) focused the attention of military forces on terrorism in a broader sense. In the maritime domain, the GWOT focused largely on possible terrorist acts against maritime security and threats of WMD. In the context of maritime interception operations three initiatives must be mentioned. The first is the expansion of maritime interception operations beyond Al Qaida and the Taliban and its supporters, resulting into maritime security operations (MSO). Second is the proliferation security initiative (PSI) and third is the updating of the SUA measures in 2005.

3.4.1 Expanded MIO and Maritime Security Operations (MSO)

Maritime embargo operations in support of economic sanctions have been called by some traditional or limited MIO.[60] AS stated above, the reaction to 9/11 expanded the use of MIO to hostilities. This subsequently introduced MIO as an instrument against the wider terrorist threat beyond Al Qaida and its supporters and beyond Afghanistan. Although the operations against terrorism are generally understood by the US Government to be based on the right of self-defence, it is not the same self-defence as was used to commence Operation *Enduring Freedom*. The MIO conducted in the general anti-terrorism scope were called 'expanded MIO, abbreviated to EMIO.[61] O'Rourke states that, 'EMIO are authorized by the President and directed by the Secretary of Defence to intercept vessels identified to be transporting terrorists and/or terrorist-related materiel that poses an imminent threat to the United States and its allies.[62] Allen adds that EMIO are, 'designed to intercept

[60] Hodgkinson 2007, p. 589.

[61] Hodgkinson 2007, p. 626.

[62] O'Rourke 2009, p. 3. See also the definition of EMIO in Joint Publication 3-03:

> Expanded maritime interception operations (EMIO) are authorized by the President and directed by the Secretary of Defense to deter, degrade, and/or disrupt or gather intelligence to prevent attacks against the US and its allies. EMIO involves interception of vessels

targeted personnel or material that pose an imminent threat to the U.S. EMIO may involve multinational forces and may be implemented even when sanctions have not been imposed.'[63] Together with the more strategic development of a focus on maritime security, this expansion of using MIO to a wider terrorist threat moved the international community in taking the path towards Maritime Security Operations (MSO): maritime policing of the seas with a view to enhance maritime security, what in the view of the US is mainly be threatened by terrorism.

3.4.2 Proliferation Security Initiative (PSI)

As the US expanded its military efforts against terrorism in a wider sense and in a broader geographical context, it also prompted new initiatives with regard to interception operations. At this point, along with terrorists, weapons of mass destruction became a focal point in the maritime dimension. NATO's Deputy Assistant Secretary-General for weapons of mass destruction policy notes in 2009: 'Looking at the past, together with the severe implications of using CBRN materials and coupled with the motivation of certain terrorists groups such as Al Qaida, we must acknowledge that WMD are a real and likely threat'.[64] In May 2003, US President George Bush, having closed the major combat operations phase in Iraq and still in search of WMD, launched the *Proliferation Security Initiative* (PSI) aiming to counter and minimize the threat of WMD at sea. The PSI connects the arms control efforts of proliferation of WMD with the terrorist threat. The *So San* incident,[65] which occurred in December 2001 in the Arabian Sea, is always mentioned in this context as *the* example that underlined that the threat of WMD was real and the legal possibilities were limited.[66] According to Davis, the PSI

identified to be transporting terrorists and/or terrorist-related materiel that pose an imminent threat to the United States and its allies. EMIO may be implemented without sanctions and may involve multinational forces or OGAs. The legal rationales required to permit boarding include those listed in subparagraph (4), above.

[63] Allen 2006, pp. 77–139.

[64] Roberts 2009, p. 1.

[65] The vessel *So San* was suspected of carrying scud missiles from North Korea to Yemen. After the boarding by Spanish forces from the Spanish warship *Navarra* upon request of the US this suspicion proved to be true. The name *So San* was freshly painted on the stern while no vessel was registered under that name in North Korea. According to Roach after being queried, the master of the vessel replied that it was registered in Cambodia. The Cambodian authorities appeared to have confirmed that a vessel meeting the description was registered in Cambodia, but under the name of *Pan Hope* instead of *So San*. No legal ground was, however, found to seize the scuds. Nothing prohibited North Korea to ship scuds to Yemen. The *So San* was released to proceed to Yemen with its original cargo still aboard.

[66] Guilfoyle 2005, pp. 735–736.

emerged from two major concerns. First, the terrorist attacks against the *USS Cole*[67] in 2000 and the French Tanker *Limburg*[68] in October 2002 had heightened the fear of more terrorist attacks in the maritime domain. Second, it was viewed that terrorist groups were trying to find weak spots in the international maritime traffic and transport systems to transport chemical, biological or nuclear weapons.[69] The essence of PSI, as Klein mentions: 'is its nature as a political and cooperative regime, which facilitates coordination between the States concerned and allows for the better flow of information and interaction at an operational level between the participants.'[70] The PSI is neither an organization nor a treaty, but an initiative based on the willingness of States to cooperate in the non-proliferation of WMD. It is based upon a set of four interdiction principles. These principles rely on already existing legal frameworks for the proliferation of WMD and focus on the interdiction of chemical, biological and nuclear weapons, their delivery systems and related material. Furthermore, to strengthen the legal grounds for actual interception within the context of PSI, the US sought to conclude bilateral shipboarding agreements with other States which were to strengthen the PSI through the ability to board foreign-flagged vessels on the high seas.[71] There is, however, hardly any public information on actual 'PSI-interceptions'. The interception of the *BBC China* in 2003[72] and *M/V Light* in 2011[73] appear to be the two publicly known cases. Apart from the US-led efforts, also the UNSC adopted SC Res. 1540 (2004) which also aims at proliferation of WMD. The resolution however lacks to provide an additional legal ground for maritime enforcement at sea.

---

[67] In October 2000, the *USS Cole* suffered a small boat attack in the port of Aden, Yemen. 17 American sailors died in the attack. The attack was claimed by Al Qaida.

[68] The tanker *Limburg* was attacked by a small boat full of explosives off the coast of Yemen that blew a hole in the hull of the tanker.

[69] Davis 2013, p. 147.

[70] Klein 2011, p. 193.

[71] Kraska and Pedrozo have published in 2013 a list of eleven US-bilateral PSI ship boarding agreements. Kraska and Pedrozo 2013, p. 794.

[72] The German-flagged vessel *BBC China* was a vessel that carried centrifuge parts for the Libyan nuclear program. The vessel was ordered by Germany to divert to the port of Taranto in Southern Italy, where agents of the US boarded the vessel for a search. It appears, however, to be debated whether the *BBC China* operation can be claimed as a PSI-operation. See: www.armscontrol.org/act/2005_07-08/Interdiction_Misrepresented.

[73] The Belize-flagged vessel *M/V Ligh t* was on its way from North Korea to Myanmar and was suspected of carrying missile parts. It was forced to turn back by the US who dispatched the *USS McCampbell* to intercept the *M/V Light*. Although authority to board was given by Belize, based on the US-Belize ship boarding agreement the master of the *M/V Light* refused to be boarded. Instead, it turned back to North Korea. Sanger 2011. At: www.nytimes.com/2011/06/13/world/asia/13missile.html?_r=0.

3.4.3 *Updating International Agreements: The SUA Protocol 2005*

Next to PSI and the UNSC putting the issue of WMD into the limelight through SC Res. 1540, other paths to enable action against threats to maritime security were also sought. One has been the path of international agreements. Treaties on maritime terrorism existed since the hijacking of the *Achille Lauro*, in October 1985.[74] Three years later, the *Convention on the Suppression of Unlawful Acts Against the Safety of Maritime Navigation* (SUA Convention) made punishable the events that had occurred on board the *Achille Lauro*. Some authors take the position that one of the major flaws of the SUA Convention is that it does not create any authority for non-flag States to board a foreign-flagged vessel to stop and arrest persons.[75] The focus on terrorism after 9/11 and a felt need to find more instruments to take effective action spurred to address this lacuna. As a result the SUA Protocol (2005) was created.[76] This protocol aims at updating the SUA Convention in two ways. It makes it firstly possible to avoid time-consuming procedures to board a foreign-flagged vessel. This enhances maritime security through the ability to act more swiftly and at the same time to adhere to the fundamental principle of exclusive flag State jurisdiction.[77] Second, a new set of offences was introduced that focuses on the use of WMD. The SUA Protocol (2005) entered into force in 2010.[78]

3.5 Strand 4: Piracy

Carvalho divides the role of naval forces in peacekeeping after the Cold War in two main legs. One is naval peacekeeping that supports land-based operations. The second is naval peacekeeping by naval forces that act autonomously from land operations. With today's focus on maritime security, he has noted a shift from land-based support operations to autonomous sea operations. Counter-piracy operations, he concludes, are; 'in a certain way, the empirical achievement of an autonomous concept of peacekeeping operations at sea envisaged by scholars engaged in the naval peacekeeping debate.'[79] Countering piracy off the coast of Somalia has since 2008 become a major activity for navies. It also pushed NATO

---

[74] Treves 1990, p. 69.

[75] MacDonald 2013, p. 492.

[76] There are two protocols to the SUA Convention. The Protocol of 2005 to the Convention for the Suppression of Unlawful Acts against the Safety of Maritime Navigation, and Protocol of 2005 to the Protocol for the Suppression of Unlawful Acts against the Safety of Fixed Platforms Located on the Continental Shelf. Whenever the 2005 Protocol is mentioned, the first protocol is meant.

[77] MacDonald 2013, p. 509.

[78] 10 July 2010.

[79] Carvalho de Oliviera 2012, p. 54.

and the EU to go beyond their usual 'maritime backyard' of the Mediterranean Sea, into the seas around the Arabian Peninsula. Although piracy has been on the agenda of the Asian States adjacent to the Strait of Malacca for years,[80] when the UNSC ultimately got involved in the issue of piracy off the coast of Somalia, the world's focus turned to piracy, and more importantly, it also pulled the criminal act of piracy within the scope of a threat to international peace and security. Interestingly, however, as SC Res. 2115 (2013) noted, piracy *by itself* is not considered as a threat to peace and security, but has linked the issue of piracy to the situation in Somalia that continues to be a threat to peace and security.

When naval operations around the Arabian Peninsula started in the context of OEF, States were confronted with piracy activities off the coast of Somalia. With regard to the conflict in Somalia discussion arose whether action against terrorists and pirates could legally be linked. Seeking to enhance possibilities to find ways to act against terrorists at sea, the law of piracy was viewed as a possible framework. Piracy, hitchhiking on the back of the efforts to find more avenues to fight terrorism at sea, rose on the international agenda.[81] Also, already earlier, since 2006, the World Food Program (WFP) sought ways to protect their humanitarian shipping from attacks and hijacking by Somali pirates and reached out to navies that were conducting their anti-terrorist task in the same region. Whereas the attention to piracy may have surfaced through the debate on how to act against terrorists at sea, current counter-piracy operations are not conceived as anti-terrorism operations. As the former legal advisor to the NATO Secretary General Peter Olson commented in regard of the nature of NATO's counter-piracy Operation *Ocean Shield*: 'Although designed for and conducted by military forces, *Ocean Shield* is neither conceived nor implemented as a counter-terrorism or combat operation.'[82]

3.5.1 Counter-Piracy Operations[83]

In August 2007, the UNSC adopted SC Res. 1772 to extend the ongoing mission of the African Union in Somalia (AMISOM). This resolution also encouraged member States with naval units in the area to be vigilant against any acts of piracy off the coast of Somalia and to protect merchant shipping, in particular shipping with humanitarian aid. Somalia had been considered a failed State for years and now also

---

[80] Bateman and Chan opine that piracy and armed robbery in the Asian regions is currently generally not a serious problem. The level is not of the sort that it needs operational involvement of non-regional actors. Bateman and Chan 2014, pp. 134–135.

[81] See on the legal difference between piracy and terrorism Guilfoyle 2014, pp. 33–52.

[82] Olson 2014, p. 183.

[83] Some view that the term 'counter-piracy' should be distinct from 'anti-piracy'. Whereas counter-piracy relates to activities of the State to protect vessels from being pirated, the latter term is reserved for practical activities of owners or masters of the vessel to minimize the risks that vessels can be boarded.

suffered attacks against the humanitarian relief shipping moving along the African coast into Somalia. France, Denmark, Canada and the Netherlands were the first States to send warships to protect merchant shipping that transported humanitarian aid for the WFP. In 2008, the UNSC adopted SC Res. 1816, which marked the active involvement of the UNSC and UN member States in the fight against piracy off the coast of Somalia.

Based on the Council's call to fight piracy to protect international trade and humanitarian aid, three different multilateral operations were set up. NATO commenced with Operation *Allied Provider* (OAP) in 2008. Its primary aim was to protect WFP-relief shipping. OAP took place from mid-October to December 2008. The NATO efforts were to help bridge the gap between the EU-decision on 8 December 2008 to send a naval force to the Somali region and the actual start of the EU operation, Operation *Atalanta*.[84] NATO opined that next to the EU operation *Atalanta* it could still have a significant role in countering piracy and commenced Operation *Allied Protector* (OAP II) in March 2009. In August 2009, NATO launched its longer-term counter-piracy effort, Operation *Ocean Shield* (OOS). This operation terminated at the end of 2016. Next to the EU and NATO initiatives, a US-led coalition was launched in January 2009 to counter piracy. These coalition efforts were brought under the command of Combined Maritime Forces (CMF).[85] One of the three taskforces (TF 151) of CMF is set up to conduct counter-piracy operations. Apart from these multilateral initiatives, individual States also decided to send warships on a unilateral basis to the seas around the Horn of Africa and the Arabian Sea. States, such as India, Russia and China, deployed warships that started contributing to enhancing the safety of shipping in the region. As is often mentioned, these different naval operations, all with their own specific mandate, cooperate and coordinate amongst each other in order to give the maximum effect to their presence in the region.[86]

The legal challenges concerning piracy are many.[87] One of the major reasons is that the fight against piracy also focuses on the aftermath of the actions taken at sea. Counter-piracy operations have underlined the challenges of ultimately prosecuting the persons in a court of law. Challenges for instance lie with gaps in the existing

---

[84] EU Council decision 2008/918/CFSP, 8 December 2008.

[85] CMF is an international partnership organization with around 30 states that contribute vessels and staff to its Headquarters in Bahrain and has three taskforces under its command: CTF 150, 151 and 152. CTF 150 focuses on maritime security and anti-terrorist operations at sea in the Arabian Sea, CTF 151 focuses on piracy and CTF 152 focuses on security and cooperation in the Persian Gulf.

[86] The *SHADE*-meeting (Shared Awareness and Deconfliction) is often mentioned in this context.

[87] In the beginning of the 20th century the focal point of piracy was still on piracy in East Asia (e.g. Beckman 2002, pp. 317–341; Menefee 1999, pp. 353–370). When the issue of maritime terrorism came more to the foreground, a focus was put on the relationship between piracy and terrorism (e.g. Garmon 2002, pp. 257–275; Jose Luis Jesus 2003, pp. 363–400; Mejia jr. 2003, pp. 153–175. When the major naval operations began after the involvement of the UN, the focus shifted to the challenges that arose with fighting pirates off the coast of Somalia. (e.g. Guilfoyle 2010a, b, pp. 1–13; Treves 2009, pp. 399–408).

international and national legal frameworks relating to piracy. These include the interaction of national and international law and the practical application of law enforcement at sea. Counter-piracy operations have also shown that conducting maritime interception operations in a successful manner planning must go beyond the operational military dimension at sea. It requires coordination with, for instance, public prosecutors, States and different governmental departments.

One significant issue that has been pointed out by counter-piracy operations is that it has underlined the shift to law enforcement operations at sea. Douglas Guilfoyle aptly noted that pirates for a number of reasons can be seen as 'agents of change'.[88] One of those changes has been the shift to the law enforcement paradigm within the context of a military response authorized by a UN Security Council resolution. It also underlined a start of more serious thoughts with regard to the application of human rights law in naval operations. Several cases concerning piracy have appeared before national courts in a number of States, among which are Germany,[89] the United States,[90] The Netherlands,[91] Kenya and the Seychelles.[92] On a more practical level, counter-piracy operations extended the need for military also to be in the courtrooms after the arrest. Crews of Dutch warships involved in counter-piracy operations were asked to make statements in courts in the Seychelles and Germany. In December 2014, the jurisprudence on piracy has also been enriched by judgments of the European Court of Human Rights. The ECtHR made judgment in two cases concerning piracy, emerging from French actions off and on the coast of Somalia.[93]

---

[88] Guilfoyle 2009, pp. 81–106.

[89] On 19 October 2012, the district court in Hamburg sentenced ten Somali pirates that had hijacked the German-flagged vessel *Taipan*. The pirates were detained after a Netherlands boarding team from *Hr. Ms. Tromp* boarded the vessel in 2010 and detained the pirates.

[90] Domestic courts in the United States have had several cases against Somali pirates, among which the case of the Hijacking of the *Maersk Alabama* in 2009.

[91] District Court of Rotterdam: *Samanyulo* (Netherlands Antilles-flagged), *Choizil* (South African-flagged) and *Al Fedda*. The first case involved the capture of pirates by the Danish warship *Absalon*, where the suspect-pirates were transferred to the Netherlands. The third case involved an incident where the pirates opened fire on the marines that where in the conduct of approaching the dhow. The public prosecutor attempted to press charges on account of murder or manslaughter against the approach marines, but they were acquitted of that charge.

[92] The UN-SG report on piracy (S/2013/623) mentions the following on Kenya and the Seychelles:

> 45. Countries in the region supported by the Counter-Piracy Programme continue to receive individuals suspected of piracy for prosecution. In total, 53 suspects remain on remand in Kenya, Mauritius and Seychelles, with the Programme supporting their trials. Another 153 convicted pirates are currently serving their sentences in Kenya and Seychelles. Prison conditions for these inmates continue to be monitored and improved where required.

[93] *Ali Samatar and other vs. France* (appl. nos. 17110/10 and 17301/10) and *Hassan and others vs. France* (appl. nos. 46695/10 and 54588/10), 4 December 2014. The first case (Samatar) related to the hijack of the French-flagged vessel *Ponant* in 2007. The hijackers were arrested on land by French authorities. The second case (Hassan) is related to the French-flagged yacht *Carre d'As* in September 2008. It was hijacked and subsequently freed by French commandos on board the French frigate *Courbet*.

Table 3.1 Counter-piracy operations off the coast of Somalia since 2008 (*Source* M. Fink)

	Operation Alias	Organization	Duration of operation
1	Operation Allied Provider (OAP)	NATO	24 October–12 December 2008
2	Operation Allied Protector (OAPII)	NATO	24 March–17 August 2009
3	Operation Ocean Shield (OOS)	NATO	17 August 2009–December 2016
4	Operation Atalanta	EU	8 December 2008–present
5	Combined maritime forces (CMF)—CTF 151	US-led coalition of forces	January 2009–present
6	Individual deployments of States	Individual States	Differs per State

In SC Res. 2067 (2012), the UNSC noted the decline of number of vessels kidnapped by pirates. A CMF press release in June 2015 mentioned that since 2012, there were no successful pirate attacks in the operational area in which the combined naval efforts were operating, but without an effective deterrent presence the threat could re-emerge again.[94] In 2016 NATO ended its counter-piracy operations. In 2018, The EU operation *Atalanta* is still ongoing (Table 3.1).

3.6 The Israeli Interception Operations

The four strands of evolution of maritime interception all, in a certain way, are part of a very broad unfolding development in international affairs. Conflict in Iraq and Afghanistan are interconnected with weapons of mass destruction and terrorism. The latter again hooked into the confrontation with piracy off the coast of Somalia. Instability in the Northern African region was the breeding ground for the Arab Spring that brought the ultimate end of Qaddafi. Maritime interception operations during these developments played an operational level role. On a separate note, Israel has also contributed to MIO with practice. The Israeli contribution lies both in large-scale naval operations and single action against vessels. With regard to the first, Operation *Change of Direction* (2006) and Operation *Cast Lead* (2009) can be mentioned, both with a significant interception role for its naval forces. In 2006, Israel commenced military operations against Hezbollah, which included establishing a blockade off the coast of Lebanon. The blockade was, albeit in a different legal context, taken over by MTF UNIFIL. In 2009, Israel established a blockade off the coast of Gaza as part of Operation *Cast Lead*. Although the naval blockade

[94] See http://combinedmaritimeforces.com/2015/06/22/international-maritime-community-works-together-to-counter-piracy-at-shade/.

operations against Hezbollah and Hamas in a way were made more palpable by the prior legal debate that occurred with regard to military operations against Al Qaida (to which the acceptance that military force in a self-defence situation could be used not only against States but also against non-state actors) it ran up against major protests when in May 2010, Israel boarded the *Mavi Marmara* which had attempted to breach the blockade off the coast of the Gaza. The action resulted in nine dead passengers of the vessel, followed by views of many legal commentators.[95] As of 2015, the Gaza blockade is still in force. Israel also intercepted the *Karine-A* (2002),[96] the *MV Francop* (2009),[97] and the *Klos-C*[98] (in 2014), all of which were considered to be a threat to Israel.

3.7 Final Remarks

In 1995, Zeigler wrote that,'Multinational interception operations are a creature of the post-World War II era, and rely on the United Nations Charter for their justification'.[99] Although maritime interception operations are indeed firmly established as a means to enforce decisions of the UNSC, at this point in time it is clear that a different conclusion must be drawn with regard to the possible legal justifications for MIO. The term MIO has gradually outgrown its original meaning connected to the maritime enforcement of UN sanctions and is now used in a much broader sense. It has lost its earlier specific legal meaning as a type of naval operations that occurs only in the context of economic sanctions imposed by the UNSC. The legal justifications for MIO can now also be found in other sources of general international law. What this short history of maritime interception operations has furthermore shown is that the scope of MIO has broadened to include the interception

[95] E.g. Farrant 2013, pp. 81–98; Heintschel von Heinegg 2011, pp. 211–236; Guilfoyle 2010a, b, pp. 171–213; Kraska 2010, pp. 367–395; Buchan 2012, pp. 264–273; Scott 2010.

[96] In 2002, Israeli Defense Forces boarded the Tonga-flagged vessel *Karine-A*, which carried 50 tons of weapons suspected to be for the Palestinian authority. See Hodgkinson 2007, pp. 623–625.

[97] On 3 November 2009, Israel boarded the *MV Francop* sailing under the flag of Antigua and Barbuda. Israel found more than three hundred tons of weapons on board, which according to Israel were meant for Hezbollah. The vessel was directed to Ashdod Port for further examination. The shipment of weapons was said to originate from Iran. In a letter to the UN SG Israel stated that the shipment constituted a breach of SC Res. 1747 and because of: 'The intended route of the *Francop* - coupled with the types of weaponry found on board - raise serious concerns that this incident also constitutes a violation of UN Security Council Resolution 1701 and 1373.' Letter to UN SG Ban Ki Moon by Ambassador Shalev, 4 November 2009. See Ministry of Foreign Affairs Israel 2009.

[98] In March 2014, Israel boarded the Panama-flagged *Klos-C* suspected of carrying a large bulk of weapons (surface-to-surface rockets). The vessel was intercepted in the Red Sea, on its way to Sudan and ultimately destined for the Gaza. The vessel was diverted to Eilat and the crew members released. According to an Israeli spokesman the crew was not aware that they carried this cargo.

[99] Zeigler 1996, pp. 1–55.

of individuals. And persons impact on MIO in a legal sense because they bring another legal regime to the scene: international human rights law. Lastly, what may also be drawn from this short history is that in the maritime dimension different legal bases and subsequent applicable legal regimes may simultaneously exist in a certain maritime area, conducted by naval forces from sometimes the same State. It poses both challenges for warship commanders and masters of merchant vessels to understand what is legally permissible in a specific interception situation at sea.

References

Adebajo A, Keen D (2007) Sierra Leone. In: Berdal M, Economides S (eds) United Nations Interventionism, 1991–2004. Cambridge University Press, New York, pp. 246–273

Allen C (2006) Limits to the use of force in maritime operations in support of WMD counter-proliferation initiatives. In: Sparks T, Sulmasy G (eds) International Law Studies 81. Naval War College, Newport RI, pp. 77–139

Bateman S, Chan J (2014) Piracy and armed robbery against ships in the South China Sea – Possible causes and solutions. In: Wu S, Zou K (eds) Non-Traditional Security Issues and the South China Sea. Routledge, Oxford, pp. 133–144

Beckman R (2002) Combating piracy and armed robbery against ships in Southeast Asia: The way forward. Ocean Development and International Law 33, pp. 317–341

Bergen P (2011) The Longest War. The Enduring Conflict between America and Al-Qaeda. Free Press, New York/London/Toronto/Sydney

Bono G (2003) NATO's 'peace enforcement' tasks and 'policy community': 1990–1999. Routledge, London

Brown N (2010) Legal Considerations in Relation to Maritime Operations against Iraq. In: Pedrozo R (ed) International Law Studies 86. Naval War College, Newport RI, pp. 127–137

Buchan R (2012) Determining the legality of Israel's interception of the peace flotilla on May 31 2010. International and Comparative Law Quarterly, 61:1, pp. 264–273

Campbell P (2009) Twenty five. Task Group Command Legal Officer SLIPPER Four, BASTILLE & FALCONER. In: Mortimer J, Stevens D (eds) Presence, Power Projection and Sea Control. The RAN in the Gulf 1990–2009, pp. 257–265

Carvalho de Oliviera G (2012) Naval peacekeeping and piracy: Time for a critical debate. International Peacekeeping 19:1, pp. 48–61

Charron A (2011) UN Sanctions and conflict. Responding to peace and security threats. Routledge, London

Cortright D, Lopez D (2000) The Sanctions Decade. Assessing UN Strategies in the 1990s. Lynne Rienner Publishers Inc., Boulder, CO

Crist D (2008) The formation of a coalition of the willing and Operation Iraqi Freedom. In: Elleman B, Paine S (eds) Naval coalition warfare. From the Napoleonic War to Operation Iraqi Freedom. Routledge, London, pp. 208–217

Davis I (2013) The Proliferation Security Initiative. Effective multilateralism or "smoke and mirrors"? In: Meier O, Daase C (eds) Arms Control in the 21st Century. Routledge, London, pp. 146–166

ECtHR, Ali Samatar and other vs. France (appl. nos. 17110/10 and 17301/10), 4 December 2014

ECtHR, Hassan and others vs. France (appl. nos. 46695/10 and 54588/10), 4 December 2014

EU Council decision 2008/918/CFSP, 8 December 2008

Farrant J (2013) The Gaza Blockade incident and the modern law of blockade. In: Naval War College Review, 66:3, pp. 81–98

Fink M (2008) De maritieme taakgroep UNIFIL. Militair Rechtelijk Tijdschrift 4, pp. 103–112

Fink M (2011) UN-mandated maritime arms embargo operations in Operation Unified Protector. Revue de Droit Militaire et Droit de la Guerre 1:2, pp. 237–260

Fink M (2012) De ontwikkeling van de strafrechtelijke rechtsmacht over het personeel van de NAVO-trainingsmissie in Irak (NTM-I). Militair Rechtelijk Tijdschrift 6, pp. 261–264

Freedman L, Karsh E (1993) The Gulf Conflict 1990–1991. Diplomacy and war in the New World Order. Faber & Faber, London

Garmon T (2002) International law of the seas: Reconciling the law of piracy and terrorism in the wake of September 12. Tulane Maritime Law Journal 27, pp. 257–275

Gordon P (2001–2002) NATO after 11 September. Survival 43:4, pp. 1–18

Gowland-Debbas V (2004) Sanctions regimes under Article 41 of the UN Charter. In: Gowland-Debbas V (ed) National implementation of UN Sanctions. Kluwer Law International, The Hague/London/Boston, pp. 3–31

Graham-Brown S (1999) Sanctioning Saddam. The Politics of Intervention in Iraq. London/New York

Guilfoyle D (2005) The Proliferation Security Initiative: Interdiction vessels in international waters to prevent the spread of weapons of mass destruction. Melbourne University Law Review 29, pp. 733–764

Guilfoyle D (2009) Somali pirates as agents of change in international law making and organization. Cambridge Journal of International and Comparative Law 1:3, pp. 81–106

Guilfoyle D (2010a) The laws of war and the fight against Somali piracy: Combatants or criminals. Melbourne Journal of International Law 11, pp. 1–13

Guilfoyle D (2010b) The Mavi Marmara incident and blockade in armed conflict. British Yearbook of International Law 81, pp. 171–213

Guilfoyle D (2014) Piracy and terrorism. In: Koutrakos P, Skordas A (eds) The law and practice of piracy at sea: European and international perspectives. Hart Publishing, Oxford/Portland OR, pp. 33–52

Heintschel von Heinegg W (2011) Methods and means of naval warfare in non-international armed conflicts. In: Watkin K, Norris A (eds) International Law Studies 88. Naval War College, Newport RI, pp. 211–236

Hirsch J (2004) Sierra Leone. In: Malone D (ed) The UN Security Council. From the Cold War to the 21st Century. Lynne Rienner Publishers, London, pp. 521–536

Hodgkinson S (2007) Challenges to Maritime Interception Operations in the War on Terror: Bridging the Gap. American University International Law Review 22:4, pp. 853–671

Jose Luis Jesus H (2003) Protection of foreign ships against piracy and terrorism at sea: Legal aspects. The International Journal of Marine and Coastal Law 18:3, pp. 363–400

Klein N (2011) Maritime Security and the Law of the Sea. Oxford University Press, New York

Kraska J (2010) Rule selection in the case of Israel's naval blockade of Gaza: Law of naval warfare or the law of the sea? In: Schmitt MN (ed) Yearbook of humanitarian International Law 13. T. M.C Asser Press, The Hague, pp. 367–395

Kraska J, Pedrozo R (2013) International Maritime Security Law. Martinus Nijhoff Publishers, Leiden/Boston

Kreps S (2007) The 1994 Haiti intervention: A unilateral operation in multilateral clothes. The Journal of Strategic Studies, 30:3, pp. 449–474

Kuijper D, Both S (2010) Combined Maritime Forces. Het belang van deelname in een unieke maritieme coalitie. Militaire Spectator, pp. 600–617

Letts D (2005) Recent Australian Experience of the Law of the Sea and Military Operations. Australian Yearbook on International Law 24

MacDonald S (2013) The SUA 2005 Protocol: A critical reflection. In: The International Journal of Marine and Coastal Law 28, pp. 485–516

Malone D (1998) Decision-Making in the UN Security Council. The case of Haiti, 1990–1997. Clarendon Press, Oxford

Marolda E, Schneller R (1998), Shield and Sword. The United States Navy and the Persian Gulf War. Naval Institute Press, Annapolis, Maryland

Mejia jr M (2003) Maritime gerrymandering: Dilemmas in defining piracy, terrorism and other acts of maritime violence. Journal of International Commercial Law 2:2, pp. 153–175
Menefee S (1999) Foreign naval intervention in cases of piracy: Problems and strategies. The International Journal of Marine and Coastal Law 14:3, pp. 353–370
Ministerie van Defensie (2008) Eindevaluatie UNIFIL Maritiem 25 April 2008
Ministry of Foreign Affairs Israel (2009) http://mfa.gov.il/MFA/InternatlOrgs/Issues/Pages/Israel-submits-letter-of-complaint-to-UN-Secretary-General-5-Nov-2009.aspx. Accessed 12 February 2017
Mobley R (2002) The Beira Patrol. Britain's Broken Blockade. Naval War College Review 55, pp. 64–84
Morabito R (1991) Maritime interdiction: Evolution of a strategy. Ocean Development and International Law 22, pp. 301–311
NATO (1992a) Ministerial Meeting of the North Atlantic Council in Oslo, 4 June 1992
NATO (1992b) North Atlantic Council. Ministerial Meeting of the North Atlantic Council in Oslo, 4 June 1992
NATO (2006) Briefing paper Active Endeavour, July 2006.
NATO (2011a) Factsheet on Libya. www.nato.int/nato_static/assets/pdf/pdf_2011_03/unified-protector-arms-embargo-factsheet.pdf. Accessed 12 February 2017
NATO (2011b) Press release, 124, 12 September 2011. www.nato.int/docu/pr/2001/p01-124e.htm. Accessed 15 August 2013
NATO (no date) Factsheet on Sharp Guard www.nato.int/ifor/general/shrp-grd.htm. Accessed 11 March 2016
NATO (no date) Factsheet on Operation Unified Protector and the NATO Arms Embargo against Libya
O'Connell D (1975) The influence of law on sea power. Manchester University Press, Manchester
Olson J (1993) Naval Interdiction Considerations in the Use of Limited Naval Force Short of War. Naval War College Paper, Newport RI
Olson P (2014) Countering piracy off the coast of Somalia: A NATO perspective. In: Koutrakos P, Skordas A (eds) The law and practice of piracy at sea: European and international perspectives. Hart Publishing, Oxford/Portland OR, pp. 183–194
O'Rourke D (2009) Navy Role in Irregular Warfare and Counterterrorism: Background and Issues for Congress. Congressional Research Service Report for Congress, 4 June 2009
Peace D (1991) Major maritime events in the Gulf. Virginia Journal of International Law 31, pp. 545–566
Pokrant M (1999) Desert Shield at Sea. What the Navy Really Did. Greenwood Press, Westport, Connecticut/London
Roberts G (2009) Hostis Humani Generis: The threat of WMD terrorism and how NATO is facing the ultimate threat. Defence against terrorism Review 2:1, pp. 1–13
Robertson H (1991) Interdiction of Iraqi Maritime Commerce in the 1990–1991 Persian Gulf Conflict. Ocean Development and International Law 22, pp. 289–299
Ruiz Palmer D (2016) A maritime renaissance. Naval power in NATO's future. In: Krause J, Bruns S (eds) Routledge Handbook on naval strategy and security. Routledge, London, pp. 364–380
Ruiz Palmer D (2007) New operational horizons: NATO and maritime security. NATO Review. www.nato.int/docu/review/2007/issue4/english/analysis4.html. Accessed 12 February 2017
Ryan M (2000) Some practical advice for a joint force commander contemplating the use of blockade, visit and search, maritime interception operations, maritime exclusion zones, cordon sanitaire, and maritime warning zones during times of international armed conflict. Paper Naval War College, Newport RI
Sanger D (2011) U.S. Said to Turn Back North Korea Missile Shipment. New York Times, 12 June 2011. www.nytimes.com/2011/06/13/world/asia/13missile.html?_r=0. Accessed 14 June 2012

Schneller R (2008) Operation Enduring Freedom. Coalition warfare from the sea and on the sea. In: Elleman B, Paine S (eds) Naval Coalition Warfare. From the Napoleonic War to Operation Iraqi Freedom. Routledge, London, pp. 193–207

Scott G (2010) Israel's seizure of the Gaza-bound flotilla: applicable laws and legality. Research paper no. 42/2010, Osgoode Hall Law School

Stigler A (2008) Coalition warfare over Kosovo. In: Elleman B, Paine S (eds) Naval coalition warfare. From the Napoleonic War to Operation Iraqi Freedom. Routledge, London, pp. 183–192

Treves T (2009) Piracy, laws of the sea, and use of force: Developments off the coast of Somalia. European Journal of International Law 20:2, pp. 399–408

Treves T (1990) The Rome Convention for the Suppression of Unlawful Acts against the Safety of Maritime Navigation. In: Ronzitti N (ed) Maritime terrorism and international law. Nijhoff, Dordrecht, pp. 69–90

United Nations (2006) A/HRC/3/2, 23 November 2006

United Nations (2009) UN SG, Letter to Ban Ki Moon by Ambassador Shalev, 4 November 2009

United Nations (2013) UN SG, Report on Piracy (S/2013/623)

US Department of Defense (2014) Press release, no. NR-126-14; March 17, 2014, DoD Statement on Boarding of Commercial Tanker Morning Glory. www.defense.gov/Releases/Release.aspx?ReleaseID=16582. Accessed 12 February 2017

Vego M (2008) On Naval Power. Joint Force Quarterly, 50:3, pp. 8–17

Zeigler D (1996) Ubi Sumus? Quo Vadimus? Charting the Course of Maritime Interception Operations. Naval Law Review 43, pp. 1–55

Chapter 4
The Right for Warships to Intervene on Foreign-Flagged Vessels on the High Seas

Contents

Abstract As a point of departure, no foreign-flagged vessel can be interfered with without a legal basis. The fundaments of this are vested in three principles: The freedom of the high seas, exclusive jurisdiction of flag States over vessels and the principle of non-intervention. These principles also lead to the conclusion that, as a point of departure, in international law interfering with a foreign-flagged vessel is considered an exception to the rule. Current focus on enhancing maritime security has put pressure on these principles as political engagement in maritime security starts from an opposite idea: everything and everyone at sea should be under a certain level of control.

Keywords Exclusive jurisdiction · Article 92 UNCLOS · maritime security · non-intervention on foreign-flagged vessels

4.1 Introduction

When a warship intervenes on a foreign-flagged vessel it may include stopping and boarding a vessel and possibly taking goods and detaining persons. Although the legal bases and regimes regulating maritime interception are not solely based on the international law of the sea, this area of international law does provide the fundamental legal framework with regard to jurisdiction over vessels at sea. It

M. Fink, *Maritime Interception and the Law of Naval Operations*,
https://doi.org/10.1007/978-94-6265-249-1_4

is, therefore, the logical point of departure for understanding the law applicable to maritime interception operations. This chapter will briefly underline three principles in the international law of the sea fundamental to maritime interception operations and will also remark on an existing tension between these principles and the issue of enhancing maritime security.

4.2 Fundamental Principles of the Law of the Sea

It is well known that the fundaments of the legal order of the oceans as we understand them today, which are codified in the UN Convention on the Law of the Sea (UNCLOS) and considered customary international law, go back to the seventeenth century debate between the concepts of *mare liberum* and *mare clausum*. The *mare liberum* approach to the legal order of the oceans underlines the importance of the freedom of the high seas. This idea, where States cannot have exclusive right of ownership over the seas and its resources were predominantly instigated by the Dutch lawyer Hugo de Groot (1583–1645).[1] His view ultimately gained the upper hand and has since served as the basis for the legal order of the oceans. In Grotius' time, the high seas were all the seas except those that were regarded as internal waters.[2] Although his idea is still the point of departure, obviously the high seas have gradually lost terrain to other maritime zones over which States possess sovereignty or exercise sovereign rights. The freedom of the high seas is codified in Article 2 of the Convention of the High Seas (HSC) and in Article 87 UNCLOS. The effect of the existence of this freedom is the notion that States do not possess sovereignty beyond their own territory. What follows from this is that States may only exercise jurisdiction over foreign-flagged vessels within their territory and in areas where they exercise functional jurisdiction for particular purposes.

Next to the principle that no State can take possession of the high seas or exercise jurisdiction over it, another fundamental principle at sea is the so-called 'flag-principle'.[3] Where the first principle focuses on the use of the sea this

---

[1] After the boarding of the Portuguese vessel *Santa Catharina* in 1603 by the Dutch Admiral Jacob van Heemskerk, Hugo de Groot was asked to legally justify the boarding and seizure of the Portuguese vessel. Accordingly, he wrote a dissertation on prize law. His view on the freedom of the seas, which was Chap. 12 of his dissertation, was edited to an independent publication and published in 1609. *Mare Liberum sive de iure quod batavis competit ad indicana commercial dissertatio* was first published anonymously, but soon afterwards it became known that it was Hugo de Groot who had written it. Vervliet 2009, p. IX. The concept of *Mare Clausum* refers to a publication of John Selden in 1635 in reaction to De Groot's work, in which he argues that the sea is not common to all under every circumstance.

[2] Rothwell and Stephens 2010, p. 145.

[3] Somewhat confusing in the military context may be that the flag-principle has in fact two meanings. First is the meaning in the maritime context, as is mentioned here. Second is the principle that wherever soldiers will go, their national laws will follow them. This principle is

principle focuses on its users. It submits that all States are entitled to exercise jurisdiction over their own vessels and take measures to safeguard vessels that are registered in that State and flying its flag. In other words, although no State can exercise jurisdiction on the high seas, States do have jurisdiction over vessels that are flying their flag. Moreover, the responsibility of jurisdiction over vessels on the high seas falls *exclusively* to the flag State. This principle, as Gavouneli points out, is 'the cornerstone on which the public order of the high seas is erected.'[4]

A third principle of importance in the context of MIO is the principle of non-intervention. It is not a principle of the international law the sea in particular, but a principle of general international law. Apart from the view that non-interference by States on foreign-flagged vessels follows from the flag principle, it is also supported by the non-intervention principle in general international law. According to this principle States need to refrain from actions that are essentially within the domestic jurisdiction of a State. The non-intervention principle, therefore, sets an extra hurdle against rushing into affairs on board foreign-flagged vessels. When applied in the maritime context, it underlines that interference by States over foreign-flagged vessels should be seen as an exception to the rule.

In sum, in the context of maritime interception operations the mentioned three principles translate into two fundamental legal points of departure. First, flag States have exclusive jurisdiction over their vessels on the high seas and other States may not interfere with those vessels. Second, if a State decides to interfere with foreign-flagged vessels by means of its warships, a State will need a legal basis. These two legal points of departure are codified in Article 92 UNCLOS. Article 92 UNCLOS reads:

> 1. Ships shall sail under the flag of one State only and, save in exceptional cases expressly provided for in international treaties or in this Convention, shall be subject to its exclusive jurisdiction on the high seas. A ship may not change its flag during a voyage or while in a port of call, save in the case of a real transfer of ownership or change of registry.
>
> 2. A ship which sails under the flags of two or more States, using them according to convenience, may not claim any of the nationalities in question with respect to any other State, and may be assimilated to a ship without nationality.

The core-sentence in Article 92 for the purpose of this chapter is: 'shall be subject to its exclusive jurisdiction on the high seas'. This sentence contains four elements that need brief attention.

The first element of importance is *jurisdiction*. As Malcolm Shaw states, jurisdiction is a vital and central feature of state sovereignty which 'concerns the power of the State to affect people, property and circumstances and reflects the basic principle of state sovereignty, equality of States and non-interference of domestic

usually supported by the Napoleonic maxim: *La ou est le drapeau, là est la France*. When, for instance, the military is deployed as vessel protection detachments (VPD) on foreign merchant vessels, both meanings of the flag-principle apply; one to the vessel and one to the military.

[4] Gavouneli 2007, p. 162.

affairs'.[5] There are three general aspects to jurisdiction which the flag State can enforce over its flagged vessels. First is the power to issue laws applicable to a vessel (prescriptive jurisdiction). A State can, for example, make its criminal law applicable on its vessels. Second is the power to enforce these laws (enforcement jurisdiction) aboard the vessel. To illustrate, this means that when a person of a different nationality is on board a vessel, and despite the active personality principle of a State over such person, the flag State will still have jurisdiction to take enforcement measures against this person. Third is the ability of the flag State to bring matters before a domestic court of law (adjudicative jurisdiction).[6] Under Article 92 UNCLOS, a flag State has jurisdiction over all three aspects of jurisdiction when its vessel sails on the high seas.

The second element is that this jurisdiction is *exclusive* to the flag State. The flag State is the only State that can enforce jurisdiction over the vessel and everyone on board the vessel. This was also underlined in the *S.S. Lotus* case brought before the Permanent International Court of Justice (PICJ) in 1927. The PICJ stated that: 'It is certainly true that – apart from certain special cases which are defined by international law - vessels on the high seas are subject to no authority except that of the State whose flag they fly'.[7] As will be discussed more elaborately, it is however generally accepted that this exclusiveness has its limits, for example in favour of suppressing universal crimes such as piracy at sea.

The third element is that exclusive jurisdiction only applies on the *high seas*. The high seas are a maritime zone in the oceans that has its particular legal regime. Article 86 UNCLOS provides that the high seas are: 'all parts of the sea that are not included in the EEZ, in the territorial sea or in the internal waters of a State, or in the archipelagic waters of an archipelagic State.' In this area, as Churchill and Lowe mention: 'From the rule that no State can subject areas of the high seas to its sovereignty, or indeed its jurisdiction, it follows that no State has the right to prevent ships of other States from using the high seas for any 'lawful purpose'.[8] Although strictly speaking the EEZ is not part of the high seas, Article 58 UNCLOS extends the freedom of the high seas onto the EEZ, under the condition that States shall have due regard to the rights and duties of the coastal State. Sub 2 of Article 58 states that Articles 88–115 apply the EEZ, which includes the freedom of

---

[5] Shaw 2000, p. 452.

[6] In the case of the Netherlands, the Netherlands Criminal Code states in Article 3 that the Netherlands Criminal Code applies to all persons on board a vessel that flies the Netherlands flag. Article 4 of the Netherlands Criminal Procedural Code contains the competence of the Netherlands courts over a criminal act on board a Netherlands-flagged vessel.

[7] *SS Lotus* case, PICJ, Series A, No. 10, 7 September 1927, 25. The Turkish vessel *Bozkourt* and the French-flagged mail boat *SS Lotus* collided on 2 August 1926 on the high seas. Eight persons on board the *Bozkourt* died because of the collision. The Turkish Government prosecuted the French first officer Demons of the *Lotus* for his share in the incident. The question whether Turkey could have jurisdiction over Demons was put before the PICJ. The Court ruled that there was no rule in international law that prohibited Turkey from prosecuting the French lieutenant.

[8] Churchill and Lowe 1999, p. 205.

navigation,[9] the rules relating to piracy[10] and the rules relating to the peacetime right of visit.[11] This explains that in naval operations a short cut is taken with regard to the high seas for practical purposes and is usually interpreted as the seas adjacent to the territorial sea, often called 'international waters'.[12]

The fourth and last element to note is *its*, which refers to the flag State of the vessel. Article 91 UNCLOS elaborates on how nationality of vessels can be granted by States. Basically, Article 91 contains two conditions for nationality: registration under domestic rules and a genuine link between the flag State and the vessel. How and under what conditions a State grants a vessel its nationality is subject to the domestic laws of States. With regard to the genuine link criterion, in 1999 the ITLOS issued its judgment in the *MV Saiga* (no. 2) case in which the Court had to determine whether the *Saiga* had the nationality of Saint Vincent and the Grenadines at the time of its arrest by Guinea.[13] The Court decided on the point of the genuine link that the genuine link criterion 'is to secure more effective implementation of the duties of the flag State and not to establish criteria by reference to which the validity of the registration of ships in a flag State may be challenged by other States'.[14] Therefore, if there is no genuine link, it does not mean that a vessel has lost its nationality, providing other States the possibility to enforce their jurisdiction over the vessel. The importance of the ability to link a vessel to a State is that it creates some level of legal order over vessels in an area that is beyond the jurisdiction of any State, as the link creates a responsibility for the flag State over its vessels. When a vessel flies under a certain flag, the flag State has duties that are summed up in Article 94 UNCLOS. One important one in this context is that the flag State must assume jurisdiction under its domestic law over each ship flying its flag and its master, officers and crew.[15]

4.3 Limited Exceptions to Non-Interference

Although the legal point of departure for maritime interception operations starts from the notion of non-interference, interference was never prohibited in its totality. It has always been accepted that States can have reasons to interfere on foreign-flagged vessels with regard to certain activities on the high seas. Reasons

---

[9] Article 87 UNCLOS.

[10] Articles 100–107 and 110 UNCLOS.

[11] Article 110 UNCLOS.

[12] One such example is the NATO naval operation conducted in Operation *Unified Protector* with regard to Libya. The term high seas that was used in SC Res. 1973, but was interpreted by NATO to mean the seas adjacent to the Libyan territorial sea.

[13] ITLOS, The M/V "Saiga" (No. 2) case (Saint Vincent and Grenadines v. Guinea), Judgment 1 July 1999. See also Chap. 10 on this case.

[14] M/V Saiga, para 83.

[15] Article 94, under 2 sub b UNCLOS.

may for instance fall within the context of international peace and security, to ensure the *bon usage* of the ocean and to maintain the public order and security interest of States.[16] These reasons legally impacted in the sense that it developed legal possibilities where States can, for instance, interfere with neutral shipping during armed conflict, act against cases of piracy on foreign-flagged vessels, allow a seaward expansion of functional jurisdiction of coastal States[17] and enter into international agreements. All have an impact on the exclusive jurisdiction over a vessel on the high seas.

During armed conflict certain activities by warships, such as the belligerent right of visit and search or the capture of vessels that attempt to breach a blockade, are well-accepted rules that infringe on the absoluteness of the principle. In peacetime circumstances, however, the scope of interference of foreign-flagged vessels by warships has been open to debate. This debate focuses primarily on the issue of whether or not States have a general policing right on the high seas. In 1955, this question was dealt with by the International Law Commission (ILC) in the context of whether warships would have a general right of verification of flags. The ILC accepted flag verification only in special 'police measures' like piracy, slave trade and stateless vessels. It rejected a *general* right for warships to verify the flag of a vessel.[18] This point of view was codified in Article 22 of the 1958 Convention on the High Seas, and later in Article 110 UNCLOS. As McDougal and Burke from thereon stated, 'no general right in warships to verify the flag of vessels ought to be provided apart from that recognized in connection with the Article on the right of visit.'[19] The starting point in the international law of the sea, therefore, is that no general policing rights other than the very limited possibilities in 110 and 111 UNCLOS exist for warships in peacetime circumstances.[20] One point to note, however, with these exceptions is that they are based on the international law of the sea. Part II of this study will underline that presently a broader international law perspective provides more exceptions to the exclusive jurisdiction of the flag State.

---

16 Papastavridis 2013, pp. 27–40.

17 The so-called creeping jurisdiction debate of seaward jurisdictional power projection has now reached the EEZ. A development which has obviously been a concern for States with an expeditionary naval force. James Kraska's study elaborates on coastal State efforts to diminish the freedom of navigation in the EEZ, taking away the advantage of maritime powers of expeditionary operations, by, as he opines 'casting doubt on the political and legal legitimacy of military activities in the EEZ. See Kraska 2011, p. 221. See also Van Dyke 2004, pp. 107–121.

18 Yearbook of the International Law Commission 1955, 1, p. 32.

19 McDougal and Burke 1962, p. 890.

20 These provisions deal with the peacetime rights of visit and hot pursuit.

4.4 Principles of the Law of the Sea Versus Maritime Security

Today's security concerns have become a reason for a need to interfere with shipping. Whereas UNCLOS does much to enhance maritime security,[21] the fundamental principles of the international law of the sea and the current trend of trying to enhance maritime security do not start from the same points of view. As said, the flag State principle and the principle of non-interference starts from the idea that interference by warships on foreign-flagged vessel must be considered as an exception to the rule. Maritime security and the manner in which enhancement of maritime security is envisaged to be put in practice at sea takes the opposite approach. It starts from the view that possibilities should exist, preferably supported by law, in which other vessels can be controlled, searched and taken action against. Emphasizing the need for more maritime security, therefore, puts a strain on the basic principles of the law of the sea. In a broader sense, basically, the discussion here is the classic dilemma of gaining more security by losing more freedom with the ultimate aim to protect those same freedoms. The mentioned tension between the legal principles of non-interference, exclusive jurisdiction and freedom of the high seas versus enhancing maritime security as we see it today, puts pressure on the principles in a number of ways.

First, in conceptual thinking it appears that the right of visit as an exceptional right is moving in the direction of the thought that the right of visit must not be seen as an exception but rather must be seen as a possibility to enable boarding foreign-flagged vessels. This way of thinking does not change anything in the strict legal sense, but it does change the underlying mindset from exceptions to possibilities. To put it differently: the thinking is shifting from 'you cannot board *unless* there is a legal basis', to 'you *can* board as long as there is a legal instrument to back you up'. Again, it does not step away from the legal situation as is, but it allows in terms of (political) mindset perhaps to more easily eroding these principles.

Second, this political thinking steers the answer to the question how to protect against threats to maritime security. As said, enhancing maritime security departs from the idea that the seas need to be policed in order to successfully protect against threats. As such, in the political and strategic arena phrases like 'policing the seas'[22] and 'securing of the commons'[23] have become fashionable wording in modern naval strategy outside situations of armed conflict. Because current strategic maritime thinking starts with the aim of trying to control what happens in the seas by means of a higher level of awareness, it is contradictory to the Grotius principles of

[21] Rothwell and Klein mention for instance the positive impact of clarity on the outer limits of maritime zones, the economic certainty that UNCLOS creates in the EEZ, the general promotion of the peaceful use of the oceans and dispute settlement. Rothwell and Klein 2009, pp. 27–29.

[22] Hammicks 2007, pp. 28–36.

[23] Smith-Windsor 2009.

the law of the sea. It insists, from a strategic-political perspective, that the legal notion of very limited policing tasks for States on the high seas must be left behind. One consequence is that States are using naval forces to police at sea, using the space under the threshold of actions that need a legal basis for interference. Warships are tasked to actively gather information on the high seas and make use of 'friendly approaches'[24] in which crews of warships come in contact with the maritime community. Crews come alongside or even step aboard other vessels, simply to exchange information and talk with each other. In practise, these "friendly approaches" to enhance maritime security are becoming a standard *modus operandi* for warships. A large part of the naval operations against piracy is conducted by coming alongside local coastal fisheries vessels to inquire and gather information that may lead to a better situational awareness of the area. On a more sophisticated level Operation *Active Endeavour* has evolved from a platform-based operation to a network based operation that tries to tie in all kinds of information in order to close the network of possible terrorist use of the sea. Huge amounts of data anomalies are filtered in this process which may lead to spot illegal activities. Part of the task of Combined Maritime Forces (CMF), a thirty nation's naval partnership, is to conduct maritime security operations. During these operations vessels conduct assist and approach visits in order to maximize general awareness at sea.[25] Ultimately, collecting this information aims to enable timely reaction against any possible threat against maritime security.[26] Policing the high seas, therefore, adds to maritime security awareness (MSA), which is an important part of current naval operations. Conceptually, however, this *modus operandi* does not sit well with the notion that foreign-flagged vessels should not be interfered with. This active politico-strategical policy of seeking out vessels at sea in the manner as described above may be considered to be under the threshold of an intervention of foreign-flagged vessels. It has, however, made some authors question whether exclusive flag State jurisdiction and in particular keeping the primary responsibility over vessel with the flag State a legal concept that possibly should today be on its return.[27] Geiss and Tams, for instance, opine that stepping away from this concept, allows for 'a wider circle of States to enforce international legal rules'.[28]

Third, as will be the main focus of study in Part II, with the collective security system, international agreements and arguments to use self-defence as a direct legal ground to board vessels, more and more exceptions to the exclusive jurisdiction of flag States have been put forward next to the traditional ones that are derived from the law of the sea. And also the objectives, through an increasing scope of issues

---

[24] This term is also institutionalized in the maritime dimension. See e.g. EUNAVFOR Operation *Atalanta* website at: http://eunavfor.eu/mission/ and the Combined Maritime Forces (CMF) webpage: http://combinedmaritimeforces.com/2013/07/04/maritime-security-operations-with-france-djibouti-yemen-and-saudi-arabia/.

[25] http://combinedmaritimeforces.com/ctf-150-maritime-security/.

[26] Boraz 2009, pp. 137–146.

[27] Geiss and Tams 2015, pp. 19–49; Brown 2015, pp. 70–71.

[28] Geiss and Tams 2015, p. 25.

brought under maritime security, for boarding foreign-flagged vessels have broadened. Such as the urge of some States to find legal ways to board vessels that are suspected of carrying WMD. Even before maritime security became central issue in the maritime domain, different authors already commented on the tension between the growing legal possibilities to interfere with the freedom of navigation.[29] Whereas these commentators primarily commented on maritime zones in which the high seas is losing terrain in relation to other maritime zones, other legal grounds to board foreign-flagged vessels, are nibbling at the rights of States with regard to the vessels at sea. These other legal frameworks also have an eroding effect on the principle of non-interference by warships of foreign-flagged vessels on the high seas. This development is not wholly without criticism,[30] and usually comes to the fore as part of more strategic debates on the influence of States and their sea power on the ocean.[31] Whereas some put the tension between the fundamental principles and politico-military strategy of States under the magnifying glass, others, such as Weinberg and Verdirame, underline that '[Yet], it would be hasty to conclude that these settled principles of the law of the sea will soon give way to the strategic necessities of powerful States and collective security.'[32]

References

Becker-Weinberg V, Verdirame G (2015) Proliferation of weapons of mass destruction and shipping interdiction. In: Weller M (ed) The Oxford Handbook of the Use of Force in International Law. Oxford University Press, New York, pp. 1017–1033

Boraz S (2009) Maritime domain awareness. Myth and realities. Naval War College Review 62:3, pp. 137–146

Brown N (2015) Jurisdictional Problems Relating to Non-Flag State Boarding of Suspect Ships in International Waters: A Practitioner's Observations. In: Ringbom R (ed) Jurisdiction over ships. Brill, Dordrecht, pp. 69–82

Churchill R, Lowe A (1999) The Law of the Sea. Manchester University Press, Manchester

Gavouneli M (2007) Functional jurisdiction in the Law of the Sea. Brill/Martinus Nijhoff publishers, Dordrecht

Geiss R, Tams C (2015) Non-Flag States as Guardians of the Maritime Order: Creeping Jurisdiction of a Different Kind? In: Ringbom H (ed) Jurisdiction over ships. Brill, Dordrecht, pp. 19–49

Hammicks D (2007) Navies Endeavour to Police the Mediterranean Sea. Jane's Navy International, July/August 2007, pp. 28–36

ITLOS, The M/V "Saiga" (No. 2) case (Saint Vincent and Grenadines v. Guinea), Judgment 1 July 1999

Kraska J (2011) Maritime power and the law of the sea. Oxford University Press, New York

---

[29] E.g. Van Dyke 2004, pp. 107–121; Soons 2000, pp. 205–211. And more recently Kraska 2011.

[30] Song 2007, pp. 101–145.

[31] For example in the tensions between the US and China on the influence of the respective States and the use of certain areas of the ocean, such as the EEZ. See e.g. Yoshihara 2016, pp. 351–363.

[32] Becker-Weinberg and Verdirame 2015, p. 1033.

McDougal M, Burke W (1962) The public order of the oceans. A contemporary International law of the Sea. Yale University Press New Haven/London

Papastavridis E (2013) The interception of vessels on the high seas. Hart Publishing, Oxford/Portland OR

PICJ, SS Lotus case, Series A, No. 10, 7 September 1927

Rothwell D, Klein N (2009) Maritime security and the law of the sea. In: Klein N, Mossop J, Rothwell D (eds) Maritime security. International law and policy perspectives from Australia and New Zealand. Routledge, New York, pp. 22–37

Rothwell D, Stephens T (2010) The International Law of the Sea. Hart Publishing, Oxford/Portland, OR

Shaw M (2000) International Law, 4th edn. Cambridge University Press, Cambridge

Smith-Windsor B (2009) Securing the Commons: Towards NATO New Maritime Strategy. Research paper, NATO Defence College 49

Soons A (2000) A “New” Exception to the Freedom of the High Seas: The Authority of the U.N. Council. In: Gill T, Heere W (eds) Reflections on the Principles and Practice of International Law: Essays in Honour of Leo J. Bouchez. Nijhoff, Dordrecht, pp. 205–211

Song Y (2007) The U.S.-Led Proliferation Security Initiative and UNCLOS: Legality, implementation, and an assessment. Ocean Development and International Law 38, pp. 101–145

Van Dyke JM (2004) The disappearing right to navigational freedom in the exclusive economic zone. Marine Policy 29, pp. 107–121

Vervliet J (2009) General Introduction. In: Grotius H (1609) Mare Liberum. Brill, Leiden/Boston

Yearbook of the International Law Commission (1955) 1

Yoshihara T (2016) Chinese views of the U.S.-led maritime order. In: Krause J, Bruns S (eds) Handbook on naval strategy and security. Routledge, New York, pp. 351–363

Part II
Legal Basis for Maritime Interception Operations

Chapter 5
The UN Collective Security System and Maritime Interception Operations

The only prediction that can be made with assurance is that the lower the level of conflict, the more localized the situation and the more restrictive the objectives, the more predominant will be the element of law in the governing of naval conduct.
—D. P. O'Connell—The influence of law on sea power

Contents

Abstract This chapter analyses the use of maritime interception operations within the context of the UN collective security system. The enforcement of UN sanctions at sea may be seen as the traditional form of maritime interception. Although naval

M. Fink, *Maritime Interception and the Law of Naval Operations*,
https://doi.org/10.1007/978-94-6265-249-1_5

forces have regularly been used to enforce UN sanctions since the fall of the Berlin wall, there has always been a debate on which precise basis, Article 41 or 42, within the collective security system these operations take place. Apart from maritime embargo operations, maritime interception can also take place within the collective security system outside the context of UN sanctions. In this regard the basis for MIO could follow from an 'all necessary means' mandate.

Keywords Maritime embargo operations · UN collective security system · Article 41 UN Charter · Article 42 UN Charter · enforcement of UN sanctions at sea

5.1 Introduction

This chapter considers the UN collective security system as a legal basis for maritime interception operations.[1] The collective security system has for a while been the primary legal basis connected to maritime interception operations. And despite other legal frameworks that have emerged or MIO, the collective security system remains one of the most important legal bases for MIO. In 2011, the UN Security Council authorized military enforcement measures against the Qaddafi-regime in Libya[2] and is still facilitating counter-piracy operations off the coast of Somalia. Maritime enforcement measures mandated by the UNSC can be divided into two types. The first type is the authorization of UN-mandated maritime embargo operations (MEO). MEO are specifically focused on the enforcement of economic sanctions at sea which are adopted by the UNSC. The second type of maritime enforcement measures by the UNSC are measures that authorize the use of armed force which is not specifically related to economic sanctions under Article 41 of the UN Charter. This is the case when the UNSC authorizes *all necessary means* to enforce a UN mandate, which, translated to actual military operations, could involve a MIO. These two types may also exist concurrently in one military campaign. During the operations with regard to Libya in 2011, naval forces were for example used both as assets to conduct a maritime embargo operation and to conduct operations to fulfil the mandate of *use all necessary means* to protect civilians.

Maritime enforcement measures adopted by the UNSC are often referred to as "UN-mandated" maritime interception operations. In fact, "UN-mandated" refers to the command and control under which the operations are carried out. Carvalho de Oliveira has made a clear distinction between so-called UN-mandated and UN-controlled naval operations. With the first, he refers to the fact that; 'The UN issues the resolutions but leaves the operational control in the hands of States,

[1] O'Connell 1975, p. 3.

[2] More recent, in March 2014, the UNSC adopted another resolution (SC Res. 2146) that allowed for stopping crude oil that is illicitly being exported from Libya.

regional organizations or international coalitions'. With the latter, he refers to operations in which, 'The Secretary-General assumes direct control of operations.'[3] Maritime interception operations based on the UN collective security system can include both UN-mandated and UN-controlled operations. To illustrate, the 2011 operations with regard to Libya in 2011 were UN-mandated because the UNSC authorized military operations that were operationally controlled by NATO (*Unified Protector*) and also for a short time by a coalition of States (*Odyssey Dawn*). MIO conducted in the context of UNIFIL are UN-controlled as it is under the operational control of the UN itself. Interestingly, this is the only naval operation that has have ever been directly controlled by the UN itself.[4] Although the MIF operations with regard to Iraq are sometimes called 'UNMIF' and parts of the Korea War naval operations have been referred to as UNBEF (United Nations Blockading and Escorting Force), neither of them were under actual operational control of the UN itself. These names, however, must be seen in the context of the period in which they were conducted and refer to the fact that they were sanctioned by the UN through a UN resolution.[5] This chapter will first briefly introduce the UN collective security system and will then consider the two types of maritime enforcement measures that can be mandated by the UN Security Council.

5.2 The UN Collective Security System

The UN collective security system is the legal basis for the UNSC to exercise its powers under Chapter VII of the UN Charter. The system takes as the obvious point of departure the use of force prohibition ex Article 2(4) of the UN Charter and provides for a graduated response for non-military and/or military measures to restore international peace and security.[6] The system revolves around Chapters VI and VII of the UN Charter. Chapter VI concerns the peaceful settlement of disputes and Chapter VII includes taking coercive measures including the use of armed force. The essential difference between Chapter VI and VII is that measures taken under Chapter VI do not include coercive powers, whereas measures taken by the UNSC under Chapter VII, through Article 25 of the UN Charter, may be binding in

---

[3] Carvalho 2012, p. 53.

[4] Rather uniquely for naval operations, the UN beret is worn by the military on board MTF UNIFIL warships.

[5] Rothwell and Stephens introduce the term "UN-sanctioned naval operations" to refer to all the naval operations authorized by the UNSC. Rothwell and Stephens 2010, pp. 262–263.

[6] Gazzini 2005, p. 7.

nature.[7] The key articles in Chapter VII are Articles 39, 41 and 42. Article 39 of the Charter is the obligatory stepping stone for taking coercive measures under Chapter VII. When a threat to peace, breach to peace or act of aggression exists, this article opens the door to the authorities that are contained in Articles 41 and 42 of the UN Charter.[8]

Based on Article 41, the UNSC can take non-military measures, such as economic sanctions. If these measures prove to be or would be inadequate under the circumstances to deal with the issue at hand, the UNSC can decide to take measures based on Article 42, which provides authority to make use of armed force to restore international peace and security. Although only Article 42 allows for the use of armed force, that is not to say that under Chapter VI and the other articles of Chapter VII no military forces can be deployed. Clearly, this has often been the case. Therefore one cannot say that the deployment of military forces by itself amounts to an Article 42-operation. Forces deployed under Chapter VI are usually called upon within the context of UN peacekeeping operations and have particular features in authority and mandate. In particular, such forces need the consent of a State to operate on their territory, are required to adhere to the principle of impartiality and are restricted to self-defence when using force.[9] Force deployed under Chapter VII of the UN Charter is often categorized as a peace-enforcing operation that bears a different legal feature than 'Chapter VI operations' in the sense that they do not need the consent of the target State, can be authorized to use force and are not necessarily impartial.

[7] Article 25 UN Charter reads:

> The Members of the United Nations agree to accept and carry out the decisions of the Security Council in accordance with the present Charter.

[8] Article 39 UN Charter reads:

> The Security Council shall determine the existence of any threat to the peace, breach of the peace, or act of aggression and shall make recommendations, or decide what measures shall be taken in accordance with Articles 41 and 42, to maintain or restore international peace and security.

[9] Gill 2010, pp. 135–142. With regard to the term self-defence within the context of UN-peacekeeping operations it must, however, be noted here that an evolution of the notion of self-defence has taken place in which it has gained a much broader meaning than that of the strict self-defence in the context of criminal law.

5.3 Maritime Embargo Operations[10]

In seven situations the UNSC has authorized maritime embargo operations to enforce economic measures at sea: Southern Rhodesia,[11] Iraq,[12] The Former Yugoslavia,[13] Haiti,[14] Sierra Leone,[15] Lebanon[16] and Libya.[17] Maritime embargo operations aim at implementing economic sanctions adopted by the UNSC at sea. That the enforcement of the embargo physically takes place at sea, distinguishes it from UN sanctions adopted by the UNSC that do not also authorize enforcement at sea, and which are restricted to implementation under national jurisdiction. Rather than only relying on national implementation of sanctions by member-states within their respective jurisdictions, maritime embargo operations add another, physical, dimension at sea directly against a sanctioned State and within the theater of conflict itself. Arguably, maritime embargo operations can be considered as a step between economic sanctions and military enforcement operations in order to put more pressure on the target state. But it can also be seen as a part of the military enforcement measures. Which one it may be or draws closes to, obviously depends on the actual circumstances in which the UNSC has authorized such activity. Since the UNSC authorized military means to implement economic sanctions at sea debate has arisen on whether these military operations, and the use of force used in pursuit of the mission, are based on either Article 41 (economic enforcement measures) of the UN Charter, or should be positioned within the context of Article 42 (military enforcement measures).[18] The '41/42' debate first arose during the imposition of economic sanctions against Iraq, after the Iraqi invasion of Kuwait in 1990. Sanctions against Iraq and their implementation at sea by the maritime interception force (MIF) lasted until the UNSC adopted, in May 2003, SC Res. 1483 (2003) that ended the sanctions regime.[19] In the years following the Iraqi experience interception operations were also conducted during the conflicts in the former Yugoslavia, Haiti and Sierra Leone. Although these maritime embargo operations made the implementation of economic sanctions at sea an accepted practice, it continued to stir the discussion on the legal basis for the naval enforcement of economic sanctions. In the maritime embargo operations that

---

[10] This section is based on my Article published in the *Netherland International Law Review* in 2013. See Fink 2013.

[11] SC Res. 217 (1965), 221 (1966), 232 (1966) and 460 (1979).

[12] SC Res. 661 (1990), 665 (1990), 670 (1990), 687 (1991) and 1483 (2003).

[13] SC Res. 713 (1991), 757 (1992), 787 (1992) and 820 (1993).

[14] SC Res. 841 (1993), 861 (1993), 873 (1993), 875 (1993) and 944 (1994).

[15] SC Res. 1132 (1997) and 1940 (2010).

[16] SC Res. 1701 (2006).

[17] SC Res. 1970 (2011), 1973 (2011), 2009 (2011) and 2040 (2012).

[18] See Politakis 1994, pp. 173–208; Schrijver 1994, pp. 153–154; Fielding 1992–1993, pp. 1191–1241; McLaughlin 2002, pp. 249–278.

[19] Goldrick 2008, pp. 201–214.

followed, during the conflicts in Lebanon and Libya, the debate did not, however, resurface. Klein has also briefly touched upon the issue but has not added a contemporary view of her own.[20]

The debate on the legal basis for naval enforcement at sea is especially relevant from a naval operator's perspective. At the operational level the core issue is whether naval forces that are deployed in maritime embargo operations to oversee and implement economic sanctions imposed at sea can resort to coercive measures, including the use of force. Do commanders of warships need flag State authority to board a vessel, or can they base their powers on the mandate of the UNSC? Can so-called disabling fire be used when a vessel refuses to comply with the warship's crew who are executing a UN mandate, or are actions only limited to monitoring and reporting? These are just a few examples of practical questions which make understanding the legal basis and legal regime under which they operate a significant issue for military practitioners. As McLaughlin states: 'It is thus essential that we understand how Articles 40, 41 and 42 interact, because it is this interaction which defines the spectrum with which UN-mandated interdiction can take place.'[21]

The next paragraphs consider the question of the legal grounds for maritime embargo operations that are utilized to implement economic measures adopted by the UNSC. To analyse this question this chapter will first argue that maritime embargo operations can broadly be categorized into two types of operations, namely *implied* and *explicit* maritime embargo operations. Second, it reassesses the main arguments of the 41/42 debate, primarily against the background of the present-day application of Article 42. It will argue that the applicability of Article 42 has evolved in such a manner that the existing reluctance in the mid-1990s concerning the possibility to position maritime embargo operations within Article 42 may now be less strong. Lastly, a few remarks are made concerning the question of whether or not the use of force within the realm of Article 41 is possible in the context of maritime embargo operations.

5.3.1 Two Types of Maritime Embargo Operations

The UNSC has made much use of the ability to impose sanctions based on Article 41 of the UN Charter. The first sanctions ever to be adopted by the UNSC were the sanctions against Southern Rhodesia in 1966, which was also the first time that a maritime interdiction operation, the so-called Beira Patrol, supported the implementation of sanctions.[22] Article 41 reads as follows:

[20] Klein 2011, pp. 276–280.

[21] McLaughlin 2002, p. 253.

[22] Gowlland-Debbas 2004, p. 7.

> The Security Council may decide what measures not involving the use of armed force are to be employed to give effect to its decisions, and it may call upon the Members of the United Nations to apply such measures. These may include complete or partial interruption of economic relations and of rail, sea, air, postal, telegraphic, radio, and other means of communication, and the severance of diplomatic relations.

Many of the sanctions imposed by the UNSC have coincided with the conduct of military peace support operations. Although some authors have suggested that the effectiveness of sanctions also depends on the willingness of States to use coercive measures, such as the use of military force,[23] most[24] of the UN sanctions are adopted without implementation instruments that include the use of military means. Following the traditional division between Articles 41 and 42 UN Charter, sanctions imposed through Article 41 have in fact very little to do with the use of military means, but form a crucial and mandatory pre-step in restoring international peace and security to what is considered to be the *ultimum remedium*: action through military means as is provided for in Article 42. Maritime strategist Geoffrey Till has argued that imposing maritime operations to enforce economic sanctions does not force the targeted State to change its policy. He claims that the relevancy of MEO on a political level is gained rather by the fact that it shows that everything possible has been undertaken to avoid to compelling compliance through the use of military force.[25]

On a number of occasions States have decided to deploy naval assets at sea to support the economic sanctions, either at the express authorization of the UNSC, but also without express authorization. Broadly speaking, two types of maritime embargo operations can be distinguished: *Implied* maritime embargo operations and *explicit* maritime embargo operations. The key difference between these two types is whether the UNSC has explicitly authorized the implementation of economic sanctions at sea. These two types of embargo operations will be considered in more detail below.

5.3.1.1 *Implied Maritime Embargo Operations*

In the past, the UNSC has adopted a number of resolutions that were based on Article 41 in the context of which the international community took the initiative to deploy naval forces.[26] Although the political developments in these cases may have been such that States or regional organizations were politically expected or even

---

[23] De Jonge Oudraat 2000, p. 112.

[24] Some implementations of sanctions also relied on the presence of a peace support operation for their implementation. See, e.g., SC Res. 1609 (2004), para 2(m), concerning Cote D'Ivoire, in which French forces were also authorized to monitor and inspect, without notice, the cargo of any transport vehicle breaching the imposed sanctions.

[25] Till 2013, p. 237.

[26] SC Res. 713 (1991) and SC Res. 757 (1992) on the former Yugoslavia; SC Res. 217 (1965) on Southern Rhodesia. In the case of SC Res. 661 (1990), it was disputed whether naval forces were

asked by the UN to deploy military means to support the decisions of the UNSC, the point to note in these resolutions is that the UNSC did not specifically adopt military measures to implement sanctions from the sea. These military operations, launched without express authorization from the UNSC to support adopted economic sanctions from the sea, can be called implied maritime embargo operations. From the wording of the resolutions it does not become apparent that the UNSC actually seeks, or authorizes any enforcement of economic sanctions at sea. The target audiences of the resolutions are the member states which, pursuant to Article 25 of the UN Charter, are obliged to take measures to implement the decisions of the UNSC. These resolutions aim to seek implementation through national procedures, rather than through military means at sea. Two examples of implied maritime embargo operations can be given:

In the case of Southern Rhodesia the UNSC adopted SC Resolution 217 (1965), shortly after SC Resolution 216 (1965) condemning the unilateral declaration of independence by the Ian Smith Government. Although with SC Resolution 217 the UNSC did not as yet take the step of mandatory economic measures under Chapter VII, the UK (the former colonial power) launched the Beira Patrol.[27] Mobley mentions that the resolution '[w]as to serve as the original (if flimsy) legal justification for later British maritime intercept operations, giving the United Kingdom reason to expect the cooperation of the flag States of suspect tankers'.[28]

In the second example, during the crisis in the former Yugoslavia, in July 1992 NATO and the Western European Union (WEU) decided to launch Operations *Maritime Monitor* and *Sharp Vigilance* in support of SC Resolutions 713 (1991) and 757 (1992) to contribute to the monitoring of sanctions adopted by the UNSC. Neither resolution contained any explicit authority for naval enforcement, but merely decided (713) that under Chapter VII 'all States shall … immediately implement a general and complete embargo on all the deliveries of weapons and military equipment to Yugoslavia'. Resolution 757 added the mandate for States to implement SC Res. 713, but only within their jurisdictional powers.

In 2011, a third example almost came into being: during the early stages of the Libya crisis NATO Secretary-General Rasmussen announced that NATO would set up an embargo operation to monitor UN sanctions that were adopted in SC Res. 1970 (2011). This resolution was expressly based on Article 41[29] and did not

operating under this resolution, or that the authorities were based on the legal regime applicable in cases of self-defence.

[27] SC Res. 460 (1979) ended the sanctions with regard to Southern Rhodesia, just before Zimbabwe emerged as a new state in 1980.

[28] Mobley 2002, pp. 64–84. Mobley also mentions that: 'in the early weeks of the operation London was required in that time to approach the tankers' flag countries and arrange to stop and board the ships, if necessary; with the passage in April of Security Council Resolution 221, Britain would no longer have to secure this approval'. See also p. 71 on which Mobley states that specific flag state consent was needed within the context of SC Res. 217 before an interception took place.

[29] UNSC Res. 1970 (2011) reads: 'Acting under Chapter VII of the Charter of the United Nations, and taking measures under its Article 41'.

contain any explicit authority to deploy naval forces to enforce the embargo with the use of armed force at sea.[30] As the situation developed, however, NATO actually started its military operations only after the UNSC adopted SC Res. 1973 (2011) that authorized explicit enforcement authority on the high seas.[31] If SC Resolution 1973 would not have contained this authorization and if NATO would have gone ahead with the deployment of naval forces off the coast of Libya, then deploying warships at sea to support a UN resolution would have been a case of implied maritime embargo operations.

5.3.1.2 Legal Basis for Implied Maritime Embargo Operations

If the maritime implementation of economic sanctions is not mentioned in the resolution, the question arises as to whether implied maritime embargo operations are actually *mandated* by the UN, or are set up in order *to support* UN decisions. It seems hard to see how a resolution can be a legal basis for maritime embargo operations if there is no mandate in the first place. If States take the initiative to deploy naval forces in support of measures taken under an Article 41 resolution that has no wording indicating that economic sanctions can also be implemented at sea, and secondly, for which the UNSC usually decides that States shall take steps to prevent by *their nationals* or from *their territory* or using *their flagged vessels* certain embargoed actions that do not go beyond the jurisdictional reach of a State and excludes foreign-flagged vessels,[32] the resolution itself may not actually be the proper legal basis, but might only serve as an argument to politically justify or to legitimize the presence of naval forces off the coast of a State which is subjected to sanctions. A decision to deploy naval forces to sea should then be sought outside Chapter VII of the UN Charter, such as the decision of a regional organization to deploy military means, made possible because of the notion of freedom of navigation on the high seas. This allows States to deploy naval forces at sea on their own initiative without any further decisions from the UNSC, or the consent of a State and without crossing third-state boundaries. The actual presence of naval assets is made possible because of the rules applicable to the different maritime zones, but is not based on explicit authorization by the Council or the consent of a State. Consequently, no enforcement authority is given to naval forces to implement economic sanctions at sea. In the absence of explicit authorization, their powers are basically restricted to monitoring and reporting. Still, however, even in a diplomatic coercion role, as Booth mentions, warships are in support of foreign policy, 'but by means of signaling rather than shooting'.[33] Zeigler mentions that the information

[30] MacAskill and Traynor 2011.

[31] See more elaborately on the Libya maritime embargo operation, Fink 2011a, pp. 1–24.

[32] See e.g. SC Res. 757 (1992), para 4(c); SC Res. 1701 (2006), para 15; SC Res. 1970 (2011), para 11.

[33] Booth 1985, p. 137.

that was reported by NATO and the WEU maritime operations during the Yugoslavia conflict 'provided sufficient information about violations to enable … the Security Council … to pass resolution 787',[34] which gave explicit authority to enforce sanctions at sea. McLaughlin views implied maritime embargo operations, which he calls 'passive naval action', more as a form of diplomatic coercion which is 'encompassed in a modern form by the peaceful settlement provisions of UN Chapter VI'.[35]

5.3.2 Explicit Maritime Embargo Operations

Explicit maritime embargo operations are maritime interception operations that are explicitly mandated by a UN resolution to enforce an embargo. A clear indication of an explicit mandate to implement economic measures at sea exists when the UNSC uses wording that resembles: 'to hold all inward and outward shipping in order to inspect and verify their cargo and destinations and to ensure strict implementation of….' This wording has been used in a number of UN resolutions and opens up the possibility to physically stop and board vessels at sea.[36]

SC Res. 665 (1990), with regard to Iraq, for the first time contained the express mandate with the above-mentioned wording that, as McLaughlin notes: 'is [thus] the fundamental conceptual precedent for modern UN naval interdiction operations'.[37] The UNSC used the 'explicit authority'-phrase possibly also to end the ongoing debate on the question as to whether naval enforcement actions against Iraqi merchant vessels were taken based on SC Res. 661 that imposed economic sanctions, or were based on Article 51 of the UN Charter.[38] The Iraqi example was followed in the former Yugoslavia crisis when the UNSC adopted economic measures in which the UNSC explicitly authorized maritime embargo operations in SC Resolution 787.[39] The NATO and WEU operations, already present in the Adriatic Sea, changed their type from implicit to explicit with the adoption of

[34] Zeigler 1996, p. 33.

[35] McLaughlin 2009, p. 128.

[36] SC Res. 665 (1990), 787 (1992), 875 (1993) and 1132 (1997).

[37] McLaughlin 2002, p. 261.

[38] See, e.g. Gill 1990, pp. 1475–1487; Peace 1991, pp. 560–561.

[39] SC Res. 787 (1992) reads:

> 12. acting under Chapter VII and VIII of the Charter of the United Nations, calls upon States, acting nationally or through regional agencies of arrangements, to such measures commensurate with the specific circumstances as may be necessary under the authority of the Security Council to halt all inward and outward shipping in order to inspect and verify their cargoes and destinations and to ensure implementation of the provisions of resolutions 713 (1991) and 757 (1992); …

explicit authority. Subsequently, NATO and the WEU changed their names for the embargo operations into *Maritime Guard* and *Sharp Fence* to reflect their new authorities. Both operations were later combined into Operation *Sharp Guard*.[40] In the cases of Haiti[41] and Sierra Leone[42] the language adopted by the UNSC more or less followed the structure of SC Res. 665.

5.4 Between Implied and Explicit

In three more recent situations, Lebanon (2006), Iran (2010) and Libya (2011), the UNSC did not use the above-mentioned boilerplate phrase. The resolutions are arguably less explicit in the wording used to authorize maritime embargo operations. In the case of Iran, it may be argued that although the possibility of embargo operations is mentioned, it does not actually mandate anything at all.

5.4.1 Lebanon

After the Israeli-Hezbollah war in the summer of 2006, during which Israel also established a belligerent blockade off the coast of Lebanon, the UN established a maritime taskforce to help the Lebanese authorities to stop arms that were meant for Hezbollah. SC Res. 1701 (2006) provides the mandate for the Maritime Task Force to UNIFIL (MTF UNIFIL) off the coast of Lebanon. Paragraph 15 imposes an arms embargo, but without any explicit enforcement authority for enforcement at sea.

---

[40] Leurdijk 1996, pp. 24–30.

[41] SC Res. 875 (1993) reads:

> 1. Calls upon Member States, acting nationally or through regional agencies or arrangements, cooperating with the legitimate Government of Haiti, to use such measures commensurate with the specific circumstances as may be necessary under the authority of the Security Council to ensure strict implementation of the provisions of resolutions 841 (1993) and 873 (1993) relating to the supply of petroleum or petroleum products or arms and related matériel of all types, and in particular to halt inward maritime shipping as necessary in order to inspect and verify their cargoes and destinations; …

[42] SC. Res. 1132 (1997) para 8 reads:

> Acting also under Chapter VIII of the Charter of the United Nations, authorizes ECOWAS, cooperating with the democratically-elected Government of Sierra Leone, to ensure strict implementation of the provisions of this resolution relating to the supply of petroleum and petroleum products, and arms and related matériel of all types, including, where necessary and in conformity with applicable international standards, by halting inward maritime shipping in order to inspect and verify their cargoes and destinations, and calls upon all States to cooperate with ECOWAS in this regard; …

No explicit authorization was included that a UN naval force was to set up a maritime arms embargo, using the boilerplate wording from SC Res. 665, or any other similar wording. The embargo operation and its authority must be read between the lines of paras 11(f), 12, 14 and 15 of the resolution. Moreover, it establishes an arms embargo without mentioning that the measures taken are based on Article 41, and without stating expressly that the measures were taken under Chapter VII, although wording indicating a Chapter VII resolution is included.[43] The political background, however, made it clear that this paragraph was to be read as establishing an arms embargo operation in support of the Lebanese authorities, which did not have sufficient capacity to close their maritime border in order to prevent arms smuggling. Also, as this embargo operation is mounted under the command of the UN itself, by broadening the existing UNIFIL operation with a maritime dimension conducting an embargo operation, one cannot say that *another* organization authorized to act may have interpreted the resolution too broadly.

The actions taken in the territorial waters of Lebanon are subject to a request of the Lebanese authorities, which to some authors made it more a peacekeeping operation rather than a peace-enforcing operation.[44] According to those authors the authorities on Lebanese territory were not derived from the resolution but from the Lebanese Government consenting to UNIFIL operating within its territorial waters. Even if this would be the proper way to construe UNIFIL's authorities within the territorial sea, the area of maritime operations of the UNIFIL MTF stretches outward to 43 nm from the Lebanese coast and thus outside Lebanese territory. The question, therefore, remains on what authority UNIFIL visits vessels outside the territorial sea. In 2009, the commander of MTF UNIFIL wrote that: 'If requested by the Lebanese Armed Forces-Navy (LAF-Navy), MTF may also board and inspect a suspect vessel'.[45] It is however unclear if this is the procedure for both inside and outside territorial waters and what legal ground the LAF would have to authorize visits outside territorial waters. The Netherlands government had a different approach and took the position that SC Res. 1701 authorized 'all necessary action' (para 12), which would also include to board vessels suspected of breaching SC Res. 1701.[46] This being the Netherlands view, interestingly, UNIFIL's website mentions that since the operation has started, it has hailed 42.500 vessels and referred 1.670 to the Lebanese authorities for further inspection; no mention is made of any boardings that have taken place. Instead: 'All merchant vessels

[43] SC Res. 1701 (2006) reads:

> Determining that the situation in Lebanon constitutes a threat to international peace and security.

[44] Weingarter 2007, pp. 116–119.

[45] Sandalli 2010, p. 6.

[46] Kamerbrief inzake beantwoording schriftelijke vragen over de maritime bijdrage aan UNIFIL (Letter to parliament answering written questions on the maritime support to UNIFIL), 11 October 2006.

classified "suspect" are monitored and, if inbound to a Lebanese harbor, are referred for inspection to LAF authorities.'[47]

5.4.2 *Iran*

In a number of resolutions the UNSC has addressed the situation with regard to Iran and the non-proliferation of nuclear weapons. Interesting to note with regard to shipboarding is SC Res. 1929 (2010), which states:

> 15. *Notes* that States, consistent with international law, in particular the law of the sea, may request inspections of vessels on the high seas with the consent of the flag State, and *calls upon* all States to cooperate in such inspections if there is information that provides reasonable grounds to believe the vessel is carrying items the supply, sale, transfer, or export of which is prohibited by paragraphs 3, 4 or 7 of resolution 1737 (2006), paragraph 5 of resolution 1747 (2007), paragraph 8 of resolution 1803 (2008) or paragraphs 8 or 9 of this resolution, for the purpose of ensuring strict implementation of those provisions.[48]

In this resolution the UNSC only 'notes' (as opposed to authorizes) the opportunity to embark on maritime interdiction operations on the high seas, but at the same time underlines the limits of the authorities only to what is allowed under general international law and the international law of the sea in particular. With this language, the Council, in this sensitive case, seems to have wanted to give States a certain justification *if* they would decide to start embargo operations against vessels that are suspected of carrying prohibited items, but at the same time made it clear that the resolution does not contain any additional authority. Besides the fact that the EU has taken this resolution to be the basis for subsequent implementation measures,[49] there has not been any international initiative to launch an actual maritime embargo operation. One can nevertheless imagine that this resolution will play an important role in *ad hoc* cases when intelligence suggests a breach of a resolution and States decide to act upon this. The resolution could, for instance, ease the path for acquiring the consent of the flag State as the resolution calls upon all States to cooperate with such a request.

---

[47] See http://unifil.unmissions.org/Default.aspx?tabid=1523. A practical reason for arriving at this operational decision could be that it may be easier to let the suspected vessel come into port where it is received to be fully inspected and where all the technical and legal facilities are present, rather than a potentially high risk visit and search at sea and having subsequent (legal) challenges of what to do with persons and material.

[48] SC Res. 1929 (2011), para 15.

[49] Dupont 2012, pp. 301–336.

5.4.3 Libya

The resolution on Libya is a case where it can easily be argued that it contains an explicit authority. In this case, however, the UNSC did not make use of the boilerplate phrases. Instead, Paragraph 13 of SC Res. 1973 (2011) took the approach of expanding the measures adopted earlier in UN Resolution 1970 to allow for the inspection of vessels on the high seas. The UNSC took the rather unique approach of replacing the paragraph in resolution 1970 with the following:

> 13. *Decides that* paragraph 11 of resolution 1970 (2011) shall be replaced by the following paragraph : "Calls upon all Member States, in particular States of the region, acting nationally or through regional organisations or arrangements, in order to ensure strict implementation of the arms embargo established by paragraphs 9 and 10 of resolution 1970 (2011), to inspect in their territory, including seaports and airports, and on the high seas, vessels and aircraft bound to or from the Libyan Arab Jamahiriya, if the State concerned has information that provides reasonable grounds to believe that the cargo contains items the supply, sale, transfer or export of which is prohibited by paragraphs 9 or 10 of resolution 1970 (2011) as modified by this resolution, including the provision of armed mercenary personnel, *calls upon* all flag States of such vessels and aircraft to cooperate with such inspections and authorises Member States to use all measures commensurate to the specific circumstances to carry out such inspections"; …[50]

The mentioning of the high seas in this resolution is reason enough to consider the text to have explicitly authorized a maritime embargo operation, albeit not in the sense that it has used the standard phrases. The Libya resolutions underline that the language that expresses or indicates maritime interdiction operations is now more diverse, the reasons for which may be manifold and driven by the particular circumstances of the conflict. Either the clarity of the language in the resolution may be subject to political aims and challenges which may require vagueness for the purpose of political progression, or it is chosen in such a way that it better applies to the actual conflict rather than the standard phrases. Indeed, it underlines that the wording of the resolution must be contextualized in the political situation to understand whether or not a maritime embargo operation is authorized or at best legitimized.

5.5 Legal Basis for Explicit Maritime Embargo Operations: Article 41 or 42?

Even when the UNSC uses phrases that explicitly state a mandate to implement economic sanctions at sea, it does not, however, clarify the applicable legal basis under which the mandate is implemented. The core problem of determining between Articles 41 and 42 with regard to explicit maritime embargo operations is

[50] SC Res. 1973 (2011), para 13.

that the aim is to impose Article 41 sanctions, but by using Article 42 means. The debate is not whether military means may be deployed under Article 41 or 42, but whether these forces can use coercive measures to implement economic sanctions.

The 41/42 debate has developed several lines of thought as to the legal basis for using military means to enforce economic measures at sea. One line centers its main arguments on a reluctance to place the naval enforcement of economic sanctions at sea wholly within Article 42. This line accepts that the enforcement of economic sanctions at sea with military means in principle falls outside the scope of Article 41, as it involves the use of armed force, but at the same time having reservations on placing it under 42. The arguments range from the intended scope and nature of Article 42, to the conditions under which Article 42 can be invoked and the level of force that is actually used during maritime embargo operations. Another line of thought is the view that the use of armed force in sanctions enforcement at sea could also be seen within the evolving scope of Article 41.[51] Military means and the use of force may be used to enforce economic measures when the purpose of the operation and the limited level of force used are such that it falls within the evolving parameters of Article 41. A last line of thought concludes that maritime embargo operations plainly fall within the context of Article 42.[52] This line focuses on the use of force as the essential dividing line between Articles 41 and 42. The following subsections will argue that in view of the evolved scope of Article 42 there may be less reluctance to position the military enforcement of economic sanctions at sea within the scope of Article 42 of the UN Charter.

5.5.1 The Evolving Scope of Article 42

Many of the arguments against Article 42 were put forward in the second half of the 1990s. Since then the applicability of Article 42 has evolved. Article 42 of the UN Charter reads:

> Should the Security Council consider that measures provided for in Article 41 would be inadequate or have proved to be inadequate, it may take such action by air, sea, or land forces as may be necessary to maintain or restore international peace and security. Such action may include demonstrations, blockade, and other operations by air, sea, or land forces of Members of the United Nations.

For the positioning of maritime embargo operations three particular points in this evolution can be highlighted. First, the scope of Article 42 operations has developed into a more and broader use of Article 42. Second, the evolution of Article 43

[51] Gowland-Debbas 2004, p. 25. Papastravidis also mentions that the UNSC has authorized maritime interdiction based on Article 41, but offers no further explanation for this statement. Papastavridis 2011, p. 60.

[52] E.g. Robertson 1991, p. 296.

has crystalized. And third, the element of 'inadequate measures under Article 41' has had more practice to determine how the UNSC deals with this phrase.

5.5.2 *Large-Scale Military Operations*

The view that Article 42 was reserved for large-scale military enforcement operations, like those in Korea (1950) and Iraq (1991) that resemble traditional warfare, has been put forward as to why the naval enforcement of economic sanctions could not fit within Article 42. It was considered that maritime embargo operations are a completely different type of operation; small and limited in scale and purpose, with potentially a very low level of the use of force. Along the same lines, it has also been argued that the naval enforcement of economic sanctions could not be part of Article 42 because the article already has the option of authorizing a blockade, which must be distinct from the more limited maritime embargo operations. As such, as Fielding mentions, in terms of scope, maritime embargo operations were more closely associated with Article 41 than Article 42.[53] In the cases of the former Yugoslavia and Haiti, Soons argues that: 'There was no situation of armed conflict between the enforcing States and the target State(s), and there was no alternative for article 41 as the basis for the resolutions, underlining the nature of article 42.'[54] Apparently, Soons at that stage considered military operations only to be within Article 42 if they went beyond the threshold of an armed conflict.

Present day application of Article 42 has however changed. First, the decisions of the Council have more frequently included the phrase 'all necessary means'. This is generally accepted as the authority given by the UNSC to implement the mandate with the use of force when necessary, and has been accepted to imply that the authorization is based on Article 42.[55] The scope of application of Article 42 has broadened to include more types of military operations beyond large-scale military operations, usually referred to as peace enforcement operations, which may not all escalate to a situation of armed conflict. The practice of peace enforcement operations has created a broader, but more moderate view of the use of armed force that can be used under Article 42. In cases where the UNSC has authorized the implementation of economic sanctions at sea, it has done so with the phrase 'to use measures commensurate to the circumstances as may be necessary'. This phrase is, strictly seen, not the same as 'all necessary means', but as McLaughlin notes, it is the equivalent of 'all necessary means' for sanctions enforcement at sea.[56] In the

[53] Fielding 1993, p. 1241.

[54] Soons 2000, p. 213.

[55] Blokker 2005, p. 22; McLaughlin 2007, pp. 389–417; Gazzini 2005, p. 43, n 70.

[56] McLaughlin 2007, p. 391.

case of Libya SC Res. 1973 uses a combination between the two and states: 'to use all measures commensurate to the specific circumstances'.

Explicit maritime embargo operations also have the characteristics of peace enforcement operations: they are not designed to pose a classic military solution and can proactively use force beyond self-defence when vessels are not compliant. All vessels can be halted for inspection without any further requirement and no flag State consent is needed to board vessels.[57] Inspection and verification to ensure strict implantation of the resolution, implies such authority. The legal ratio of these powers is that the UNSC through Chapter VII of the UN Charter can take coercive measures that all States, pursuant to Article 25 of the Charter need to comply with. What follows is that flag States cannot object to the boarding of their flagged vessels. Furthermore, it is argued that Article 103 of the UN Charter trumps the exclusive jurisdiction of the flag State. Neither practice nor literature on the subject records any protests against this way of interpreting the resolutions. In the Yugoslavia embargo the standard phrase was adopted in SC Res. 787 (1992). Leurdijk mentions that this resolution was interpreted by NATO, in close coordination with the UN, as 'permitting the boarding and searching of all merchant traffic entering the Adriatic…'[58] The commander of the Netherlands warship *Hr. Ms. Kortenaer*, who participated in the embargo in the Adriatic, wrote in line with Leurdijk's comments that boarding operations were only authorized after the adoption of SC Res. 787.[59]

Secondly, apart from the broader scope of military operations conducted under Article 42, Blokker mentions an evolving tendency of defining the mandate in more detail, as opposed to the broad authorization of Iraq in SC Res. 678 (1990), to gain more control over the use of force, also arguably limiting the use of force.[60] It minimizes the possible political fear that too much force is unleashed in a particular situation. Interestingly, in this context, Weller comments with regard to SC Res. 665 that Article 42 was specifically not included in the resolution to '[p]reclude an expansive interpretation of the authority that was granted.'[61] Explicit maritime embargo operations to enforce economic sanctions at sea are precisely the kind of balanced and controlled actions towards which the UNSC has been moving. Maritime embargo operations are, in other words, a good example of how the powers of Article 42 can be used. In that sense, the wording of Article 42, which states: 'such action … as maybe necessary', may now be interpreted to include limited military operations using force to implement economic sanctions. Article 42 authorizes the ultimate and broadest authority in terms of the use of force, but does not preclude the lesser.[62] Maritime embargo operations may generally be

[57] Soons 2000, p. 214.

[58] Leurdijk 1996, p. 25.

[59] Van Maanen 1994, p. 15.

[60] Blokker 2005, p. 24.

[61] Weller 1993, p. 36.

[62] Dinstein 2003, p. 250.

considered as low scale operations in terms of the use of force. But how can one characterize a maritime embargo operation if it is an integral part of a military peace enforcement operation as a whole? This was the case in the NATO-led operation Unified Protector in Libya, generally viewed as an operation that was conducted under Article 42 that also rose up to the level of an armed conflict. The overall campaign, of which the embargo operation was part, was not a low-scale operation.

Additionally, apart from the arguments mentioned above, one other argument according to which maritime embargo operations could fit Article 42 is that nothing in Article 42 suggests that the measures taken on that basis cannot also involve economic measures that are enforced by military means. In fact, the use of a blockade, specifically mentioned in Article 42, is a method of naval warfare that traditionally falls under economic warfare. As Conforti noted, 'the forces mentioned in article 42 ought to be set up and employed not only for military action but in furtherance of measures under article 41'.[63]

5.5.3 *Article 43 UN Charter*

During the Iraq conflict, a case for the impossibility of Article 42 to be invoked was made as Article 43 of the UN Charter has remained dormant. No arrangements had yet been made for UN standing forces.[64] As the evolution of the working of the UN collective system on this point had not yet reached fruition in that period, this argument was then highly relevant.[65] At present, however, the argument has lost its strength. The practice of the UNSC has developed in a different way, authorizing the use of force through other agencies pursuant to Article 53 UN Charter. This practice has been accepted by the member states as a legitimate way for the UNSC to operate.[66] Member states are authorized to implement the decision of the Council taken on the basis of Article 42. Gazzini concludes on the connection between Articles 42 and 43: 'Although supported in the past by the Secretary General, this view is now rather marginal.'[67] Therefore, Article 43 does not preclude explicit embargo operations that authorize the use of force from being characterized as Article 42-measures.

[63] Conforti 1991, p. 113.

[64] Schrijver 1994, pp. 153–154.

[65] Which was underlined by Cuba during the Iraq-Kuwait crisis. UN Doc. S/PV.2938, 25 August 1990, pp. 13–17.

[66] Blokker 2000, p. 554.

[67] Gazzini 2005, p. 35.

5.5.4 *Inadequate Measures Under Article 41*

For Article 42 to be invoked, the UNSC must consider that measures under Article 41 'would be inadequate or have proved to be inadequate'. The wording suggests that Article 41 can also be skipped from the outset if the view is that economic measures will not provide the desired result. The Council does not first have to impose sanctions, wait for them to fail, and then move to military enforcement. Schrijver has noted in the case of UNSC Resolution 665 (Iraq) that the resolution cannot be considered an Article 42 resolution because the UNSC did not determine that the measures taken in SC Resolution 661 were inadequate.[68] However, the Council's practice appears to be that the UNSC only determines that the sanctioned State has failed to comply with the adopted obligations, but does not explicitly State that therefore those measures are inadequate before moving on to measures that involve the use of armed force.[69] Whether the condition of inadequacy is met must be derived from wording that does not express the condition in detail, like 'determining that the measures taken under such and such resolution have proven inadequate'. Interestingly, this approach also leaves open the opportunity for it to be repeated in subsequent resolutions without having to make the decision to move to military enforcement measures. Furthermore, if the UNSC decides from the outset of a conflict to use military enforcement measures, it is not likely that any mention or reasoning will be made with the view that measures under Article 41 would have been inadequate; this must be implied from the decision itself not to use economic measures.

5.6 Article 41 and the Use of Force

It is not debated that military means can be deployed in both Articles 41 and 42, nor is it debated that no consent is needed to board a vessel. Rather, the question is whether naval forces can actually take coercive measures when vessel is not compliant. As mentioned above, the UNSC must use language that indicates that

[68] Schrijver 1994, p. 154.

[69] In SC Res. 665, the preamble mentioned that: 'Iraq continues to refuse to comply with resolutions…'. SC Res. 678 was the basis for Operation *Desert Storm*, in which states were authorized 'to use all necessary means to uphold and implement resolution 660 and all subsequent resolutions…' Also in this resolution the preamble stated that Iraq refused to comply with its obligations despite all efforts by the UN. In SC Res. 787 (1992) the Council stated that it was deeply concerned about the continued violations of the embargo imposed by SC Res. 713 (1991) and 724 (1991), and in the case of Haiti, the preamble of SC Res. 917 referred to SC Res. 783 (1993), in which the Council said that it was ready to take additional measures if Haiti continued to fail to comply in full with relevant resolutions. Finally, in the 2011 Libya crisis, the UNSC mentioned the failure to comply with Res. 1970 (2011) by the Libyan authorities.

armed force can be used. The question arises as to whether Article 41 could imply such use of force. Four points can be made.

First, Article 41 does not preclude the use of force *in toto*. When the Council adopts economic measures based on Article 41, the target audience to implement these measures is the member states. They are obliged pursuant to Article 25 of the UN Charter to implement the decisions of the UNSC. Although the UNSC takes economic measures, such as prohibiting trade or imposing an asset freeze, which by their nature are measures that do not involve the use of armed force, member states are obligated to take, as Gazzini mentions: '[w]ithin their respective jurisdiction, all necessary measures to implement the economic enforcement measures'.[70] The possibility to use force or coercive measures for the implementation does not directly flow from the resolution, but is based on national legislation, for instance in the pursuance of an arrest of persons who have breached the embargo, or to stop a vessel in territorial waters that is believed to be carrying prohibited items. Whereas domestic laws would provide a basis to enforce within the States' jurisdictional areas, it, however, will not be sufficient to also enforce an embargo outside the States' jurisdictional areas.

Second, at a minimum what is necessary to imply the authorization for the use of force at sea is that the resolution uses language that actually mandates the implementation of economic sanctions at sea. Without this there is nothing at all to imply the use of force. In other words, at least what is needed is a maritime embargo operation that is explicitly mandated. Although States may take the decision to send warships to sea, it is a step too far to also derive authority for the additional use of force where the UNSC has not even authorized economic sanctions to be enforced at sea. Klein, in the context of SC Resolution 733 (Somalia), argues that implying the use of force in cases where the UNSC did not give explicit authorization 'seems unwarranted in view of the Security Council's practice at the time of explicitly authorizing that ships be halted and cargo inspected and verified under Chapter VII'.[71] This line also appears to have been followed in practice. During Operations *Maritime Monitor* and *Sharp Vigilance* no enforcement powers were given to warships as they 'merely monitored merchant shipping entering into the Adriatic'.[72] With regard to the Beira Patrol, the UK took the view that boarding a vessel and arresting persons and cargo could only be done with the consent of the flag State. No authority was derived from SC Resolution 217.

Third, current practice does not provide any examples in which maritime embargo operations were expressly based on Article 41, authorized an explicit mandate for naval forces to implement sanctions at sea, *and* also authorized the use of force to implement these sanctions.[73] In the case of Sierra Leone and Iran it is

---

[70] Gazzini 2005, p. 16.

[71] Klein 2011, p. 278.

[72] Pugh 1994, p. 208.

[73] The case of Southern Rhodesia has been confusing in the determination of whether the use of force was also possible under Article 41. The Beira Patrol started as an implied maritime embargo

clear that sanctions are taken under Article 41. In the first case, the UNSC also authorized maritime embargo operations, but it states that the implementation must be done in cooperation with the government of Sierra Leone and 'in conformity with applicable international standards'.[74] The UNSC did not use the 'necessary measures' phrase that indicates that force can be used. In the case of Iran, Article 41 is explicitly mentioned and also has the slightest indication of possible implementation through maritime embargo operations in SC Resolution 1929 with regard to Iran.[75] This resolution at the same time underlines that there are no additional enforcement powers based on the resolution itself. In relation to the sanctions imposed against Iran, Gray makes an important point which underlines the importance of the division of Articles 41 and 42. She mentions that the UNSC carefully specified that the sanctions against Iran are based on Article 41, 'in order to ensure that no claim could be made that the Security Council was implicitly authorizing the use of force'.[76] Although she does not say whether force can be used under Article 41, she does point out the danger of blurring the dividing lines between 41 and 42.

Fourth, when explicit authority for a maritime embargo operation is given *and* the language also indicates the authority to use force, the actual level of force used has been an argument to place authority for enforcement still under Article 41. Politakis has argued that actions taken in practice—rare instances of using warning shots across the bow[77]—'have very little to do with what one would understand as use of force'.[78] This discourse could lead to the conclusion that very low-scale use of force should be implied in the enforcement of economic sanctions under Article 41. Apart from the view by some that, for example, warning shots are a traditional and inherent authority for warships, it may not be completely accurate to draw

operation based on SC Res. 217 (1965). The resolution only called upon, but did not decide under Chapter VII to impose sanctions. SC Res. 221 (1966), however, first reaffirmed in the preamble 'its call to all states to do their utmost to break off economic relations with Southern Rhodesia', and secondly, expressly authorized, with the use of force if necessary, the stopping of the Greek-flagged tanker *Joanna V*. The resolution clearly indicates that the *former* resolutions were taken with Article 41 in mind, but not SC Res. 221 itself that included the use of force against Joanna V. Uniquely, the UNSC first authorized force to stop the oil and petroleum flows, and then posed in SC Res. 232 (1966) for the first time in the Council's existence mandatory sanctions specifically based on Article 41, whilst also reaffirming resolution 221. Since the adoption of SC Res. 232 it may seem as if force was authorized under a specific Article 41 mandate. In fact, SC Res. 232 adopted a wide range of economic sanctions under Article 41 without the use of force. Next to that, only the oil embargo could be enforced with the use of force if needed, which, as said, was based on a resolution that did not mention any article.

[74] SC Res. 1132 (1997), para 8.

[75] SC Res. 1929 (2010) states: 'Acting under Article 41 of Chapter VII of the Charter of the United Nations…'

[76] Gray 2008, p. 266.

[77] Morabito mentions that a warning shot was used during the Iraq conflict on 18 August (before SC Res. 665 was adopted). More interestingly, he considers a warning shot to be '[a]n accepted international signal by which a warship tells a merchant vessel to stop'. Morabito 1991, p. 307.

[78] Politakis 1994, p. 192.

conclusions solely on the view of what force *has been* used during maritime embargo operations. If one wants to derive conclusions from practice in terms of the use of force, more important would be the question of what force *can* be used to compel compliance in circumstances that require a step up in coercive measures. Even though the practice may have been that maritime embargo operations are usually of a very low scale on the use of force ladder, this may only mean that commanders of warships have not been confronted with situations in which more force was needed to compel the vessel to comply with the orders of an interdicting warship. The rules of engagement (ROE) may in fact provide for a more robust use of force. The question should, therefore, be raised, for example, whether the crew have ROE that contain the ability to escalate the use of force when necessary and may use disabling fire, detain persons, or use force to protect themselves against hostile acts or the intention to engage in such acts by the vessel's crew or passengers. When a commander of a warship has been given these types of coercive measures, it may be less logical to argue that the use of force is in fact so limited that it can be neglected and therefore positioned within Article 41. At the same time, one must however also keep in mind that coercive action in maritime embargo operations are actions against civilians who, even when they resist, do not take part in hostilities. As such, it limits the overall scope of military measures that can be taken under these circumstances.

5.7 Sub-Conclusion Maritime Embargo Operations

Imposing economic measures against a State is not an unfamiliar task for navies. On the contrary, economic warfare has always been part of the operational oeuvre and the conditions under which the economy of the adversary can be targeted are for instance well presented in the law of naval warfare. Maritime embargo operations executed within the context of the collective security system have been another, and nowadays well-established, step in the evolution of economic warfare at sea. In the past, authors have suggested that there is no strict separation between Articles 41 and 42 of the UN Charter when it comes to enforcing economic sanctions at sea. The different views in this debate have led to conclusions that maritime embargo operations are based on '41½ resolutions'[79] or were found to be venturing in uncharted waters halfway between economic sanctions and military enforcement.[80] To envisage the relationship between Articles 41 and 42 as a continuum would in the first instance indeed be a suitable view for the positioning of the naval enforcement of economic sanctions at sea. The heart of the UNSC decision to authorize naval assets to implement economic sanctions at sea clearly lies with

[79] Blokker 2000, p. 544.

[80] Politakis 1994, p. 197.

Article 41, but the justification and authority to act with military means to enforce implemented economic measures seems more closely related to Article 42.

In determining whether or not maritime embargo operations fall under Article 41 or 42 of the UN Charter, this chapter first tried to make clear that maritime embargo operations are not one of a kind and can largely be divided into implied and explicit maritime embargo operations. The latter can furthermore be divided into operations that are and are not authorized to use force. Consequently, the question as to whether or not maritime embargo operations fit Article 41 or 42 cannot therefore be answered in general, but must be reassessed per situation on every occasion. Secondly, the practice of maritime embargo operations shows that in cases in which the UNSC specifically adopted sanctions under Article 41, and maritime embargo operations were authorized or brought up as a possibility, the use of force was not authorized in the same resolution. In cases in which explicit maritime embargo operations were authorized, including the use of force to enforce the economic sanctions at sea, Article 41 is never explicitly mentioned. Whether Article 41 includes the use of force to implement economic sanctions at sea cannot be sufficiently answered through the current practice of maritime embargo operations because there has not been any situation in which the UNSC has specifically adopted an Article 41 resolution and also explicitly mandated a maritime embargo operation that was authorized to use force. The resolutions on Sierra Leone and Iran do however suggest that the UNSC is very reluctant to use wording that indicates the use of force to implement economic sanctions under Article 41. It is therefore tempting to conclude that only when a maritime embargo operation is based on all three conditions of the existence of economic sanctions, an explicit authority to implement at sea and an authorization to use coercive measures can a maritime embargo operation fall under Article 42. In all other cases of explicit embargo operations it falls back on Article 41. In cases of implied maritime embargo operations the legal basis falls outside the scope of Chapter VII. This conclusion may be even more tempting within the context, as these paragraphs have argued, of the view that presently there are arguments which would take away the initial reluctance to base the use of force in maritime embargo operation under Article 42. Over past years Article 42 has evolved in such a way that it allows for a broader and more moderate scope of military operations within the context of Article 42, particularly military operations that are more limited in scope and the use of force. Furthermore, other restraints in the original set-up of the UN Charter, such as Article 43 and the condition of inadequate measures, no longer form an obstacle to positioning the military enforcement of economic sanctions in Article 42. With the experience we now have, explicit maritime embargo operations that fulfill the three mentioned conditions may well be positioned within Article 42 of the UN Charter.

5.8 UN-Mandated Interception Operations Under 'All Necessary Means'

The above section has analysed the legal basis for maritime embargo operations to implement economic measures adopted by the UNSC. Besides economic measures the UNSC can also decide to take other measures that can be enforced by naval assets based on Chapter VII of the UN Charter. These measures can either be specific measures against specific threats, such as piracy, or to use a specific method, such as the method of blockade, but can also be more general to authorize the use of armed force to fulfil a mandate. In such cases the UNSC can *authorize all necessary means* to fulfill the mandate, which translated in operational conduct may lead to the need of conducting MIO.

5.8.1 All Necessary Means

When the UNSC adopts a resolution within a Chapter VII context that authorizes the use of *all necessary means*,[81] it is generally accepted as giving authority for the use of military force based on Article 42 of the UN Charter.[82] The phrase *all necessary means* is translated on an operational level into authorities for the military, such as the rules of engagement (ROE). Based on the circumstances of the conflict conducting maritime interception operations may be one of the means necessary and will therefore be granted through the specific mission ROE. Clearly, the phrase does not provide any specific methods, but rather very broadly sets the outer limits within which the military operations need to operate to fulfill its mandate. How far *all necessary means* to enforce a mandate can go, is highly contextual. One author has suggested this possibility within the context of maritime operations in East Timor.[83] Rogers, writes that in the East Timor case "all necessary means in SC Res. 1264 (1999); "was arguably broad enough to encompass a right

[81] Interestingly, in SC Res. 2249 (2015), regarding the Council's reaction to the terrorist attacks in Paris in November 2015, the UNSC used the *all necessary means*-phrase, but did not pre-worded it with the term "authorize". Instead, it "called upon" states, rather than it authorized states to use all necessary means. It led to discussion whether or not the resolution actually gave powers to use military force based on resolution 2249.

[82] McLaughlin 2007; Papastavridis 2007. Papastavridis notes that:

> The example par excellence of that could not be other than the ritual incantation of the magic formula "to use all necessary means" from Resolution 678 (1990) onwards in every case of authorization to use force. The above phrase was accepted to have a different meaning than the ordinary and to denote the authority to use force, illustrating thus the common will of the Council to that effect. The existence of this formula in a Resolution is perhaps the most decisive factor as to whether the latter has authorized the use of force.

[83] Rogers 2005, p. 579.

of approach and visit if required".[84] Klein also states that *all necessary means*: '[m]ay be considered as sufficient authority for interdictions at sea to enforce the Security Council's sanctions regime'.[85] Such a view has also been part of discussion during Operation *Unified Protector* (OUP) with regard to Libya in 2011. The military operations with regard to Libya between March and November 2011 consisted also of a significant maritime element in which both a maritime arms embargo was enforced and naval forces were deployed to contribute to the protection of civilians based on UNSC Res. 1973 (2011). Paragraph 4 of UNSC Res. 1973 (2011) reads:

> 4. Authorizes Member States that have notified the Secretary-General, acting nationally or through regional organizations or arrangements, and acting in cooperation with the Secretary-General, to take all necessary measures, notwithstanding paragraph 9 of resolution 1970 (2011), to protect civilians and civilian populated areas under threat of attack in the Libyan Arab Jamahiriya, including Benghazi, while excluding a foreign occupation force of any form on any part of Libyan territory, and requests the Member States concerned to inform the Secretary-General immediately of the measures they take pursuant to the authorization conferred by this paragraph which shall be immediately reported to the Security Council;

Because of the manner in way the text of resolution 1973 was construed, enforcement of the arms embargo was limited to the sea outside the Libyan territorial waters. Paragraph 4 was, however, not limited in such a way. If necessary for the fulfilment of the mandate of protecting civilians, all necessary means could have been operationally translated into stopping and boarding vessel in the territorial sea. What matters in this is that the action taken must be in concordance with the purpose of the mandate. If, for instance, the general practice of the UNSC is to explicitly authorize oil embargos against a State, discussion can emerge on whether an operation that practically result in an oil embargo and based on 'all necessary means' really is in line with the purpose of the mandate. Although such matters depend on the actual situation in a given conflict, it is submitted here that 'all necessary means' may include the use of naval forces to conduct MIO to enforce the mandate, if this is in line with the purpose of the mandate.

5.9 Specific Measures

Apart from the general *all necessary means*-phrase, the UNSC can also adopt specific measures in which the Council authorizes interception operations for a specific aim and purpose, or through a specific method. Specific measures can be taken with regard to a wide range of subjects, such as piracy, or WMDs, but the Council can also decide to establish a naval blockade or take a specific measure to

[84] Rogers 2005, p. 579.

[85] Klein 2011, p. 279.

help support a State that is trying to stabilize internal unrest. These four will be briefly touched upon in the next paragraphs.

5.9.1 "Article 42" Blockade

A type of maritime interception operations, albeit under a more traditional name, is explicitly mentioned in Article 42 of the UN Charter. Article 42 mentions as an example of measures that can be taken under Article 42, the use of a blockade to enforce measures taken by the UNSC. By nature, a blockade is different than an embargo operation. Whereas the embargo is a control-mechanism to inspect inward and outward shipping where vessels may pass if it does not carry any of the prohibited items, a blockade closes the target port or coastal stretch completely and lets no one and nothing in in or out, save a few specific exceptions.[86] In that sense, MEO are closer to contraband law than blockade law as they establish a selective barrier rather than a complete one. A blockade is impartial and not focused on certain goods or persons, but simply closes the sea routes to and from the targeted State completely.

A difference must be made between the UNSC specifically authorizing a blockade under Article 42 UN Charter and the decision of military commanders to establish a blockade when the factual situation of the conflict and the given mandate allows them to resort to such a method. The first authorizes, as a legal basis, a *de facto* blockade operation under the authorities that will be determined in the resolution. The second is a method of the law naval warfare, which can be applied when the factual circumstances of the conflict rise to an international armed conflict, and allows for the law of naval warfare to be applied. A third option would be that an *all necessary means*-mandate is neither explicitly stating to use a blockade, nor does the conflict rise to an international armed conflict. A *de facto* blockade could in this case still be argued, but within limited purpose of the mandate.

At this stage, no resolution has ever been adopted by the UNSC in which it explicitly called for a blockade. Decisions by military commanders to resort to blockade operations under the law of naval warfare have, however, taken place. During the Korea War the method of blockade was used by the naval force, shortly after the North Korean invasion of South Korea in July 1950, which was made possible by SC Resolutions 83 and 84 (1950).[87] Taskforce 95 was called the *UN Blockading and Escort Force* (UNBEF). In this case, the UNSC declared that members of the UN may furnish such assistance that may be necessary to repel the attack of North Korea. The military operations resulting from this UNSC-authorization can be characterized as an international armed conflict, to which the law of war, including the law of naval warfare, applied. The operations

[86] See on these exceptions Fink 2011b.

[87] Baer 1993, p. 323.

came under unified command of the US, led by General MacArthur. US President Truman then ordered a naval blockade against North Korea.[88]

During the Iraq crisis in 1990, the media quickly moved to the use of the term blockade after the adoption of SC Res. 665.[89] Although the US and UK, still operating under the legal basis of article 51 UN Charter, could have established a blockade, they did not. The measures taken by the Council could be seen as complementary measures to self-defence. The authorities given by Council, however, did not authorize a blockade and did not go beyond maritime embargo operations. At that stage of the conflict, a possible blockade would not have been connected to the measures taken by the Council. From the adoption of the 'ultimatum-resolution' SC Res. 678 that led to Operation *Desert Storm* in January 1991, arguably, either these UNSC-measures can be seen as part of necessary measures within the context of self-defence, or as the Council taking measures within the collective security system.[90] Either way, the subsequent military operations rose to an international armed conflict, to which the law of naval warfare applied. Although not actually executed, one example of the third option can be mentioned here. During the Cyprus crisis in 1974, when Turkey decided to invade the island, a British Task Force set off to sail to Cyprus. The commander of these British forces in Cyprus suggested blockading the northern coast of Cyprus to stop the Turkish reinforcements on Cyprus on behalf of the UN. The UN peacekeeping force UNFICYP[91] had been established on Cyprus since 1964. Although the UK naval Task Group went to position itself at sea, the initiative was called off, amongst other reasons, because it was questionable whether UNFICYP mandate would support such an action when performed as an official declared part of UNFICYP.[92]

5.9.2 *Piracy*

The UNSC adopted several UN resolutions concerning the fight against piracy off the coast of Somalia.[93] Although piracy has been a longstanding issue in these and also other parts of the world, these resolutions brought the issue of piracy off the coast of Somalia onto the international peace and security agenda. Through its resolutions the UNSC has mainly served as a vehicle for international action with

---

[88] Politakis 1994, pp. 64–66.

[89] See e.g. 'Comprehensive mandatory sanctions imposed against Iraq - Kuwait: The Crisis - Cover Story', in U.N. Chronicle, December 1990; Marolda and Schneller 2001, pp. 83–96.

[90] See discussion on this point for instance in Gill 2015, pp. 737–751; Dinstein 2003, pp. 242–245.

[91] *United Nations Peacekeeping Force in Cyprus.*

[92] Asmussen 2008, pp. 133–134.

[93] SC Resolutions 1814 (2008), 1816 (2008), 1838 (2008), 1844 (2008), 1846 (2008), 1851 (2008), 1897 (2009), 1918 (2010), 1950 (2010), 1976 (2011), 2015 (2011), 2020 (2011), 2077 (2012) and 2125 (2013) 2184 (2014).

regard to piracy in the seas around the Horn of Africa. It has furthermore helped to enable to take measures against piracy within the Somali territorial sea and also even on land. The counter-piracy resolutions are adopted under Chapter VII of the UN Charter and also include an *all necessary means*-mandate. SC Res. 1816 (2008) mentions that States cooperating with the Somali Transitional Federal Government in the fight against piracy may:

> (b) Use, within the territorial waters of Somalia, in a manner consistent with action permitted on the high seas with respect to piracy under relevant international law, all necessary means to repress acts of piracy and armed robbery;[94]

A number of important limitations have, however, been brought into the resolutions. First, and as eluded to in the chapter on consent, to operate in the Somali territorial sea the Chapter VII authorities are restricted by the consent of the Somali authorities. Second, the authorities of the participating States must be consistent with action permitted on the high seas, which means that actions must be concordance with the law of the sea. Additionally, in terms of legal regime, the use of force is limited to force that is allowed within the context of human rights law standards.

5.9.3 Weapons of Mass Destruction and Terrorism

The prohibitions regarding weapons of mass destruction, commonly regarded as chemical, biological, nuclear and radiological weapons, are regulated by treaties such as the BWC,[95] CWC[96] and the NPT.[97] In 2004, the UNSC adopted SC Resolution 1540 with regard to non-proliferation of WMD, in which it decided that; ‘all States shall refrain from supporting by any means non-State actors that attempt to acquire, use or transfer nuclear, chemical or biological weapons and their delivery systems’.[98] Although it has been adopted under Chapter VII of the UN Charter, this resolution does not authorize any maritime enforcement actions on the high seas.[99] For its enforcement it primarily relies on other treaties, all of which do not contain provision that allow non-consensual interception on the high seas of foreign-flagged vessels by warships when the provisions of the treaties are breached. Just after the 9/11 attacks, the UNSC adopted SC Res. 1373(2001), determining that terrorists acts are a threat to international peace and security. Also this

[94] SC Res. 1816 (2008), para 7(b).

[95] *The Convention on the Prohibition of the Development, Production and Stockpiling of Bacteriological (Biological) and Toxin Weapons and on their Destruction,* 10 April 1972.

[96] *Chemical Weapons Convention*, 3 September 1992.

[97] *The Treaty on the Non-Proliferation of Nuclear Weapons,* 1968.

[98] Press release SC/8076. UN Security Council, 4956th Meeting (PM), 28 April 2004.

[99] See e.g. Dafrancia 2012, pp. 705–783.

resolution does not contain a specific authority for enforcement of the adopted measures on the high seas.

The UNSC has the possibility to adopt military measures to enforce that States will comply with their WMD non-proliferation and disarmament obligations when it considers that breaching them is a threat to international peace and security. Apart from the non-proliferation resolution 1540, the UNSC has adopted a number of other resolutions with regard to specific States, such as North Korea[100] and Iran.[101] In these specific cases thus far, and although measures are taken under Chapter VII, the UNSC has not authorized any coercive enforcement measures *at sea* that would include the boarding of a foreign-flagged vessel to stop WMD.[102] In fact, with regard to Iran under SC Res. 1747 (2007)[103] and 1929 (2010)[104] the UNSC specifically adopted the wording that states that inspection measures on the high seas could only be taken based the consent of the flag States. As a last, in the context of acting against WMD, the failure of Iraq to comply with SC Resolutions 678, 687 and 1441 was interpreted by the US and UK to invade Iraq and to overthrow Saddam Hussein in the Gulf War of 2003. The military operations also had a naval dimension which included MIO.[105] The justification for the start of military operations against Iraq based on these resolutions has been very widely criticized.[106]

---

[100] SC Res. 1695 (2006) and 1718 (2006).

[101] SC Res. 1696 (2006), 1737 (2006), 1747 (2007), 1803 (2008), 1835 (2008), 1887 (2009) and 1929 (2010).

[102] See on North Korea Yong-Joong Lee 2007.

[103] Operative para 5 of SC Res. 1747 (2007) reads:

> Decides that Iran shall not supply, sell or transfer directly or indirectly from its territory or by its nationals or using its flag vessels or aircraft any arms or related materiel, and that all States shall prohibit the procurement of such items from Iran by their nationals, or using their flag vessels or aircraft, and whether or not originating in the territory of Iran;

[104] SC Res. 1929 (2010), para 15 reads:

> 15. Notes that States, consistent with international law, in particular the law of the sea, may request inspections of vessels on the high seas with the consent of the flag State, and calls upon all States to cooperate in such inspections if there is information that provides reasonable grounds to believe the vessel is carrying items the supply, sale, transfer, or export of which is prohibited by paragraphs 3, 4 or 7 of resolution 1737 (2006), paragraph 5 of resolution 1747 (2007), paragraph 8 of resolution 1803 (2008) or paragraphs 8 or 9 of this resolution, for the purpose of ensuring strict implementation of those provisions;

[105] Kidd 2004, pp. 134–144.

[106] The US and participating States opined that the authority to use force derived from the earlier resolutions in the beginning of the 1990s could in 2003 still be used to use force after the failure of Iraq to comply with SC Res. 1441. (See e.g. Rostow 2006, pp. 21–42.) Other States disagreed on this point of view and opined that a further resolution from the Council was needed to resort to the use of military force. See Franck 2006, pp. 15–20; Gazzini 2005, pp. 227–230.

5.9.4 Crude Oil Export: Libya 2014

The Libya conflict of 2011 resulting in the overthrow and death of Qaddafi did not result in the peaceful rebuilding of Libya. Internal struggles between local militias demanding autonomy and the government continued to be a challenge for the State. Local militias kept their weapons and took control of some of the oil ports in parts of Libya.[107] This situation led to the adoption of SC Res. 2146 (2014) authorizing under Chapter VII the stopping, albeit with consent, of designated vessels that illicitly transport crude oil from rebel held ports. Days before the adoption of this resolution, US Navy SEALS stopped the tanker *Morning Glory* that was trying to leave Libya in order to sell oil.[108] The actions of the UNSC in this case are very specific in a particular phase of state building and appear to be an attempt to canalize Libyan political developments for the better.

5.10 Conclusions

The UN collective security system provides a legal basis for maritime interception operations. Two types of MIO can be distinguished. The first are the maritime interception operations that aim to enforce economic measures taken by the UNSC under Article 41 UN Charter. These operations are often termed maritime embargo operations. The second are interception operations, based on Chapter VII, that do not per definition aim to enforce economic measures. This category can either authorize the use of armed force to fulfill a mandate through general indications such as all necessary means, which may include MIO, or can explicitly authorize MIO in relation to a specific subject, such as piracy or WMD. States can also mount maritime interception operations outside the scope of Chapter VII, but this will impact on the authorities that warships may have to support the UN efforts. Arguably, in such case it must be questioned whether the UN collective security systems is actually providing the legal basis or that States are in fact using the freedom of the seas to support UN efforts in controlling a conflict.

Maritime embargo operations based on the UN collective security system are, as noted in Chap. 3, the type of MIO that were first meant by the term MIO and have since their inception been used by the UNSC as an instrument to restore international peace and security. The legal parameters of this legal basis have now for the most been crystallized. Next to standard phraseology to indicate that embargo operations are authorized, even in the event that those phrases are not used, such as

[107] 'Libya asks UN and the world for help', in *Times of Malta*, 20 March 2014, p. 12.

[108] US Department of Defense, press release, 17 March 2014, NR-126-14, 'DoD Statement on Boarding of Commercial Tanker Morning Glory'.

in the case of Libya and Lebanon, it has led to a standard maritime embargo operation, matched to the details of the text of the resolution and other specific circumstances of the conflict.

References

Asmussen J (2008) Diplomacy and conflict during the 1974 crisis. Cyprus at war. I.B. Tauris, London/New York

Baer G (1993) One hundred years of seapower. The U.S. Navy 1890–1990. Stanford University Press, Stanford, CA

Blokker N (2000) Is the Authorization Authorized? Powers and Practice of the Security Council Resolution to Authorize the Use of Force by "Coalitions of the Able and Willing". European Journal of International Law 11, pp. 541–568

Blokker N (2005) The Security Council and the Use of Force – On Recent Practice. In: Blokker N, Schrijver N (eds) The Security Council and the Use of Force. Theory and Reality – A Need for a Change? Martinus Nijhoff Publishers, Leiden

Booth K (1985) Law, Force and Diplomacy at Sea. George Allen & Unwin, London

Carvalho de Oliviera G (2012) Naval peacekeeping and piracy: Time for a critical debate. International Peacekeeping, 19-1: 48–61

Conforti B (1991) Non-coercive Sanctions in the United Nations Charter: Some Lessons from the Gulf War. European Journal of International Law 2, pp. 110–113

Dafrancia C (2012) Enforcing the Nuclear Non-proliferation Regime: The Legality of Preventive Measures. Vanderbilt Journal of Transnational Law 45:705, pp. 705–783

De Jonge Oudraat C (2000) Making Sanctions Work. Survival 42, pp. 105–127

Dinstein Y (2003) War, Aggression and Self-Defence. Cambridge University Press, Cambridge

Dupont P (2012) Countermeasures and Collective Security: The Case of the EU Sanctions against Iran. Journal of Conflict and Security Law 17, pp. 301–336

Fielding L (1992–1993) Maritime Interception: Centrepiece of Economic Sanctions in the New World Order. Louisiana Law Rev 53, pp. 1191–1241

Fink M (2011a) UN-Mandated Maritime Arms Embargo Operations in Operation Unified Protector. Military Law and the Law of War Review 50, pp. 1–24

Fink M (2011b) Contemporary views on the lawfulness of naval blockades. Aegean Review of the Law of the Sea and Maritime Law 1:2, pp. 191–215

Fink M (2013) Maritime embargo operations: Naval implementation of UN sanctions at sea under Articles 41 and 42 of the UN Charter. Netherlands International Law Review, 60:1, pp. 73–92

Franck T (2006) Iraq and the law of armed conflict. In: Jacques R (ed) International Law Studies 80. Naval War College, Newport RI, pp. 15–20

Gazzini T (2005) The Changing Rules on the Use of Force in International Law. Manchester University Press, Manchester

Gill T (1990) De Golf crisis. De volkenrechtelijke regels inzake het gebruik van militair geweld. Nederlands Juristenblad 31, pp. 1475–1487

Gill T (2010) Peace operations. In: Gill T, Fleck D (eds) The Handbook of the International Law of Military Operations. Oxford University Press, New York, pp. 135–142

Gill T (2015) When does self-defence end? In: Weller M (ed) The Oxford Handbook of the Use of Force in International Law. Oxford University Press, New York, pp. 737–751

Goldrick J (2008) Maritime Sanctions Enforcement against Iraq, 1990–2003. In: Elleman B, Paine S (eds) Naval Blockades and Seapower. Strategies and Counter-strategies, 1805–2005. Routledge, London, pp. 201–214

Gowland-Debbas V (2004) Sanctions regimes under Article 41 of the UN Charter. In: Gowland-Debbas V (ed) National implementation of UN Sanctions. Kluwer Law International, The Hague/London/ Boston, pp. 3–31
Gray C (2008) International Law and the Use of Force. Oxford University Press, New York
Kamerbrief inzake beantwoording schriftelijke vragen over de maritime bijdrage aan UNIFIL (Letters to parliament answering written questions on the maritime support to UNIFIL), 11 October 2006
Kidd J (2004) Campaign analysis: Maritime forces. In: Cornish P (ed) The conflict in Iraq, 2003. Palgrave Macmillan, pp. 134–144
Klein N (2011) Maritime security and the law of the sea. Oxford University Press, New York
Leurdijk D (1996) The United Nations and NATO in Former Yugoslavia. Partners in International Cooperation. Netherlands Institute of International Relations 'Clingendael', The Hague
MacAskill E, Traynor I (2011) Libya: NATO defence ministers agree on minimal intervention. Victory for US as agreement to move warships closer to Libya falls far short of measures called for by Britain and France. The Guardian, 10 March 2011. www.guardian.co.uk/world/2011/mar/10/libya-gaddafi-nato-us-minimal-intervention. Accessed 17 February 2017
Marolda J, Schneller Jr R (2001) Shield and Sword. The United States Navy in the Persian Gulf War. Naval Institute Press, Annapolis Maryland
McLaughlin R (2002) United Nations Mandated Naval Interdiction Operations in the Territorial Sea? International and Comparative Law Quarterly 51, pp. 249–278
McLaughlin R (2007) The Legal Regime Applicable to Use of Lethal Force When Operating under a United Nations Security Council Chapter VII Mandate Authorising "All Necessary Means". Journal of Conflict and Security Law 12, pp. 389–417
McLaughlin R (2009) United Nations Naval Peace Operations in the Territorial Sea. Martinus Nijhoff Publishers, Leiden
Mobley R (2002) The Beira Patrol. Britain's Broken Blockade. Naval War College Review 55, pp. 64–84
Morabito R (1991) Maritime interdiction: Evolution of a strategy. Ocean Development and International Law 22, pp. 301–311
NATO Operation Maritime Monitor www.manp.nato.int/NAVSOUTH/OperationMaritimeMonitor.htm. Accessed February 2013
O'Connell D (1975) The influence of law on sea power. Manchester University Press, Manchester
Papastavridis E (2007) Interpretation of Security Council Resolutions under Chapter VII in the Aftermath of the Iraqi Crisis. International and Comparative Law Quarterly 83, pp. 83–118
Papastavridis E (2011) The Right of Visit on the High Seas in a Theoretical Perspective: Mare Liberum versus Mare Clausum Revisited. Leiden Journal of International Law 24, pp. 45–69
Peace D (1991) Major Maritime Events in the Persian Gulf between 1984 and 1991. Virginia Journal of International Law 31, pp. 545–566
Politakis G (1994) UN-Mandated Naval Operations and Notion of Pacific Blockade: Comments on Some Recent Developments. Revue Africaine de Droit International et Comparé 6, pp. 173–208
Pugh M (1994) Peacekeeping, Monitoring and Verification. In: Haydon P, Griffiths A (eds) Maritime Security and Conflict Resolution at Sea in the Post-Cold War Era. Centre of Foreign Policy Studies Halifax, NS, pp. 207–224
Robertson H (1991) Interdiction of Iraqi Maritime Commerce in the 1990–1991 Persian Gulf conflict. Ocean Development and International Law 22, pp. 289–299
Rogers F (2005) The international force in East Timor – legal aspects of maritime operations. UNSW Law Journal 28:2, pp. 566–580
Rostow N (2006) International Law and the 2003 Campaign against Iraq. Jacques R (ed) International Law Studies 80. Naval War College, Newport RI, pp. 21–42
Rothwell D, Stephens T (2010) The international Law of the Sea. Hart Publishing Oxford/ Portland, OR
Sandalli P (2010) Maritime task force's role in UNIFIL. Al Janoub, 6 January 2010

Schrijver N (1994) The Use of Economic Sanctions by the Security Council: An International Law Perspective. In: Post H (ed) International Economic Law and Armed Conflict. Martinus Nijhoff Publishers, Dordrecht, pp. 153–154
Soons A (2000) A "New" Exception to the Freedom of the High Seas: The Authority of the U.N. Council. In: Gill T, Heere W (eds) Reflections on the Principles and Practice of International Law: Essays in Honour of Leo J. Bouchez. Martinus Nijhoff Publishers, Dordrecht, pp. 205–211
Till G (2013) Seapower. A guide for the twenty-first century. Routledge, London/New York
Times of Malta (2014) Libya asks UN and the world for help, 20 March 2014, p. 12
UN (1990) UN Doc. S/PV.2938, 25 August 1990
UN (2004) UN Press release SC/8076. UN Security Council, 4956th Meeting (PM), 28 April 2004
UN Chronicle (1990) Comprehensive mandatory sanctions imposed against Iraq - Kuwait: The Crisis - Cover Story December 1990
US Department of Defense (2014) Press release, 17 March 2014, NR-126-14, 'DoD Statement on Boarding of Commercial Tanker Morning Glory'
van Maanen M (1994) Embargo operaties in de Adriatische zee. Militair Rechtelijk Tijdschrift, pp. 15–18
Weingarter J (2007) Das Unifil-mandat der Bundeswehr – politische und rechtliche Aspekte. Journal of International Law of Peace and Armed Conflict, 20:2, pp. 116–119
Weller M (1993) The United Nations and the Ius ad Bellum. In: Rowe P (ed) The Gulf War 1990–1991 in International and English Law. Routledge, London, pp. 29–54
Yong-Joong Lee Y (2007) Legal Analysis of the 2006 U.N. Security Council Resolutions Against North Korea's WMD Development. Fordham International Law Journal 31:1, pp. 1–33
Zeigler D (1996) Ubi Sumus? Quo Vadimus? Charting the Course of Maritime Interception Operations. Naval Law Review 43, pp. 1–55

Chapter 6
Self-Defence and Maritime Interception

As a practical guideline naval planning staffs should take it for granted that the employment of force...will be regarded as overstepping the boundaries of the legitimate, except when resorted to in self-defence. The real problem is what is meant by self-defence against an armed attack?
—D. P. O'Connell, The Influence of Law on Seapower

Contents

Abstract This chapter analyses self-defence as a legal basis for conducting maritime interception operations. Generally speaking, there are two manners in which way self-defence is argued as a legal basis. The first manner is as a legal basis for larger scale naval operations, among which the naval forces could also perform maritime interception operations. The second is that self-defence is used as a direct legal basis to board foreign-flagged vessels. The latter is often discussed in the context of effectively dealing with terrorist threats and possible weapons of mass destruction at sea. Self-defence in this regard is argued in an anticipatory manner.

Keywords Self-defence · weapons of mass destruction · Enduring Freedom · Active Endeavour · anticipatory self-defence

M. Fink, *Maritime Interception and the Law of Naval Operations*,
https://doi.org/10.1007/978-94-6265-249-1_6

6.1 Introduction

Self-defence as a legal basis for military operations has since the 9/11 attack been under much scrutiny, in particular with regard to how this legal basis should be applied in contemporary threats.[1] In the maritime dimension self-defence is often argued in two different contexts. It is firstly argued as the legal basis for the deployment of large-scale military campaigns that, including a naval component. Recent examples are Operations *Enduring Freedom*, *Active Endeavour*, *Cast Lead* and *Change Direction.* Self-defence is also argued as a basis to stop weapons of mass destruction and terrorists, or a combination thereof, at sea, outside the context of large scale military campaigns.[2] The latter approach applies the right of self-defence against single threats in individual cases. This second approach has particularly emerged since the fight against terrorists was broadened against persons and cargo beyond Al Qaida, the Taliban and its affiliates. It was primarily initiated by the US National Security Strategy (2002), in which the former US president George W. Bush coined the much debated idea of pre-emptively countering threats to US national security, in particular terrorists who obtain and use weapons of mass destruction. Interestingly, back in 1956, the International Law Commission noted on the issue of whether the right of self-defence could be another exception to the exclusive jurisdiction of the flag State that it was not 'deemed to be advisable', because of the vagueness of terms as 'imminent danger' and 'hostile acts', which leaves them open to abuse.[3] To some, the issue implied the recognition of the idea itself.[4] To others, the ILC-commentary closed the subject.[5] Today, however, the discussion of self-defence in relation to the exclusive jurisdiction over a vessel has received new attention in the legal arena. This chapter analyses the right of self-defence in relation to maritime interception operations. It will first start with a brief introduction to the right of self-defence and remark on the application of

---

[1] O'Connell 1975, p. 54.

[2] Guilfoyle 2005, p. 750; Fitzgerald 2008; Shulman 2006; Von Dyke 2004; Heintschel von Heinegg 2004. Klein also points in this direction as an emerging trend. See Klein 2005, pp. 307–308 and 2011, pp. 297–300.

[3] UN Doc A/3159, *YILC* 1956 vol. II. Comment 4 to Article 46, p. 284. Comment 4 is worthwhile quoting here because it remains of relevance to this day. It reads:

> The question arose whether the right to board a vessel should be recognized also in the event of a ship being suspected of committing acts hostile to the state to which the warship belongs, at a time of imminent danger to the security of that state. The commission did not deem it advisable to include such a provision mainly because of the vagueness of terms like 'imminent danger' and 'hostile acts', which leaves them open to abuse.

[4] Syrigos 2006, p. 163.

[5] Somers 2010, p. 291.

self-defence through both large-scale military campaign naval operations in an interception role, and self-defence in response to single threats of WMD and terrorists.

6.2 The Right of Self-Defence

Similar to the UN collective security system the legal basis of self-defence takes as starting point the prohibition on the use of force laid down in Article 2(4) of the UN Charter. The sources of the right of self-defence are usually considered to be based on both the UN Charter and international customary law. These sources result in the view that there are specifically written conditions for self-defence in Article 51 of the UN Charter and additional conditions that are derived from customary international law. Article 51 of the UN Charter reads as follows:

> Nothing in the present Charter shall impair the inherent right of individual or collective self-defence if an armed attack occurs against a Member of the United Nations, until the Security Council has taken measures necessary to maintain international peace and security. Measures taken by Members in the exercise of this right of self-defence shall be immediately reported to the Security Council and shall not in any way affect the authority and responsibility of the Security Council under the present Charter to take at any time such action as it deems necessary in order to maintain or restore international peace and security.

The threshold condition that must be fulfilled in order to invoke the right of self-defence is the existence of an armed attack. Once an armed attack exists the reaction to the armed attack must fulfill the substantive customary conditions of necessity, proportionality, and immediacy.[6] Necessity relates to the existence of an armed attack or an immediate threat of attack and focuses on the question whether the use of force under self-defence is a measure of last resort to which there are no other means or alternative available than the use of force. Proportionality focuses on a balanced response to the armed attack, against the background of the purpose of self-defence. This purpose is to halt and repel the attack, and, to some authors, also includes ensuring that the attacker cannot mount future attacks.[7] Immediacy considers the temporal link between the attack and the start of the reaction to the attack once the attack has occurred.

The answer to the question whether an armed attack has occurred, has been part of extensive legal debate since the 9/11 attacks, in particular from a material, temporal and *personae* perspective. These three perspectives deal with the questions of what amounts to an armed attack, at what moment in time can the right of self-defence be invoked and against whom can it be invoked. The debates have

[6] Next to these conditions, there is also a procedural condition that obliges to inform the UNSC that use of force is used in the context of self-defence. This procedural obligation is explicitly stated in Article 51 of the UN Charter.

[7] Kretzmer 2013, p. 264; Gill 2007, p. 124.

concentrated on whether self-defence could exist in an anticipatory manner, whether it can be invoked against non-state actors and which scale and effect the attack must have be to be considered an armed attack. This is not the place to extensively repeat those debates, but it generally appears that, although the jurisprudence of the ICJ is more reluctant,[8] scholars are moving into the direction that the general answer to the first two questions relating to the expanding scope of self-defence might well be a positive one.[9] Indeed an evolution in thought appears to have taken place with regard to the scope of the armed attack, which now more readily considered to include anticipatory attacks and attacks mounted by non-state actors. As Van Steenberghe has concluded om the latter based on a study of recent state practice; '…the interpretation of recent state practice amounts to considering that the latter evidences a clear tendency towards allowing States to act in self-defence in response to attacks, even if these attacks are committed only by non-state actors'.[10] In relation to self-defence in the context of maritime interception operations, this evolution of thought opens the possibility to act against non-state actors that are on board a vessel or use the vessels as an instrument in an armed attack. The material aspect of self-defence emerges as an issue in the context of attacks against warships and the possibilities a State and the individual warship commander might have to react against it.[11] But more importantly, the broadened scope of self-defence in the temporal aspect is particularly of interest for proponents of the view that foreign-flagged vessels that pose an imminent threat by virtue of threatening cargo can be boarded based on self-defence. In this context anticipatory self-defence, which is seen through the now generally accepted *Caroline-criteria*—the armed attack must be instant, overwhelming, leaving no choice for other means, and no moment for deliberation—[12]and the interpretation of immediacy is of importance. Anticipatory self-defence in essence questions whether a State can act

[8] Dinstein 2005; Schmitt 2008. Schmitt underlines that there is a difference in view between jurisprudence of the International Court of Justice and state practice in the case of Operation *Change Direction*.

[9] See e.g. Kretzmer 2013; Waxman 2013.

[10] Van Steenberghe 2010, p. 207.

[11] In the *Oil Platform* case, the ICJ dealt with the case of the US attacking a number of Iranian oil platforms. The attacks came as a reaction to a missile attack during the Iran-Iraq War that caused damage to the Kuwaiti owned but US-reflagged oil-tanker vessel *Sea Isle City* in 1987, and the damage caused by mines, a year later, to the warship *USS Samuel B. Roberts*. The US chose to attack the oil platforms because it was believed that the platforms collected and reported intelligence concerning passing vessels, acted as military communication link for Iranian naval forces and as military staging bases. The ICJ noted that although in the specific circumstances of the incident with the *USS Samuel B. Roberts* being struck by a mine, the Court considered that attacking the platforms was not justifiable in response to an armed attack, the Court did, however, state it does not exclude the possibility that; 'the mining of a single military vessel be sufficient to bring into play the "inherent right of self-defense"'. See ICJ, *Oil Platform* (Islamic Republic of Iran v. United States of America), Judgment, I.C.J. Reports 2003, 161 (Oil Platforms case).

[12] Gill 2007, p. 125.

when the use of force against the State is about to happen and whether a State needs to wait until an actual attack has occurred.

6.3 Large-Scale Military Campaigns

In several recent military operations the right of self-defence has been a legal ground for States to deploy their warships in a maritime interception role. With regard to the military campaigns, from 1990 onwards most notably, the first days of the military operations against Iraq (1990), the operation with regard to Afghanistan from September 2001 onwards, and the Israeli operations against Hezbollah (2006) and Hamas (2009) are generally considered to be based on self-defence. Although the latter three operations have their peculiarities with regard to the application of self-defence against non-state actors, there is not much controversy on whether self-defence could be used as a legal basis. Moreover, this practice has been taken to support the broadened scope of the application of the right of self-defence. The four conflicts mentioned, produced five different military operations in which maritime assets were also deployed in a maritime interception role: First, the immediate military response to the invasion of Iraq in Kuwait in 1990; second and third, the military response against the attacks on the United States on 11 September 2001, Operations *Enduring Freedom* and *Active Endeavour*; fourth, Israel's military operations against Hezbollah in Lebanon (Operation *Change Direction*) in the summer of 2006 and finally the fifth, the Israeli operations against Hamas since the end of 2008 (Operation *Cast Lead*).

6.3.1 Iraq (1990–1991)

The affirmation by the UN Security Council that the Iraqi invasion of Kuwait on 2 August 1990 was considered a situation activating the right of self-defence in light of the UN Charter followed four days later, on 6 August, when the Council adopted SC Res. 661 (1990). In addition, the UNSC in SC Res. 661 also imposed a trade embargo on the import into the territories of all member nations of all the commodities and products originating in Iraq or Kuwait. Debate existed on the legal basis of the maritime interception operations that occurred between the adoption of SC Res. 661 and 665, because SC Res. 661 was considered to be based on Article 41 of the UN Charter[13] and did not authorize any seaborne enforcement actions. The US, and later the UK,[14] stated that it intercepted vessels at the request of

[13] Gill 1990, p. 133.

[14] Westra 2007, pp. 113–114.

Kuwait who were in violation of the UN resolution, but considered those actions to be based on a continued right of self-defence, thereby acting in consistency with the Council's resolution.[15]

6.3.2 Enduring Freedom, Change of Direction *and* Cast Lead

Whereas the invocation of the right of (collective) self-defence against Iraq in support of Kuwait in 1990 was straightforward in the sense that it was a state-to-state situation, invoking self-defence against Al Qaida in 2001, a non-state actor supported by the *de facto* Taliban government of Afghanistan, initiated quite some legal debate. While this debate on applicability of the law self-defence to non-state actors raged from 11 September onwards in the academic arena, on 7 October 2001 the US and its coalition allies started Operation *Enduring Freedom* (OEF). For the coalition the legal basis for the military response to the attacks was clear from the outset: Article 51 of the UN Charter. Their view was backed up by the UNSC in SC Res. 1368 (2001). On the legal debate of invoking self-defence against non-state actors that emerged after the 9/11-attacks the statist presumption, as Gill notes, was eventually left behind to include the possibility of invoking the right of self-defence against non-state actors.[16] This view also paved the way to more practice in which the right of self-defence was used against non-state actors, in particular in Operations *Change Direction* and *Cast Lead*.[17] In July 2006, Israel launched Operation *Change Direction* after Hezbollah raided the Israeli border from Lebanese territory and ambushed Israeli soldiers. Eight Israeli soldiers died and two were captured. Israel's military operation as a reaction was considered to

[15] Fielding 1997, pp. 46–47; Fielding 1993; McNeill 1991, p. 641. The announcement ran as follows (quoted from Robertson 1991, p. 295):

> U.S. Forces participate in a multinational effort that will intercept ships carrying products and commodities that are bound to and from Iraq and Kuwait. This action is consistent with UN Security Council Resolution 661, which imposed mandatory sanctions on trade with Iraq and occupied Kuwait.

See also a more recent comment by Heintschel von Heinegg 2015, p. 942 on this episode that underlines this view.

[16] Gill 2002, p. 9.

[17] Ruys 2010, pp. 419–462.

be based on the right of self-defence, which was presented so to the UNSC.[18] Part of the military campaign that Israel launched against Hezbollah consisted of a belligerent naval blockade off the coast of Lebanon. Israel argued that "[T]he ports and harbours of Lebanon are used to transfer terrorists and weapons by the terrorist organizations operating against the citizens of Israel from within Lebanon, mainly Hezbollah". The blockade was lifted again on 7 September 2006 after which the UN implemented a maritime embargo operation (MTF UNIFIL) in support of Lebanon against Hezbollah.

Israel's naval operations against Hamas in the Gaza strip established since January 2009 has another particularity. First, Israel seems to have taken the approach in which it has based its military operations on the right of self-defence and accepts that an armed conflict exists them Israel and Hamas, which in first appearance would be non-international in nature. But secondly, Israel's position towards the imposed blockade established on 3 January 2009 is that: 'A maritime blockade is in effect off the coast of Gaza. Such blockade has been imposed, as Israel is currently in a state of armed conflict with the Hamas regime that controls Gaza.' This is an odd legal construction as the law of naval warfare does not apply in non-international armed conflicts. Although the blockade has been established since January 2009, the *Freedom Flotilla* incident in May 2010 finally grasped the attention of the international community and commentators of the existence of this blockade.[19]

6.3.3 *Operation* Active Endeavour

To support the US-led coalition after 9/11, NATO took eight measures, one of which was to deploy the NATO standing maritime force to the Eastern Mediterranean Sea to demonstrate NATO's 'resolve to help deter, defend, disrupt and protect against terrorism'. A day after the 11 September attacks the NAC stated that if it could be proved that the attacks were directed from outside the United States NATO would consider it an armed attack under the terms of Article 5 of the NATO Treaty, which includes reference to Article 51 UN Charter. To NATO, satisfactory evidence was given to the NAC by the US on 2 October, which

---

[18] S/2006/515, 12 July 2006. The latter states:

> Israel thus reserves the right to act in accordance with Article 51 of the Charter of the United Nations and exercise its right of self-defence when an armed attack is launched against a Member of the United Nations. The State of Israel will take the appropriate actions to secure the release of the kidnapped soldiers and bring an end to the shelling that terrorizes our citizens.

[19] Farrant 2013; Sanger 2010; Heintschel von Heinegg 2011; Guilfoyle 2010; Kraska 2010; Scott 2010; Buchan 2012.

triggered the start of Operation *Active Endeavour* (OAE). In the years following, the NATO operation underwent several geographical evolutions with regard to the operation to ultimately cover the complete Mediterranean Sea. OAE however never extended its naval operations to operate in the seas around the Arabian Peninsula, the operational area of *Enduring Freedom*.[20] Whereas separate members of NATO did take part in OEF, NATO as an organization neither took part in the OEF-coalition, nor did it participate in the early stage of offensive military operations in Afghanistan.

6.4 Self-Defence Against Vessel-Borne WMD and Non-State Actors

Self-defence is also argued as a legal basis to legitimize military action to thwart a threat from vessels that may be carrying WMD, terrorists, or both.[21] In this context, Operation *Enduring Freedom* quickly expanded from the war against Al Qaida and its affiliates into the global war on terror. In the maritime dimension of this operation the expansion resulted into conducting so-called expanded maritime interception operations (EMIO). EMIO aimed primarily at denying and disrupting the movement of terrorists and weapons of mass destruction, and, importantly, its target audience went beyond only Al-Qaida and its affiliates.[22] The actions taken against these potential terrorists are not covered by the same invocation of self-defence that covered the use of force against Al-Qaida and its affiliates. Instead, self-defence is argued to thwart individual terrorist threats. Although this approach of using self-defence against threats coming from vessels that may be carrying WMD, terrorists, or both is argued, there is no publicly known record to the author of a situation in which this has occurred in practice that would confirm the use of self-defence as an in practice accepted approach by States to thwart terrorist or WMD vessels at sea.[23] The interception of the *Karin-A* by Israel is often used as an example. This is, however, in technical terms not a very good example because the *Karin-A* carried conventional weapons rather than WMD. In January 2002, the *Karin-A* was carrying more than 50 tons of (conventional) weapons destined for the Palestinian Authority and was intercepted by the Israeli Defence Forces in

---

[20] Becker mentions one action that occurred in July 2002 against Al Qaida terrorists, which was according to him presumably conducted within the context of OAE. Although it could have been warships from NATO-members, considering that the area of operations did not go beyond the Suez Canal, I hesitate to believe that the action was taken under NATO-command. See Becker 2005, p. 152.

[21] E.g. Schulman 2006; Nincic 2005; Doolin 2006; Garvey 2005.

[22] Hodgkinson 2007.

[23] Papastavridis 2011, pp. 45–69.

international waters, on its way to the Gaza. Israel argued self-defence in its letter to the UN-Secretary General.[24] Later, in March 2014, the *Klos-C* was boarded by Israel. Although the Israeli political message maintained that Israel must be able to defend itself, the Israeli boarding of the *Klos-C* appeared to be with the consent of the Panamanian authorities.[25] Even though there may be no or hardly any practice, it remains that the concept is often argued to stop emerging threats from or via the sea, or to use Allen's more popular words, to stop cargoes of doom. Within this scenario, vessels can for example be used for transportation of WMD to ports of a State, brought close to governmental vessels or critical infrastructure and pose a grave threat to those objects. Whether self-defence can be invoked in such cases, have to be assessed like any other claim to self-defence. The main question, therefore, is whether such situations meet the condition of armed attack.

6.4.1 WMD and Armed Attack

In order to be able to react in self-defence against these *cargoes of doom,* one must in the first place consider whether the situation of a WMD on board a vessel constitutes an armed attack. This is already challenging enough because the question that arises is whether the existence of dangerous cargo on board a vessel (or the combination of vessel and cargo) can constitute an armed attack. The only manner in which way this could be considered as such, would be through an anticipatory manner. 'At most', as Klein mentions, 'the shipment of weapons to support a terrorist attack against another State is a threat of force'.[26] The conditions for using self-defence in an anticipatory manner are the generally accepted Caroline-criteria: The danger or threat must be instant, overwhelming, leaving no choice for other means, and no moment for deliberation. Apart from the fact that there must be a meaningful threat against the State (Joyner mentions that non-state actors that merely possess or are developing WMD, without the existence of a meaningful threat, do not satisfy the Caroline-criteria),[27] the main point of contention with regard to the anticipatory self-defence criteria and vessel-borne WMD

[24] In a letter to the UN-Secretary General (4 January 2002, A/56/766) Israel told the UNSC the following:

> The attempt by the Palestinian Authority to smuggle this unprecedented number of weapons is a flagrant violation of agreements reached between the parties and is an ominous sign of Palestinian intentions to continue their terrorist campaign well into the future. These weapons were capable of striking deep into Israel and their seizure constitutes a vital act of self-defence and an important counter-terrorist measure, that has saved Israeli civilians from an untold number of terrorist attacks against Israeli population centres.

[25] Williams 2014.

[26] Klein 2011, p. 270.

[27] Joyner 2015, p. 1043.

is related to the temporal dimension of self-defence, and in particular with the interpretation of the condition of imminence.

Whereas in 'traditional' armed attacks the condition of immediacy relates to the temporal link between the attack and the reaction to the attack, in which no undue time-lag can take place between the attack and the reaction to the attack.[28] In the anticipatory context immediacy does not relate to the situation after the attack, but is interpreted in a different temporal perspective. As Gill states: 'Immediacy in the context of the *Caroline*-criteria for anticipatory self-defence is synonymous with the existence of imminent or immediate threat of an armed attack.'[29] The temporal dimension in this case is not related to the reaction to an actual attack, but has to be interpreted in the context of when the armed attack might—in future—occur. Ruys has noted in this respect that some scholars view that the temporal aspect of immediacy in anticipatory self-defence should not be part of what imminence in this case should entail.[30] If this is taken out, imminence becomes primarily a consideration of gravity of danger and the likelihood that it will occur. Akande and Liefländer, who also seem to be supporters of this view, argue that when severe threat exists, but still temporally remote one can still react as long as the action is necessary and proportionate.[31] Proponents of this view support the so-called *last window of opportunity*-standard, in which a State must act or otherwise loses the opportunity to defend itself.[32] If it is only the *gravity* of the threat that must be considered, the ICJ in the *Nicaragua*-case has indicated that the existence of an armed attack must also be measured against the scale and effects of the use of force, to rule out mere frontier incidents.[33] Apart from the fact that this viewpoint has been much criticized,[34] it may easily be argued that the use of chemical, nuclear of biological weapons can in fact have an enormous grave effect. As Guilfoyle notes, 'The critical justification for pre-empting WMD is that attack's potential scale, not its temporal imminence'.[35] Giving less importance to the more traditional approach of the temporal aspect of imminence would ultimately lead to support the position that WMD in the wrong hands are an imminent danger against which action can be taken, when also necessary and proportionate.

Still, the temporal aspect cannot be completely discarded, as other factors, such as the ability to connect the danger to the potential victim State, become harder to assess. It is in such circumstances also difficult to show that there is an intention of attack that is directed against a particular State. As Klein states, drawing a conclusion from the *Oil Platforms* case; '…the armed attack must clearly be targeted

[28] Dinstein 2003, p. 184.

[29] Gill 2007, p. 151.

[30] Ruys 2010, pp. 320–321.

[31] Akande and Liefländer 2013, p. 565.

[32] Mordarai et al. 2013, p. 823.

[33] ICJ, *Nicaragua* (merits), para 191.

[34] Ruys 2010, pp. 520–524.

[35] Guilfoyle 2005, p. 758.

against the State that acts in self-defense.'[36] The difficulty, therefore, is that something may in terms of gravity be a real threat, but at the same it is hard to argue that it may be a specific threat directed against a specific State. The very detail of the situation, such as the particular type and reach of the imminent threat, the whereabouts of the vessel, the intelligence or situational facts available to assess whether the threat is directed against a specific State would have to fill in the puzzle in order to answer a situation would fulfill the conditions of anticipatory self-defence. The challenging issue of how imminence should be interpreted in the context of modern threats is at this stage still without consensus.[37] In the author's opinion, it goes too far to state that the gravity of the threat alone is the only factor that needs to be considered for it to be an armed attack.

Another question that is connected with the question whether an armed attack exists, is the question of imputability. As mentioned by Van Steenberghe, cited earlier, practice seems to suggest that it is accepted that self-defence can also be invoked against non-state actors and is less dependent on a 'statist link'. In this respect, also Bethlehem states: 'It is by now reasonably clear that states have a right of self-defence against attacks by non-state actors'.[38]

6.4.2 Reaction to Armed Attack: Flag State Jurisdiction and Self-Defence

In the traditional sense, when an action is considered to be an armed attack, the reaction of the State can be directed against the territory of the State that launched the armed attack. A relationship between the non-state actor and the State where the actions of the first can be attributable to the latter will justify an attack on the territory of that State. It gets more complex when the attack is launched by a non-state actor from the territory of another State and where the action of the non-state actor is not attributable to that State. Basically, two views to this issue exist. Firstly, the starting point that sovereignty is irrelevant because self-defence has never been dependent on the will of other States. And secondly, that the competing rights of self-defence and sovereignty need to be balanced. In the latter view it is argued that where there is no sufficient relationship between the non-state actor and the State, defence against an armed attack by a non-state actor can still be undertaken on that territory when the State is unable and/or unwilling to take action and the military operations are directed only against the non-state actors which are

[36] Klein 2011, p. 264.
[37] Bethlehem 2012, pp. 769–777.
[38] Bethlehem 2012, p. 774.

located on that territory.[39] The conditions that need to be fulfilled in of case defence against these so-called non-attributable armed-attacks try to reconcile the use of force in self-defence against non-state actors with the interstate prohibition of the use of force and the idea that self-defence is not dependent on the will of another State.[40] This view is for instance supported by Schmitt, who mentions that the US, and he himself, take the position that:

> if the sanctuary State fails to remedy the situation because it is either unwilling to do so (perhaps out of sympathy for the attackers) or unable to do so (for instance, due to a lack of the necessary military equipment), the victim State, in realization of its right of self-defence, may cross into the sanctuary State's territory for the sole purpose of defending itself.[41]

The doctrine however lacks clarity, for instance in terms of the question when a State is in fact unable or unwilling, and who decides when this is the case. As regards the state of the law with regard to the doctrine of unable and unwilling, this may be summed up by Dawood Ahmed, who opines:

> It is thus fair to summarize then that the legality of the "unwilling or unable" doctrine under international law, remains, as Jack Goldsmith has written, "unsettled". Considering that a right of self-defence in effective host states does not have any foundations in treaty law, its existence as customary law is debated, the ICJ has refused to recognize it and victim states' uses of force in allegedly ineffective host states have not met with universal approval, it can only be safely asserted that the rules in this area remain murky.[42]

Getting back to the maritime dimension, on the high seas it is not the territory of a State but the jurisdiction of a flag State that is called into question in relation to self-defence. If one applied the doctrine as mentioned above, its argumentation would lead to the view that States could act against non-state actors on board foreign-flagged vessels under the limited circumstances that a flag State is unable or unwilling to act in order to remedy the situation, for instance in cases of vessels carrying WMD.[43] In the context of stopping WMD and non-state actors the doctrine is tempting because it would provide a way of sidestepping the exclusive jurisdiction of a flag State. Theoretically, it allows for the boarding of a foreign-flagged vessel without any form of consent of the flag State. Heintschel von Heinegg is very articulate in the context of interception operations at sea and a strong proponent of the view that interception operations can be based on self-defence, which in his opinion prevails over the flag state principle.[44] He opines that consent of the flag State or the master in the context of self-defence is irrelevant, 'as the right of self-defence has never been made dependent upon the will of

---

[39] See on this practice Trapp (2015), who mentions Al Qaida (2001) and Hezbollah (2006) as examples in which self-defence was used to act against non-state actors who deeds where not attributable to the State they were in (Afghanistan and Lebanon).

[40] Schmitt 2013, p. 87; Paust 2010.

[41] Schmitt 2013, p. 89.

[42] Ahmed 2013, p. 12.

[43] E.g. Walker 2009; Fitzgerald 2008.

[44] Heintschel von Heinegg 2010, pp. 389–390.

Third States or of individuals'.[45] To the author's opinion, self-defence does not by definition prevail over the exclusive jurisdiction of the flag State over its vessel. Although a vessel is not territory in a legal sense, a State holds exclusive jurisdiction over its flagged vessels as if it were floating territory. The conditions of an unwilling and/or unable flag State might help to solve the tension as a guideline between both rights of law, but is trickled with un-clarity in its substance. Especially in a maritime environment, being far away from the flag State's territory, a State may also be more quickly considered to be unable to effectively deal with the threat that is extant on its vessels. In between self-defence and exclusive jurisdiction there is also space to consider consent of the flag State. Even if a State is unable or unwilling, consent by the flag State allowing another State to react continuous to stay relevant. Lastly, apart from the legal tension between the exclusive jurisdiction of the flag State and the right of self-defence with regard to boarding vessels, the latter obviously also includes considerations of proportionality and necessity.

6.4.3 Advantages of the **Ius ad Bellum** *Approach to Boarding*

An attractive point of the above-mentioned argumentation of basing a ship boarding on the right of self-defence is that boarding of a vessel is now directly connected to self-defence instead of an applicable legal regime. Taken against the reality of modern conflict, this view has its operational advantages. In the first place, it circumvents the operationally challenging issue of flag State consent to board a foreign-flagged vessel. When the stringent conditions of self-defence are met, such argumentation potentially opens the door to boarding vessels that within the political scheme of things would never have consented to let its vessels be boarded.

A second advantage of connecting to right to board to the *ius ad bellum* instead of the *ius in bello* is that it bypasses the question of whether the law of naval warfare applies in non-international armed conflict or against non-state actors. To take the Afghanistan example, it is widely viewed that the situation in Afghanistan changed after the Taliban had been brought to a fall and the *Loya Jirga* was convened in June 2002. First, many commentators view that the status of conflict changed from that point onwards from an international armed conflict to a non-international armed conflict.[46] A common view with respect to the applicability of prize law, which the belligerent right of visit is part of, is that prize law is only applicable in international armed conflicts.[47] The application of the belligerent right of visit and search, therefore, poses extra challenges in applying it in new threats.

[45] Heintschel von Heinegg 2004, p. 154.

[46] See e.g. Pejic 2007, p. 345.

[47] Heintschel von Heinegg 2010; Kraska 2010.

This subject in particular, with regard to the right of visit during NIACs will be further discussed in Chap. 9. As the law of self-defence is gradually moving into the direction of accepting the use of force against non-state actors without State attribution, the essence of the issue relates to the question whether prize law can also be applicable in non-international armed conflicts or transnational armed conflicts. With regard to the latter type of conflict, which has no distinct legal regime, there is a tendency to view that in transnational armed conflicts the regime of non-international armed conflict applies.[48] Taking the above-mentioned views as the point of departure, for States that apply the authorities of the law of naval warfare, the status of the conflict has impact on the authorities. But when the right to board another vessel is based on self-defence rather than the belligerent visit and search, the change of status of the conflict is in fact irrelevant. It stops, in other words, the need to articulate the status of the conflict.

One author has noted the use of a so-called "third-tier", in which the conditions of self-defence are used as a third legal regime, next to IHRL and LOAC.[49] In this approach the law of self-defence provides both a basis *and* a legal regime for and during military operations. The law of self-defence is not only used to determine whether force can be used, but also provides the scope of authorities—in a MIO context—during the boarding, based on the conditions for the application of military force under the law of self-defence (proportionality, necessity, immediacy). Hodgkinson opines that an Article 51 UN Charter boarding in the context of acting against WMD could firstly be a legal basis to board a vessel suspected of harboring terrorists and secondly opines that 'boarding such a vessel, mounting an inspection, and obtaining biometric data from its crews or passengers, even without the ship master's consent, could be viewed as proportional to a great enough threat'. Geoffrey Corn, who is a fervent opponent of the third-tier view, has noted that proponents of the third tier can avoid assessing the nature of hostilities and how they implicate *ius in bello* applicability.[50] This is a convenient argument in current day conflict and fits neatly in the view that WMD can be stopped and seized on board a foreign-flagged vessel, solely based on self-defence. This argument of using self-defence as a right to visit in the context of maritime interception operations is also found in a document from the US Defence Department organization *Defense Institute of Legal Studies* (DILS), which notes that:

> The maritime interception operation has, through accepted practice and custom, developed a new legal regime under which, with the proper legal antecedents (i.e., UN authorization or national or collective self-defense under Article 51 of the UN Charter) warships may intercept foreign flag commercial vessels on the high seas, without resorting to any classical belligerent right. In fact, this expansion is now well seasoned through over ten years of continuous, unchallenged operations. Indeed, a substantial number of maritime nations have actively participated in the Arabian Gulf MIO.[51]

[48] Kreß 2010, pp. 245–274.

[49] Corn 2012.

[50] Corn 2012, p. 73.

[51] US DoD, DILS, Maritime interception operations, 13 June 2005.

As mentioned earlier, apart from the *Karin-A* incident, it is hard to tell whether practice actually exists where self-defence was used as a legal basis to stop WMD or terrorists. Although the above blurb from DILS concludes otherwise and the US has taken the position that OEF was conducted on the basis of self-defence, the US has left it unspecified whether it used LOAC to regulate its boardings in OEF. With regard to the implicit acknowledgement of this practice as 'a substantial number of maritime nations have actively participated', it can be said that in this coalition operation the participating States have individually considered on which legal bases and within which legal regime their participating warships would operate. It cannot be said, therefore, that participating States have accepted this approach only by participating in OEF. Lastly. in this context one historical case can be noted. During the Algerian War of independence (1955–1962), the visits and searches conducted by French naval forces are mentioned by some[52] as MIO conducted based on self-defence, rather than the law of armed conflict. O'Connell notes on this case that: 'The competence of the French Navy to carry out such visits and searches, although challenged apparently at the diplomatic level, did not form the subject of action in French courts. This is because in French law it is possible to test in the courts the validity of a seizure of cargo but not the preliminary issue of the validity of visit and search, which is an act of government'.[53]

6.5 Final Remarks

Current day conflict is characterized by non-state actors, NIACs and WMD, which pose challenges for maritime interception operations. In the quest to counter these challenges different views are embraced on how self-defence can be a legal basis. The right of self-defence is argued as a basis for maritime interception operations in two different approaches. Firstly in a traditional way, where self-defence serves as a legal basis upon which large scale naval operations are conducted that may include maritime interception operations. Secondly, in the fight against non-state actors in NIACs and WMD, self-defence serves as a direct legal basis to conduct MIO. The difference is that in the traditional approach, self-defence is a condition that allows for the application of the law of armed conflict; LOAC provides the right to board vessels, albeit limited to international armed conflicts. In the other approach, related to NSA and WMD, the right to board a foreign-flagged vessel is derived from the *ius ad bellum* itself, which brings unique characters into play, such as the argument that the use of self-defence is not dependent on other States. Connecting to the debate on crossing borders, it is viewed that non-state actors can, under certain conditions, be dealt with beyond the attacked State's borders in other States.

[52] Churchill and Lowe 1999, pp. 216–217; Heintschel Von Heinegg 1995, pp. 56–57.

[53] O'Connell 1970, p. 36. He mentions a French note that contended that the visits were justified by the French based on self-defense.

A translation to the maritime dimension would lead to the conclusion that foreign-flagged vessels could be boarded based on self-defence when the flag State is unable and/or unwilling to act. Advantages to use self-defence in such a way are primarily that it circumvents the issue of flag state consent. It is advantageous both in the fact that there is no need to gain timely consent, and in situations where the State will politically not give consent. A further advantage is that it allows one to disregard the position that the right to board a vessel in the law of naval warfare only applies in international armed conflicts, which does not make it very useful in current conflicts, which are often characterized as non-international. There is some attractiveness to such an argument when one needs to deal with current threats and conflicts. Regardless of this attractiveness, still the stringent conditions of the law of self-defence have to be met, and as such self-defence is not a *carte blanche* to circumvent flag State consent or LOAC.

References

Ahmed D (2013) Defending Weak States Against the "Unwilling or Unable" Doctrine of Self-Defense. Journal of International Law and International Relations 9, pp. 1–37

Akande D, Liefländer T (2013) Clarifying necessity, imminence, and proportionality in the law of self-defense. American Journal of International Law 107, pp. 364–570

Becker M (2005) Shifting public order of the oceans. Harvard International Law Journal 46:1, pp. 131–230

Bethlehem D (2012) Self-defense against an imminent or actual armed attack by non-state actors. American Journal of International Law 106, pp. 769–777

Buchan R (2012) The Palmer Report and the legality of Israel's naval blockade of Gaza. International and Comparative Law Quarterly 61, pp. 264–273

Churchill R, Lowe A (1999) The Law of the Sea. Manchester University Press, Manchester

Corn G (2012) Self-defense targeting: Blurring the line between the ius ad bellum and the ius in bello. In: Watkin, K, Norris R (eds) International Law Studies 88. Naval War College, Newport RI, pp. 57–92

Dinstein Y (2003) War, Aggression and Self-Defence. Cambridge University Press, Cambridge

Dinstein N (2005) The conduct of hostilities under the law of international armed conflict. Cambridge University Press, Cambridge

Doolin J (2006) The Proliferation Security Initiative. Cornerstone of a new international norm. Naval War College Review 59:2, pp. 29–57

Farrant J (2013) The Gaza Blockade incident and the modern law of blockade. Naval War College Review 66:3, pp. 81–98

Fielding L (1992–1993) Maritime Interception: Centrepiece of Economic Sanctions in the New World Order. Louisiana Law Review 53, pp. 191–1241

Fielding L (1997) Maritime interception and U.N. Sanctions. Austin & Winfield, San Francisco/London/Bethesda

Fitzgerald M (2008) Seizing weapons of mass destruction from foreign-flagged ships on the high seas under Article 51 of the UN Charter. Virginia Journal of International Law 49:2, pp. 473–506

Garvey J (2005) The international institution imperative for countering the spread of weapons of mass destruction: Assessing the Proliferation Security Initiative. Journal of Conflict and Security Law 10:2, pp. 125–147

Gill T (1990) De Golf crisis. De volkenrechtelijke regels inzake het gebruik van militair geweld. Nederlands Juristenblad 38, pp. 1475–1487

Gill T (2002) The 11th September and the International Law of Military Operations. Vossiuspers, UVA, Amsterdam

Gill T (2007) The Temporal Dimension of Self-Defence: Anticipation, Pre-Emption, Prevention and Immediacy. In: Schmitt M, Pejic J (eds) International Law and Armed Conflict: Exploring the Faultlines - Essays in Honour of Yoram Dinstein. Martinus Nijhoff Publishing, Leiden, pp. 113–157

Guilfoyle D (2005) The Proliferation Security Initiative: Interdiction vessels in international waters to prevent the spread of weapons of mass destruction. Melbourne University Law Review 29, pp. 733–764

Guilfoyle D (2010) The Mavi Marmara incident and blockade in armed conflict. British Yearbook of International Law 81, pp. 171–213

Heintschel von Heinegg W (1995) Visit, search, diversion and capture – condition of applicability. In: Reports and commentaries of the round table of experts on international humanitarian law applicable to armed conflict at sea, Bochum, pp. 1–93

Heintschel von Heinegg W (2004) Current legal issues in maritime operations: Maritime interception operations in the global war on terrorism, exclusion zones, hospital ships and maritime neutrality. Israel Yearbook of International Law 34, pp. 151–178

Heintschel von Heinegg W (2010) Maritime interception/interdiction operations. In: Gill T, Fleck D (eds) The Handbook of the International Law of Military Operations. Oxford University Press, New York, pp. 375–393

Heintschel von Heinegg W (2011) Methods and means of naval warfare in non-international armed conflicts. In: Jacques R (ed) International Law Studies 88. Naval War College Newport RI, pp. 211–236

Heintschel von Heinegg W (2015) Blockade and interdictions. In: Weller M (ed) The Oxford Handbook of the Use of Force in International Law. Oxford University Press, New York, pp. 925–946

Hodgkinson S (2007) Challenges to Maritime Interception Operations in the War on Terror: Bridging the Gap. American University International Law Review 22:4, pp. 853–671

ICJ, Case concerning military and paramilitary activities in and against Nicaragua (Nicaragua v. United States of America) Merits. 27 June 1986

ICJ, Oil Platform (Islamic Republic of Iran v. United States of America), Judgment, I.C.J. Reports 2003

Joyner D (2015) The implications of the proliferation of Weapons of mass destruction for the prohibition of the use of force. In: Weller M (ed) The Oxford Handbook of the Use of Force in International Law. Oxford University Press, New York, pp. 1034–1056

Klein N (2005) The right of visit and the 2005 Protocol on the suppression of unlawful acts against the safety of maritime navigation. Denver Journal of International Law and Policy 35:2, pp. 287–332

Klein N (2011) Maritime security and the law of the sea. Oxford University Press, New York

Kraska J (2010) Rule selection in the case of Israel's naval blockade of Gaza: Law of naval warfare or the law of the sea? In: Schmitt M (ed) Yearbook of Humanitarian International Law 13, pp. 367–395

Kreß C (2010) Some reflections on the international legal framework governing transnational armed conflicts. Journal of Conflict and Security Law 15:2, pp. 245–274

Kretzmer D (2013) The inherent right to self-defence and proportionality in ius ad bellum. European Journal of International Law 24, pp. 35–282

McNeill J (1991) Neutral rights and maritime sanctions: The effects of two Gulf Wars. Virginia Journal of International Law 31, pp. 631–643

Mordarai G, O'Connell D, Kelly T, Farrant J (2013) The seizure of Abu Anas Al-Libi: An international law assessment. International Law Studies 89, Naval War College, Newport RI, pp. 817–839

Nincic D (2005) The challenge of maritime terrorism: Threat identification, WMD and regime response. The Journal of Strategic Studies 28:4, pp. 619–644
O'Connell D (1970) International Law and Contemporary Naval Operations. British Yearbook of International Law 44, pp. 19–68
O'Connell D (1975) The influence of law on sea power. Manchester University Press, Manchester
Papastavridis E (2011) The right of visit on the high seas in a theoretical perspective: Mare Liberum versus Mare Clausum revisited. Leiden Journal of International Law 24, pp. 45–69
Paust J (2010) Self-defense targeting of non-state actors and permissibility of U.S. use of drones in Pakistan. Journal of Transnational Law and Policy 19:2, pp. 237–280
Pejic J (2007) Unlawful/enemy combatants: Interpretations and consequences. In: Schmitt M, Pejic J (eds) International law and armed conflict: Exploring the faultlines. Martinus Nijhoff Publishing, Dordrecht, pp. 335–355
Robertson H (1991) Interdiction of Iraqi Maritime Commerce in the 1990–1991 Persian Gulf Conflict. Ocean Development and International Law 22, pp. 289–299
Ruys T (2010) 'Armed attack', and Article 51 of the UN Charter. Cambridge University Press, Cambridge
Sanger E (2010) The contemporary law of blockade and the Gaza Freedom Flotilla. Yearbook of International Humanitarian Law 13, pp. 397–444
Schmitt M (2008) "Change Direction" 2006: Israeli operations in Lebanon and the International law of self-defense. Michigan Journal of International Law 29:2, pp. 127–164
Schmitt M (2013) Extraterritorial Lethal Targeting: Deconstructing the Logic of International Law. Columbia Journal of Transnational Law 52, pp. 79–114
Scott G (2010) Israel's seizure of the Gaza-bound flotilla: Applicable laws and legality. Research paper no. 42/2010, Osgoode Hall Law School
Shulman M (2006) The Proliferation Security Initiative and the evolution of the law on the use of force. Houston Journal of International Law 28:3, pp. 771–828
Somers E (2010) Inleiding tot het internationaal zeerecht. Kluwer, Mechelen
Syrigos A (2006) Development on the interdiction of vessels on the high seas. In: Strati A, Gavouneli M, Skourtos N (eds) Unresolved issues and new challenges to the law of the sea. Time before and time after. Publication on Ocean Development 54, pp. 149–202
Trapp KN (2015) Can Non-State Actors Mount an Armed Attack? In: Weller M (ed) The Oxford Handbook of the Use of Force in International Law. Oxford University Press, New York, pp. 679–719
UN (1956) UN Doc. A/3159, Yearbook of the International Law Commission, 1956 vol. II
UN Security Council (2006) UN Security Council, S/2006/515, 12 July 2006
UN SG, 4 January 2002, A/56/766
US DOD, DILS, Maritime interception operations, 13 June 2005
Van Dyke J (2004) The disappearing right to navigational freedom in the exclusive economic zone. Marine Policy 29, pp. 107–121
van Steenberghe R (2010) Self-defence in response to attacks by non-state actors in the light of recent state practice: A step forward. Leiden Journal of International Law 23, pp. 183–208
Walker G (2009) Self-defense, the law of armed conflict and port security. South Carolina Journal of International law and Business 5:2, pp. 347–410
Waxman M (2013) Regulating resort to force: form and substance of the UN Charter regime. European Journal of International Law 24:1, pp. 151–189
Westra J (2007) International Law and the Use of Armed Force. Routledge, London/New York
Williams D (2014) Israel seizes arms shipment. www.reuters.com/article/us-israel-gaza-ship-idUSBREA240X720140305. Accessed 22 March 2017

Chapter 7
(Ad Hoc) Consent

Contents

Abstract This chapter analyses *ad hoc* consent as a legal basis for maritime interception operations. Consent is a legal basis that within the context of ever-growing importance of enhancing maritime security is used regularly as a legal basis for MIO. The legal parameters for consent as a legal basis during maritime interception operations have always been under discussion. Proponents exist for both flag State and master's consent.

Keywords Master consent · flag State consent · Statelessness · friendly approaches · consenting authority

7.1 Introduction

Consent of a State to allow another State the use of its armed forces on its territory or aboard its flagged vessels may serve as a legal basis for maritime interception operations. Within the maritime context this could firstly mean that a coastal State will consent to allow maritime interception operations by foreign warships within its territorial sea or internal waters. Secondly, this could mean that a flag State allows the boarding of its vessels by foreign warships on the high seas. The legal basis of consent for military operations,[1] and for maritime interception operations in

[1] To illustrate with a recent military operation, in 2013 the French operation *Serval* was based on the consent of the Mali authorities to rid the State of terrorists that had taken control of parts of Mali. On this operation, see Bannelier and Christakis 2013.

M. Fink, *Maritime Interception and the Law of Naval Operations*,
https://doi.org/10.1007/978-94-6265-249-1_7

particular, is in fact often used. Guilfoyle mentions that consent-based interceptions are much used in law enforcement operations, for instance in relation to drug smuggling, fisheries management and transnational crime.[2] A well-known situation that addressed consent in the maritime context and has reached the ECtHR is the *Medvedyev* case.[3] In early June 2002, the French authorities requested permission from Cambodia to intercept the Cambodian-flagged vessel *Winner* that was suspected of carrying large quantities of drugs. France requested and got the authority via a diplomatic note exchange between France and Cambodia.[4] The French warship *Lieutenant de vaisseau Le Henaff* was instructed to intercept the *Winner* and did so near the Cape Verde Islands. France based its action on three legal bases.[5] Article 108 UNCLOS, the diplomatic note, and the argument that the vessel was not flying a flag and refused to identify itself. The ECtHR dismissed the first argument because Cambodia is not a party to UNCLOS and also because Article 108 does not cover situations of requests to board third State vessels. The ECtHR also dismissed the second legal basis because the nationality was in fact already known before the *Le Henaff* physically encountered the *Winner* and as such considered the argument contradictory to the claim it was without nationality. The third legal basis, the diplomatic note, however was considered by the court as an *ad hoc* agreement between France and Cambodia and thus a source in international law. Although the ECtHR considered the *Note Verbale* not sufficiently clear on the fate of the crew, it did not reject the view that the note could be a legal basis to board the vessel.

There are also a few other incidents in which the boarding of a vessel were carried out on the basis of consent. In March 2014, Israel boarded the Panama-flagged *Klos-C* on suspicion of carrying a large bulk of weapons (surface-to-surface rockets) in the Red Sea on its way to Sudan, ultimately destined for the Gaza in an operation code-named Operation *Full Disclosure*. According to the Foreign Affairs minister of Israel, it had obtained permission from Panama to board the vessel.[6] The vessel was diverted to port of Eilat and the crew members, who according to an Israeli spokesman were not aware of the content of the cargo, were released. In addition to individual cases, the NATO-led Operation *Active Endeavour* (OEA) is a MIO whereby the boarding operations are entirely based on consent. In 2003 NATO decided to undertake interception operations in the context of OAE. With regard to the authorities to perform boardings by participating warships, NATO decided that such boardings can

---

[2] Guilfoyle 2009, p. 342.

[3] ECtHR, *Medvedyev and others v. France*, application no. 3394/03. Judgment 29 March 2010.

[4] *Medvedyev*, para 10.

[5] *Medvedyev*, paras 82–101.

[6] Williams 2014. Williams reports that:

> Foreign Minister Avigdor Lieberman said Israel had obtained Panama's permission to board the ship. "We followed international law to the letter. The ship travelled under a Panamanian flag, the company was listed in Marshall Islands, the captain was Turkish and the crew was from various different countries," he told a conference in Tel Aviv.

At: www.reuters.com/article/2014/03/05/us-israel-gaza-ship-idUSBREA240X720140305.

only be undertaken when they were of a *compliant manner*.[7] NATO understood compliant boardings in the case of OAE as requiring prior authorization from both the State *and* the master to board a foreign vessel. UNSC-practice also exists in relation to consent based maritime interception operations. In SC Res. 1929 (2010) relating to Iran, the UNSC has underlined the possibility of boarding foreign-flagged vessels under the condition that the flag State consents to the boarding. Also SC Res. 2146 (2014) with regard to the Libyan crude oil export prohibition, the UNSC notes that States should first make efforts to ask the flag State for authorization before boarding the vessel.[8] In sum, therefore, it is accepted in both practice and jurisprudence that consent is an internationally accepted legal basis for maritime interception operations. The application in the maritime dimension of the conditions under which consent can be a legal basis are, however, not crystal clear. The main point of contention is whether alongside the authorities of the flag State, the master of the vessel is authorized to validly consent to a boarding.

In his commentary on the ILC Draft Articles on State Responsibility, James Crawford has given two meanings to the notion of consent in international law.[9] In the first meaning consent is seen in the context of State responsibility and viewed as a circumstance that precludes wrongfulness of State actions when the other State has consented to this action. In the second meaning consent must be seen within the context of the law of treaties and as a basis for the existence of international agreements and the suspension of international obligations that flow from such agreements. The legal basis to the use of force on the territory of another State or on board a foreign-flagged vessel is viewed as part of the first meaning, and will be dealt with in this chapter. Consent as used in the second meaning will be dealt with in the chapter on international agreements. Consent, in any case, is an attribute of sovereignty in which a State may always (not) consent to a foreign State conducting activities that would otherwise violate its sovereignty. This chapter aims to consider some points of contention with regard to consent-based maritime interception operations. Consent can manifest itself as a legal basis for maritime interception operations from three vantage points. The first is consent from a State to board its vessel on the high seas. This type of consent concentrates on the vessel itself. Second is the notion of the statelessness of vessels. This type of consent is realized by the lack of a responsible flag State. And third is the consent of a State to conduct MIO in the maritime zones over which a coastal State has jurisdiction. This type of

---

[7] The term "compliant boarding" is not often used anymore. It is more common to speak of *consensual boardings*. See Chap. 2 on the terminology of boarding operations.

[8] SC Res. 2146 (2014), para 6 reads:

> *Requests* that Member States, before taking the measures authorized in paragraph 5, first seek the consent of the vessel's flag State;

[9] Commentary no. 2 on Article 20 of the Draft Articles of State Responsibility. See also Farhang 2014.

consent focuses on the geographical area over which a State has jurisdiction. As this last subject falls outside the scope of the study, it will not be discussed here.[10]

This chapter will address the above-mentioned contexts in two parts. It will first consider the conditions for consent in general international law, and will apply these conditions in the context of consent in maritime interception operations on the high seas. The second will discuss MIO in relation to stateless vessels. Obviously, the issue of statelessness is not a matter of consent *strictu sensu,* but it relates in so far that challenges exist when there is no State that can give consent.

7.2 Legal Framework Consent

Consent is not generally considered from the perspective of the prohibitions of the use of armed force within the framework of the UN Charter, but as a circumstance that precludes the wrongfulness of actions by a State.[11] Article 20 of the Draft Articles on State Responsibility states that valid consent by a State to the commission of a given act by another State precludes the wrongfulness of that act in relation to the former State to the extent that the act remains within the limits of that consent. Sovereignty implies that within the limitations of international law a State may allow another State to use its military within the area over which the consenting State has sovereign powers. Consequently, consent of a State can allow another State to engage in operations in relation to areas, objects, or persons subject to its jurisdiction. Or, in the words of Wendel in the context of MIO: 'The fact that the flag State authorizes another State to board a vessel flying the flag of the former State, precludes the wrongfulness of the boarding in relation to the flag State.'[12]

The point to note regarding consent, as also underlined in the ICJ-case *DRC v. Uganda*[13] and mentioned by Crawford under commentary no. 4 of Article 20 DARS, is that that a consent must be *valid.* This includes issues of whether the agent or person who gave the consent is authorized to do so on behalf of the State, or whether a consent was achieved through coercion or some other factor.[14] Based on Crawford's commentary, Gill considers within the context of military operations in general that the primary three conditions for consent to be a true legal ground are: a consent, which must be (1) granted freely, and (2) issued by the lawful authority of

[10] See on this subject McLaughlin 2009.

[11] UNGA resolution 56/83 (12 December 2001): Responsibility of states for internationally wrongful acts, Article 20. Crawford mentions under commentary no. 4 that: A consent must be valid, which includes issues of whether the agent or person who gave the consent is authorized to do so on behalf of the state, or whether the consent was vitiated by coercion or some other factor.

[12] Wendel 2007, p. 165.

[13] ICJ, *Case concerning armed activities on the territory of the Congo (Democratic Republic of the Congo v. Uganda)* judgment of 19 December 2005.

[14] Crawford 2002, p. 73.

the (3) consenting State.[15] The first condition underlines that there should not be any form of threat or compulsory action aimed at the State to give consent. It is also always subject to any condition that the State may pose and may always be terminated. As such, military operations based on consent must be conducted within the limits of the given consent. This condition interrelates with both legal basis and regime: if on the one hand action is taken based on consent which goes beyond the substantial scope of the consent (legal regime) that is given, the consent may lose its validity to serve as a legal basis. The third condition underlines that consent must ultimately be attributed to the State as the authority that can decide on whether or not to allow military operations within its jurisdiction. What also flows from this is that the consenting State may not grant more authority than it possesses. In particular, condition two and three raise debate within the context of maritime interception.

7.2.1 *The Consenting Authority*

Conditions 2 and 3 essentially deal with the question of the consenting authority to allow a boarding to take place on a foreign-flagged vessel. In the first place, consent to board a foreign-flagged vessel cannot be implied to exist. This may for instance be the case in instances where a State requests to board another vessel, but no answer to the request is given. In the prompt release case between The Netherlands and the Russian Federation before the ITLOS, concerning the Netherlands-flagged Greenpeace vessel *Arctic Sunrise*, this point was also argued by the Netherlands, who opined that: 'Any exceptions to the general prohibitive rule to exercise enforcement jurisdiction over foreign vessels are explicit and cannot be implied'.[16]

With regard to the consenting authority within the context of maritime interception operations there are two main questions that are part of the current debate. The first question is the issue of who the consenting authority can be. The second is the question of the actual scope of the consent. The latter question is a question of applicable legal regime, but has significant impact on whether or not a consensual boarding is legal and is therefore difficult to separate. The first question refers to the core debate whether or not consent of the flag State is needed (flag State consent) before a boarding party boards a merchant vessel that flies a different flag than the warship, or whether the consent of the master of the vessel provides an adequate authority to do so (master's consent). The existence of these two views could raise confusion when a warships' crew that is allowed to visit based on master's consent according to its national view, boards a vessel of a nation that views flag State consent as the only legally correct ground of visit. Although it is in fact immaterial what the view of the boarding State is, the commander of the visiting warship may

[15] Gill 2010, p. 230.

[16] ITLOS, case no. 22. *Arctic Sunrise*, order of 22 November 2013, para 63.

—incorrectly—view that he has handled the situation correctly based on the national legal view. One can imagine that this is a recipe for potential legal and diplomatic problems.

7.2.1.1 Flag State Consent

The principal argument for flag State consent is the view that sovereignty, on which the principle of non-interference of vessels is based, is a State instrument and cannot be waived by individuals like the master of a ship. The view is taken that the master of the vessel is in most instances not an official representative of a State and therefore cannot waive the State's jurisdiction,[17] particularly when the master of the vessel does not have the same nationality as the flag State. Proponents of flag State consent furthermore argue that because of its nature and purpose it is difficult for a visiting warship to be conducting activities that could not be considered as being the prerogative of the flag State. When flag State consent is given by the State concerned, the master should then comply with the visit of a foreign warship.

7.2.1.2 Master's Consent

Both master's and flag State consent take the same principle of sovereignty of the flag State over vessels as the legal point of departure. The proponents of master's consent however argue that the consent of the flag State in certain cases is not needed and that the consent of the master proved sufficient authority. The *Commander's Handbook on the Law of Naval Operations* of the United States views master's consent as follows:

> A consensual boarding is conducted at the invitation of the master (or person-in-charge) of a vessel which is not otherwise subject to the jurisdiction of the boarding officer. The plenary authority of the master over all activities to the operation of his vessel while in international waters is well established in international law and includes the authority to allow anyone to come aboard his vessel as his guest, including law enforcement officials.
>
> The voluntary consent of the master permits the boarding, but it does not allow the assertion of law enforcement authority (such as arrest or seizure). A consensual boarding is not an exercise of law enforcement jurisdiction per se. Nevertheless, such boardings have utility in allowing rapid verification of the legitimacy of a vessel's voyage by obtaining or confirming vessel documents, cargo, and navigation records without undue to the boarded vessel.[18]

In other words, the master of the ship has the authority to allow persons on board as long as the boarding party does not perform any law enforcement activities. Therefore, proponents of the concept of master's consent argue that visits by

[17] See Van der Kruit 2007, p. 84.

[18] Thomas and Duncan 1999, p. 240, Section 3.11.2.5.2.

foreign-flagged warships can be authorized by the master of the vessel as long as the visiting warship's crew does not perform any law enforcement activities.

Several arguments are put forward to support this view, such as the existence of *flags of convenience* that cause a certain level of legal disconnect between the flag State and the vessel that flies its flag[19] and the view that visiting a vessel does not mean that the boarding team is actually stepping on the territory in the legal sense of the flag State.[20] The main argument for master's consent is however a practical one. As Becker states, it is viewed that: "Where procedure for requesting and authorizing flag State consent are not predetermined by agreement, the process can be slow or, in the worst case, a failure if the target is allowed to escape before operations can begin".[21] The reasons for the delay could be many. For instance, a nation does not have a single point of contact or an internal procedure to find a fast answer. Often many actors need to be consulted before consent can or cannot be granted. The second PSI principle therefore also underlines that States undertake to streamline procedures "for rapid exchange of relevant information concerning suspected proliferation activity (…)".[22] Also more political reasons could explain why a nation does not want to answer or consent to boarding. One could imagine that, for example, Iran will not consent to the United States boarding a vessel flying its flag. Also revealing information to support the request for boarding may give difficulties as the intelligence may be classified. As Brown writes: "However, for States with strained diplomatic relations with the United States, particularly if the evidence of terrorism activity is withheld as classified intelligence, consent may be more difficult to obtain".[23] Also Wilson's argument with regard to flags of convenience to support master's consent seems to come from a practical point of view.[24] He asserts that States with open registries, next to the fact that there is no genuine link between the vessel and the flag State, are often also vulnerable to political upheaval and do not take jurisdictional responsibility over the vessel. As such: "The recognition and continued existence of master's consent is crucial as a valid alternative where the flag State consent is not possible or practical".[25]

[19] Wilson 2008, pp. 170–185.

[20] Brown 2010, p. 81.

[21] Becker 2005, p. 178.

[22] Shulman 2006, p. 827.

[23] Brown 2010, p. 83.

[24] Another more practical point is that a warship can have a potentially threatening posture. By analogy, as Greenwood remarked, in the context of confiscation of goods in enemy territory, 'the request by a heavily armed soldier that is requesting to search the house may in fact not be an actual request'. It cannot be ruled out that law-abiding merchant vessel captains will be overwhelmed by an approaching warship and will readily invite the boarding party at the warships request aboard, without also knowing where the limits of the authorities of the crew are. In this sense, flag state consent at least supposes that the requestor and the requested remain on a more equal level.

[25] Wilson 2008, p. 185.

7.3 Analysis

There is a common understanding that a captain of a vessel is free to invite persons on board as his guests, which could include military personnel.[26] No one will disagree that also military personnel can be invited for instance to a cocktail party aboard a merchant vessel without the captain having to show the guest list to the flag State for approval. The purpose of such a visit is, however, significantly different than from a visiting warship's crew in pursuit of their official duties. There is also a deep-rooted understanding in maritime law that the master of a vessel has responsibility for the safety of his vessel, from which certain legal authorities are derived. Some domestic legislation may under certain circumstances even allow the master of the vessel to perform specific law enforcement activities over the crew of the vessel. These activities are, however, limited to the purpose of safeguarding the safety of the vessel and cargo and do not extend to authorities for the master according to which the exclusive jurisdiction of a flag State can be waived. Some argue that for the safety of his vessel a master can invite third States to support the master. This view is also underlined by Article 27 UNCLOS,[27] which mentions that whilst sailing through the territorial sea of a coastal State the master can ask for the assistance of the coastal State authorities. This is, however, a different situation than a situation when the vessel's safety is not at stake and it is not the master that is asking for assistance, but is being asked to be boarded on the suspicion, for instance, that the vessel is used to transport prohibited cargo or possible criminals.[28]

That the principle of master's consent exists is, therefore, not contested. Be that as it may, an invitation of the master does, in the first place, not provide any sort of law enforcement authority to the boarding party aboard the vessel. Second, persons in their official capacity in the pursuit of their task must take into account the limits of their authority. The crux of the matter essentially lies in the nature of the activities of the boarding party and whether or not the boarding party does something that would fall under the authority of the flag State. In other words, the purpose of the visit is essential to the question whether a master's or flag State consent is needed. What is in fact contested is which authority master's consent will create to a boarding party of a foreign warship.

The difficulty lies in drawing the line between action by naval personnel that does or does not imply some form of law enforcement, or does not involve any activities that may threaten the sovereignty of the flag State. The example of the cocktail party is easy, but gathering intelligence that may end up supporting military or law enforcement action becomes more blurry. When one accepts that a master can invite persons on board, the dividing line between an authorized and an unauthorized visit may even be as thin as a difference in the manner of querying the crew of the vessel. The US *Commander's Handbook on the Law of Naval*

---

[26] See also Kraska 2010, p. 16.

[27] Article 27 sub 1 (c) UNCLOS.

[28] Hodgkinson 2007, p. 583.

Operations mentions that checking paperwork during a boarding granted by the master's consent is a permitted activity. Roach supports this view to argue that checking the vessel's documents, cargo and records, are "non-jurisdictional actions".[29] Another view would be that checking the validity of paperwork and cargo manifests are actions that are usually performed by government officials and in that sense could fall within the realm of law enforcement activities. Von Heinegg appears to draw the line at verification of the vessel's true nature. This for him includes verifying cargo, documents and destination, but does not go as far as enforcement measures if in case irregularities of some sort would come from the verification.[30] In the authors' view, if consent is given by a master to come on board, they are basically nothing more than his guests and no law enforcement authority can flow from this. The master is not required to hand over any documentation of vessel or cargo, unless this is permitted through domestic legislation. In this sense, one can relate to the view of Matteo Tondini, who mentions that: 'the legal basis for boarding a vessel with the master's consent only [...] remains questionable when exercised other than for maritime safety reasons.'[31]

7.3.1 The "Broken Taillight-Approach"

Interestingly, in practice a *modus operandi* has evolved which at times is characterized as the so-called "broken-taillight-approach".[32] The approach refers to the police officer that stops a car because of a broken taillight, but then discovers (or already knew beforehand) the drugs on the backseat of that same car, which will subsequently be taken by the police officer. The scenario has been used in the context of trying to find ways to board vessels in order to stop WMD at sea.[33] The broken taillight-approach, in other words, is used as an argument to find whatever ways to be able to board a vessel.[34] Whereas the broken-taillight approach signals 'pushing the envelope' on the legal limits of existing legal possibilities, the search for lawful boarding options on a practical level and within the context of MSO has also resulted into a practice in which master's consent plays a significant role. In the naval operators' dimension, these actions are familiar under the term 'friendly approaches' or 'approach and assist visits' (AAV).[35] Lieutenant Marsden explains:

[29] Ashley-Roach 1993, p. 337.

[30] Heintschel von Heinegg 2015, p. 942.

[31] Tondini 2012.

[32] Kraska 2010.

[33] Su 2012, p. 103.

[34] Kraska 2010, p. 14.

[35] See e.g. CMF press release, 24 March 2013, 'HMS Monmouth Conducts Maritime Approach and Assist Operations'. At http://combinedmaritimeforces.com/2013/03/24/hms-monmouth-conducts-maritime-approach-and-assist-operations/. US Navy press release, Ramage VBSS team

> Over the course of an average day we will conduct between 5 and 20 Approach and Assist visits to fishing and trading dhows of various sizes", said Deputy Logistics Officer and Boarding Officer Lt Chris Marsden RN [Royal Navy, MDF]. "The boats' crews are generally pleased to see us and we are often able to help out by providing them with supplies and information ranging from deteriorating weather conditions to the latest cricket scores! In return the crews are able to provide us with details of any suspicious activity in the area, which we can then act upon.[36]

The information gathered through engaging the maritime community in a certain area adds to the maritime awareness and may ultimately be a piece of the puzzle which results in actionable intelligence. Allen mentions that this practice during maritime security operations in which crew of warships board at the invitation of the master to approach the maritime community point into the direction that master consent is in practice in fact tacitly accepted even by States such as the United Kingdom, who are proponents of flag State consent.[37] An AAV may also include coming on board the vessel in which the warship is engaged with. This *modus operandi* is supported also by the definition of approach used by the EU Operational Order (OPORD) for Operation *Atalanta*, which is quoted by Papastavridis:

> An approach is defined by a de-escalatory low key interaction. This may include visits on board if invited, but does not include 'boarding exploitation' of the vessel (crew checks, searching cargo/crew)...the approach is an informal means of engaging with the maritime population to continue the conversation on board his vessel...this is not considered as a boarding in a legal sense.[38]

In performing 'friendly approaches' or AAVs, therefore, naval operators seem to take care of staying away from any activity that may be seen as a law enforcement activity. Interestingly, the EU, possibly in order to try to create some clarity, seems to have divided in boardings in the legal sense and boardings in the non-legal sense. The latter is a boarding in which the boarding party is physically on board another vessel at the invitation of the master and does not perform any activities that may possible be seen as law enforcement actions. Although this is essentially a form of master's consent, this EU-approach with regard to the purpose, therefore, goes less far as the view of the United States, underlined by Kraska, who mentions: 'Nevertheless, such boardings have utility in allowing rapid verification of the legitimacy of a vessel's voyage by obtaining or confirming vessel documents, cargo, and navigation records without undue delay to the boarded vessel.'[39] With

---

conducts 100th Approach and assist visit', at http://www.navy.mil/submit/display.asp?story_id=42177.

[36] CMF press release, 24 March 2013, 'HMS Monmouth Conducts Maritime Approach and Assist Operations'. At http://combinedmaritimeforces.com/2013/03/24/hms-monmouth-conducts-maritime-approach-and-assist-operations/.

[37] Allen 2014, p. 259. Examples from UK practice can be found at http://eunavfor.eu/eu-naval-force-ship-rfa-lyme-bay-conducts-friendly-approach-with-local-seafarers/.

[38] Papastavridis 2013, p. 59, footnote 107.

[39] Kraska 2010, p. 17.

this practice, we see a certain level of acceptance of master consent, but still a difference in opinion with regard to the scope of authority that a boarding party has under the invitation of a master.[40]

In summary, the above paragraphs have shown that with regard to *ad hoc* consent in the context of MIO, basically two—closely related—points of contention exist. The first is a difference in view whether a State allows either master or flag State consent boardings with regard to their vessels. The second is a difference in view, or rather debate, on what the scope of authorities would be when a master consent boarding is carried out. These two points are, as said, closely related because whether a State would allow a master consent boarding may also depend on the scope the activities of a boarding party. A State may find itself in agreement with a *de facto* boarding in order to acquire information about the area or to support its vessels with any safety issues, but may not agree with a boarding that is set up to actively search for any criminal activity. Ultimately, whether flag State or master consent applies in a particular situation depends on the position of the flag State of the vessel and on what level or detail the flag State has authorized to the master in domestic law to act on behalf of the flag State.[41] Current practice in maritime security operations seems also to be moving into the direction that master consent boardings of the kind that merely allows to engage with the maritime community is a more and more an accepted *modus operandi*.

7.4 Stateless Vessels

One particular issue to note with regard to flag State jurisdiction over vessels in the context of consent is statelessness. In general, consent presupposes the existence of a State that can exercise its jurisdiction over a vessel and can give its consent to another State to board a vessel. If a vessel is considered to be stateless, there will be no State that can be requested for permission. Statelessness as a legal basis to board a vessel does not flow from the inability to obtain consent from a State. Rather, reasonable ground to believe that a vessel is stateless by itself provides a legal basis for warships to visit the vessel.[42] The legal consequence of a stateless vessel is that is considered to be without nationality. This is codified in UNCLOS,[43] and arguably also a rule of customary law.

Boarding stateless vessels by means of warships is, in fact, not a rare activity. It is a much discussed topic in drug interdiction operations, for instance in the Caribbean region. France also used statelessness as an argument to board the

[40] Arguably, when a boarding team encounters something illegal during an AAV, they would have to obtain consent from the flag State if it decides that it wants to take action.

[41] Papastavridis 2013, p. 65.

[42] See Article 92 sub 2 and Article 110 sub 1 under (d) UNCLOS.

[43] See Article 110 UNCLOS.

Winner in the *Medvedyev* case. But also in the realm of international peace and security, since 9/11 the use of statelessness as a legal basis has spread in the effort of enhancing maritime security. Spanish forces operating within the context of Operation *Enduring Freedom* in the search for Al Qaida and the Taliban members at sea, boarded the *So San* after concluding that the vessel could be considered as stateless. In March 2014, US Navy Seals boarded and stopped the *Morning Glory* from trying to sell crude oil coming from a Libyan port, as the vessel was a Libyan rebel held vessel that was said to be stateless after it was stolen by Libyan individuals upon which North Korea deregistered the vessel.[44]

7.4.1 Conditions for Statelessness as a Legal Basis

In order for statelessness to be a proper legal basis, the commander of the visiting warship must have *reasonable suspicion* that the vessel is stateless. A vessel is determined to be stateless under three different circumstances: if the vessels shows a flag but is suspected of flying a false flag, shows more than one flag[45] and when the vessel does not fly a flag at all. Article 110 UNCLOS provides that under these circumstances a warship can board a stateless vessel. In terms of process, Meyer states that the visiting State first has a duty to try to verify the nationality of the vessel without boarding the vessel. Basically, Meyer sums up three conditions that should justify the boarding of the vessel: (1) The determination of reasonable suspicion that the vessel is indeed without nationality, (2) there are no other means available to verify its registration and, (3) that there is no 'reasonable excuse', why the vessel is trying to conceal its nationality.[46] Meyers' view therefore underlines that even though a legal basis may exist, some reticence must still be observed to board the vessel.[47]

With regard to Meyer's second condition, one can argue whether the duty must not solely be on the commander of the warship, but also on the State of the

---

[44] 'U.S. Navy hands over North Korean-flagged oil tanker Morning Glory to Libya after seizing it from rebels in dramatic raid', in *Daily Mail*, 22 March 2014. At: http://www.dailymail.co.uk/news/article-2586995/U-S-Navy-hands-North-Korean-flagged-oil-tanker-Morning-Glory-Libya-seizing-rebels-dramatic-raid.html.

[45] See also Article 92(2) UNCLOS.

[46] Oppenheim (Oppenheim 1906) writes on the manner in which flag verification is demonstrated:

> A man-of-war which meets a suspicious merchantman not showing her colours and wishes to verify the same, hoists its own flag and fires a blank cartridge. This is the signal for the other to hoist her flag in reply….if the suspicious vessel, in spite of this warning [warning shot across the bow] still declines to hoist her flag, the suspicion becomes so grave that the man-of-war may compel her to bring to for the purpose of visiting her and thereby verifying her nationality.

[47] Meyer 1967, pp. 309–323.

warship. In other words, must a State do all which is feasible under the circumstances at the time to find out what the nationality of a vessel is, or is the local situation *at sea* and the communication between commander and the vessel enough for determining that there is a reasonable suspicion that the vessel is stateless? The ECtHR in the *Medvedyev* case seems to point in the direction that it is not only a commander's duty, but, when possible, also a State's duty. The ECtHR judged the fact that the *Winner* at sea did not show the flag and kept resisting the boarding not sufficient to consider the vessel as stateless against the background that the French authorities at that stage already knew it was a Cambodian-flagged vessel.[48] As such, the ECtHR appears to take the path that it is not solely the information that is physically verifiable at sea, but also includes other information within the government that may be available to the commander. In the case of the *So San* that occurred in December 2002, according to Doolin, the decision to board the vessel came about based on three suspicions.[49] First, the vessel zigzagged, something that vessels ordinarily would not do; the crew of the *So San* raised and lowered the North Korean flag; third and most importantly the name *So San* was freshly painted on the stern while no vessel was registered under that name in North Korea. According to Roach after being queried, the master of the vessel replied that it was registered in Cambodia. The Cambodian authorities appeared to have confirmed that a vessel meeting the description was registered in Cambodia, but under the name "*Pan Hope*" instead of *So San*. So a State-to-State loop of confirmation was closed in that incident. What the authority of the boarding team is once the vessel is boarded, is however the real subject of debate. No real clarity exists on the jurisdiction that can be exercised over a stateless vessel. This subject will be touched upon in Chap. 9.

7.5 Final Remarks

Consent is a generally accepted legal basis for maritime interception operations. The conditions for consent are clear, but the question when these conditions are met in the context of maritime interceptions operations raise certain issues, in particular with regard to the consenting authority. This debate centers on the question whether a State itself or the master of a foreign-flagged vessel provides sufficient authority to board the vessel. As a result of different views on this matter NATO in Operation *Active Endeavour* has taken a cautious approach in which both master's and flag State consent is needed.[50] Whereas the principle of master consent exists and the notion by itself is not debated, the scope of master consent is. To what boarding by a foreign warship's crew can a master consent and what can the boarding-team undertake during a master consent boarding? Factors to be considered in the

---

[48] *Medvedyev*, paras 87–89.

[49] Doolin 2006, pp. 29–30.

[50] NATO Review 2005.

answers to these two questions are the position of the flag State of the vessel and to what purpose the boarding is taking place. With regard to the latter, it is generally clear that no jurisdictional activities can take place during such boarding. The contention, however, is that there is a thin line between non-jurisdictional and jurisdictional actions. Practise within the context of conducting maritime security operations is now leaning toward a higher acceptance of master consent under the conditions that no jurisdictional activities are undertaken. This approach is, therefore, stepping away from the more strict approach that boarding without State consent is in general not permitted. It may not have been a significant shift in thinking based on legal arguments, but rather the need to police the seas against current threats that has moved *ad hoc* consent in this more forward leaning direction. The matter is, however, unsettled in a more general sense, at least for the present until such time as an authoritative ruling is issued or international agreement on this issue is reached.

References

Allen C (2014) International law for seagoing officers, 6th edn. Naval Institute Press, Annapolis MD

Ashley-Roach R (1993) Developments in the Law of Naval Operations. In: Lefeber R (ed) Contemporary International Law Issues: Opportunities at a Time of Momentous Change. Martinus Nijhoff Publishers, Dordrecht

Bannelier K, Christakis T (2013) Under the UN Security Council's watchful eyes: Military intervention by invitation in the Malian Conflict. Leiden Journal of International Law 26, pp. 855–874

Becker M (2005) Shifting public order of the oceans. Harvard International law Journal 46:1, pp. 131–230

Brown T (2010) For the "Round and Top of Sovereignty": Boarding Foreign Vessels at Sea on Terror-related Intelligence Tips. Naval Law Review 59, pp. 63–104

CMF (2013) Press release, 24 March 2013, HMS Monmouth Conducts Maritime Approach and Assist Operations. http://combinedmaritimeforces.com/2013/03/24/hms-monmouth-conducts-maritime-approach-and-assist-operations/ Accessed 18 February 2017

Crawford J (2002) ILC Draft Articles on State Responsibility: Articles and commentaries, pp. 72–74

Daily Mail (2014) U.S. Navy hands over North Korean-flagged oil tanker Morning Glory to Libya after seizing it from rebels in dramatic raid, 22 March 2014. www.dailymail.co.uk/news/article-2586995/U-S-Navy-hands-North-Korean-flagged-oil-tanker-Morning-Glory-Libya-seizing-rebels-dramatic-raid.html. Accessed 13 February 2017

Doolin J (2006) The Proliferation Security Initiative. Cornerstone of a new international norm. Naval War College Review 59:2, pp. 29–57

ECtHR, Medvedyev and others v. France, application no. 3394/03. Judgment 29 March 2010

Farhang C (2014) The notion of consent in part of the draft articles on State responsibility. Leiden Journal of International Law 27, pp. 55–73

Gill T (2010) Military intervention at the invitation of the government. In: Gill T, Fleck D (eds) The Handbook of the International Law of Military Operations. Oxford University Press, New York, pp. 229–234

Guilfoyle D (2009) Somali pirates as agents of change in international law making and organization. Cambridge Journal of International and Comparative Law 1:3, pp. 81–106

Heintschel von Heinegg W (2015) Blockade and interdictions. In: Weller M (ed) The Oxford Handbook of the Use of Force in International Law. Oxford University Press, New York, pp. 925–946
Hodgkinson S (2007) Challenges to Maritime Interception Operations in the War on Terror: Bridging the Gap. American University International Law Review 22:4, pp. 853–671
ICJ, Case concerning armed activities on the territory of the Congo (Democratic Republic of the Congo v. Uganda). Judgment of 19 December 2005
ITLOS, case no. 22. Arctic Sunrise, order of 22 November 2013
Kraska J (2010) Broken taillight at sea: The peacetime international law of visit, board, search and seizure. Ocean and Coastal Law Journal 16:1, pp. 1–46
McLaughlin R (2009) United Nations naval peace operations in the Territorial Sea. Martinus Nijhoff Publishers, Leiden/Boston
Meyer H (1967) The Nationality of ships, Martinus Nijhoff, The Hague
NATO Review (2005) De strijd tegen het terrorisme in het Middellandse Zeegebied. NATO Review 3. www.nato.int/docu/review/2005/issue3/dutch/art4.html. Accessed 13 February 2017
Oppenheim L (1906) International Law. A Treatise. Vol. II. War and Neutrality. Longmans and Green and Co, London/New York/Bombay
Papastavridis E (2013) The interception of vessels on the high seas. Hart Publishing, Oxford/Portland, OR
Shulman M (2006) The Proliferation Security Initiative and the evolution of the law on the use of force. Houston Journal of International law 28:3, pp. 771–828
Su J (2012) The Proliferation Security Initiative (PSI) and Interdiction at Sea: A Chinese Perspective. Ocean Development and International Law 43, pp. 96–118
Thomas A, Duncan J (1999) Annotated Supplement to the Commander's Handbook on the Law of Naval Operations. International Law Studies 73. Naval War College, Newport RI
Tondini M (2012) The legality of intercepting boat people under search and rescue and border control operations. The Journal of International Maritime Law 12, pp. 59–74
UN GA (2001) Resolution 56/83 (12 December 2001)
US Navy press release. Ramage VBSS team conducts 100th Approach and assist visit. www.navy.mil/submit/display.asp?story_id=42177. Accessed 17 February 2017
Van der Kruit PJ (2007) Maritime drug interdiction in international law. Dissertation, Den Helder
Wendel P (2007) State Responsibility for Interferences with the Freedom of Navigation in public international law. Hamburg Studies on Maritime Affairs 11, Springer, Berlin/Heidelberg
Williams D (2014) Israel seizes arms shipment. Reuters, 5 March 2014. www.reuters.com/article/2014/03/05/us-israel-gaza-ship-idUSBREA240X720140305. Accessed 13 December 2016
Wilson D (2008) Interdiction on the high seas: The role and authority of a master in the boarding and searching of his ship by foreign warships. Naval Law Review 55, pp. 170–185

Chapter 8
International Agreements on Maritime Interception

Contents

Abstract Enhancement of maritime security has become important in the maritime dimension in the last decennia. International agreements between States are considered to be another legal solution to seek effective enhancement of maritime security. International agreements are not only useful for the actual interception phase at sea, but also facilitate the cooperation before and after the interception at sea. This chapter touches upon a number of international agreements that can be the basis for maritime interception operations.

Keywords SUA Convention · SUA Protocol · UNCLOS · bilateral ship boarding agreements

8.1 Introduction

States have the power to agree with other States to allow those States to intercept and board vessels under their jurisdiction on the high seas for certain specific activities. Obviously, international agreements are a form of consent, most commonly agreed between States. Treaties primarily aim to agree or set out the conditions between States in a more structural and permanent manner. The general advantage of international agreements over *ad hoc* consent, apart from the agreement being a more

M. Fink, *Maritime Interception and the Law of Naval Operations*,
https://doi.org/10.1007/978-94-6265-249-1_8

structural form, is that the provisions of the agreement itself upon which the interception takes place, provides more narrowly described authorities and also defines the scope of activities that may take place under the treaty-regime.

The contemporary focus on the use of international agreements as a legal basis for maritime interception operations is connected to the efforts to enhance maritime security. First, making use of international agreements fits the idea that maritime security is reached through cooperation on mutual security issues that States share.[1] This is a different idea than the classic naval power view in which naval power is used for competing with other States over command of sea. Second, international agreements have become more interesting where on the global level security interests cannot be sufficiently dealt with due to challenges of the involvement of the many States and their interests, States may still pursue their security interests on a more bilateral or regional level. To illustrate, the UN efforts on proliferation of WMD have until now not reached as far as providing non-consensual boarding authority to stop vessels suspected of carrying WMD on the high seas. Instead, States try to achieve this through agreements on a bi- and multilateral level. As some States may find that the particular issue of WMD is not sufficiently addressed through either the UN collective security system or the international law of the sea, international agreements are the tool that provides the legal basis in order to fill that gap. On the one hand, therefore, while global maritime security issues force States to cooperate with each other, on the other hand, because of the multitude of interests and factors involved these issues can develop slowly or in an unsatisfactory manner, States can approach issues from the bottom up with smaller bi-, regional- or multilateral level solutions.

International agreements with regard to maritime interception operations do not aim to take a step away from the basic ground rules of the law of the sea. Rather, one reason to enter into international agreements is that they make things work better or run more smoothly within the international system of States, which may be especially true for treaties that seek to enhance safety at sea. International agreements in this context try on a more operational level to overcome the hurdles that initially come with the fundamental principles of international law. They focus on mutual cooperation between States. Aspects like setting up procedures, intensifying coordination, points of contact, or obligations to criminalize acts under domestic laws all seek to strengthen maritime security, without in fact having to step away from fundamental principles derived from the sovereignty of States. It firstly operationalizes the issue of sovereignty versus mission accomplishment into workable details. And secondly, it can subject any possible boarding to strict control measures.

Still, using the tool of the international agreement for maritime interception operations is not without criticism. The bilateral boarding agreements between the US and other States have brought some to argue against such treaties. For one reason because the procedural provisions set up in the agreements while not explicitly violating the basic principles of the law of the sea, do seem to nibble at

[1] Kraska 2009.

those fundamental principles. As such, as the argument runs, an implied consent regime which is set up in these agreements is a procedure that may not seriously allow the requested State to exercise their sovereignty.[2] The fear may be that these procedures may be the start of something that ultimately can result in impairing the sovereignty and the equality of States.[3]

There are a number of international agreements on a wide range of topics that can form the basis for maritime interception operations. Examples of topics are drug-interdiction (1988 Vienna Convention),[4] criminal acts at sea (SUA Convention and its Protocols), piracy (UNCLOS), hostages (Hostages Convention 1979) and WMD (bilateral boarding agreements between the US and others). These treaties all fall within the realm of minimizing criminal acts at sea. As such, most of these fall outside the scope of this study. But because certain topics are now also brought within the realm of restoring international peace and security, such as piracy, terrorists and proliferation of WMD, these topics will be touched upon in this chapter. Apart from the international agreements that are meant to work in a more global manner on specific thematic topics, also regional mutual cooperation arrangement are made between States to counter a maritime threats in specific areas. For instance, the cooperation treaty between the ASEAN States[5] laid down in the ASEAN Convention on counter-terrorism[6] and the so-called *San Jose Treaty* on drug trafficking between a number of States in the Caribbean hemisphere.[7]

8.2 The Increasing Role of International Agreements in MIO

Although this study focuses on the legal basis for MIO at sea, international agreements can play a role in the whole maritime interception process in the broadest sense, which extends further than to activities at sea alone. First, international agreements can play a role in the preconditions for successful MIO. This could for instance be setting up an intelligence gathering and sharing network between States and relevant organizations.[8] But this could also include authority to operate in certain geographical areas where naval operations are subject to authority of a State. A State can agree by international arrangement to allow foreign vessels

[2] Klein 2011, p. 313.

[3] Syrigos 2006, p. 201.

[4] See Article17 of the *Vienna Convention against illicit traffic in narcotic drugs and psychotropic substances* (1988).

[5] Association of Southeast Asian Nations, which includes 10 member states in South Asia.

[6] *ASEAN Convention on Counter Terrorism*, Cebu, 13 January 2007.

[7] *Agreement concerning co-operation in suppressing illicit maritime and air trafficking in narcotic drugs and psychotropic substances in the Caribbean area*, San Jose, 10 April 2003.

[8] Klein 2010, pp. 224–241.

to operate in its territorial sea. Another example of where international agreements can play a role in MIO is in international (shiprider) agreements to allow foreign shipriders[9] or law enforcement agents (LEDETs)[10] on board a warship. The purpose of shiprider agreements is to provide a jurisdictional link between a suspect person and the State officials. It is a frequently used agreement in maritime drug interdiction[11] and has also been a subject of discussion in counter-piracy operations off the coast of Somalia. Whereas these examples focus on setting the conditions to ultimately enable a successful operation at sea, international agreements can also play a role in the aftermath of the interception. Some treaties set out provisions that codify the principle of *aut judicare aut dedere*, such as the SUA Convention.[12] With regard to piracy, the UNCLOS provisions on piracy do not contain such a provision, but in recent counter-piracy operations off the coast of Somalia further agreements were made to transfer persons from one State to another. For instance, the EU concluded a transfer-agreement with Kenya on the conditions of transfer of suspected pirates.[13] Apart from the fact that such agreements lessen the logistical burden of out-of-area counter-piracy operations, it also supports the political view that piracy should be prosecuted in the region rather than in the far off State of the intervening warship.

In terms of agreements that focus on the aftermath, also mention can be made of so called diversion port agreements that be concluded in order to agree with a State to have a port available where suspect vessels can be inspected, in a more thorough fashion as can be done at sea. Apart from the practical issues of inspecting at sea, the advantage of in-port inspection is that it takes place within the jurisdiction of a State who can take more appropriate measures against possible breaches of a UN embargo. Although a diversion port agreement would very much take away much of the un-clarity as to what to do with suspected goods and persons encountered at sea, States seem to be reluctant to agree on authorizing one of its ports to function as a diversion port during military operations.[14]

Narrowing MIO again to operations at sea, a number of international agreements have specific provisions that deal with the right of visit by warships on foreign

---

[9] Voetelink 2013, p. 150. Shipriders should not be confused with vessel protection detachments (VPD). The first are law enforcement agents who 'ride' on board a warship of another State through which specific authorities are provided that enables an arrest of a person at sea. VPD are protection teams that protect a vessel from being boarded. These are frequently used in the context of piracy. See for the Dutch experiences Fink and Voetelink 2013.

[10] Law Enforcement Detachment.

[11] See Van der Kruit 2007, pp. 274–294.

[12] Article 10 SUA Convention.

[13] *Exchange of Letter between the European Union and the Government of Kenya on the conditions and modalities for the transfer of persons suspected of having committed acts of piracy and detained by the European Union-led naval force (EUNAVFOR), and seized property in possession of EUNAVFOR, from EUNAVFOR to Kenya and for their treatment after such capture*, 25 March 2009.

[14] Based on the author's experience during OUP.

vessels on the high seas. The most obvious three treaties, used within the context of international peace and security, are the UNCLOS, *Treaty on Suppression of Unlawful acts at Sea against the Safety of Maritime Navigation,* 1988 (SUA Convention) and its 2005 Protocol, and lastly, the bilateral boarding agreements between the United States and other nations that are agreed against the background of the PSI. These agreements will be discussed below in the following paragraphs.

8.3 International Agreements and the Law of the Sea

Article 92 UNCLOS mentions that the convention itself (itself a treaty) or an international treaty may deviate from the fundamental principle of exclusive jurisdiction over a vessel by the flag State. As such, UNCLOS clearly opens the door for States to agree on treaties that may give enforcement jurisdiction to other States over a foreign-flagged vessel. As Chap. 4 has set out, on the high seas the State has exclusive jurisdiction on board its flagged vessels. As mentioned there, Article 92 UNCLOS provides for the exception to the ground-rule in 'exceptional cases expressly provided for in international treaties or in this Convention…' UNCLOS, therefore, opens the door specifically to consent through treaties. It does, however, not say anything on the use of consent within the meaning of precluding the wrongfulness of actions of a State. A strict reading of this provision would lead to the conclusion that it does not consider consent through other forms of State consent, such as consent within the meaning an *ad hoc* agreement. As international agreements are form free and may also exist in very rudimentary forms as long as it consists of the will of an authorized body or person within both States, this still could fit the *ad hoc* agreement of consent. This seems also to be the line taken by the ECtHR in the *Medvedyev* case.

There are only a few international agreements that allow third States to enforce jurisdiction over a flag State vessel without prior *ad hoc* permission in the context of international peace and security. The obvious one is UNCLOS. And next to UNCLOS one could mention the UN Charter of which the collective security system provides for binding decisions for States and can take mandatory measures under Chapter VII to intercept third state vessels.[15] Interestingly, although an international agreement may give options to overcome the issue of exclusive jurisdiction, treaty-making practice in the maritime dimension has not jumped immediately in that direction. Apart from the two mentioned, there are in fact no treaties that specifically step away from prior permission. Instead, against the background of trying to promote more instruments to minimize the threats of terrorists and WMD, solutions in recent treaties are sought primarily in shorter

[15] Churchill 2008, p. 147.

timelines and more efficient procedures to be able to obtain consent to board a foreign-flagged vessel. As Hodgkinson concludes: 'Boarding agreements save time'.[16] As was mentioned in Chap. 2, the SUA Protocol 2005 endeavored to enhance the use-ability of the SUA Convention in light of the increased threats against maritime security. The main principle enshrined in Article 8 bis of the 2005 SUA Protocol is still that: 'The requesting Party shall not board the ship or take measures set out in subparagraph 5(b) without the express authorization of the flag State'. A prior request thus needs to be sent to the flag State. A minor procedural step away from this principle is however made in Article 8 bis sub 5 under (d), which creates a 'silent consent' procedure or a 'presumption of consent' when a State party does not react within 4 h.[17] As Ashley Roach mentions, 'The boarding procedures do not change existing international maritime law or infringe upon the traditional principle of the freedom of navigation. Instead, the procedures eliminate the need to negotiate time consuming *ad hoc* boarding arrangements when facing the immediacy of ongoing criminal activity.'[18]

The PSI is not a treaty and the interdiction principles by themselves do not give a legal basis for boarding foreign-flagged vessels. Instead, the PSI contains a political basis for subsequent treaty making between PSI-participants.[19] The bilateral ship boarding agreements between the US and other States are based on this. A construct of implicit authorization by the flag State is used in these ship boarding agreements.[20] For example, the agreement between the US and Liberia has a time-lapse

---

[16] Hodgkinson 2007, p. 665.

[17] Article 8 bis, sub 5 (d) 2005 Protocol to the 1988 Convention for the Suppression of Unlawful Acts against the Safety of Maritime Navigation, London, 14 October 2005, IMO Doc. LEG/CONF.15/21, reads as follows:

> Upon or after depositing its instrument of ratification, acceptance, approval or accession, a State Party may notify the Secretary-General that, with respect to ships flying its flag or displaying its mark of registry, the requesting Party is granted authorization to board and search the ship, its cargo and persons on board, and to question the persons on board in order to locate and examine documentation of its nationality and determine if an offence set forth in article 3, 3*bis*, 3*ter* or 3*quater* has been, is being or is about to be committed, if there is no response from the first Party within four hours of acknowledgement of receipt of a request to confirm nationality.

[18] Ashley-Roach 2012, p. 50.

[19] The fourth principle states that:

> Take specific actions in support of interdiction efforts regarding cargoes of WMD, their delivery systems, or related materials, to the extent their national legal authorities permit and consistent with their obligations under international law and frameworks...

[20] Ship boarding agreements have been agreed between the US and Antigua & Barbuda (2010); Nassau (2008), Belize (2005); Croatia (2007); Cyprus (2006); Liberia (2004); Malta (2007); Marshall Islands (2004); Mongolia (2008); Panama (2004); Saint Vincent and the Grenadines (2010).

limit of 2 h before an authority to board is assumed.[21] The agreement between the US and Croatia appears to be an exception to this construct. Although there is a time limit of 4 h, there are no consequences when time has run out. Express authorization of the flag State is still needed.[22]

Both the 2005 SUA Protocol and the ship boarding agreements appear to have effectively dealt with the fear that explicit flag State consent may take too long. This approach seems to be moving away from a hard-line view of the principle of flag State consent. Primarily because, as Garvey mentions: 'Two hours is obviously a period of time grossly inadequate to assess the credibility of a request for interdiction and the interests involved. Under these bilaterals, if consent is not provided within two hours, interdiction can proceed by default'.[23] Whether it is possible to obtain consent within 4 h will depend on how the national institutions are organized to deal with the question when it arises.

8.4 UNCLOS

UNCLOS contains provisions based on which it is allowed to interfere with foreign-flagged vessels on the high seas. These provisions are laid down in Articles 98, 110 and 111 UNCLOS.[24] Arguably, these provisions codify existing international customary law. These provisions contain six subjects altogether: rendering

---

[21] Article 3(d) Agreement Between the Government of the United States of America and the Government of the Republic of Liberia concerning Cooperation to Suppress the Proliferation of Weapons of Mass Destruction, their Delivery Systems, and Related Materials by Sea, Washington, 11 February 2004, http://www.state.gov/t/isn/trty/32403.htm, reads as follows:

> If there is no response from the Competent Authority of the requested Party within two hours of its acknowledgment of receipt of the request, the requesting Party will be deemed to have been authorized to board the suspect vessel for the purpose of inspecting the vessels documents, questioning the persons on board, and searching the vessel to determine if it is engaged in proliferation by sea.

[22] See Articles 4(b) and (d) Agreement between the Government of the United States of America and the Government of the Republic of Croatia concerning Cooperation to Suppress the Proliferation of Weapons of Mass Destruction, their Delivery Systems, and Related Materials, Washington, 1 June 2005 (at:http://www.state.gov/t/isn/trty/47086.htm). Article 4d of this agreements states:

> d. Except as otherwise permitted by international law, the requesting Party shall not board the vessel without the express written authorization of the Competent Authority of the requested Party.

[23] Garvey 2005, p. 133.

[24] Article 110 sub 1 UNCLOS reads:

> 1. Except where acts of interference derive from powers conferred by treaty, a warship which encounters on the high seas a foreign ship, other than a ship entitled to complete immunity in accordance with articles 95 and 96, is not justified in boarding it unless there is reasonable ground for suspecting that:

assistance, piracy, slave trade, unauthorized broadcasting, statelessness and hot pursuit.

Articles 100–107 and 110 UNCLOS relate to the law of piracy. A lot has been written on the law of piracy laid down in UNCLOS since the multinational efforts of navies started to patrol the seas around the Horn of Africa supported by UN resolutions. In this context however Articles 105 and 110 are UNCLOS are of particular importance. Article 105 UNCLOS allows States to establish universal jurisdiction over piracy on the high seas, or any other place outside the jurisdiction of any State.[25] When properly authorized through national legislation, warships of all States can board a vessel suspected of piracy, arrest the persons and seize the property on board. Article 110 UNCLOS provides the authority to board a foreign-flagged vessel, under the condition that there is a reasonable ground for suspecting that the vessel engaged in piracy.

Obviously, the piracy provisions in UNCLOS have been well used in recent years, but also, as mentioned in Chap. 7, the notion of statelessness is used as a reason to board a vessel within the context of enhancing maritime security.

Apart from the more traditional provisions of 110 and 111 UNCLOS, one could argue that in the interest of saving human lives in danger of the perils of the sea, Article 98 UNCLOS concerning the rendering of assistance implies also that under circumstances of distress the boarding of a foreign-flagged vessel is permissible. The situation of distress allows (or rather: obliges) for immediate action taken by any mariner—man of war or merchantman—that can do so without serious danger to one's own ship, crew or passengers. No consent of a flag State is needed to board a vessel in distress. Rendering assistance in a maritime context has a specific and long developed context, is codified not only in UNCLOS but also in other maritime law treaties,[26] and focuses on the safety of the vessel and persons of the dangers that exists from the perils *from* the sea, for instance the lack of seaworthiness of a vessel drifting at sea. But it is, however, not meant to permit boarding when life-threatening danger arises between, for instance, persons on board. Rendering assistance has, in other words, a limited meaning and cannot be used in all circumstances of danger at sea.

(a) the ship is engaged in piracy;

(b) the ship is engaged in the slave trade;

(c) the ship is engaged in unauthorized broadcasting and the flag State of the warship has jurisdiction under article 109;

(d) the ship is without nationality; or

(e) though flying a foreign flag or refusing to show its flag, the ship is, in reality, of the same nationality as the warship.

[25] Presumably, this is Antarctica. Some have, however, argued that maritime areas that belong to failed States would also fall under this.

[26] Such as the SOLAS Convention and the Salvage Convention.

8.5 The SUA Convention and Protocol

States have sought to take appropriate measures against criminal acts that occur on board a vessel via the SUA Convention (1988), which came about as a result of the *Achille Lauro* incident.[27] The Convention is supplemented by the SUA Protocol (2005), which entered into force in 2010. The SUA Protocol is not yet a broadly ratified protocol.[28] The importance of the 2005 SUA Protocol is that it adds four new offences to the SUA Convention and includes a right of visit regime.[29] The offences are important for the proliferation of WMD because they make punishable an act the intention of which is to intimidate a population, or to compel a government or an international organization to do or to abstain from any act, by using NBC-material on or from the vessel. The provisions that allow for boarding a foreign flag vessel under SUA are Articles 8*bis* under 5(c) and (d). With Article 8*bis* under 5(c)(i) a flag State can authorize another State to board its vessel. With Article 8*bis* under 5(d) a flag State can also opt for the 4-h rule regime, in which a requesting boarding State can board the vessel if there is no response from the flag State within 4 h of acknowledgment of receipt of a request to confirm nationality. The visit-provisions are further analysed Chap. 9. Although the Protocol is, as Kraska and Pedrozo mention,[30] more robust than many other international agreements, it still takes the exclusive jurisdiction of the flag State over its vessels as the point of departure. Article 8*bis* under 5(c) states that no party shall board the ship or take measures without the express authorization of the flag State.

8.6 PSI Bilateral Boarding Agreements Between the US and Others

The United States has entered into a number of bilateral ship boarding agreements (BSA) for the purpose of stopping WMD. Kraska and Pedrozo mention that within the different agreements that exist (11 in 2014) three models exist for a legal ship boarding action.[31] First is the situation where the US needs flag state consent under all circumstances. Second is the situation in which boarding is presumed to be authorized when a certain period of time has lapsed without response. And third is the situation where the boarding can take place if the registry of the vessel cannot be

[27] The Italian-flagged *Achille Lauro* was hijacked by Palestinians off the coast of Egypt, demanding the release of 50 Palestine prisoners. The hijackers were given safe passage in Egypt and allowed to board an airplane to fly to Tunisia. US fighters then forced the plane to land in Italy. See Bryant 2004; Cassese 1989.

[28] The IMO website states that as of February 2016, 35 states ratified the Protocol.

[29] Article 4 under 5 SUA Protocol.

[30] Kraska and Pedrozo 2013, p. 835.

[31] Kraska and Pedrozo 2013, p. 788.

confirmed within a certain timeframe. There is not much available on the practical use of these BSA. Only the *MV Light* incident can be connected to BSA.[32] But apart from its actual use in practice, one can also see agreements as a mechanism to close the net on terrorists that try to use the maritime environment for their actions.

8.7 Final Remarks

International agreements can form the legal basis for maritime interception operations. Where some treaties (UNCLOS and the UN Charter) have provisions that ultimately allow States under certain circumstances to interfere with other vessels without prior permission of the flag State, other relevant treaties, such as SUA and the bilateral ship boarding agreements, have explicit regulations on boarding foreign-flagged vessels. The latter, however, do not reach as far as not needing prior permission. Rather, against the background of the need to act rapidly authority in treaties has moved to implied authority, or silent procedures: the condition for the legal basis to come into play is the passage of time, after which consent is presumed to be given. Even so, this procedure is still based on the overall explicit authority given by a State through an agreement, and in that sense, has agreed to such undertaking.

References

Ashley-Roach J (2012) Global Conventions on piracy, ship hijacking, hostage taking and maritime terrorism. In: Beckmann R, Ashley-Roach R (eds) Piracy and international maritime crimes in ASEAN. Prospects for cooperation. NUS center for international law, pp. 38–61

Bryant D (2004) Historical and Legal Aspects of Maritime Security. University of San Francisco Maritime Law Journal 1:3–4, pp. 1–27

Cassese A (1989) Terrorism, politics and law. The Achille Lauro affair. Polity Press, Oxford

Churchill R (2008) UN Security Council Resolutions and 1982 LOS Convention. In: Carsten M (ed) International Law Studies 84. Naval War College, Newport RI, pp. 143–157

European Union (2009) Exchange of Letter between the European Union and the Government of Kenya on the conditions and modalities for the transfer of persons suspected of having committed acts of piracy and detained by the European Union-led naval force (EUNAVFOR), and seized property in possession of EUNAVFOR, from EUNAVFOR to Kenya and for their treatment after such capture, 25 March 2009

Fink M, Voetelink J (2013) De status van militaire Vessel Protection Detachments. Militair Rechtelijk Tijdschrift 106, pp. 41–53

[32] The Belize-flagged vessel *M/V Light* from North Korea on its way to Myanmar and suspected of carrying missile parts was forced to turn back by the US who dispatched the *USS McCampbell* to intercept the *M/V Light*. Although authority to board was given by Belize, based on the US-Belize ship boarding agreement the master refused. Instead it finally turned back to North Korea.

Garvey J (2005) The international institution imperative for countering the spread of weapons of mass destruction: Assessing the Proliferation Security Initiative. Journal of Conflict and Security Law 10:2, pp. 125–147

Hodgkinson S (2007) Challenges to Maritime Interception Operations in the War on Terror: Bridging the Gap. American University International Law Review 22:4, pp. 853–671

Klein N (2010) Intelligence gathering and information sharing for maritime security purposes under international law. In: Klein N, Mossop J, Rothwell D (eds) Maritime security. International law and policy perspectives from Australia and New Zealand. Routledge, London/New York, pp. 224–241

Klein N (2011) Maritime security and the law of the sea. Oxford University Press, New York

Kraska J (2009) Grasping the influence of law on sea power. Naval War College Review 62:3, pp. 113–135

Kraska J, Pedrozo R (2013) International Maritime Security Law. Martinus Nijhoff Publishers, Leiden/Boston

Syrigos A (2006) Development on the interdiction of vessels on the high seas. In: Strati A, Gavouneli M, Skourtos N (eds) Unresolved issues and new challenges to the law of the sea. Time before and time after. Publication on Ocean Development 54, pp. 149–202

van der Kruit P (2007) Maritime drug interdiction in international law. Dissertation, Den Helder

Voetelink J (2013) Militair operationeel recht. Wolff Legal Publishers, Oisterwijk

Part III
Legal Regimes for Maritime Interception Operations

Part III
Legal Regimes for Maritime Interception Operations

Chapter 9
The Right of Visit

> *The belligerent right of visit is not a substantive and independent right, it is a means justified by the end.*
>
> —A. P. Higgins

Contents

Abstract The visit of a foreign-flagged vessel is the core activity of maritime interception operations. The right of visit of foreign-flagged vessels comes in different manifestations, depending on the legal basis. This chapter analyses these different manifestations of the right of visit. One challenge is that today's conflicts are often characterized as non-international in nature. As the law of naval warfare does not apply to non-international armed conflicts, the question remains whether a non-international armed conflict right of visit should exist and under what legal parameters.

M. Fink, *Maritime Interception and the Law of Naval Operations*,
https://doi.org/10.1007/978-94-6265-249-1_9

Keywords Right of visit · belligerent right of visit and search · NIAC right of visit · blockade · right of visit and non-international armed conflict · Article 110 UNCLOS · contraband

9.1 Introduction

The right of visit is of key importance to maritime interception operations. It is at the very heart of maritime interception.[1] Traditionally, the right of visit is generally separated into peacetime rights of visit and the right of visit during international armed conflict. The first are codified in Articles 110 and 111 UNCLOS. The second refers to the belligerent right of visit and search, which is part of the law of naval warfare. Generally, the peacetime rights of visit are called 'the right of visit'. The right of visit during international armed conflict appears usually under the term 'the right of visit and search', 'the belligerent right of visit and search', or even more extensively under the term 'the belligerent right of visit, search and capture'. In line with the view that there are several legal bases for MIO, it is argued here that the right of visit has more manifestations than the traditional separation into peacetime and wartime rights and may include manifestations arising from different legal bases. For example, a right of visit is now also accepted to exist on the basis of an authorization by the UNSC, derived from *ad hoc* consent or based on international agreements.

The right of visit in this chapter is defined as the rules that regulate the authority during a visit of a foreign-flagged vessel by a warship. In principle, a visit contains three aspects that relate to both the legal basis and legal regime: the legal basis to board, the authority for boarding crew during the visit and the legal regimes that apply during the conduct of the visit. To illustrate, if a boarding is based on an international agreement, the agreement itself is the legal basis that will also detail the scope of authorities during the boarding. Added to this is the manner in which way force may be used or persons are detained, which is based on the applicable legal regime. These three aspects together make up the complete scope of rules that a boarding-team must consider during the boarding of a vessel (see Fig. 9.1).

Separating these three legal aspects of a visit is relatively easy done for existing manifestations of the right of visit or for visits derived from an international agreement. For visits that do not have a pre-existing legal framework addressing the scope of authority, this is less clear. For example, when an *ad hoc* consent is the legal basis for the boarding, the scope of consent given should also detail the scope of authority for the boarding. The legal regimes that apply depend on the factual situation, which can be either IRHL or LOAC. Similarly, a UN resolution can be the legal basis for the boarding, which may detail some of the scope of authority for the boarding itself. The manner in which way the authority is enforced depends on the applicable legal regime. This chapter focuses on the rights *during* the visit. The

[1] Higgins 1926, p. 43.

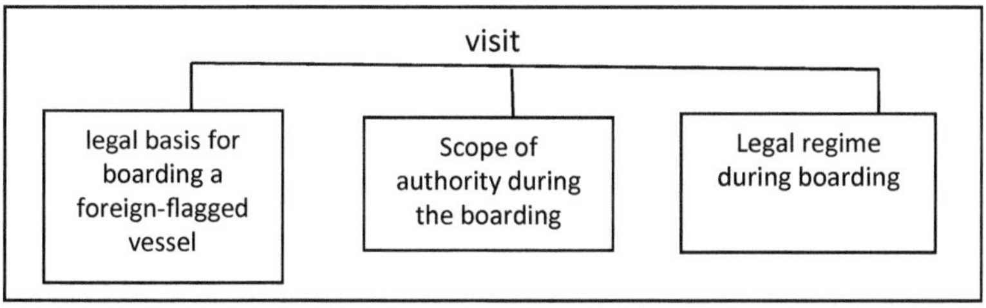

Fig. 9.1 Three legal aspects of a visit (*Source* M. Fink)

first aspect (legal basis) has already been discussed in Part II. The third aspect will be discussed in Chaps. 10 and 11. This chapter will first start with three general remarks concerning the right of visit during maritime interception operations and then proceed to analyse the different manifestations of the right of visit.

9.2 General Remarks on the Right of Visit

As will be outlined in this chapter, there are different manifestations of the right of visit. A first general remark is on conjuncture of these rights. Different manifestations can be used simultaneously in one military campaign. As pointed out in Chap. 2, during one military operation warship commanders can be authorized to act based on different types of right of visit. For example, a warship that takes part in an international armed conflict could exercise the belligerent right of visit and search and at the same time be authorized to act against piracy[2] or against a SUA offence.[3] This was for example the case during the Dutch contribution to Taskforce 150 in the Arabian Sea. The maritime operating area of Taskforce 150 was both an area of interest with regard to terrorists and Somali pirates. Netherlands warships assigned to the operation had both the authority to use the belligerent right of visit and search to search for possible terrorists at sea and the authority to act against piracy off the coast of Somalia. As an another example, it can be mentioned that the fact that a warship is, for instance, assigned to a multinational UN-mandated maritime embargo operation does not preclude that the ship may also be authorized to board vessels that are stateless or suspected of piracy. It may, however, have an impact on the command and control of the contributing warships. Where an international commander can order a visit in line with the mandate, other types of authority stay, in principle, with the State of the contributing State unless it has delegated its authority to an international commander.

[2] Ministerie van Defensie, Eindevaluatie CTF 150, 18 September 2006.

[3] Interestingly, Article 2*bis* sub 2 of the SUA-Protocol mentions that the Convention does not apply to the activities of armed forces during an armed conflict, but does not exclude that the Convention applies also during armed conflict.

Second, as a consequence from the above, different manifestations of the right of visit can exist simultaneously within one area of operations. During the US/UK naval operations in the Persian Gulf in March 2003 against Iraq (OIF), in which the belligerent right of visit and search applied, the right of visit derived from a UNSC resolution to enforce the maritime embargo against Iraq still existed in the area of the Persian Gulf.[4] Moreover, if the State has assigned ships to both operations, the rights can be applied in the same area and conducted by warships of the same State.[5] As this chapter will show, there are significant differences between these different manifestations of the right of visit. It is, therefore, important to know which right of visit applies to a particular situation, even though the execution of the right from an operational perspective may be quite similar. For a warship commander, the rules of engagement designed for a particular operation often provide some assistance in this regard.

Third, it must also be underlined that the quote by A. P. Higgins in the heading of this chapter signals an important point with regard to the nature of the right of visit. The activity of visiting a foreign-flagged vessel by a warship is not an *end* to itself, but a *means* that serves another, and specific, purpose. The right exists to enable States by means of a visit of another vessel to verify and, if needed, subsequently stop an illicit activity, a breach of a UN resolution, or exercise an authority under the law of naval warfare. It is not a right that is meant for the sole purpose to gain access to a foreign-flagged vessel, and after which a range of new opportunities may arise from the fact that a State is physically on board the vessel. The right of visit is a means to support something else, which must be sufficiently concrete so that lawful access to a vessel cannot be used for other purposes. As such it cannot be separated from the reason why a visit is undertaken. The lawfulness of the visit will also depend on this connected reason. To illustrate the operational challenge this comment raises, I will sketch the following dilemma:

> During an international armed conflict a neutral vessel suspected of carrying contraband to the enemy is sailing from (not to) enemy territory to a neutral destination. The latter information bars a commander from using the right of visit based on the law of naval warfare, as this authority is limited by a suspicion of carrying contraband and (ultimate) enemy destination of the vessel. The commander has, however, noticed that the vessel does not fly a flag and therefore views the vessel to be stateless. This allows him, based on a peacetime right of visit, to board the vessel. While checking for nationality on board the vessel, his suspicion that the vessel is carrying contraband appears to be correct. Because lawful capture of contraband still depends on the condition of destination, it means that in this case, although access to the vessel was gained lawfully, it is still not lawful to seize the goods that are deemed contraband.

---

[4] See also McLaughlin 2015, pp. 267–268.

[5] In this context McLaughlin refers to an interesting situation during the 2003 operations against Iraq, in which the belligerent visit and search does not allow a warship to visit a vessel that comes from the enemy state (based on the fact that contraband needs to have an enemy destination), and where the co-existing resolution does provide the authority to stop merchant vessels for inspection of prohibited goods. McLaughlin 2015, p. 267.

The above dilemma shows how complex the interaction between the different manifestations of the right of visit can be. It also, perhaps, shows how quickly mistakes or misuse of the right can be made when no attention is paid to the fact that the right of visit is a means rather than an end.

9.3 Ad Hoc Consent-Based Right of Visit

As was noted in Chap. 7, consent between States is a legal basis for visiting a foreign-flagged vessel. The situation in which an *ad hoc* consent visit takes place must usually be sought within the realm of law enforcement type of operations. For instance for the purpose of stopping illicit activities on board foreign-flagged vessels. When authority to board is given through consent this does not, however, also automatically clarify the scope and authority of the visit as there is no specific legal framework that automatically comes into play. Important to note is that *ad hoc* consent does not per definition include the authority to perform jurisdictional enforcement activities. As Gill mentions: ‘The intervention will be subject to any conditions posed by the consenting State’.[6] Through consent a State can waive the exclusive enforcement jurisdiction, but only to the extent the waiver permits. As Kraska notes: ‘Permission to board may be narrowly circumscribed, however, and does not necessarily entail consent to inspect, search or seize the vessel’.[7] The purpose and the range of the enforcement measures during the visit depend therefore on what is agreed between the States, which, as a guideline, must also be sufficiently concrete. The latter point has also been illustrated in the *Medvedyev* case. The Cambodian diplomatic note of consent included the authority to intercept, inspect and take legal action against the *Winner*.[8] The ECtHR accepted the diplomatic note as the legal basis but also opined that the fate of the crew was not sufficiently covered by the note and therefore did not establish that the deprivation of liberty of the crew was subject to an agreement between France and Cambodia.[9] The enforcement jurisdiction of France to arrest and detain the persons on board the vessel was not considered granted by the Cambodian authorities. In this case, the legal certainty that had to arise from the note also emerged from human rights standards on deprivation of liberty, which will be elaborated upon in Chap. 11. At this point it is enough to conclude that what is allowed based on the consent must be made sufficiently clear.

Based on Article 92 UNCLOS the flag State will have exclusive jurisdiction over the vessel. Based on the (passive) nationality or universality principle, the boarding State may have jurisdiction over the persons when for instance the persons on board (e.g. the suspected criminal or the victims of the crime) have the same nationality as

---

[6] Gill 2010, pp. 229–234.

[7] Kraska 2010b, p. 11.

[8] *Medvedyev*, para 10.

[9] *Medvedyev*, paras 98–99.

the boarding State. In other words, situations of concurrent jurisdiction can exist. As the flag State has exclusive jurisdiction over the vessel, primary jurisdiction is with the flag State, unless the waiver of consent allows the boarding State to enforce its own jurisdiction. The consenting State can therefore choose to either allow the boarding State to enforce jurisdiction on behalf of the flag State, or decide to waive its enforcement jurisdiction in favor of enforcement jurisdiction of the boarding State. The first situation is foreseen, albeit agreed in an international agreement, in the SUA-Protocol boarding provisions and the bilateral ship-boarding agreements between the US and other States. It is, furthermore, unlikely that a State will give consent to a boarding of one of its flagged vessels without any reasons given by the requesting boarding State. The boarding State will have to make clear to the flag State that there are grounds for suspicion that a certain criminal or prohibited act is taking place on board against which actions must be taken. It would seem that the threshold to board the vessel will be at least a reasonable ground for suspicion that persons on board the vessel are engaged in something illicit.

9.4 International Agreements and the Right of Visit

In Chap. 8 it was noted that a legal basis for MIO exists when States agree to conclude international agreements. When the visit finds its legal basis in an international agreement the purpose and scope of the visit is detailed in the agreement itself. In the following paragraphs the UNCLOS, the SUA provisions and the bilateral boarding agreements between the US and others States will be touched upon as illustrative examples of such agreements.

9.4.1 The Limited Character of the Right of Visit in UNCLOS

Primarily,[10] Article 110 UNCLOS deals with the peacetime right of visit on the high seas. This provision has been subject to much analysis, in particular after the emergence of piracy off the coast of Somalia became a much debated topic. The purpose of the right of visit is limited to piracy, slave trade, stateless vessels and unauthorized broadcasting. It is explicitly stated that warships may exercise this

[10] Other peacetime rights of visit may be found in article 111 UNCLOS, which regulates the right of hot pursuit. Arguably, also Article 98 UNCLOS implies a right of visit to secure the safety of persons in distress at sea. Also, outside the realm of international peace and security, more implicit rights of visit exist, for example, a right of visit that is implied in other authorities in which a state asserts their rights in the different maritime zones. The practical side to conduct the authorities given under Article 33 UNCLOS in the contiguous zone implies such a right for certain specific purposes.

right. Klein notes on this right: 'The fact that these exceptions are narrowly construed reflects that the preference of States still accords with the overarching construct of *mare liberum*'.[11] The right of visit under UNCLOS follows both the notion that the right of visit must be considered as an exception to the exclusive jurisdiction of a flag State, and the notion that States do not have general policing rights on the high seas. Apart from the fact that Article 110 UNCLOS characterizes these rights as acts of interference, the exceptional character of this right is also manifested in a number of other limitations.

First, Article 110 UNCLOS puts up the threshold of 'reasonable grounds to suspect' for the application of the right.[12] The information of this suspicion itself may either come from the commander of the visiting warship on the spot, or via other channels, such as received intelligence. To underline this threshold, UNCLOS also mentions that when the suspicion on a later point appears to be unfounded, a ground for compensation for any loss of damage will exist.[13] Obviously, this signifies that losses or damages which result from a boarding that is undertaken without any suspicion at all, must also be compensated. As Wendel states: 'Object and purpose of Art. 110 para. 3 LOSC is to prevent abusive interference and to increase the degree of diligence exercised by the naval officers considering a boarding.'[14]

Second, as mentioned previously, the purpose of the visit it is limited to certain types of situations, namely in the cases of piracy, slave trade, stateless vessels and unauthorized broadcasting. The purpose is clearly defined. It does not leave room to apply the right of visit to, for instance, drug-trafficking or suspected terrorist boarding operations.

Third, the authorities are limited to visit and search only. They do not expressly possess authority to attain seizures, or exercise enforcement jurisdiction. This authority still lies with the flag State.[15] Based on reasonable suspicion, Article 110 UNCLOS only allows to board for the purpose of determining whether one of the four situations are ongoing. It does not mention what happens after the moment the warship's crew has found that the suspicion was right. This indicates also that the right of visit is very limited in the sense that well founded suspicion which after inspection appears to be correct still does not give any further authorities for the boarding warship

---

[11] Klein 2005, p. 302.

[12] Article110 UNCLOS (excerpt) reads:

> 1. Except where acts of interference derive from powers conferred by treaty, a warship which encounters on the high seas a foreign ship, other than a ship entitled to complete immunity in accordance with articles 95 and 96, is not justified in boarding it unless there is reasonable ground for suspecting that:

[13] Article 110 sub 3 UNCLOS reads:

> 3. If the suspicions prove to be unfounded, and provided that the ship boarded has not committed any act justifying them, it shall be compensated for any loss or damage that may have been sustained.

[14] Wendel 2007, p. 113.

[15] Guilfoyle 2009, p. 78; Papastavridis 2013, p. 80.

to act against it and the persons on board. The one exception to this is piracy. Article 105 UNCLOS[16] explicitly states that enforcement jurisdiction exists for other States over vessels that are suspected of piracy. As such, Article 105 provides that piracy is a crime over which every State has jurisdiction. In order to use this possibility, domestic legislation must, however, be in place.[17] Whereas some authors, such as Guilfoyle and Papastavridis, adhere to the strict approach of authorities based on Article 110, Heintschel von Heinegg goes a step further and submits that also for the other rights in Article 110, based on the precedent of the piracy articles, 'there are good reasons to assume that those measures may also be taken against a vessel if the suspicions that they are engaged in any of the other activities prove to be well founded'.[18] His view ensures for instance in cases of statelessness of a vessel that enforcement jurisdiction is guaranteed. However, positive this may be, it is clear that enforcement jurisdiction based on Article 110 UNCLOS is not a given and remains under discussion in every particular case.

Fourth, Article 110 UNCLOS is geographically limited to the high seas. Via Article 87 UNCLOS, Article 110 also applies also in the EEZ. For operational purposes during military operations the limits given to warships for conducting these authorities can be further limited to a specific operational area. It does not mean, however, that outside that operational area acting against for instance piracy becomes unlawful. It does, however, mean that a commander will act outside his given military orders. To illustrate this in an international setting, the EUNAVFOR counter-piracy operation *Atalanta* has limited its operational area to up to 500 nm from the Somali coast, which was expanded in 2009 to the Seychelles.[19] If a State wishes to capture and prosecute pirates outside the EU-operational area, it would have to do it outside the EU orders, and base itself on national orders.

---

[16] Article 105 UNCLOS reads:

> On the high seas, or in any other place outside the jurisdiction of any State, every State may seize a pirate ship or aircraft, or a ship or aircraft taken by piracy and under the control of pirates, and arrest the persons and seize the property on board. The courts of the State which carried out the seizure may decide upon the penalties to be imposed, and may also determine the action to be taken with regard to the ships, aircraft or property, subject to the rights of third parties acting in good faith.

[17] The Netherlands Criminal Code has made piracy punishable under Articles 381–385. The Netherlands Criminal Procedural Code in Article 359d opens the possibility that commanders of Netherlands warships are authorized to act against piracy.

[18] Heintschel von Heinegg 2010, p. 389.

[19] Article 1 of the EU Council Joint Action 2008/851/CFSP states:

> 2. The forces deployed to that end shall operate, up to 500 nautical miles off the Somali coast and neighbouring countries, in accordance with the political objective of an EU maritime operation, as defined in the crisis management concept approved by the Council on 5 August 2008.

Fifth, the jurisdictional consequence of a stateless vessel with regard to the exercise of jurisdiction by other States is not entirely clear in international law. Most authors take the view that a vessel without nationality does not breach international law. The notion of statelessness of vessels on the high seas, however, does not sit well with the basic concepts of the international law of the sea. Statelessness goes against the public order of the oceans because no State can exert jurisdiction and take responsibility over such vessels. It is also not an automatism that a stateless vessel is subject to the universal jurisdiction of all States. UNCLOS in this respect goes as far as a right to board and identify a stateless vessel, but does not mention what to do next, if indeed no State can be linked to the vessel. Obviously, jurisdiction on board can be established on other points than only the flag of the vessel, for instance focusing on the persons and establishing jurisdiction based on the nationality principle. Even though this still does not solve the issue of (the lack of) jurisdiction on the vessel itself, chances that a State will object to actions against a stateless vessel are not very probable. One school of thought on this point is, as Den Heijer mentions:

> …the school of thought that ships without a nationality do not enjoy the protection of any State and that, in the absence of competing claims of State sovereignty, any State can apply its domestic laws to a stateless vessel and to that purpose proceed with the boarding, searching and seizure of that vessel.[20]

A balance, therefore, ought to be struck based on the specific circumstances of the case between the totally unwanted consequence of statelessness in which stateless vessels become effectively immune because no one can exert jurisdiction and automatically applying the boarding State's jurisdiction as a standard consequence of statelessness.

Apart from the issue whether statelessness implies that the boarding State can assert jurisdiction over a vessel,[21] another point to note is the purpose behind the authority to board under circumstances of statelessness. Interestingly, in both *Medvedyev* and *So San* the ultimate aim of the boarding of both vessels was not to check whether or not the vessel was in fact stateless, but to stop something else from happening: a criminal act and a weapons delivery. One cannot escape the feeling that the legal framework of statelessness is not used in the scope for what this framework has been set-up to do, namely a very restrictive authority to check the nationality of the vessel. In a restrictive approach, the consequence of statelessness can be that the vessel and crew is detained in order to further determine who is responsible for the vessel. If the crew is suspected of any criminal acts during a check on nationality, it should be referred to the State that has jurisdiction once it is established which State has responsibility over the vessel, or otherwise via the nationality of the crew. Statelessness should, however, not be used to gain

---

[20] Den Heijer 2011, p. 236.

[21] Guilfoyle notes that this issue remains unclear. He concludes that some States, including the US, take the approach that jurisdiction may be asserted over a stateless vessel, which is a practice that, as he states, is unprotested. Guilfoyle 2009, pp. 341–342.

access on board a vessel for the purpose of stopping other illegal activities actions on board, but for which there is no legal ground to board at hand.

9.4.2 The SUA Provisions

The SUA provisions are quite detailed regarding the scope of authority during the visit. The purpose of the visit within the SUA framework is to act against the offences stated in Article 3 SUA Convention and Article 4 sub 5 SUA Protocol. The latter provision has been added to make punishable acts by *any* person from or with a ship (the ship used as a weapon) which also involves WMD. Article 5 of the SUA Protocol requires States to make these SUA offences punishable under their domestic laws and Article *3quater* mentions *any* person, the State who acts on the basis of the SUA Convention will have enforcement jurisdiction on the basis of their domestic laws. Also, the SUA framework requires reasonable suspicion to be able to exercise the right, which is codified in Article 8*bis* sub 4 of the SUA Protocol. Article 8*bis* sub 5 of the SUA Protocol allows a State to take appropriate measures with regard to that ship which may include the stopping, boarding and searching the ship, its cargo and persons on board and questioning the persons on board, *only* in order to determine if an offence is being is about to be committed. Article 8*bis* sub 5 therefore merely authorizes another State to determine whether a SUA offence has taken place, but does not authorize primary enforcement jurisdiction. In this respect, the article follows the same construct of Article 110 UNCLOS. When an offence has indeed taken place, with regard to jurisdiction over the offenses Article 8*bis* sub 6–8 of the Protocol are of importance. Once it is found that such an offence as indeed taken place, sub 6 then goes on to state that the flag State may authorize the requesting party to detain the ship, cargo and persons pending receipt of disposition instructions from the flag State. Sub 8 underlines that the flag State has primary jurisdiction, but can waive its jurisdiction to allow for taking measures by another State. In summary, in the SUA-framework the flag State stays in charge of the issue, but has through the means of an international agreement quickened the process for boarding to consent to boarding under specific circumstances.

The geographical limitation of the right of visit based on the SUA Protocol is connected to Article 4 of the SUA Convention. Paragraph one reads: ‘This Convention applies if the ship is navigating or is scheduled to navigate into, through or from waters beyond the outer limit of the territorial sea of a single State, or the lateral limits of its territorial sea with adjacent States.’ It suggests that it not only applies in the maritime zones outside the territorial sea but applies also to vessels that are within the territorial sea of another State and are scheduled to navigate into other maritime zones.

9.4.3 Bilateral Ship Boarding Agreements Between the US and Other States

As noted in Chap. 3, bilateral ship boarding agreements between the US and other States are pursued in the context of PSI and SC Res. 1540 (2004). Its scope, therefore, is related to the suppression of activities related to WMD and its purpose is to engage in operational agreements that authorize boarding of foreign-flagged vessels to interdict WMD in order to disrupt the trafficking of WMD.[22] As of 2015, the US has concluded agreements with 11 different States.[23] That does not seem much, but it is argued by the US that these eleven States account for 60% of the world's tonnage. The authorities under which a boarding can take place differ per agreement. As mentioned in Chap. 8, Kraska and Pedrozo state that the bilateral ship boarding agreements (BSA) make use of three different models with regard to the authorization to board the vessel.[24] First is that the State will have to give consent. Second is that consent is presumed to have been given, when there is no reaction of the flag State within a certain period after the request. And third is the model that boarding authority is presumed within a certain period of time only if the State cannot confirm the registry of the vessel. The BSA list a number of conditions that forges the right during the visit in these circumstances. Firstly, boarding is only allowed outside the territorial sea of any State. Secondly, the threshold of reasonable grounds is introduced. There must be a reasonable ground to suspect that the vessel is engaged in illicit trafficking of WMD. The BSA mention in Article 1 (definitions) that: '"Suspect vessel" means a vessel used for commercial or private purposes in respect of which there are reasonable grounds to suspect it is engaged in proliferation by sea.' Third, the BSA also consider the jurisdiction over detained vessel, cargo, other items or persons on board the vessel. The principle is that primary jurisdiction remains with the flag State and the boarding party effectively operates on behalf of the flag State. It is still for the flag State to decide how to proceed further once action has been taken.

9.5 Self-Defence and the Right of Visit

In Chap. 6 two approaches were noted as to how self-defence is argued as a legal basis for MIO. First, the traditional approach in which the use of force in self-defence triggers the situation of an armed conflict, to which the law of armed conflict applies. And second, the approach in which self-defence is argued as a legal

[22] Kraska and Pedrozo 2013, pp. 785–787.

[23] Antigua and Barbuda, Bahamas, Belize, Croatia, Cyprus, Liberia, Malta, Marshall Islands, Mongolia, Panama, St. Vincent and the Grenadines. See www.state.gov/t/isn/c27733.htm. All the BSA have also been published on this website.

[24] Kraska and Pedrozo 2013, p. 788.

basis to stop vessels that carry WMD or terrorists. The following paragraphs will first go into the right of visit regulated by the law of naval warfare in particular. It will then place some remarks in the context of the second use of self-defence, which arguably could be called 'self-defence right of visit' or 'NIAC right of visit'.

9.5.1 The Belligerent Right of Visit and Search

The law of naval warfare is a specialized subset of rules in the law of armed conflict that applies during international armed conflict at sea. They regulate naval warfare issues such as blockades, contraband, hospital ships and the protection of wounded and shipwrecked at sea. It also includes the law of maritime neutrality. The law of naval warfare also contains the belligerent right of visit and search. There is no modern treaty[25] that explicitly codifies this right, although it is implied in some provisions of the law of naval warfare.[26] The belligerent right of visit and search is however a longstanding and accepted right for States during international armed conflict. Pyke, in his treatise on the law of contraband in 1915 mentions that:

> The right of visiting and searching merchant ships upon the high seas, whatever be the ships, whatever be the cargoes, whatever be the destinations, is an incontestable right of the lawfully commissioned cruisers of a belligerent nation'...the right is equally clear in practice, for practice is uniform and universal upon the subject.[27]

Also Colombos opines that the belligerent right of visit is uncontested.[28] The practice in the 1980–1988 Iran-Iraq war, as Gioia and Ronzitti mention: 'has clearly demonstrated that belligerents still enjoy the right to visit and search neutral merchant vessels in order to ascertain whether they are carrying contraband of war'.[29] And even more currently, during the Iraq War of 2003, US naval forces operated under the law of naval warfare and relied upon the belligerent right of visit and search.[30] Point 3 of *Special Warning no. 121* for the Persian Gulf promulgated by the US on 20 March 2003 also used wording that indicates such a use:[31]

---

[25] It is mentioned, however, in historical treaties. See Heintschel von Heinegg 1995.

[26] In, for instance, provisions of the (unratified) London Declaration of 1909, the Hague Convention (XI) relative to certain restriction with regard to the exercise of the right of capture in naval war of 1907 and the Paris Declaration of 1856, there is mention of capture, rather than explicitly expressing that there is a belligerent right of visit and search. Article 63 of the London Declaration (resistance to search) specifically mentions search.

[27] Pyke 1915, pp. 196–197.

[28] Colombos 1962, p. 712.

[29] Gioia and Ronzitti 1992, p. 232.

[30] It appears also that the US Coast Guard vessels during OIF have made use of the right. See Tripsas et al. 2004.

[31] Special warnings are warnings issued by the US to alert the maritime community of risks for maritime shipping in maritime zones. It can also contain information on what to expect when a merchant vessel is entering an operational area.

> 3. Vessels operating in the Middle East, Eastern Mediterranean Sea, Red Sea, Gulf of Oman, Arabian Sea, and Arabian Gulf are subject to query, being stopped, boarded and searched by US/Coalition warships operating in support of operations against Iraq. Vessels found to be carrying contraband bound for Iraq or carrying and/or laying naval mines are subject to detention, seizure and destruction. This notice is effective immediately and will remain in effect until further notice.[32]

In short, the belligerent right of visit and search is a longstanding right and has certainly not become an obsolete means to exercise maritime interception. With regard to the scope and purpose of the belligerent right of visit and search, a number of remarks can be made.

First, the belligerent right of visit and search is a procedural right. It allows enforcing the law of contraband, blockade and un-neutral service and is primarily applicable to neutral merchant vessels, but also to hospital ships.[33] Arguably, this right also exists in relation to enemy merchant vessels and against all vessels that are breaching a blockade. This is because the view that enemy merchant vessels and blockade-runners can be captured implies inevitably that as matter of practical circumstances, they can also be visited, although they do not need to be searched.[34] The same point of view is taken in the *San Remo Manual*, that in its rule 118 on the right of visit and search does not distinguish between neutral and enemy merchant vessels, and adds in the commentary that its drafters did not hesitate to acknowledge the right to 'visit and search all merchant vessels, be they enemy or neutral'.[35] Arguably, therefore, two different types of belligerent rights of visit can be distinguished. The first is explicit and against neutral merchant vessels for the purpose of finding contraband or to determine whether a vessel is engaged in un-neutral services. The second is implied in the fact that enemy merchant vessels and blockade runners can be captured, implying a visit necessary to take control over the vessel.

Second, the belligerent right of visit and search is a right for belligerent warships and is only applicable in international armed conflicts. With regard to the latter point, it is still the general consensus that the law of naval warfare is only applicable in interstate conflict.[36] Interestingly, this point of departure immediately puts a stop to the application of this right in most of the contemporary conflicts, which tend to be non-international in character.

---

[32] Special Warning no. 121 Persian Gulf is reproduced in Kraska and Pedrozo 2013, p. 95.

[33] Colombos 1962, para 870.

[34] Heintschel von Heinegg (2003, p. 407) states that:

> Enemy merchant vessels may not be attacked unless there is sufficient proof that they serve a function that renders them legitimate military objectives. They are, however, subject to visit, search and capture, unless they are in neutral waters.

[35] San Remo Manual, Commentary, p. 196.

[36] Heintschel von Heinegg 2010; Kraska 2010a, b.

Third, the belligerent right of visit and search is not a right that can be used in general, but is a right connected to the seizure of contraband or in relation to un-neutral service. And when one agrees that in the context of capturing blockade-runners and enemy merchant vessels such a right is implied, it is only limited to those purposes. It is, as Higgins states; 'not a substantive and independent right, it is a means justified by the end.'[37]

Fourth, and most important for maritime interceptions, the operational advantage of this right is that the Party to the conflict does not need prior authorization from the flag State to board the vessel. The underlying rationale of this right is based upon the consideration that States do not take responsibility over the trade in which their nationals are engaged.[38] A vessel that carries contraband does not, in principle, endanger the neutrality of the flag State.

Fifth, the threshold to use this right is that the commander of the visiting warship needs to have a reasonable ground for suspicion that a vessel is not neutral, either by carrying contraband or by flying the enemy's flag, or by breaching a blockade. The *San Remo Manual* notes in its Chapter V, Rule 118, that in order to exercise the right of visit during a conflict, reasonable grounds for suspicion must exist.[39] The commentary to Rule 118 adds that, 'The right of visit and search may not be exercised arbitrarily. An unrestricted practice of visit and search has never been considered to be in accordance with international law.'

Sixth, the capture of goods or vessels is subject to a further judicial scrutiny by a prize court or an equivalent competent judiciary body. Many of the doctrines and military manuals still mention that the fruits of the visit and search must be put before a prize court. Whether national legislation will still have prize court regulations, however, may be less obvious today. A prize court adjudicates the lawfulness of the seizure of the confiscated vessel and goods. Only after the prize court has given its judgment, will the goods or vessels change ownership. As there is still no international prize court, all prizes are brought before a national court.[40] Although the Helsinki Principles on the law of maritime neutrality have adopted a principle which states that: confiscation without a prize court decision is prohibited,[41] some States appear to deviate from this position.[42]

---

[37] Higgins 1926, p. 43.

[38] Colombos 1962, para 866.

[39] Rule no. 118 SRM reads:

> In exercising their legal rights in an international armed conflict at sea, belligerent warships and military aircraft have a right to visit and search merchant vessels outside neutral waters where there are reasonable grounds for suspecting that they are subject to capture.

[40] Although Hague Convention no XII (1907) was supposed to establish an international prize court to adjudicate prizes in appeal, the Convention has never come into working.

[41] Paragraph 5.2.2. Helsinki Principles.

[42] The UK Manual on the Law of Armed Conflict (2005) mentions that:

> The United Kingdom has not used prize courts for many years and unlikely to do so in the future. Where a vessel or aircraft is captured by United Kingdom armed forces it will

As a last and seventh point to note here is that the belligerent right of visit and search is a *right*. This means that there is no obligation to use it. If, politically or operationally, it may be opportune to decide not to use it and instead use the peacetime right of visit, or perhaps an extant right of visit based on a UN Security Council mandate, a State is free to do so. Examples from practice of this are mentioned in Chap. 3 in relation to the right of visit during Operation *Iraqi Freedom*.

In sum, the belligerent right of visit and search seems in first instance be a far reaching authority in the sense that it does not need the consent of the flag State to be applied to foreign-flagged vessels, which makes it a very effective tool for warships to use. It is however also restricted to a number of ways. And if one delves deeper into the legal weeds of the law of naval warfare, even more limitations become apparent.[43]

9.5.2 The Subregimes of the Law of Naval Warfare

As mentioned above, the belligerent right of visit and search is a means to ascertain other rights of the law of naval warfare and as such connected to a number of subsets of the law of naval warfare. The main subsets are the law of contraband, the law of blockade, the law of un-neutral service and the law that allows capturing enemy merchant vessels. What these subsets have in common is that they primarily aim to limit the opponent's margin of economic means during international armed

---

normally be deemed to be the property of Her Majesty's government UK Ministry of Defence, *The Manual of the Law of Armed Conflict* (Oxford, 2005), para. 12.78.1. It is, however, remarkable that this paragraph is not repeated in the chapter on maritime operations.

The US and Israel still appear to accept the validity of having prize courts. Israel has submitted the Finnish vessel *Estelle*, captured while trying to breach the Gaza blockade in 2012, before a court (see http://opiniojuris.org/2014/01/13/lieblich-guest-post-yet-another-front-israelipalestinian-lawfare-international-prize-law/). According to Brown, during the Iraq War in 2003, the US prepared for prize taking and assigned competent court to do so. In 2002, The Netherlands has deleted from its domestic laws the competency of the *Hoge Raad (the Supreme Court of the Netherlands)* to judge prize cases, even though the Netherlands Maritime doctrine of the Netherlands Navy still recognizes the need for prize courts. See more elaborately on the current state of Dutch Prize Law, Fink 2013. The Hoge Raad (The Supreme Court of the Netherlands) has only once made use of its prize law competency. This took place in the *Nyugat*-case (1956) that concerned the capture made by the Netherlands Navy (*Hr. Ms. Kortenaer*) during the beginning of the Second World War in the Far East.

[43] For instance with regard to convoying neutral merchant vessels by neutral warships and the position that reasonable suspicion must exist that a vessel is carrying contraband at that very moment, not a reasonable suspicion that the vessel has carried contraband but is now empty and is already on its way back to a neutral port.

conflict: They regulate economic warfare. Simply said, blockade and the capture of enemy merchant vessels aims to stop vessels, the law of contraband aims to stop goods, and un-neutral service focuses on stopping persons and communication on board neutral-flagged vessels. The following paragraphs briefly touch upon the essence of these subsets.

9.5.2.1 The Law of Contraband

Neutrality is breached when a neutral vessel carries goods that are considered to be contraband by one of the belligerent parties *and* is bound for the enemy.[44] To capture a neutral ship or goods, these two conditions need therefore to be considered. The latter condition of destination has been developed into the 'doctrine of continuous voyage', which accepts that goods that *ultimately* end up in enemy hands can be captured, even if the vessel with contraband may sail into the direction of a neutral harbor. If the goods from there will be transferred to an enemy destination, they can be considered as contraband. Interestingly, the condition of destination excludes capturing vessel that sail *from* enemy territory. With regard to the first condition relating to contraband, belligerent parties should make public which goods they consider contraband, although the practice of publishing contraband lists and the distinction between different types of contraband seems under debate.[45] The law of contraband does not focus on persons. When during the inspection the vessel's cargo appears to be contraband, the belligerent warship can capture the goods and vessel and bring them before a prize court that adjudicates the status of captured goods and vessel. The consequence of carrying contraband, therefore, is the loss of goods, and possibly the vessel.[46]

Inspecting neutral vessels for contraband is not geographically limited under the law of naval warfare, other than that it is only allowed in the maritime areas where military operations can take place. These are the maritime areas outside the territorial sea of a neutral State. Visit and search by belligerents is not allowed in neutral waters. In practice, the belligerent right of visit and search could, for operational and political reasons, be limited to the proximity of the theater of operations. Furthermore, the *ius ad bellum* may have a limiting impact in the sense that the proportionality principle could limit, for instance, the extent as to which visit and search could be conducted in waters far removed from the actual theatre of operations.[47] Lastly, a number of exceptions to the belligerent right of visit and search

[44] The conditions of contraband and destination is also underlined in paras 5.2.1. and 5.2.3. of the Helsinki Principles on the law of maritime neutrality (1997).

[45] Gioia and Ronzitti 1992, p. 232. They mention that legal writers opine that the belligerent practice of enlarging contraband lists to comprise all goods considered to be useful for the enemy makes the difference between absolute and conditional obsolete.

[46] Conference report Council on Ocean Law and the Law of the Sea Institute 1988, p. 306.

[47] See on the effect of *ius ad bellum* on *ius in bello* Gill 2015.

against certain particular vessels exist. One such exception exists when neutral vessels are sailing under convoy of a neutral warship.[48]

9.5.2.2 The Law of Un-Neutral Service

Whereas the law of contraband focuses on goods, the law of un-neutral service focuses on persons and dispatches carried for one of the belligerents.[49] An example is the carrying of persons or troops who belong to the armed forces of the enemy State by a neutral merchant vessel.[50] The scope of activities that is considered as un-neutral, however, is unclear. Furthermore, the line between un-neutral service and directly taking part in hostilities (DPH) may also be hard to draw. One dividing line, however, may be that DPH focuses on activities of persons, and un-neutral service focuses on activities of the vessel, although the vessel is operated by persons. The difference in consequences between the two concepts is, however, significant. In the first situation a vessel may not subject to direct attack, whereas in the latter this may be possible. It thus depends on the nature of the service that is rendered by the neutral vessel. Articles 45–47 of the (unratified) London Declaration give examples of what can be viewed as un-neutral service by a neutral vessel.[51] These provisions do not resolve the former question but at least underline that, as a minimum, belligerents can take action (including the boarding and seizure) against neutral vessels that display such assistance to the enemy.

9.5.2.3 The Law of Blockade

A right of visit is also implied in the law of blockade. A blockading belligerent force can stop and capture vessels that breach or attempt to breach a belligerent blockade, under the condition that the blockade is lawfully established. To establish a blockade in a lawful manner, it must be notified, conducted impartially and effective.[52] Apart from the one rule in the Declaration of Paris (1856) on effectiveness,[53] the law of blockade is not codified, but rather based on customary law.

---

[48] Rule 120 SRM, Article 61 LD. Heintschel von Heinegg 1994, pp. 5–34.

[49] Tucker 1955, p. 318.

[50] In the *Asama Maru* incident (1940) the UK took the position that even persons that were not yet military, but were returning to their homeland and could possible take up military service could also be taken prisoner. The Japanese Government protested against this view. See Dunham 1997.

[51] E.g. transporting passengers that are embodied in the armed forces of the enemy, gathering intelligence for the enemy or transporting a military detachment of the enemy.

[52] See generally on the conditions of establishing belligerent blockades, Heintschel von Heinegg 2012; Fink 2011b.

[53] Which, in rule number 4, states that a blockade must be effective for it to be established lawfully.

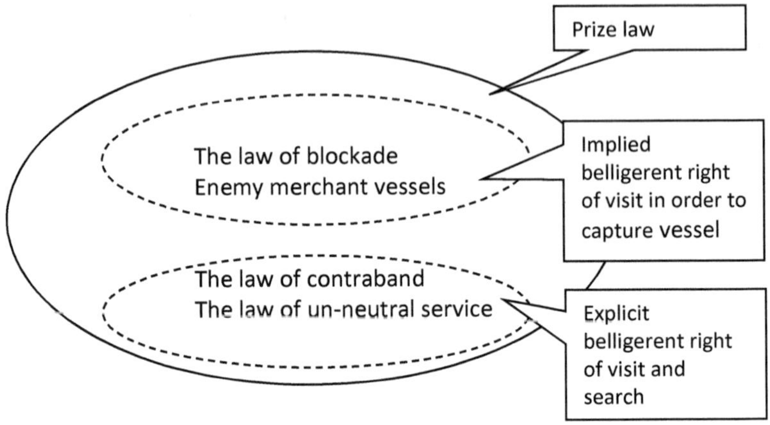

Fig. 9.2 Relationship between prize law, belligerent visit and search and implied belligerent right of visit and search (*Source* M. Fink)

The *London Declaration* (1909) attempted to codify the rules on blockade,[54] but the Declaration remains unratified. Although no codified nor specific rule exists that expresses the belligerent right of visit within the context of blockade, the right clearly exists implicitly as vessels that breach or attempt to breach a blockade are liable to capture.[55] The right of visit must be implied in order to stop a vessel from breaching the blockade. Captured vessels are brought before a competent court that can deal with prize cases. Although the question of application of the law of blockade by Israel against the Gaza was widely contested, which produced several reports and many scholarly articles, the right to visit a foreign-flagged vessel within the context of a blockade was not (Fig. 9.2).[56]

9.5.2.4 Enemy Merchant Vessels

The law of naval warfare accepts that not only enemy warships or State vessels are subject to capture, but also enemy merchant vessels.[57] Capturing enemy vessels, much in the same way the law of blockade does, implies an authority to board the vessel to physically enable the capture of the vessel. It is obvious that no advance consent is needed to capture an enemy merchant vessel. A number of exemptions to

[54] One attempt of codifying the law of blockade can be found in the first 21 articles of the London Declaration (1909).

[55] SRM, rule 126(f), Articles 14, 17, 20 LD.

[56] A/HRC/15/21, for instance in para 56, by stating that 'Thus, if there is no blockade, the only lawful basis for intercepting the vessel would be …' implies that a right of visit is accepted within the context of blockade.

[57] See Heintschel von Heinegg 2013; Section IV SRM.

capturing enemy merchant vessels however exist. Examples are hospital ships, vessels (under conditions agreed to by the belligerent parties) that carry relief goods for the civilian population or carry cultural property, cartel ships, vessels charged with religious or non-military scientific activities, and small coastal fishing vessels employed in local trade, all under the condition that they do not misuse their exempted status to support military operations.[58] Although specific enemy merchant vessels may be exempt from *capture*, the vessel can, however, still be visited and searched. In the event that there is no certainty as to the character of the vessel, the right of belligerent visit and search allows for inspection of the vessel to ascertain its neutral character or its exempted status.[59]

9.6 Non-International Armed Conflicts

As mentioned above, the general point of view is that the law of naval warfare does not apply to non-international armed conflicts. Against the background of adapting maritime operations to counter contemporary threats some begin to propose its applicability to non-international armed conflicts, albeit with certain modifications. McLaughlin for instance already noted that: 'I think it uncontentious, for example, that a State may impose a blockade…against territory substantially controlled by a terrorist group which is also an OAG [organized armed group] engaged in an armed conflict with that State….'[60] Even Heintschel von Heinegg, who usually appears to be straightforward in his non-applicability of the law of naval warfare to NIAC, has stated that the law of naval warfare can be applied in a NIAC, 'albeit modified, between parties to the conflict'.[61] The San Remo Manual noted the possible application of the law of naval warfare in NIAC as follows:

> Although the provisions of this Manual are primarily meant to apply to international armed conflicts at sea, this has intentionally not been expressly indicated…in order not to dissuade the implementation of these rules in non-international armed conflicts involving naval operations.[62]

Apart from academic opinions spurred by the evolving nature of conflict and discussion of practice derived from the Gaza blockade and more historical cases,[63] the view of non-application in a NIAC remains the starting point in recent debates on application of the law of naval warfare. The Israeli blockades against Hezbollah in the Summer War of 2006 and against Hamas since 2009 did trigger some debate

---

58 See Article 4 Hague Convention no. XI (1907), Article 25 GCII and Section 136 SRM.

59 Section 135 SRM. Heintschel von Heinegg 2013, p. 495.

60 McLaughlin 2011, p. 403.

61 Heintschel von Heinegg 2007, p. 213.

62 SRM, p. 73.

63 During the Algerian Crisis of 1955–1962 in which France, based on self-defence, controversially used the belligerent visit and search during a NIAC. See Papastavridis 2013, pp. 95–97.

on the applicability of the law of naval warfare, in particular the law of blockade to be more precise, to NIACs,[64] but it has not yet matured in any way that we can solidly conclude that the traditional standpoint has actually changed. The most important conclusion for maritime interception is that the belligerent right of visit and search does not apply in a NIAC. This obviously poses challenges in modern conflict that is often characterized as such and is not restricted to the land territory. Also naval forces can therefore be confronted with a situation that is characterized as a NIAC and a non-state opponent, in which there is no generally accepted right to visit foreign-flagged vessels in order to take action against these non-state actors at sea. Two examples from practice are Operation *Enduring Freedom* and Operation *Active Endeavour*.

9.6.1 Operation Enduring Freedom

With regard to Operation *Enduring Freedom* States have reacted differently on both the issue of the legal characterization of the conflict at sea and its consequences for the right of visit. It is widely viewed that the legal character of the conflict in Afghanistan changed after the Taliban had been brought to a fall and the *Loya Jirga* was convened in June 2002. The military operations were then in support of a newly chosen Afghan Government. From that point onwards, the status of the armed conflict changed from an international to a non-international armed conflict.[65] If indeed an international armed conflict existed before June 2002, it was during a period of only about 7 months.[66] From the point of view of the limited application of the law of naval warfare only in international armed conflict, the naval dimension would lose a valuable tactical tool for deterring terrorists at sea if the conflict were to be considered a non-international armed conflict.

Participating warships in the OEF-coalition boarded and searched merchant vessels for possible terrorists. States, however, had different views on which right of visit applied, which is connected to the question of applicable legal regime. The UK viewed that the legal basis for military force as a reaction to 9/11 was based on Article 51 of the UN Charter, but considered only the land operations in Afghanistan to be conducted under the law of armed conflict. The approach was taken that the factual situation at sea was not considered an armed conflict situation. Because the UK chose this position, it meant that the belligerent right of visit could not be applied by British warships and that any persons captured would not be prisoners of war. The UK thus considered that parts of the same military campaign

[64] Obviously, questions as to whether Israel invoked the right of self-defence against Hezbollah or Lebanon, or how symbiotic Al-Qaida and the Taliban were considered all play a role. See on these issues; Ruys 2010, pp. 450–457; Ducheine and Pouw 2009; Gill 2003, p. 26.

[65] See e.g. Pejic 2007, p. 345.

[66] From October 2001 to June 2002.

that operated in a completely different geographical area and contextual situation can be governed by a different legal regime. Brown indicates that the authorities for British warships were not beyond what was authorized under peacetime visit and search.[67] By reliance upon peacetime right of visit, the change of conflict status did not have any effect on the right used.

The Netherlands considered itself to be in an armed conflict with Al Qaida and the Taliban.[68] In contrast to the UK, the Netherlands did not distinguish between land and sea operations and viewed the conflict *as a whole* as an armed conflict. As such, it also considered the law of naval warfare applicable, which opened the door to the belligerent right of visit and search.[69] The Netherlands government in its documents did not explicitly distinguish between an international and a non-international armed conflict. It also did not change the boarding authority after June 2002.[70] The belligerent authority was, however, watered down in the sense that—as a matter of policy rather than law—master's consent was asked before a vessel was boarded. In practice, therefore, a certain watering down of the authorities was made to avoid possible unnecessary controversy.[71] The Netherlands appears not to be the only State who thought it could use the belligerent right of visit. According to the Canadian Rear-Admiral Bob Davidson the Canadian naval

[67] Brown 2003, pp. 303–307.

[68] Letters to parliament, 27 September 2004.

[69] Eindevaluatie CTF 150, *Ministerie van Defensie*, 18 September 2006, p. 4.

[70] The *Eindevaluatie CTF 150* (18 September 2006) mentions (in Dutch):

> *De status van gewapend conflict heeft tot gevolg dat op het maritieme deel van OEF het zeeoorlogsrecht van toepassing is. Dit vormt dan ook de juridische grondslag voor het kunnen uitvoeren van boarding operaties, dat een wezenlijk onderdeel is van het maritieme optreden. Onder het zeeoorlogsrecht zijn combattanten bevoegd om neutrale scheepvaart te controleren, om vast te stellen of zij ook daadwerkelijk neutraal zijn. Daarbij wordt onder andere gekeken naar de scheepspapieren en de lading, zodat kan worden bezien of er geen mensen of goederen worden vervoerd ter ondersteuning van de tegenpartij.*
>
> *[...]...Zoals gebruikelijk bij deelname aan OEF heeft Nederland de ROE voor de Nederlandse militairen zelf geschreven en ter beschikking gesteld aan de andere coalitiepartners. Hoewel CTF 150 deel uitmaakt van OEF en derhalve, zoals gesteld, deelneemt aan een gewapend conflict is alleen het mogen boarden van scheepvaart daarvan een weerslag in de ROE.*

[71] During the beginning of the operation The Netherlands first did not authorize participating warships to board other vessels, but this changed during the course of the operation. See Leijnse and Weijne 2002, pp. 149–154. Also, in the *Letters to Parliament* of 27 September 2004 it is stated that:

> *Bij inspecties treden overigens alle maritieme eenheden van de operatie Enduring Freedom zoveel mogelijk op met instemming van de vlaggenstaat van het te onderzoeken schip.* [Inspections will be conducted as far as possible with the consent of the flag State.]

contribution to OEF was also able to board vessels based on the law of naval warfare.[72]

With no sufficiently official public source available, it is hard to determine which right of visit the US used for its boardings in OEF. Although the general guidance for the US in OEF was that hostilities in Afghanistan were to be in accordance with the law of war, the US did not—systematically, it appears[73]—articulate the legal regime under which the boardings conducted under OEF took place. It kept underlining that its operations were based on the right of self-defence.[74] Also the *Special Warning no. 120*, published shortly after the 11 September attacks, underlined that US forces were to exercise appropriate measures of self-defence if warranted by the circumstances. It did not use any law of naval warfare terminology.[75] Views on the legal regime applied by the US range from a right of visit directly based on self-defence,[76] to assumptions that the belligerent visit and search was used, primarily because the US considered itself in a state of armed conflict.[77] One reference to the actual authorities for US warship on visits is found with Van Dyke, who states: 'Attempts have been made to undertake these boarding operations with the consent of the masters of the vessels, but the US notification made to the maritime industry made it clear that vessels suspected of transporting or assisting bin Laden and senior al Qaeda leadership would be subject to the use of force to compel a boarding.'[78] If this is an accurate statement, one interpretation could be that (and leaving aside for the moment debate on master's or flag state consent) the US interception operations in OEF appear firstly not to overstep the peacetime right of visit, but in situations where Al Qaida is actually spotted, the fact that the person is on board foreign vessel does not stop US military in what is viewed as a necessary and proportional action of self-defence.[79] Here, it seems that the right to visit is, interestingly enough, derived from the *ius ad bellum* itself.

---

[72] Davidson 2008/9, p. 18. But see also Papastravidis 2013, p. 92 who appears to opine the belligerent right of visit and search also applies during a NIAC.

[73] Tabori-Szabo 2015.

[74] Klein 2011, p. 274. Interestingly, with regard to this operation Klein refers to the specific legal basis for action, whereas in fact the specific legal regime may be meant, as the legal basis for the military operation has been clear from the outset.

[75] *Special Warning no. 120* is printed in Kraska and Pedrozo 2013, p. 95. They also explain that *Special Warnings* are used by the US to publish information about potential hazards that are caused by the political climate (at p. 88).

[76] O'Rourke 2003.

[77] Hodgkinson (2007) mentions that LIOs are legitimate as an exercise of self-defence as part of armed conflict. My assumption is that the latter part of the phrase implies the use of the law of naval warfare. In discussing the issue with several US Navy JAGs this point has not become any clearer.

[78] Van Dyke 2004, p. 25.

[79] This view is also coined by Wendel. Wendel 2007, p. 32.

9.6.2 *Operation* Active Endeavour

The 9/11 attacks induced NATO to take naval action. In the early stages of OAE, the NATO's naval forces were not authorized to board vessels. This authorization was, however, acquired at a later stage of the operation, in 2004.[80] Interestingly, NATO's anti-terrorist operation OAE, although based on the collective self-defence provisions of Article 5 of the NATO Treaty, authorized participating warships only to board when both flag State and master consent existed. The following text is found in a NATO report on the visits-regime of OAE:

> 105. Once a suspicious ship is identified, OAE assets could hail the ship, request to board, and eventually track the ship into territorial waters where a properly alerted national maritime authority would take appropriate action. Boarding takes place only with the compliance of the captain of the ship and the flag State, in accordance with international law. If the captain of the suspicious ship does not wish to be boarded, NATO forces will follow the vessel and alert the port in which it is coming to rest, whose authorities will have the legal right to examine it.[81]

Lieutenant Ioannis Kizanis (Hellenic Navy) mentions the visits regime in OAE:

> Initially the main task of NATO's naval units was to "hail" merchant vessels transiting their patrolling areas (i.e., to call them on a VHF channel, ask questions about the ships' identity, cargo, and activity, visually identify them, and monitor their movement for as long they were in sensor range). In other words, NATO's activities were limited to the right of approach. This information was then related to CCMAR Naples, Italy and NATO's shipping center in Northwood, UK. In April 2003 the mission was modified to include compliant boarding operations on suspect vessels, "compliant" in this case meaning with the prior consent of the ships' masters and flag States, which gives the boarding full legitimacy under international law.[82]

Vice-Admiral Cesaretti, commander of OAE in 2005, in his article in the *NATO Review* underlined also that inspection of foreign-flagged vessels were conducted with the consent of both flag and master.[83] There is, however, no official public record available regarding the legal framework on the legal regime used in OAE. The relevant question would be whether NATO considered itself to be in an armed conflict. Possibly, NATO considered that the visits were based on the law of naval warfare, but for various political reasons opted for a very restrictive use of the belligerent right of visit and search. Another reason can be that, despite the fact that Article 5 was invoked, against the background of the actual situation at sea and that NATO actions were an act of solidarity rather than acts of war or the start of actual hostilities against terrorists, it would be problematic to consider that participating

---

[80] NATO Parliamentary Assembly, Committee Reports 2008 Annual Session (158 DSC 08 E bis) —NATO Operations: Current Priorities and Lessons Learned, para 105. At: www.nato-pa.int/default.asp?SHORTCUT=1476.

[81] 158 DSC 08 E BIS—NATO Operations: Current Priorities and Lessons Learned, para 105.

[82] Kizanis 2008.

[83] Cesaretti 2005.

States in this NATO operation were engaged in an armed conflict. Furthermore, even if this would have been the case that NATO states considered themselves to be in an armed conflict, the status of the conflict would have been non-international after June 2002. This bars the possibility of making use of the belligerent right of visit and search.

Whatever decision NATO made in the past to decide not to use the belligerent right of visit and search during OAE, it subsequently fell back upon the peacetime visit and search framework. One legal possibility of boarding of foreign-flagged can be to get consent of the flag State. The multitude of participating States within NATO, however, has generated another discussion which is focused on the master/flag state consent issue. Because individual States within NATO have different opinions on this issue, it may be that the only politically acceptable way within NATO was to authorize visits through consensual boarding with both flag State and master consent. Be that as it may, the approach taken by NATO meant that they did not have to change their ROE because of the changing character of the conflict in 2002.[84]

9.6.3 A NIAC Right of Visit?

The preceding paragraphs on non-international armed conflict and the challenge of the non-existence of a right of visit in NIACs may have given rise to a phenomenon that could be termed 'self-defence right of visit' or 'NIAC right of visit'. Chapter 6 has noted that self-defence is also argued as a direct legal basis to board foreign-flagged vessels, in which the conditions and characteristics of self-defence serve as the legal basis to board the vessel. Chapter 6 noted that the characteristics of the current state of self-defence (not dependent on the will of another State, possible to invoke against non-state actors and an emerged view that acting against non-state actors may, under conditions, not be limited to one's own territory) is balanced against the sovereignty of a State to allow for cross-border operations in situations where a NIAC exists. The consequence of an evolving right of self-defence for maritime interception could be that when the right of self-defence applies to armed attacks conducted by non-state actors, potentially opening the door to action on the territory of a State where the non-state actor is located and operating from, it seems counter-intuitive to say that no right of visit would be available to counter seaborne (threats) of attack. This would, arguably, be both necessary and proportionate if there were clear indications that the vessel was transporting members of the opponent armed group under the flag of a vessel where the group

[84] Differently than OEF, OAE is a NATO operation with a set of rules of engagement (ROE) that has been drafted according to the usual NATO process of ROE drafting. Instead of coalition ROE, such as in OEF where in principle all states bring their national ROE, NATO ROE are usually one set that applies to all participating states, but with possible caveats attached if States for political, legal or operational reasons cannot concur with the ROE.

has a substantial presence, or where the vessel itself has come under the control of the armed group or otherwise posed a threat of attack. Since the right of self-defence does not apply to the territory of third States, one limitation to this is that only vessels of that particular State can be boarded. When a NIAC exists between a non-state actor and State A and State B is involved only in so far as that their territory is used by the non-state actor, the vessels of State B could be the vessels on which a right of visit is allowed. When non-state actors use a vessel from State C, a right of visit would not exist. This limitation however impacts highly on the possible effect of a NIAC right of visit. In the same vein as that third States are exempt from this right, it would also only apply on the high seas and within the territorial and internal waters of State B. In contradiction to the situation in which consent has been given, where States waive their exclusive jurisdiction over a vessel and set the scope of authority for the boarding State, this is not needed in case of a NIAC right of visit.

Another argument to circumvent flag State jurisdiction is that, rather than considering the non-state actor as passenger on board the vessel, the use of the vessel by the non-state actor could be such that the non-state actor has complete and factual control over the vessel and uses it solely for the purpose of its military operations. In this scenario it could be argued that the vessel has lost its link with the flag State, who has *de iure* jurisdiction, but is *de facto* completely under the control of the non-state actor. If the vessel is under the factual control of members of an organized armed group and the vessel is used solely as a means to undertake military operations, it becomes a military objective. When the character of the conflict amounts to a non-international armed conflict and the vessel can lawfully be considered a military objective, attacking it would be a legally permissible action.

Once on board, the actions of the boarding team are regulated by LOAC applicable to non-international armed conflict. Therefore, although such a boarding cannot make use of the more elaborate law of naval warfare, which allows the boarding State to seize goods or vessels, it does require the State to act in accordance with NIAC regulations when on board the vessel. The US asserted that in the war between the US and Al Qaida and its affiliates the Geneva Conventions would not apply because it fitted neither the regime applicable to international armed conflicts nor that of a non-international armed conflict. This approach was later overturned by the US Supreme Court in *Hamdan v. Rumsfeld* (2006) to at least apply the mini-convention of Common Article 3 GCI-IV. Accordingly, Common Article 3 would also apply during a NIAC right of visit.

Important to note is that the purpose for boarding a foreign-flagged vessel is different than the primary purpose of why the right of visit and search exists in an international armed conflict. The belligerent visit and search exists as a means to pursue economic warfare against an opponent in order to enforce the rules on prize, such as the capture of contraband that is destined for the enemy. Quite differently, a NIAC right of visit applies this means against the non-state actor itself or it instruments, such as WMD or the vessel as a military objective. In other words, the right is used directly to be able to act against the opponent. Remotely, it may possibly resemble an implied right of the belligerent in an international armed conflict to board an enemy merchant vessel in order to capture it. Taken this different purpose of the right of visit in non-international armed conflict, it therefore does not make sense to start from the point of view to question whether the existing belligerent right of visit and search in an international armed conflict should apply to a non-international armed conflict.

9.7 The Right of Visit Conferred Through the UN Collective Security System

The collective security system is a legal basis to authorize maritime interception operations. Interestingly, the resolutions of the Council never *explicitly* mention that vessels can be boarded and searched to enforce adopted sanctions. This must be read from the word "inspect" that will in a practical sense include the boarding of the vessel for physical inspection of papers, vessel and cargo. In order to be effective in enforcing sanctions, ultimately, it also means that any illicit goods may be seized. What the exact authority is during a MIO that is conferred through the UN collective security system will depend on the applicable resolutions in the specific conflict. Additionally, where such measures involve persons, human rights law will also be applicable. And where the factual situation of an international armed conflict may arise, the law of naval warfare would start to play a part. As the scope, purpose and content depend on the extant UN resolution, measures may vary per operation. In the early maritime embargo operations since the MIF, a standard phrase was introduced in the resolutions that mandate the scope of the authorities. The resolutions relating to the embargoes of Iraq, Former Yugoslavia, Haiti and Sierra Leone all authorized measures "*to halt all inward and outward*[85] *maritime shipping in order to inspect and verify their cargoes and destinations and to ensure strict implementation*" of applicable resolutions. The embargo with regard to Lebanon and Libya used other language, which related more specifically to the situations at hand in those conflicts.

The above-mentioned phrase in the early resolutions did not contain any threshold of suspicion. This would seem logical, because naval commanders were to halt *all* inward and outward bound shipping in the operational area. The phrase "all inward and outward shipping" implied that every vessel in the given area could be stopped, even if there was no suspicion. Interestingly, the Libya resolution 1973 (2011), did adopt through the use of different wording, a reasonable suspicion standard.[86] In the case of the Libyan embargo, the enforcement power conferred by the Council was therefore different than the 'blanket authority' to halt every vessel,

[85] In the case of Sierra Leone the resolution only authorized inward, not outward bound traffic. See SC Res. 1132 (1997).

[86] See para 13 of SC Res. 1973.

as provided in earlier resolutions. Vessels were not totally denied from entering or leaving Libyan ports. In practice, the reasonable suspicion standard is derived from different factors and may even be satisfied by the fact that vessels were sailing into the direction of one of the Libyan ports.[87] Additionally, the purpose of the visit depends entirely on the text of the resolution. The UNSC can choose from a wide range of sanctions, from sanctioning the influx of arms[88] or oil,[89] to a comprehensive trade embargo,[90] to all types of commodities. In the case of Former Yugoslavia, the embargo started as an arms embargo[91] and then expanded to an export embargo of the import of all commodities and products originating from Serbia and Montenegro.[92] SC Res. 2146 (Libya), on the other hand, was very limited in its purpose. It only allowed the boarding of vessels that illicitly exported crude oil from Libya and only consisted of vessels that had been designated by the UN Libya Sanctions Committee.

The operational level challenge is that there is often a level of uncertainty relating to the goods that can be stopped and taken, which is derived from the text of the resolutions. Resolutions that allow stopping for instance "arms related material" leave a margin to commanders to decide within the context of the conflict what can be considered as arms related material. To illustrate, if the State under sanctions uses a specific type of civilian vehicle to support its military operations, then arguably these are arms related material. But it leads to complex questions. If fuel is not sanctioned, can fuel than still be stopped if there a reasonable certainty that the fuel is used for military vehicles or aircraft? This obviously leads to a need for more detailed understanding of the situation in order to make these decisions. Also interesting is that, whereas maritime embargo operations have always focused on goods, SC Res. 1973 expanded this to include stopping mercenaries at sea who were bound for the conflict.[93] As such, persons have come into the maritime embargo operations arena.

As mentioned, effective enforcement of such resolutions implies that items can also be confiscated. However, notwithstanding this authority, this is a challenge from an operational perspective, because usually the ultimate mission aim is to stop the traffic of sanctioned items, and confiscation at sea poses many logistical challenges, confiscation of goods is not automatically the *modus operandi*. Vessels can

[87] In general vessels will be hailed for inspection and directed to a waiting area to await inspection at sea. For different reasons such as that inspection at sea is not opportune due to weather circumstances, because the suspicion endures but needs more thorough inspection, or that prohibited items are found that need to be of leaded, vessels can be diverted to a port.

[88] E.g. MTF UNIFIL, Libya, Former Yugoslavia and Haiti.

[89] E.g. Libya, after the 2011 conflict, with SC Res. 2146 (2014).

[90] E.g. Iraq. The UNSC established a trade embargo of all products exported from Iraq and Kuwait and sale and supply to Iraq and Kuwait. SC Res. 678 relaxed embargo to allow humanitarian supplies. SC Res. 688 ended embargo against Kuwait.

[91] SC Res. 713 (1991).

[92] SC Res. 757 (1992).

[93] SC Res. 1973 (2011), para 13.

instead also be diverted to a port for inspection of simply turned back so that sanctioned goods will not arrive at the State under sanctions. In the case of MTF UNIFIL, UNIFIL's website mentions that since the operation has started, it hailed 42.500 vessels and referred 1.670 to the Lebanese authorities for further inspection; no mention is made of any boardings that have taken place. Instead: 'All merchant vessels classified "suspect" are monitored and, if inbound to a Lebanese harbor, are referred for inspection to LAF authorities.'[94] Apart from the discussion on the legal basis for the MIO in UNIFIL, a practical reason for this is that it may be easier to let the suspected vessel come into port where it can to be fully inspected in port and where all the technical and legal facilities are present, rather than a potentially high risk visit and search at sea.

Unlike the belligerent or peacetime manifestations of the right of visit, there is no procedure that regulates the confiscation of the goods at sea in these types of operations. Under the law of naval warfare a prize court will judge whether the prize was lawfully taken. In peacetime circumstances a criminal court may judge whether a suspected individual is criminally punishable and the person can instigate civil actions against the State. On land, States will have adopted national laws to enforce the UN sanctions. Such laws may apply at sea, but often will not have specific language to that effect making it essentially a discretionary matter for the operational commander as to how sanctions can be enforced. Article 110 UNCLOS includes a compensation clause for losses and damages if suspicion is determined to be unfounded. Such procedures do not automatically exist in relation to maritime embargo operations when goods are confiscated at sea. If legal proceedings with regard to the confiscation are instigated, one legal avenue to take would be against the State of the intercepting warship. The only known legal case to this author is the *Lido II*-incident, which occurred during the Former Yugoslavia embargo and came before an Italian court, as the vessel was brought within the geographical jurisdiction of Italy.[95] During that court case, the European Court of Justice (ECJ) was asked to advise on the incident, in particular whether a breach of the embargo had actually taken place now that the vessel had not enter the territorial sea of Montenegro but was stopped just before.[96]

The resolutions usually do give some guidelines as the geographical limitations of the embargo authorities. When it mentions that it allows the inspection of inward and outward bound shipping, it implies a certain proximity to the target State is the operational area in order to be able to separate the inward and outward shipping from the rest of the maritime traffic. The geographical and operational circumstances obviously will have an impact on the naval operational areas in which the embargo will take place. In the MIF operation, for example, maritime interception operations were conducted in the Gulf of Aqaba to ensure that no prohibited

---

94 http://unifil.unmissions.org/Default.aspx?tabid=1523.

95 See Chap. 3 on this incident.

96 *ECJ*, case. no. C-177/95, 27 February 1997.

products were indirectly shipped to Iraq.[97] In the case of Libya the resolution was explicit as to geographical limitations by stating that the enforcement authority existed on the high seas,[98] which, as a result, meant that the territorial waters of Libya were outside the embargo zone. NATO, therefore, dedicated a maritime area of operations in the Southern Mediterranean Sea close to Libya itself, but outside the territorial waters.[99] The area is usually also published so that maritime traffic is made aware of in what location they can expect warships to enforce an embargo.[100]

Absent specific limitations derived from the specific resolution, Chapter VII maritime enforcement measures can be conducted both inside and outside the territorial sea of the targeted State. They cannot be conducted within the territorial waters of other States without the permission of the coastal State.[101] In early MEO that resembled maritime peacekeeping operations, questions were raised on operating inside the territorial seas of the State under sanctions. In essence because of the fact that one of the conditions of peacekeeping operations is that the forces operate with the consent of a State within its territory. MIO conducted under Article 42 are coercive peace-enforcing operations and need not have the consent of a State. As said, a-typical in this respect are the UNIFIL and Libya operations. The latter because it explicitly stated that the embargo could be enforced on the high seas, which was interpreted by NATO to the effect that enforcement of the embargo

[97] Fielding 1993, pp. 1220–1221. The area of operations for the MIF was established by special warning no. 80 (1990).

[98] Although this could have resulted into a completely different enforcement model, military planners derived from the resolution a military activity that resembled traditional maritime embargo operations off the coasts of the targeted State. That decision-makers had a traditional maritime-arms-embargo-type operation in mind when the resolution was adopted, can perhaps be deduced from the fact that there was no opposition against the implementation of these military activities; not even by the Sanctions Committee. In the end, NATO's maritime operation was conducted only in the central Mediterranean Sea off the coasts of Libya. An established Maritime Surveillance Area (MSA) tied the actual maritime operations area to the Libyan coast. Notifications were sent out to inform the shipping community of the embargo's existence and to establish a reporting system for vessels that were sailing to or from Libya.

[99] SC Res. 1973 (2011) and 2146 (2014). In the Libyan conflict the UNSC did not so much focus on the area of crisis, but authorized measures that could be taken on the territory of each member State. Before revising some paragraphs of Resolution 1970 through the adoption of Resolution 1973, the Council seemed to consider member States' territory as the main geographical starting point for the embargo. Resolution 1973 then extended to the high seas the powers of member States with regard to the arms embargo (which had already been established by Resolution 1970). For naval enforcement operations at sea, this different 'expanded authority' approach brought the operational effect that the embargo could be enforced in the Libyan territorial sea. See more elaborately on this point, Fink 2011a.

[100] See for instance in the case of Libya: NAVAREA III 170/11 (081415 UTC Apr 11). Following the adoption of SC Res. 2009, NAVAREA III 170/11 was replaced by NAVAREA III 395/11. With NAVAREA 445/11, the MSA was terminated.

[101] During the MIF operations this led to oil smugglers that tried to reach Iranian territorial waters and then proceed to the Strait of Hormuz during which time the MIF was not able to stop them. See Shaw 1999, p. 5.

could not take place within the territorial sea of Libya.[102] The former because the resolution is construed on a double legal basis in order to support to Lebanese authorities. Chapter 5 has touched upon the discussion on the exact legal basis for MTF UNIFIL, which in practice is not challenged because apparently no vessels are boarded. Instead, information on suspected vessels is transferred to the Lebanese authorities to deal with the vessel in port. Because the Area of Maritime Operations (AMO) of UNIFIL lies both in the territorial sea and on the high seas (43 nm wide from the coastline and 110 nm long), UNIFIL and Lebanon have made detailed arrangements where in the AMO UNIFIL is allowed to take measures.[103] UNIFIL units only operate within the zones that are in the territorial sea on request of Lebanon.[104] These circumstances signify that UNIFIL naval forces can only conduct operations within the Lebanese territorial sea at the request of the designated authorities.

9.7.1 All Necessary Means

More challenging in terms of understanding the scope of authority during visits that are authorized by the collective security system, is when the UNSC does not explicitly authorize the enforcement of sanctions at sea, but when a MIO is based on the wording of *all necessary means*. As was discussed in Chap. 5, it is widely accepted that the phrase *all necessary means* implies that the mandate includes using military force to fulfill the mission as an ultimate means. On the level of coercive measures all necessary means can also be translated into the need to visit and search vessels in the pursuit of the mandate. One argument to support this is that because lethal means are ultimately possible, lesser means such as maritime

[102] In the case of Libya, the restriction to the high seas resulted in a gap in which vessels could move prohibited materiel from one city to another through the territorial sea only, or entered the Libyan territorial sea through the territorial seas of the neighboring States. When, however, one looks at the geographical limitation of the arms embargo in a wider perspective, including the whole mandate of SC Res. 1973, one also ends up bringing to light some discrepancy with other authorized operations. The mandate to protect civilians under para 4 of the same resolution, for instance, does not state that enforcement operations have only to take place outside the Libyan territory. On the contrary, this part of the mandate solely focuses on the territory of Libya, which also includes the territorial sea. Maritime operations carried out under this part of the mandate—as long as they would not turn into occupation operations—were allowed to be implemented in the Libyan territorial waters. Since para 4 of Resolution 1973 authorized all necessary means to protect civilians and civilian-populated areas, arguably this could have also been an authority to enter the Libyan territorial sea. However, for the interception operations to be legitimately carried out, the latter should be aimed at stopping a threat to civilians and civilian-populated areas, and not at enforcing UN sanctions.

[103] Haussler 2011, pp. 161–211.

[104] *Kamerbrief inzake beantwoording schriftelijke vragen over de maritime bijdrage aan UNIFIL* (Letters to parliament answering written questions on the maritime support to UNIFIL), 11 October 2006.

interception operations may arguably also fall within the scope of the mandate. But in contrast to explicitly authorized enforcement, in these cases there is no detailed guidance at all on how and against whom maritime interception operations may be conducted. The filling in of the detailed purpose, scope and content of authority is basically left to the State or the commander that is interpreting the mandate, against the further legal environment of applicable legal regimes. If the operational situation necessitates the authority to stop fuel from coming into a State which will end up to supporting the fighting capacity of the opponent, or to stop individuals that would likely take part in the conflict, would *all necessary means* suffice to take those measures? This example could lead to indirect economic sanctions, which are usually provided for through a resolution that adopts such sanctions. Such action could therefore go beyond the scope of the mandate. If, however, the vision behind the mandate is to authorize such actions against the target State, this could well include actions, or even the applicability of the law of naval warfare including blockade. In other words, the scope, purpose and content of authority of visits based on *all necessary means* must be read in context of the aim and purpose of the resolution itself. Also here, and as will be discussed more elaborately in Chap. 11 on detention at sea, further conditions apply in cases where visits based on *all necessary means* are used to detain persons to which human rights law apply.

9.7.2 The Law of Blockade and Article 42 of the UN Charter

Article 42 of the UN Charter explicitly mentions the possibility of authorizing a blockade. Whether this also means that the law of blockade applies to this blockade is not entirely clear. Different options as how to interpret the use of a blockade within the context of the collective security system were already discussed in Chap. 5. Historically, Article 42 was focused on large-scale military operations in which the factual situation amounted to an international armed conflict. From this perspective, there is therefore some logic assuming the purpose of authorising a blockade as a military enforcement measure under Chapter VII of the UN Charter would coincide with applying also the law of blockade. Nowadays, however, military operations that are authorized under Article 42, arguably, firstly do not automatically rise to the level of an armed conflict. And if they do, these conflicts are often characterized as non-international in character. Blockade as a method of warfare to which the law of blockade applies can only exist in cases where there is an international armed conflict. These points basically put an end to any assumption that the law of blockade automatically applies where the UNSC authorizes a blockade as a military enforcement measure. Following this line of argument it still leaves the UNSC with the possibility of using the *method* of blockade, without using the *law* of blockade to automatically fill in the authorities. The scope, purpose and content of such a blockade would then depend on the text of the resolution, in which the UNSC can tailor the law of blockade in such a way to fit the specific circumstances. The advantages of a blockade based on Article 42, is in the first place that a blockade would not become unlawfully established when it does not fulfil all the conditions in order to legally establish a blockade.[105] Secondly, an Article 42 blockade could also be established in circumstances that can be characterized as a NIAC in which the UNSC could decide that the relevant legal features of the law of blockade apply in the given situation. At this stage, however, there appears to be no practice that could underline this view.

9.8 Final Remarks

This chapter has examined the different manifestations of the right of visit that can apply during maritime interception operations. As the scope, purpose and content differs per type of visit, it is, obviously, of importance that warship commanders must ensure to keep them apart. Some manifestations are detailed because they are part of either international agreements, or its details have been widely accepted in customary international law, such as the belligerent right of visit and search. Some are, however, less clear and must either be detailed in the State's consent that waives the flag state authority, or must be interpreted through the actual texts and background of UN resolutions. Generally, however, the different types of right of visit require a threshold (a reasonable ground for suspicion) before a boarding can take place. The exception is the early maritime embargo operations, which authorized the halting of all vessels for inspection. Although during the military operations with regard to Libya the threshold was also introduced for maritime embargo operations it is not unthinkable that the early resolution of resolutions will be used in future conflicts as this depends on the possible future need in conflicts. Second, a right of visit does not mean that once on board, automatically enforcement jurisdiction exists whenever it becomes clear that the suspected ship or person is in breach of law or a mandate. As Guilfoyle already noted: 'The general position is that authority to visit and inspect a vessel does not automatically extend to a right of arrest and prosecution. Unless relinquished or waived, a flag State has 'primary jurisdiction' to conduct any subsequent prosecution.'[106]

One challenge with regard to the right of visit lies in the fact that contemporary conflicts are often characterized as non-international armed conflicts. Whereas regulations related to international armed conflict allow the use of the right of visit and search which is longstanding and accepted as customary international law, this right does not exist in non-international armed conflicts. From an operational point of view, it is quite unsatisfying that existing rules related to the belligerent right of visit and search do not always fit current conflict in the sense that the means are not available to effectively act against non-state actors at sea. Possible legal solutions to what seems to be a gap have been suggested, through the argument of a self-defence

[105] Notification, impartiality and effectiveness.

[106] Guilfoyle 2011, p. 84.

or NIAC right of visit. In this approach, the legal basis for the actual boarding of the vessel is regulated by the *ius ad bellum* and the scope of the boarding authorities by NIAC regulations or self-defence itself.

References

Brown N (2003) Panel III, Commentary – maritime and coalition operation. In: Borch F, Wilson P (eds) International Law Studies 79. Naval War College, Newport RI, pp. 303–307

Brown N (2010) Legal Considerations in Relation to Maritime Operations against Iraq. In: Pedrozo P (ed) International Law Studies 86. Naval War College, Newport RI, pp. 127–137

Cesaretti R (2005) Combating terrorism in the Mediterranean. NATO Review, Autumn 2005

Colombos C (1962) The International Law of the Sea, 5th edn. Longmans Green, London

Council on Ocean Law and the Law of the Sea Institute. Conference Report. The Persian/Arabian Gulf Tanker War: International Law and international chaos. Ocean Development and International Law 19, pp. 299–321

Davidson B (2008/9) Modern naval diplomacy - a practitioner's view. Journal of Military and Strategic Studies 11:1–2, pp. 1–47

den Heijer M (2011) Europe and extraterritorial asylum. Dissertation, Amsterdam

Ducheine P, Pouw E (2009) Operation Change of Direction: A short survey on the legal basis and applicable legal regimes. NL ARMS, Netherlands Defence Academy, Breda, pp. 51–96

Dunham C (1997) The Asama Maru incident of January 21, 1940. Paper prepared for the thirteenth annual Ohio Valley History Conference, October 1997

ECJ, (Lido II) case. no. C-177/95, 27 February 1997

ECtHR, Medvedyev and others v. France, application no. 3394/03. Judgment 29 March 2010

EU Council (2008) Joint Action 2008/851/CFSP

Fielding L (1993) Maritime Interception: Centrepiece of Economic Sanctions in the New World Order. Louisiana Law Review 54, pp. 1191–1241

Fink M (2011a) UN-Mandated Maritime Arms Embargo Operations in Operation Unified Protector. Military Law and the Law of War Review 50:1–2, pp. 237–260

Fink M (2011b) Contemporary views on the lawfulness of naval blockades. Aegean Review of the Law of the Sea and Maritime Law 1:2, pp. 191–215

Fink M (2013) Toute prise doit être jugée. Opmerkingen over het Nederlandse prijs(proces)recht. Militair Rechtelijk Tijdschrift 106:6, pp. 211–219

Gill T (2003) The Eleventh of September and the Right of Self-Defense. In: Heere W (ed) Terrorism and the Military: International Legal Implications. T.M.C. Asser Press, The Hague, pp. 23–37

Gill T (2010) Military intervention at the invitation of the government. In: Gill T, Fleck D (eds) The Handbook of the International Law of Military Operations. Oxford University Press, New York, pp. 229–234

Gill T (2015) Some considerations concerning the role of ius ad bellum to targeting. In: Ducheine P, Schmitt MN, Osinga F (eds) Targeting. The challenges of modern warfare. T.M.C. Asser Press, The Hague, pp. 101–120

Gioia A, Ronzitti N (1992) The law of neutrality: Third states' commercial rights and duties. In: Dekker I, Post H (eds) The Gulf War of 1980–1988. Martinus Nijhoff Publishers, Dordrecht, pp. 221–242

Guilfoyle D (2009) Shipping interdiction and the law of the sea. Cambridge University Press, New York

Guilfoyle D (2011) Human Rights Issues and Non-Flag State Boarding of Suspect Ships in International Waters. In: Symmons C (ed) Selected Contemporary Issues in the Law of the Sea. Brill Nijhoff, Dordrecht, pp. 83–104

Haussler U (2011) Crisis response operation in maritime environments. In: Odello M, Piotrowicz R (eds) International Military Missions and International Law. Brill Nijhoff, Dordrecht, pp. 161–21

Heintschel von Heinegg W (1994) The current state of international prize law. In: Post H (ed) International Economic Law and Armed conflict. Martinus Nijhoff Publishers, the Netherlands, pp. 5–34

Heintschel von Heinegg W (1995) Visit, search and capture – conditions for applicability. In: Heintschel von Heinegg W (ed) Reports and Commentaries of the Round-Table of experts on international humanitarian law applicable of armed conflicts at sea. Bochumer Schriften zur Friedessicherung und zum Humanitarischen Volkerrecht 24, Berliner Wissenschafts-Verlag GmbH, Berlin, pp. 1–92

Heintschel von Heinegg W (2003) The protection of navigation in case of armed conflict. The International Journal of Marine and Coastal Law, 18:3, pp. 401–422

Heintschel von Heinegg W (2007) "Benevolent" third states in international armed conflicts: The myth of the irrelevance of the law of neutrality. In: Schmitt M, Pejic J (eds) International law and armed conflict: Exploring the faultlines. Martinus Nijhoff Publishers, Leiden, pp. 543–568

Heintschel von Heinegg W (2010) Maritime interception/interdiction operations. In: Gill T, Fleck D (eds) The Handbook of the International Law of Military Operations. Oxford University Press, New York, pp. 375–393

Heintschel von Heinegg W (2012) Naval blockade. In: Schmitt M, Heintschel von Heinegg W (eds) The conduct of hostilities in International Humanitarian Law 1. Ashgate, Farnham, Burlington, pp. 203–228.

Heintschel von Heinegg W (2013) The law of armed conflict at sea. In: Fleck D (ed) The Handbook of International Humanitarian Law, 3rd edn. Oxford University Press, New York, pp. 486–498

Higgins AP (1926) Visit, Search and Detention. British Yearbook of International Law 43, pp. 43–53

Hodgkinson S (2007) Challenges to Maritime Interception Operations in the War on Terror: Bridging the Gap. American University International Law Review 22:4, pp. 853–671

Kizanis I (2008) 'Probable cause' for maritime interdictions involving illicit radioactive materials. Thesis for the Naval Postgraduate School, California

Klein N (2005) The right of visit and the 2005 Protocol on the suppression of unlawful acts against the safety of maritime navigation. Denver Journal of International Law and Policy 35:2, pp. 287–332

Klein N (2011) Maritime security and the law of the sea. Oxford University Press, New York

Kraska J (2010a) Rule selection in the case of Israel's naval blockade of Gaza: Law of naval warfare or law of the sea. Yearbook of International Humanitarian Law 13, pp. 367–395

Kraska J (2010b) Broken taillight at sea: The peacetime international law of visit, board, search and seizure. Ocean and Coastal Law Journal 16:1, pp. 1–46

Kraska J, Pedrozo P (2013) International Maritime Security Law. Martinus Nijhoff Publishers, Leiden/Boston

Leijnse M. Weijne J (2002) De bijdrage van de Koninklijke Marine aan de strijd tegen het terrorisme. Marineblad, May 2002, pp. 149–154

Letters to parliament, 27 September 2004, Inzet Nederlands fregat in Operatie Enduring Freedom (conduct of Dutch Frigate in Operation Enduring Freedom)

Letters to parliament, 11 October 2006, answering written questions on the maritime support to UNIFIL

Lieblich E (2014) Yet Another Front in Israeli/Palestinian Lawfare–International Prize Law. Opinio Iuris. http://opiniojuris.org/2014/01/13/lieblich-guest-post-yet-another-front-israelipalestinian-lawfare-international-prize-law/. Accessed 18 February 2017

McLaughlin R (2011) Terrorism as a Central Theme in the Evolution of Maritime Operations Law Since 11 September 2001. Yearbook of International Humanitarian Law 14, pp. 391–409

McLaughlin R (2015) United Nations Security Council Practice in relation to the use of force in no-fly zones and maritime exclusion zones. In: Weller M (ed) The Oxford Handbook of the Use of Force in International Law. Oxford University Press New York, pp. 251–271
Ministerie van Defensie (2006) Eindevaluatie CTF 150, 18 September 2006
Ministerie van Defensie (2008) Eindevaluatie UNIFIL maritiem, 25 April 2008
NATO Parliamentary Assembly (2008) Committee Reports 2008 Annual Session (158 DSC 08 E bis) - NATO Operations: Current Priorities and Lessons Learned
O'Rourke K (2003) Commentary – Maritime & Coalition operations. In: Borch F, Wilson P (eds) International Law Studies 79. Naval War College Newport RI, pp. 297–299
Papastavridis E (2013) The interception of vessels on the high seas. Hart Publishing, Oxford/ Portland, OR
Pejic J (2007) Unlawful/enemy combatants: Interpretations and consequences. In: Schmitt MN, Pejic J (eds) International law and armed conflict: exploring the faultlines. Martinus Nijhoff Publishers, Leiden, pp. 335–355
Pyke H (1915) The law of contraband of war. Clarendon Press, Oxford
Ruys T (2010) 'Armed attack', and Article 51 of the UN Charter. Cambridge University Press, Cambridge
Shaw T (1999) Arabian Gulf Maritime interception operations: balancing the ends, ways, means and risks. Paper Naval War College, Newport RI
Tabori-Szabo K (2015) Self-defence and the policy of drone strikes. Journal of Conflict and Security Law 3, pp. 381–413
Tripsas B, Roth B, Fye R (2004) Coast Guard Operations during Operation Iraqi Freedom, Center for Naval Analysis
Tucker R (1955) The law of war and neutrality at sea. NAVPERS 15031, Government Printing Office, Washington
UK Ministry of Defence (2005) UK Manual on the Law of Armed Conflict, Oxford University Press, New York
UN General Assembly (2010) A/HRC/15/21, 27 September 2010
Van Dyke J (2004) Balancing Navigational Freedom with Environmental and Security Concerns. Colorado Journal of International Environmental law and Policy 19, pp. 19–28
Wendel P (2007) State Responsibility for Interferences with the Freedom of Navigation in public international law. Hamburg Studies on Maritime Affairs 11, Springer, Berlin/ Heidelberg

Chapter 10
The Application of Force in Maritime Interception Operations

Contents

Abstract The use of force during maritime operations has traditionally been approached from the perspective of the law of the sea, even though this area of law does not have explicit rules on the application of force. Arguably, the standards that the Courts have used in cases to define the use of force during maritime operations were the human rights law standards. As human rights law has, however, always been regarded to apply within the territory of a State, and although this includes the jurisdiction of a State over its vessels and planes, the use of force in actions circumstances at sea between vessels were apparently never explicitly set within realm of human rights law. Today, it is clear that the standards for the application of the use of force flow from the legal regimes of human rights law or the law of armed conflict.

Keywords Right to life · laws of armed conflict · application of force · human rights in MIO · use of force in maritime operations

M. Fink, *Maritime Interception and the Law of Naval Operations*,
https://doi.org/10.1007/978-94-6265-249-1_10

10.1 Introduction

The term use of force can have different connotations. First, it can have the meaning interstate military force in the context of the *ius ad bellum*. This has been discussed in Part II. Part of the *ius ad bellum* issues with the use of force is whether force must be seen in the context of 2(4) UN Charter, or whether it is in fact a State's legitimate use of force in pursuit of law enforcement activities at sea. On this question of threshold, the answer, as Nevill concludes; 'turns on an objective assessment of the State's intentions and the surrounding circumstances, not the gun or ammunition used, the number of shots fired, or the identity of the State authority…'[1] Another connotation of the use of force *is* related to the ammunition used or the number of shots fired. This is the actual use or application of force itself. *How* must force be applied during maritime interception operations? This question, which relates to the application of force during a maritime interception operation and the applicable legal regimes that regulates such force, is central to this chapter.

With regard to the legal regimes that regulate the use of force in maritime interception operations both human rights law and the law of armed conflict obviously play a key role. The use of force at sea is often discussed in the context of the international law of the sea. All three regimes have different perspectives with regard to the use of force. As this chapter will underline, the law of the sea has no specific use of force regulations, but developed some guidance through case law on the subject, basically through applying human rights law standards to situations at sea. Within the law of the sea the focus lies on the application of force against vessels. Human rights law primarily relates to the exercise of public power in relation to individuals. Also human rights law has no specific use of force regulations, but these are derived from other human rights, primarily the right to life. The law of armed conflict comes into play when a situation of armed conflict exists. This framework has very particular rules on the use of force, against both vessel and persons, as it is specifically meant to regulate force during armed conflict. As one can see, and which will be discussed in this chapter, the applicable frameworks thus differ in concept on the matter of the application of force.

How these legal frameworks interact with each other is a matter of debate. It relates to the extraterritorial applicability of human rights law and to the relationship between human rights and the law of armed conflict. Although these debates have primarily emerged in land based military operations, human rights law has now also received increased attention in the maritime context, for example in counter-piracy operations off the coast of Somalia and with regard to maritime border patrol operations in the context of dealing with refugees at sea. The law of the sea, as a separate body of law, does not deal with the application of human rights in the maritime dimension, although the rendering of assistance at sea expresses a duty for States aiming to protect the seafarer against the perils of the sea that may arguably be seen as a human right obligation for States stemming directly

[1] Nevill 2015, p. 282.

from the international law of the sea.[2] The relationship, however, between human rights and the law of the sea is an issue that has yet to further crystallize.[3] A first step in this discussion has been taken by the ECtHR in the *Hirsii Jamaa v. Italy* case, which has focused on the relation between the duty to render assistance and the human rights principle of *non-refoulement*. In this context, Klein underlines the need to further harmonize the, as she calls it, 'fragmented legal frameworks applicable to maritime interception'.[4] This not only holds true for the interrelationship between the law of the sea and human rights, but also with regard to the relationship between human rights and the law of naval warfare. Whereas the discussion on the relationship between the law of naval warfare and the international law of the sea since the adoption of UNCLOS III has now slowly moved to the background, and extensive debate exists covering the relationship between human rights law and the law of armed conflict, little attention is paid to the relationship between the laws of naval warfare and human rights.

Various types of situations in the maritime dimension exist in which a necessity to apply force can arise. These include the performance of law enforcement at sea, personal self-defence in response to unlawful assault and the execution of a UN mandate. As stated previously, this chapter focuses on the question how force is applied. In the broadest sense, every form of coercion may be considered as an application of some sort of force. Also boarding and visiting a foreign-flagged vessel or the detention of a person[5] may arguably be considered as a form of coercion as it impacts on the free will of the master of the vessel and the detained individual. This chapter will be limited to the use of armed and potentially lethal force during an interception operation. In other words, if arms are used in the course of a maritime interception, what are the conditions under which such force can be applied?

This chapter will first underline three preliminary thoughts with regard to the use of force in relation to naval forces. Then it will continue analysing the application of force in the context of the law of the sea, human rights law and the law of armed conflict. Further remarks are made with regard to the use of force in UN-mandated maritime interception operations and finally, the relationship between human rights law and LOAC in relation to MIO is touched upon.

---

[2] Cacciaguidi-Fahy 2007.

[3] Treves 2010.

[4] Klein 2014.

[5] See also Petrig 2014, pp. 113–114, who states: 'Since arrest and detention of persons suspected of piracy or armed robbery at sea is a form of use of force going beyond self-defence and defence of others, …'.

10.2 Naval Forces and the Use of Force

Three general comments should be placed here on the use of force by naval forces. The first is that naval forces can be assigned several tasks within one military campaign, which, in terms of the application of force, can lead them to operate in both the lower and higher spectrum of using force within one overall campaign. In one campaign, naval forces can, for example, be assigned to conduct embargo operations against shipping, while also providing naval gunfire support to land operations. One such example is Operation *Desert Storm* in which naval forces were used to fire Tomahawk missiles at land targets in Iraq, while simultaneously enforcing the embargo, at the lower end of the use of force spectrum.[6] Another example is Operation *Unified Protector*, where some of the naval forces of the NATO operation were used to enforce the UN-mandated embargo and at the same time apply naval gunfire support to support the ongoing air-campaign. The latter was clearly a war-fighting activity as opposed to the maritime embargo operation. At the operational level, an organizational separation is usually made where ships are assigned to a certain specific task. It is, however, not excluded that warships may quickly change from one tasking to another. Many factors will have a bearing on this decision, such as the capabilities of the forces available and geographical positioning. But also the limitations that States put on the conduct of their participating warships may play a part. Be that as it may, a change to the task requires the commander and its staff to change mind-set quickly from, say, the administration of force against suspect merchant vessel on one day, to attacking military targets on the next.

The second general comment is that on a tactical level the application of force can be directed against both the *vessel* and the *persons* on board the vessel. Force can be directed to make the vessel stop, to take over control over the vessel or arrest persons on board. The military actions against the persons on board the *Ibn Khaldoon* and the *Mavi Marmara* are examples of the latter.[7] The actions of the *Niels Ebbessen* are an example of the former. In the context of applicable law, it is interesting to note that the law of the sea and the law of naval warfare have developed through a focus on force against vessels, whereas human rights law, obviously, focuses on persons. Two perspectives of how the application of force at sea should be administered (against vessel and/or person), therefore, may exist.

---

[6] Benbow 1999.

[7] The *Ibn Khaldoon* was a merchant vessel, dubbed the "peace-ship", which sailed in 1990 from Algeria to the port of Basra in Iraq during the MIF-period. The *Ibn Kaldoon*, similarly to the *Mavi Marmara*, had protestors, congressmen and women on board and purposely attracted a lot of media attention. After helicopter insertion of the US boarding team passive resistance occurred by the passengers to try to stop the boarding team to take control of the vessel. After the boarding-team discovered prohibited items on board a port needed to be found to offload the prohibited cargo. Ultimately the cargo was offloaded in Oman. See http://articles.latimes.com/1990-12-26/news/mn-6714_1_peace-ship; Pokrant 1999, pp. 193–194.

As a third general comment it is important to note that the application of force can, obviously, be directed against the military opponent, such as enemy warships or combatants. Force can, however, also be applied against civilian merchant vessels and persons on board those vessels. This is for instance the case in the context of embargo enforcement or blockades. In fact, most of the naval operations that deal with economic warfare or the enforcement of economic sanctions at sea are directed against civilian vessels and their crews and passengers, who may not have anything to do with the conflict, but are subject to coercive measures once they sail through a specific area of operations.

10.3 International Law of the Sea

The international law of the sea is primarily meant to be peacetime law and does not concern itself with military operations at sea. Also, no provisions of UNCLOS explicitly mentions any rule or guideline on how to use force during interception operations on the high seas, in either circumstances of peacetime or conflict.[8] Some provisions, such as Article 225 UNCLOS,[9] are seen implicitly as referencing to the use of force. And others find implicit grounds for arguing that force at least can be used in the conduct of certain UNCLOS authorities for the simple reason that during an arrest of suspected pirates under Article 105 one can assume that there is a chance they will resist.[10] Without the possibility of any coercive measures, such authorities would become useless. Gosalbo-Bono and Boelaert see this implied use of force authority also in Articles 110 and 111 UNCLOS.[11] Tullio Treves argues in this context that '[g]eneral international law, in authorising stopping and boarding for the purpose of exercising the right of visit under Article 110 of UNCLOS or the seizure of a pirate ship under Article 105, presupposes that force may be used to reach these objectives.'[12] An argument against this line of thinking is that the authorization for the use of force when conducting an UNCLOS-authority is derived from domestic law to, for instance, arrest a suspected pirate or to stop a vessel in hot pursuit when it has breached a coastal State's national laws. By that as it may, it is clear that UNCLOS does not contain explicit powers for the application of force.

---

[8] Stephens 1999, p. 292. Rothwell and Stephens 2010, p. 419.

[9] Article 225 UNCLOS reads:

> In the exercise under this Convention of their powers of enforcement against foreign vessels, States shall not endanger the safety of navigation or otherwise create any hazard to a vessel, or bring it to an unsafe port or anchorage, or expose the marine environment to an unreasonable risk.

[10] See e.g. McLaughlin 2009, p. 80; Gosalbo-Bono and Boelaert 2014, p. 103.

[11] Gosalbo-Bono and Boelaert 2014, pp. 106–107.

[12] Treves 2009, p. 413.

Case law on the use of force in the context of the law of the sea does, however, provide some guidelines. There are several classics on the use of force in relation to the international law of the sea and maritime interception. Most notably, the *I'm Alone* (1929),[13] *Red Crusader* (1961),[14] *M/V Saiga, no. 2* (1999)[15] and the Guyana *v. Suriname* (2007)[16] cases. In the *MV Saiga* case the ITLOS-tribunal held that:

> Although the Convention does not contain express provisions on the use of force in the arrest of ships, international law, which is applicable by virtue of article 293 of the Convention, requires that the use of force must be avoided as far as possible and, where force is unavoidable, it must not go beyond what is reasonable and necessary in the circumstances.[17]

After this introductory point, taking in the whole of international law within the context of the law of the sea, the Tribunal then proceeded to state on a more practical level:

> These principles have been followed over the years in law enforcement operations at sea. The normal practice used to stop a ship at sea is first to give an auditory or visual signal to stop, using internationally recognized signals. Where this does not succeed, a variety of actions may be taken, including the firing of shots across the bows of the ship. It is only after the appropriate actions fail that the pursuing vessel may, as a last resort, use force. Even then, appropriate warning must be issued to the ship and all efforts should be made to ensure that life is not endangered.[18]

---

[13] The Canadian-flagged vessel *I'm Alone* was sunk in March 1929 by the US coast guard cutter *Dexter* in hot pursuit on the high seas in the Gulf of Mexico. The vessel was engaged in prohibited liquor trafficking.

[14] Permanent Court of Arbitration (PCA), 23 March 1962. In 1961, the Danish fisheries inspection vessel *Niels Ebbessen* boarded the British-flagged vessel *Red Crusader* and arrested the crew. They were suspected of fishing within a prohibited area. After agreeing to follow the *Niels Ebbessen* to the Faroe Islands, it stopped cooperating to follow the *Ebbesen.* As a reaction, the *Ebbessen* first fired warning shots upon the Red Crusader, hailed it to stop and then proceeded to aim and fire at the *Red Crusader.* The Court concluded that firing upon the *Red Crusader* was not justified and that other means should have been sought to pursue arrest.

[15] ITLOS, *MV Saiga no. 2, Saint Vincent and the Grenadines vs. Guinea,* judgment, 1 July 1999. The oil tanker *MV Saiga* was attacked and boarded by Guinean officials in 1997. The vessel and persons were brought to Conakry and placed under arrest. The Tribunal found that Guinea under the specific circumstances of the case used excessive force against the *MV Saiga,* which was fully loaded with fuel, was unarmed and travelling at a speed of 10 knots. See paras 158–159.

[16] Award of the Arbitral Tribunal constituted pursuant to Article 287, and in accordance with annex vii, of the United Nations Convention on the Law of the Sea, *Guyana vs. Suriname* 17 September 2007. The underlying issue in this case was a border dispute between the two neighbouring States. The case emerged from an incident in 2000 in which Suriname threatened to use force by means of two gunboats of the Suriname Navy to expel the vessel *C. E. Thornton,* which was in the service of Guyana, from the disputed area between both States.

[17] ITLOS, *MV Saiga* no. 2, para 155.

[18] ITLOS, *MV Saiga* no. 2, para 156.

The force in the mentioned cases is force used in the context of constabulary purposes, in pursuit of legitimate law enforcement actions. Those actions were considered to be below the threshold of the prohibition of the use of force under Article 2(4) of the UN Charter. The legality of the application of force during law enforcement action by a State on the high seas against foreign-flagged vessels was, therefore, not considered through the *ius ad bellum*. Guilfoyle has supported this view by stating that force against a foreign (merchant) vessel is not force against the political or territorial integrity of a State.[19] Obviously, other factors matter also in this debate, such as to what the degree the State itself is involved in, for instance, protecting the vessel (e.g. convoys with warships), or with its relationship with the vessel (is the vessel conducting a contractual governmental task?). How thin the line between enforcing rights based on law enforcement activities and the use of force in contravention of the use of force prohibition of Article 2(4) UN Charter is, is shown by the Tribunal in the *Guyana-Suriname* case. In this case:

> The Tribunal accepts the argument that in international law force may be used in law enforcement activities provided that such force is unavoidable, reasonable and necessary. However in the circumstances of the present case, this Tribunal is of the view that the action mounted by Suriname on 3 June 2000 seemed more akin to a threat of military action rather than a mere law enforcement activity. This Tribunal has based this finding primarily on the testimony of witnesses to the incident, in particular the testimony of Messrs Netterville and Barber. Suriname's action therefore constituted a threat of the use of force in contravention of the Convention, the UN Charter and general international law.[20]

The general principle that force may be applied in law enforcement activities at sea provided that such force is unavoidable, reasonable and necessary, is codified in different international agreements that deal with matters on the law of the sea. For instance, the *Agreement for the Implementation of the Provisions of the United Nations Convention on the Law of the Sea of 10 December 1982 Relating to the Conservation and Management of Straddling Fish Stocks and Highly Migratory Fish Stocks* states in Article 22, para 1(f) that:

> 1. The inspecting State shall ensure that its duly authorized inspectors: … (f) avoid the use of force except when and to the degree necessary to ensure the safety of the inspectors and where the inspectors are obstructed in the execution of their duties. The degree of force used shall not exceed that reasonably required in the circumstances.

Also, the SUA Protocol has a provision on the use of force which, interestingly, also focuses on the use of force *on board* the vessel. Article 8*bis* sub 9 of the SUA Protocol mentions, apart from the general principle that any force shall not exceed the minimum degree of force which is necessary and reasonable in the circumstances, that force shall be avoided except when necessary '*to ensure the safety of its officials and persons on board, or when the officials are obstructed in the execution of the authorized actions*'. The latter condition might apply when a vessel is not compliant with orders to stop and no other means are available to stop the

[19] Guilfoyle 2009, p. 273.

[20] *Guyana-Suriname*, para 445.

vessel. Once on board, the officials need to avoid any use force during their activities unless to ensure their safety and those of the persons on board. The bilateral ship-boarding agreements between the US and other States also contain a provision on the use of force. The agreement between Belize and the US, for instance, states that:

> 2. Each Party shall avoid the use of force except when and to the degree necessary to ensure the safety of Security Force Officials and ships, and of persons on board the suspect ship, and where Security Force Officials are obstructed in the execution of their duties.
> 3. Only that force reasonably necessary under the circumstances may be used.
> 4. Boarding and search teams and Security Force ships have the inherent right to use all available means to apply that force reasonably necessary to defend themselves or others from physical harm.[21]

The point to underline is that when an international agreement on a specific subject exists, it may have a specific provision on the application of force. Those provisions may deal with force, both against the vessel and the persons on board. The scope of these international agreements is usually aimed to facilitate law enforcement activities, during the course of which persons may be arrested and force goes beyond the situation of personal self-defence.

In sum, three points can be noted on the application of force from a law of the sea perspective. First, UNCLOS does not contain explicit rules on the use of force. Through case law it is, however, accepted that force based on general international law is under strict conditions allowed in the pursuit of lawful law enforcement activities at sea by a State. Case law has developed via a route in which the rules on the use of force has emerged in the context of law enforcement activities against vessels, not against persons directly. Persons are, however, part of the proportionality consideration when applying force against a vessel. Furthermore, and secondly, in specific agreements related to law enforcement at sea, provisions exist that regulate force. The regulations in agreements related to the law of the sea have added a person-focused part to using force. And third, which may perhaps be the most important point to underline, is that the case law and agreements, in fact, apply general international law on the use of force within a maritime context. Arguably, the general international law on which this is based is the human rights law standard

[21] See Article 9 of the *Agreement Between the Government of the United States of America and the Government of Belize Concerning Cooperation to Suppress the Proliferation of Weapons of Mass Destruction, Their Delivery Systems, and Related Materials By Sea*, October 2005. The US-Croatia agreement (2005), for example, mentions words alike. Article 9 states:

> 1. Rules. When carrying out the authorized actions under this Agreement, the use of force shall be avoided except when necessary to ensure the safety of its officials and persons on board, or where the officials are obstructed in the execution of the authorized actions. Any use of force pursuant to this Agreement shall not exceed the minimum degree of force which is necessary and reasonable in the circumstances.
> 2. Self-defense. Nothing in this Agreement shall impair the exercise of the inherent right of self-defense by Security Force or other officials of either Party.

for applying the use of force. As human rights law has, however, always been regarded to apply within the territory of a State, and although this includes the jurisdiction of a State over its vessels and planes, the use of force in actions circumstances at sea between vessels were apparently never explicitly set within realm of human rights law. As extraterritorial applicability of human rights law is today a more generally accepted legal concept, it may now perhaps be more to the point to state that the legal regime for the application of force at sea stems from the human rights law standards applied in the maritime context, rather than following the evolutionary route in which the principles for the use of force trickled into and became part of the international laws of the sea the based on general international law.

10.4 Applicability of Human Rights to High Seas Interceptions

During the early stages of maritime interception operations the thought of applying human rights law to MIO was not as developed or relevant as it is today. One reason could be that maritime embargo operations after the Cold War were focused on goods rather on persons. The 'early writers' on MIO, such as Fielding and Politakis, did not consider human rights as a legal regime possibly applicable in the context of maritime interception operations. Today, the interception of persons has come more the foreground in MIO. And when individuals become involved, human rights become important. To illustrate, SC Res. 1973 (2011) uniquely embargoed both goods and certain persons (mercenaries)[22] and counter-piracy operations have firmly stressed the fact that human rights law is an important legal regime to consider within the context of applying coercive measures against pirates. Another reason for the rise of the importance of human right in military operations is obviously the above-mentioned continuously growing acceptance that human rights law also applies extraterritorially. The naval dimension is certainly not excluded from this trend. In 1993, Captain Lyon (RN), for instance, still considered the possibility of using force during the MIF MIO against persons mainly from a law of the sea perspective and did not consider that the UK might have had jurisdiction based on human rights law.[23] Today, this question would immediately have been analysed from a human rights law perspective.

The applicability of human right in maritime interceptions outside the sovereign waters of a State is an issue of extraterritorial application of human rights. The applicability of human rights revolves around the question whether a State has jurisdiction over persons. From a European law perspective, Article 1 ECHR states that:

---

[22] SC Res. 1973 (2011), para 13.

[23] Lyons 1993, pp. 163–164.

> The High Contracting Parties shall secure to everyone within their jurisdiction the rights and freedoms defined in [Section I of] this Convention.

Against the background of the growing acceptance that—albeit still in an exceptional fashion—jurisdiction may also exist extraterritorially on the high seas, the applicability of human rights can be established in two ways. First, because States have exclusive jurisdiction over vessels that fly their flag their flag, States have responsibility over human rights law issues that may arise on board that vessel. This applies in particular to State vessels, such as warships, which can be considered as representatives of a State. Actions by the crew of warships can be considered to be attributable to the flag State. Once a person is brought on board a warship there is no discussion that human rights law applies on board even when the warship is on the high seas.

Second, a State can have extraterritorial jurisdiction based on factual circumstances. Case law on extraterritorial application of human rights is extensive and developing. In essence, it centres on the notion of *effective control*. If in case a State has effective control over a person (state agent authority, SAA) or an area (effective control over an area, ECA), there may be ground to conclude that a jurisdictional link is established between the person and that State, which allows human rights law to be applicable in the relation between the acting State and the individual. ECA exists when, as a consequence of military action a State exercises effective control of an area outside its national territory. As the ECtHR states: 'The obligation to secure, in such an area, the rights and freedoms set out in the convention derives from the fact of such control, whether it be exercised directly, through its armed forces, or through a subordinate local administration'[24] SAA refers to the situation where a State can be held accountable for violations of human rights when persons are under the authority and control of its agents and outside the territory of the State.[25] It does not matter whether there is a legitimate legal basis which underpins the action. Human rights law may, for example, apply also where a State did not have the consent of a flag State where it should have and has acted against the persons on board that vessel.

The State's actions through the use of their warships and crews make it possible that human rights apply in the area of the high seas. Because international[26] and

[24] ECtHR, *Loizidou v. Turkey*, application no. 40/1993/435/514, (Preliminary objections), 23 March 1995. Paragraph 62 reads as follows:

> Bearing in mind the object and purpose of the Convention, the responsibility of a Contracting Party may also arise when as a consequence of military action - whether lawful or unlawful - it exercises effective control of an area outside its national territory. The obligation to secure, in such an area, the rights and freedoms set out in the Convention derives from the fact of such control whether it be exercised directly, through its armed forces, or through a subordinate local administration.

[25] See Milanovic 2012 on these two notions of establishing extraterritorial jurisdiction.

[26] E.g. *Medvedyev v. France, Hirsi Jamaa v Italy, Rigopoulos v. Spain, Xhavara v. Albania.*

national[27] case law has dealt with the matter of application of human rights law on the high seas, this is rather undisputed. As Papastavridis mentions in respect of the *Medvedyev*-judgment; 'Hence, the Medvedyev case comes to complement the above decisions and provide cogency to the argument that the Convention applies on the high seas, in so far as control, and therefore, jurisdiction is exerted by organs of the States parties.'[28] Also, apart from the threshold question, the UNSC has underlined in its resolutions in the case of counter-piracy[29] and with respect to the Libya MIO in SC Res. 2146 (2014) that measures shall be undertaken in accordance with human rights law.[30] The Council does not state that every action taken during counter-piracy operations will meet the conditions for extra-territorial application of human rights law, but the Council requires actions to be in accordance with human rights law by stating that measures shall be undertaken in such a manner.

With regard to the threshold question of applicability of human rights law on the high seas, if one would divide a maritime interception into phases, broadly speaking a distinction can be made between (1) the phase that leads up to boarding the vessel, (2) the phase of being on board the vessel, and (3) a possible phase of bringing persons on board the warship.[31] As said, in the latter phase there is no discussion on whether human rights apply. Most recently, the ECtHR in the *Hirsi* case underlined that persons brought on board the warship are under *de jure* and *de facto* control of the authorities of that State.[32] Earlier, in the *Bankovic* case, the Court held that jurisdiction of a State exists on board crafts and vessels registered in, or flying the flag of, that State.[33] National court cases, in particular with regard to procedural human rights, also do not dismiss that human rights law apply when the suspects are brought on board the warship.[34] Once persons have been brought on board a warship, there is no doubt that IHRL applies to these individuals.

---

[27] E.g. counter-piracy cases.

[28] Papastavridis 2010, p. 871.

[29] See e.g. SC Res. 2077, para 17.

[30] Paragraph 5 of SC Res. 2146 (2014) reads:

> 5. Authorizes Member States to inspect on the high seas vessels designated by the Committee pursuant to paragraph 11, and authorizes Member States to use all measures commensurate to the specific circumstances, in full compliance with international humanitarian law and international human rights law, as may be applicable, to carry out such inspections and direct the vessel to take appropriate actions to return the crude oil, with the consent of and in coordination with the Government of Libya, to Libya;

[31] Petrig 2013, p. 36 identifies two phases: 'The question of application of human rights on board the warship and application 'beyond its railing''.

[32] *Hirsi Jamaa*, paras 81–82.

[33] ECtHR, *Bankovic vs Belgium et al.*, appl. No. 52207/09, Decision Grand Chamber, 21 December 2001, para 73.

[34] For instance, in the Netherlands court case on the pirated vessel *MS Samanyolu*, it was never disputed that human rights applied on board the Danish warship *Absalon*. The District Court of Rotterdam held that the prolonged detention on board the *Absalon* was a breach of Article 5(1) ECHR, but did not regard it a breach by the State of the Netherlands.

With regard to the first two phases, there may be more discussion. Do human rights already apply at the stage in which the warship commander is using force against a vessel to persuade it to stop the vessel? In the *Xhavara v. Italy and Albania* case,[35] in which during the boarding procedure of the Albanian-flagged *Kater I Rades* carrying Albanian refugees by the Italian warship *Sibilia* the ships collided and caused the Albanian vessel to sink, a plea of Article 2 ECHR was brought before the court. However, the Court held that the complaint was inadmissible because at that stage not all local remedies were exhausted.[36] This case unfortunately for the academic question involved provided, therefore, no answer. In the *Women on Waves v. Portugal* case, however, the Court applied human rights (in this case Articles 10 and 11 ECHR) to be applicable even when the (Netherlands-flagged) vessel *Borndiep* was not boarded.[37] In 2004, the *Borndiep* was not allowed into Portuguese territorial waters and warships were sent to obstruct the passage into the territorial waters of Portugal. Arguably, here the Portuguese warships exercised public authority over the vessel, by prohibiting it to sail its intended course and denying access to Portuguese territorial waters. Papastavridis states that 'it seems difficult to sustain that anything less than actual physical interference or by boarding, would trigger the extra-territorial application of the ECHR'.[38] A broader approach than actual physical control, but rather already through military presence, would be to accept that human right would apply when a State exercises public authority over persons and objects. As Den Heijer mentions in this context:

> …it transpires from the evolving case law on the extraterritorial application of human rights that the form or manner of state activity is generally not considered decisive for enlivening the state's extraterritorial obligations but rather the question whether there is a factual assertion of state sovereignty which affects a person in such a way that he can be considered a victim of an alleged infringement of a human rights obligation.[39]

Consequently, this threshold would widen the application of human rights in the context of maritime interception operations to include a situation in which there is not yet physical control of persons and objects, but the State has started to exercise its public authority. In other words, before the boarding and physical control of the vessel and persons on board has occurred, human rights law would start to apply.

Another way to approach the applicability of human rights in the context of approaching vessels by warships, or vessels in the vicinity of individuals not being on board of the warship itself, is via the concept of effective control over an area (ECA). The ECA concept in this maritime context aims, rather than control over the

[35] ECtHR, *Xhavara and others v. Italy and Albania appl. no 39473/98*, 11 January 2011.

[36] *Xhavara and others v. Italy*, p. 8.

[37] ECtHR, *Women on Waves and others v. Portugal*, (appl. no. 31276/05), 3 February 2009.

[38] Papastavridis 2013, p. 126.

[39] Den Heijer 2011, p. 254.

individuals themselves, to see whether there may be a jurisdictional link on the basis of the idea that a warship (or a fleet) has effective control over a maritime area. This approach is advocated by Petrig who seems to have taken on board the idea that a group of warships may have control over an operational area. She mentions that; 'it could be argued that effective territorial control cannot only be established within the (geographically changing) operational radius of an individual military ship, but even over a joint operational area by the entirety of ships and aircraft deployed.'[40] She then proceeds to take the Internationally Recommended Transit Corridor (IRTC) to be an example of such control. Assuming that at sea a certain degree of control of sea areas may indeed be established, the level of control in that area varies with the type, purpose and conditions within the area. Arguably, when the area is smaller, such as an area of amphibious operations (AOA) off the coast of another State, control may be assumed earlier than within a more general—and larger—area of operations (AOO).[41] If one would follow this reasoning to establish applicability of human rights law, it should be recalled that from an operational perspective, the operational areas may be enormous and the military assets may be few. In which case it would take days arrive at any incident. From this perspective, it would seem very difficult to readily accept that effective control exists within such an operational area at sea. Put differently, establishing an operational area does not automatically indicate that naval forces will have control over it. And consequently, one should not automatically conclude that effective control necessarily exists simply on the basis that an operational maritime area is assigned to a mission.

With regard to the second phase, where a boarding team is on board another foreign-flagged vessel, both Papastavridis and Guilfoyle take the view that the mere presence of an armed boarding party on board a foreign-flagged vessel would satisfy the condition of effective control.[42] In the case of captured suspected pirates on board a small pirate *dinghy*,[43] this could very much be the case. But in the context of a huge container vessel, it may be less easy to readily accept this view. In the *Al Skeini* case, the ECtHR stated:

> The Court does not consider that jurisdiction [in the above cases] arose solely from the control exercised by the Contracting State over the buildings, aircraft or ship in which the individuals were held. What is decisive in such cases is the exercise of physical power and control over the person in question.[44]

Effective control, therefore, should not automatically be assumed solely on the basis that a boarding party is inserted on a foreign-flagged vessel. In the case of an

[40] Petrig 2013, pp. 39–41.

[41] The theatre of operations (TOO) is the widest operational area, more specific is the area of operations (AOO), and then smaller specific areas can be assigned, such as an amphibious operations area (AOA).

[42] Papastavridis 2013, p. 76; Guilfoyle 2009, p. 268.

[43] A small motor boat.

[44] ECtHR, *Al-Skeini and others v. The United Kingdom* (application no. 55721/07), judgment, 7 July 2011, para 136.

opposed boarding with substantial armed resistance, outside the situation of an armed conflict, the human rights law paradigm applies. In terms of the question whether extraterritorial jurisdiction exists, one has to question whether effective control of the vessel or persons on board in fact exists during the phase of the boarding where there is armed resistance. In any case, in line with from the Court's view as stated above, the mere fact that a boarding party is on board a vessel does not automatically mean that it has effective control over the vessel or persons. In cases of friendly approaches, for instance where the boarding party is invited on board and engages solely in general and friendly communication with crew of the vessel, there may be no actual exercise of public authority. That it is very possible that jurisdiction can exist whilst being on board a foreign-flagged vessel, is underlined by the *Medvedyev* case, in which the ECtHR considered that jurisdiction ex Article 1 ECHR existed because the French boarding team was obliged to use their weapons to defend themselves, kept the crew under guard in their cabins and rerouted and towed the *Winner* into the Port of Brest, all under orders of the French authorities. The Court therefore concluded that France had jurisdiction, at least *de facto*, from the moment of interception until the persons were tried.[45]

10.5 The Right to Life in a Naval Operations Dimension

If international human rights law applies during maritime interception, the next step is to consider the substantive law on the use of force within the context of human rights law. Requirements for the use of force under international human rights are dealt with through the human right of the right to life. In the *European Convention on Human Rights* (ECHR), Article 2 ECHR has codified the right to life.[46]

Which conditions apply to the military when using force in relation to the right to life under human rights law, has been extensively discussed, *inter alia* by Nils Melzer,[47] Louise Doswald-Beck[48] and Eric Pouw.[49] In essence, the general conditions for the use of force in the context of the right to life may be summarized by five requirements: The requirement of an adequate legislative framework, necessity, proportionality, precaution and investigation. The first requirement in essence obliges a State to have a legal framework for the use of force, train personnel and

[45] *Medvedyev*, paras 66–67.

[46] Article 2(1) ECHR states:

> Everyone's right to life shall be protected by law. No one shall be deprived of his life intentionally save in the execution of a sentence of a court following his conviction of a crime for which this penalty is provided by law.

[47] Melzer 2006.

[48] Doswald-Beck 2011.

[49] Pouw 2013.

adequately plan for operations.[50] The second requirement (necessity) obliges States to only use force in circumstances when it is absolutely required to achieve the legitimate objective. The threat must be such that the use of lethal force must be unavoidable under the circumstances of the case and the use of force is strictly limited to achieve the legitimate objective. Within the context of this requirement the use of force is also limited to the *actual* moment when the threat is manifestly concrete and specific. With regard to the third requirement (proportionality) Pouw states that when the nature and scale of the threat does not outweigh the harm or injury to life resulting from the use of force applied in support of a legitimate aim, the deprivation of life violates the right to life.[51] The fourth requirement (precaution) obliges a State to take precaution throughout the whole process of the planning, execution and aftermath of the action. The requirement of precaution obliges the State to plan, organize and control the operation with a view towards restricting the use of lethal force, to the greatest extent possible.[52] The fifth requirement (investigation) means that a State has a duty to conduct an independent and impartial investigation in every instance of use of force that can be attributed to a State.

At this stage, there is no case law from the European Court of Human Rights that has dealt with the right to life at sea.[53] The only case that came close was the *Xhavara* case, but, as mention earlier, which was not admissible to the Court. No substantive views on the application of the right to life in the maritime environment have therefore emerged from its decisions to date. Nevertheless, the above-mentioned five requirements exist in every situation where government officials (military) are required to use force to achieve their legitimate objectives. The requirements mentioned above clearly do not limit themselves to the actual moment of the use of the force, but cover a wide range of obligations and conditions related to the use of force before and after using the lethal means itself. The question within the context of MIO is whether the use of force under human rights law may be any different in the maritime context than the application of force outside the maritime dimension. As a point of departure, it is safe to say that the maritime environment does not change anything in relation to the requirements. If differences exist, they must be sought in the practical application of these requirements. Operating in the maritime environment may involve practical issues that could lead to a different interpretation of the requirements at sea.

One of the challenges in terms of adequate legal framework may be that, although international agreements may give warship commanders the authority to act, naval personnel need to be given law enforcement authority to act through domestic law in such a way that naval personnel can lawfully perform law enforcement activities. The maritime environment may also have an impact on the

[50] Doswald-Beck 2011, pp. 165–167.

[51] Pouw 2013, p. 245.

[52] Pouw 2013, p. 247.

[53] Papastavridis 2013, pp. 126–130.

feasible precautions requirement. What is feasible at sea may be quite different than in a normal law enforcement scenario on land. For example, an interception at sea involving the use of force can occur hours or even days away from supporting elements, such as sufficient medical facilities, and will depend on the location of the target vessel. Hence, the fact is that the maritime environment will often signify that fewer supporting resources are immediately available than in the land environment. With regard to proportionality, the circumstances of the case may lead to the decision not to board at sea when the vessel will ultimately sail into port and where the port authorities can be requested to inspect the vessel and take relevant actions. This must also be seen in the context of the fact that fewer means are available at sea for the application of precautionary measures. Furthermore, practical challenges may arise relating to investigations after the use of force on a foreign-flagged vessel with regard to the ability to investigate. When an intervention on a foreign-flagged vessel occurs and there would be reason to conduct an investigation, more States would be involved which could lead to more coordination efforts during such investigation. This, however, does not mean that under these circumstances investigations cannot be conducted impartially.

10.5.1 Counter-Piracy Operations off the Coast of Somalia

Piracy is a crime subject to universal jurisdiction under UNCLOS and customary law. By its nature, it is subject to the law enforcement standards of human rights law. In the particular case of piracy off the coast of Somalia, the UNSC has adopted *all necessary means* in relation to act against piracy in the Somali territorial sea. The general understanding of the phrase is that it authorizes the use of military force.[54] It does not, however, also provide a separate legal regime to use force. As mentioned in previous chapters, although the counter-piracy resolutions use the

---

[54] See SC Res. 1816 (2008). The resolution, in operative para 7, states:

> 7. Decides that for a period of six months from the date of this resolution, States cooperating with the TFG in the fight against piracy and armed robbery at sea off the coast of Somalia, for which advance notification has been provided by the TFG to the Secretary General, may:
> (a) Enter the territorial waters of Somalia for the purpose of repressing acts of piracy and armed robbery at sea, in a manner consistent with such action permitted on the high seas with respect to piracy under relevant international law; and
> (b) Use, within the territorial waters of Somalia, in a manner consistent with action permitted on the high seas with respect to piracy under relevant international law, all necessary means to repress acts of piracy and armed robbery;

See also EU Council joint action 2008/851/CFSP, 10 November 2008 in which the EU underlined this authority in its mandate. Article 2d states:

phrase *all necessary means*, the given authorities are limited by the fact that action has to be in accordance with relevant international law, which in this case are UNCLOS and human rights law. Guilfoyle, Blank and others have sufficiently argued that counter-piracy operations are not military operations that are conducted under the regime of the law of armed conflict.[55] The phrase *all necessary means* by itself also does not, as Guilfoyle mentions, 'necessarily implicate IHL, which is applicable only in an international or non-international armed conflict'.[56] The use of force by naval forces in counter-piracy operations is, therefore, firstly force used in the legitimate pursuit of a law enforcement action. Naval personnel can be assigned a law enforcement task to take action against piracy.[57] The limits on the use of force are the limits posed on law enforcement actions.[58] These law enforcement actions go beyond the situation of personal self-defence and have the purpose to arrest a criminal suspect. The function of counter-piracy operations, to quote Guilfoyle again, 'is clearly a constabulary one: it is the power to arrest suspects and bring them to trial, one which necessarily carries with it an authorisation to use force'.[59] During these actions, fire can sometimes be directed against military personnel, which can trigger the right of personal self-defence, the legal parameters of which are defined by domestic law. In November 2008, British Royal Marine Commandos from *HMS Cumberland* approaching a Yemen-flagged dhow, believed to be attacking the Danish merchant vessel *MV Powerful*, in Rhibs shot two pirate-suspects when they were fired upon from a dhow.[60] In another instance in 2009, Netherlands Royal Marines from *Hr. Ms. Tromp* in a Rhib were fired upon when approaching a dhow that also held hostages. Their reaction led to the death of two hostage takers.[61] Secondly, Bono and Boelaert pose the view that the phrase *all necessary means* is important in light of the different activities with regard to defending against piracy, which may go beyond the strict action of arresting pirates during a law enforcement actions.[62] Examples they mention are escorting or convoying vessels with warships or armed personnel on board the vessel. Although the force applied must still be within the realm of human rights, the legal ground for the

(d) take the necessary measures, including the use of force, to deter, prevent and intervene in order to bring to an end acts of piracy and armed robbery which may be committed in the areas where it is present;

[55] Guilfoyle 2010b; Blank 2013.

[56] Guilfoyle 2015, p. 1062.

[57] It is apt to quote a phrase coined by Allen 2006, p. 82 in this context, who stated: 'It is the mission, not the uniform worn by the actor, that determines how force should be classified and which doctrine controls that use of force'.

[58] Treves 2009, pp. 412–414.

[59] Guilfoyle 2010b, p. 10.

[60] http://www.theguardian.com/world/2008/nov/13/pirates-killed-gulf-aden.

[61] District Court of Rotterdam, The Netherlands. *Al Feddah* case. 12 October 2012.

[62] Gosalbo-Bono and Boelaert 2014, pp. 109–110.

use force would arguably be based on the authority of the resolution. The difference with using force in personal self-defence would be that in such case there is no duty to try to escape from the danger. Zwanenburg, discussing the use of force for Dutch VPDs on board escorted vessels which are not part of the UN resolution based operations, has therefore argued that vessels being attacked by pirates must first try to escape from the attack before any necessity for the VPD exists to act in self-defence.[63] Obviously, the factual circumstances of the case, however, will influence whether this may be the manner in which the element of necessity in self-defence must be operationally translated.

10.6 The Law of Armed Conflict

Maritime interception operations may also be conducted in the context of an international armed conflict. In the context applying force, a number of essential conceptual differences exist between the legal regime of LOAC and human rights law. In essence, whereas LOAC is a legal regime is concerned with the rules to apply force, the rules on force in IHRL derived from different substantial rules, such as the right to life, for which States have an obligation to ensure and secure. Whereas human rights law is meant to protect the individual against government actions, LOAC concentrates on the balance between the principles military necessity and humanity. The general concept, therefore, of the application of force within LOAC can be described as that force is generally allowed but limited by the rules of LOAC. Within the context of LOAC not every individual is protected against the use of force. The general concept of IHRL, however, is that force cannot be used as a legal principle and must be considered as an *ultimum remedium.* This point results in the general view that under IHRL actions of a State should be focused on arrest, rather than killing the person.[64] Another conceptual difference is that the purpose of LOAC is that it is meant to operate within the complex circumstances of conflict. This leads to open norm provisions for a commander. IHRL is meant to operate under peacetime circumstances and is judged also by its effects *after* the use of force rather than by the circumstances at the time the commander made the decision. The use of force in LOAC and IHRL is, therefore, conceptually based on opposite ideas. Clearly, whether force is used under the legal regime of LOAC or IHRL, therefore, does make much difference. Both legal regimes have their own conditions of application, which means that the question needs to be

[63] Zwanenburg 2014, pp. 210–212.

[64] Droege 2008, p. 525.

considered separately for both regimes. Moreover, it could also result in the conclusion that both apply. Indeed, the more generally accepted view is that human rights law continues to apply during armed conflict.[65]

Whether the law of armed conflict applies depends on either the situation in which a State has declared war or when armed conflict exists.[66] The applicability of the LOAC centralizes primarily around the term 'armed conflict'. This is a factual term which is not defined in LOAC treaties. Jurisprudence has provided tools to define whether or not an armed conflict exists.[67] The well-known *Tadic* formula states that an armed conflict exists when there is a resort to armed force between States or protracted armed violence between governmental authorities and organized armed ground, or between such groups with the States.[68] With regard to the existence of non-international armed conflicts, jurisprudence has developed indicative factors to be considered, such as the number, duration and intensity of individual confrontations; the type of weapons and other military equipment used; and the number and calibre of munitions fired, against which the intensity of the violence and the ability to resort to protracted armed violence must be considered.[69] The essence, however, is that the factual existence of an armed conflict is the threshold for application of the law of armed conflict.

Obviously, the law of armed conflict is of importance in relation to the use of force and maritime interception. That part of LOAC that deals with hostilities will apply in military operations against the enemy opponent during conflicts at sea and is essentially guided by the fundamental principles of humanity, military necessity, distinction, proportionality and chivalry. But apart from the law that regulates the conduct of hostilities, of particular importance to maritime interception is a specialized part of LOAC applicable to international conflict at sea: the law of naval

[65] Contrary views also exist, namely, the separatist-approach. This approach contains the view that LOAC applies during armed conflict and IHRL applies during peacetime circumstances. See on these approaches Gill 2014.

[66] See Common Article 2 of the Geneva Conventions.

[67] Bartels 2008.

[68] E.g. *Prosecutor v. Dusko Tadic*, IT-94-1, 2 October 1995, para 70.

[69] The Trial Chamber of the ICTY in its judgment of 3 April 2008 in the Haradinaj case noted (para 49):

> 49. The criterion of protracted armed violence has therefore been interpreted in practice, including by the Tadić Trial Chamber itself, as referring more to the intensity of the armed violence than to its duration. Trial Chambers have relied on indicative factors relevant for assessing the "intensity" criterion, none of which are, in themselves, essential to establish that the criterion is satisfied. These indicative factors include the number, duration and intensity of individual confrontations; the type of weapons and other military equipment used; the number and caliber of munitions fired; the number of persons and type of forces partaking in the fighting; the number of casualties; the extent of material destruction; and the number of civilians fleeing combat zones. The involvement of the UN Security Council may also be a reflection of the intensity of a conflict.

warfare. This regime not only regulates hostilities between belligerent naval and aerial forces at sea during an international armed conflict, but also contains rules relating to economic warfare and maritime neutrality. Conceptually, for the purpose of analysing the use of force within the legal regime of LOAC it is important to underline that many of the provisions of the law of naval warfare deal with operations that involve dealing with civilians rather than operations that are solely directed against the military forces of the opponent. The use of force in the naval dimension and within the context of the legal regime of LOAC therefore has two main prongs: One is the use of force against enemy warships; the other is the use of force in relation to action directed against civilian merchant shipping. Whereas the land dimension of this legal regime has distinction and the rule of direct participation to hostilities as its guiding principles, the law of naval warfare contains an extra legal framework that details under which circumstances force can be used against civilian merchant shipping. Important also, is that these regulations focus mainly on *shipping*, and not on persons. Because the law of naval warfare is a part of LOAC, the applicability follows the same conditions. One major difference, however, is that the law of naval warfare is viewed not to be applicable in non-international armed conflicts.[70] Be that as it currently is, naval forces are certainly not unused in NIACs. Whereas the overall LOAC framework of obligations and principles with regard to the use of force apply in maritime operations during a NIAC, the specific rules of the law of naval warfare, in particular the rules relating to economic warfare and maritime neutrality which are confined to IACs, do not apply in a NIAC.

10.6.1 Use of Force Against Neutral and Enemy Merchant Vessels

As underlined above, it must first be underlined that force can be used against military *and*, under certain conditions, against civilian shipping. In that sense, a separation can be made between the use of force against vessels that are considered to be military objectives and are objects that are subject to attack. The obvious example of a military objective is an enemy warship. An example of an object that is subject to attack is a neutral merchant vessel.

The use of force against an enemy warship is regulated by the targeting-rules. Although nowadays extremely unlikely, situations may exist where enemy warships are boarded and ultimately taken as booty. If the maximum authority of

[70] Heintschel von Heinegg 2010.

directly attacking the vessel on sight is lawful, the lesser means of boarding and capturing the vessel would also fall within the lawful scope of actions.

More complex, however, within the context of military objective are the rules that apply when force may be used against neutral or enemy civilian merchant vessels. Enemy or neutral merchant shipping can under certain conditions also be subject to attack. As mentioned, the fundamental principle with regard to the use of force in LOAC starts with that distinction must be made between persons that take part in hostilities and persons that do not. The latter are protected against the use of force. Interestingly, many of the instruments available to a State under the law of naval warfare involve not just the opponent, but rather focus on other users of the sea against which, under specific circumstances, force can be used. These other users are civilian merchant shipping ('civilian' and 'merchant' may be considered as in fact the same thing, but for the purpose of underlining its character both terms are used). The law of naval warfare specifies under what conditions force may be used against civilian merchant shipping. These can be either neutral or enemy, but the essence is that they are civilian in nature.

In 1991, William Fenrick wrote that the question of when a merchant vessel can be considered a military target as one of the most unsettled questions of modern naval warfare.[71] His arguments as to why it is difficult lie mainly in the way naval warfare has developed throughout history. Although there is general agreement on the legal point of departure that merchant vessels cannot be attacked, one of the difficulties is that distinction between naval forces and civilian shipping has in history been blurred by incorporating the merchant fleet into the war effort. Further back in history, the use of privateers caused a very close tie between merchant and naval fleets, and also later, during the World Wars of 1914–1918 and 1939–1945 naval and merchant vessels were closely related during conflict, for instance by the confiscation of the whole merchant fleet by the State and in using them in the war efforts, for transport, evacuation and supply. Also the ruses used in naval warfare, such as Q-ships and the use of false flags, have done much to continue to blur the distinction between combatants and civilians at sea. States themselves have also used the tool of arming their merchant vessels to defend but also attack enemy warships. '*The first British counter-move, made on my responsibility in 1915, was to arm British merchantmen to the greatest possible extent with guns of sufficient power to deter the U-boat from surface attack*', wrote Winston Churchill in his history of the First World War.[72] Historical practice shows that distinction at sea has, therefore, not been without any challenges, and certainly not as easy as

---

[71] Fenrick 1991, p. 425.

[72] Churchill 1927, p. 353. The second countermove was the use of Q-ships, ultimately followed by the convoy system.

identifying a grey hull as the enemy and all other vessels as civilian. Although everyone will have a picture in mind of what a warship looks like, the definition of warships in UNCLOS, states that a warship should bear the external markings to distinguish such ships of its nationality, which is left to the flag State.[73] The *Hague Convention 1907 no. VII* on transformation of merchant vessels to warships follows the same requirement in terms of external markings.[74] The external difference between merchant vessels and enemy warships can thus be as little as the marking of the war-flag. Legally, the use of force against such vessel may shift as fast as the flag is raised. History, therefore, has given rise to ideas that enemy merchant vessels could or should be attacked. H. A. Smith, in 1950, and after going over a number of hybrid examples during the Second World War even came to the conclusion that: '*Unless a firm and clear line can be drawn between the warship and the merchantman it is inevitable that the latter must be exposed to the same risks as the former.*'[75] There should be no other legal point of departure than the presumption that all merchant vessels—enemy or neutral—are exempted from attack, unless they can be deemed military objectives.[76] In that sense, there is no difference in the law then and now regarding the attack of merchant vessels. This general point of departure is also underlined in the basic targeting guidelines of the *San Remo Manual*.[77] Today, however, conflicts have generally not risen to the level of the Great Wars in which merchant vessels fulfilled the conditions to be attacked as military objectives, and where merchant vessels were transformed to participate as warships, or where States made them participate in the war effort.

The law of naval warfare considers certain activities by enemy or neutral merchant vessels to render the vessel a military objective or subject to attack. The SRM,

[73] Article 29 UNCLOS reads:

> For the purposes of this Convention, "warship" means a ship belonging to the armed forces of a State bearing the external marks distinguishing such ships of its nationality, under the command of an officer duly commissioned by the government of the State and whose name appears in the appropriate service list or its equivalent, and manned by a crew which is under regular armed forces discipline.

[74] Article 2 HC VII. The only external marking to distinguish a warship from a civilian vessel in Netherlands domestic law is the war flag (*oorlogswimpel*) and nothing else.

[75] Smith 1950, p. 83.

[76] See e.g. Dinstein 2005, p. 102; Klein 2011, p. 289. Heintschel von Heinegg 2010, p. 359; 2014, p. 152.

[77] See part III SRM, specifically paras 40, 41 and 59.

in Section 60[78] and 67,[79] has prelisted with regard to enemy merchant vessels and neutral merchant vessel a number of activities that may render an enemy merchant vessel as a *military objective* and a neutral military vessel *subject to attack*. Both these lists are interesting, first in the sense that the enemy merchant vessel and the neutral merchant vessel are apparently considered to be different in character with regard to when they can be considered as military objective. It begs the question whether there is any difference between 'military objective' and 'subject to attack'. The SRM-Commentary answers this question by stating that the definition of military objective does not apply in the legal relationship between a belligerent and

---

[78] Section 60 SRM reads:

> 60. The following activities may render enemy merchant vessels military objectives:
>
> (a) engaging in belligerent acts on behalf of the enemy, e.g., laying mines, minesweeping, cutting undersea cables and pipelines, engaging in visit and search of neutral merchant vessels or attacking other merchant vessels;
>
> (b) acting as an auxiliary to an enemy s armed forces, e.g., carrying troops or replenishing warships;
>
> (c) being incorporated into or assisting the enemy s intelligence gathering system, e.g., engaging in reconnaissance, early warning, surveillance, or command, control and communications missions;
>
> (d) sailing under convoy of enemy warships or military aircraft;
>
> (e) refusing an order to stop or actively resisting visit, search or capture;
>
> (f) being armed to an extent that they could inflict damage to a warship; this excludes light individual weapons for the defence of personnel, e.g., against pirates, and purely deflective systems such as chaff; or
>
> (g) otherwise making an effective contribution to military action, e.g., carrying military materials.

[79] Section 67 SRM reads:

> 67. Merchant vessels flying the flag of neutral States may not be attacked unless they:
>
> (a) are believed on reasonable grounds to be carrying contraband or breaching a blockade, and after prior warning they intentionally and clearly refuse to stop, or intentionally and clearly resist visit, search or capture;
>
> (b) engage in belligerent acts on behalf of the enemy;
>
> (c) act as auxiliaries to the enemy s armed forces;
>
> (d) are incorporated into or assist the enemy s intelligence system;
>
> (e) sail under convoy of enemy warships or military aircraft; or
>
> (f) otherwise make an effective contribution to the enemy's military action, e.g., by carrying military materials, and it is not feasible for the attacking forces to first place passengers and crew in a place of safety. Unless circumstances do not permit, they are to be given a warning, so that they can re-route, off-load, or take other precautions.

a neutral.[80] In other words, it seems that the term military objective cannot be used when a belligerent targets a neutral vessel. In terms of ultimate result with regard to the use of force it is, however, the same: force can both be used against a military objective and a vessel that is subject to attack.

Secondly, and more important, the list in Section 60 (enemy merchant vessels) is interesting because on the one hand it lists actions that under the current API targeting rules may indeed turn the vessels into military objectives.[81] One such example is "engagement in acts of war on behalf of the enemy".[82] But on the other hand, it also includes an action that arguably does not pass the threshold of military objective under the API-targeting rules. Of particular importance is the use of force during maritime interception after "refusing an order to stop or active resistance to visit, search or capture".[83] The SRM-commentary mentions that the vessel becomes a military objective by *behaviour*, which is not a standard in API.[84] Article 52 API only renders a civilian object military by nature, location, purpose or use, and not by behaviour. Section 60 SRM, therefore, has listed on the one hand the historical grown ideas that at least the enemy merchantman could be related to the enemy war efforts, which gives rise to the customary law notion that civilian merchant vessels can be targeted if they show a number of activities. On the other hand, there are the contemporary LOAC-targeting rules that aim to make a strict distinction between military targets and civilian objectives. Of note, however, in this context is that Article 49(3) API mentions that the API-provisions on targeting do not otherwise

[80] SRM-Commentary, para 67.7. In a discussion with a Professor Heintschel von Heinegg who was intensely involved in the drafting of the San Remo Manual, he mentioned that the difference and the commentary made here was made in order for some to accept the current draft of the sections, but not to underline a legal distinction between 'subject to attack' and 'military objective'.

[81] The key article is Article 52 API, which reads:

> 1. Civilian objects shall not be the object of attack or of reprisals. Civilian objects are all objects which are not military objectives as defined in paragraph 2.
>
> 2. Attacks shall be limited strictly to military objectives. In so far as objects are concerned, military objectives are limited to those objects which by their nature, location, purpose or use make an effective contribution to military action and whose total or partial destruction, capture or neutralization, in the circumstances ruling at the time, offers a definite military advantage.
>
> 3. In case of doubt whether an object which is normally dedicated to civilian purposes, such as a place of worship, a house or other dwelling or a school, is being used to make an effective contribution to military action, it shall be presumed not to be so used.

[82] Paragraph 60(a) SRM.

[83] Paragraphs 60(e) and 67(a) SRM.

[84] SRM-Commentary, 60.6.

affect the rules of international law applicable in armed conflict at sea or in the air.[85] The provision suggests that customary rules of warfare at sea are not automatically set aside by Article 52 API. This has also led to early comments on these API-provisions in the sense that they did not apply to naval operations.[86] While the general rules of API on targeting apply to naval warfare (as set out in Part III of the *San Remo Manual*), API does not apply as treaty law to naval warfare. Nor does it set aside accepted customary rules on the loss of protection from attack or becoming a military objective during naval warfare. What follows from this, is the view that the customary rule of becoming subject to attack or a military objective when a merchant vessel is resisting submitting itself to belligerent visit and search, cannot be barred through the application of API. It may be arguable and depending on the circumstances whether an enemy merchant vessel without any further suspicion of contributing to the war effort, that refuses an order to stop or actively refusing to be boarded the vessel, is in fact making an effective contributing to military action and the destruction of it will give definite military advantage. If that is the case, in Sections 61 and 68 SRM it is underlined that subsequent measures must be in accordance with the basis targeting rules that includes proportionality. The vessel becomes a military objective, the person on board may or may not be part of the balancing test of proportionality. To illustrate, an enemy passenger liner that sails under convoy of enemy warships may be deemed a military objective, but attacking it may be a disproportionate measure when the passenger liner has many civilians as passengers on board. Another example more closely connected to interception is the situation in which a vessel refuses to let itself be subjected to visit and search and is deemed to be subject to attack. Sinking the vessel may, however, not be a proportionate action depending on the risk posed to the persons on board and the question whether these persons can be seen as having lost their protection as civilians.

10.6.2 Use of Force Under the Prize Law Rules

Next to the situation where force is used against a vessel that may be considered as military objective, the other situation is the use of force against merchant vessels under the prize law rules. These rules apply to the use of force against neutral and enemy merchant vessels. The unique thing, that has already been noted, is that the

---

[85] Article 49(3) API reads:

> 3. The provisions of this Section apply to any land, air or sea warfare which may affect the civilian population, individual civilians or civilian objects on land. They further apply to all attacks from the sea or from the air against objectives on land but do not otherwise affect the rules of international law applicable in armed conflict at sea or in the air.

[86] Politakis (1997), p. 639, who cites Michael Bothe's view on this.

law of naval warfare accepts a limited number of circumstances in which the use of force against merchant vessels is not prohibited.

With regard to neutral merchant vessels, situations can occur in which the activities of a neutral merchant vessel do in fact conform to the definition of military objective, for instance when it is engaged in belligerent acts on behalf of the enemy.[87] There are also instances were a neutral merchant vessel does not become a military objective, but still can be subject to attack. In the context of maritime interception two situations are interesting to note, which are both listed in Section 67(a) SRM. First, it is considered that carrying contraband to the enemy makes the vessel subject to attack.[88] Still, the decision to attack must fulfil the question if the vessel by carrying contraband actually effectively contributes to the military action and its destruction offers military advantage. It is may be easy for absolute contraband such as weapons and other military materiel, but less easy when it is a cargo of flour meant for the civilian population but put on the contraband list by a belligerent. Contraband can consist of many different things ranging from actual war materiel to other material that may support the war effort in the most widest and remote sense, for instance luxury goods that alleviates the hardships of conflict on the population of the enemy State. It would not seem that there is a clear military advantage in these cases to render the vessel a military objective. Furthermore, questions can be posed whether a vessel that is suspected of carrying contraband and in which the commander of the warship decides to check its paperwork, is immediately considered a military objective because it intentionally and clearly resists the orders of the commander? Although reasonable suspicion of carrying contraband is enough to use the belligerent right of visit and search, is it also enough to consider it a military objective? Probably not, more likely is that based on the targeting-rules the vessel actually needs to be positively identified as carrying contraband. It, however, still allows for using force against the vessel according to the SRM.

Second, neutral merchant vessels are also subject to attack when they (attempt to) breach a blockade.[89] Apart from the overall notifications, the blockading power in stopping the vessel must first issue appropriate warnings when a merchant vessel is trying to breach a blockade after which he can use force to stop it.[90] The mere fact that the vessel breaches a blockade is enough to use force against it. It does not have to fulfil the conditions of a military objective. It might very well be a neutral merchant vessel that is simply taking its chances to escape or enter a blockade port without having anything to do with the conflict. The Netherlands government after

---

[87] Section 67(b) SRM.

[88] Section 67(a) SRM.

[89] Section 67(a) SRM.

[90] Section 98 SRM.

the *Flotilla* incident underlined in its answers to parliament that under these circumstances the rule of using force to stop a blockade-runner still applies.[91]

Both enemy and neutral merchant vessels if captured must be brought before a prize court. If a vessel, however, can be targeted because it is deemed to be a lawful military objective but is captured as a lesser means, this would arguably not be the case. Somewhat outside the discussion is the issue of the use of force rules to sink a vessel *after* it has been captured. In the case of a capture of a military objective this would be possible. In other cases of capture, destruction, for instance because there is no practical opportunity to bring the captured vessel into port or another military necessity arises which necessitates destruction rather than prize court procedures, is debated. If destruction is authorized it is strictly limited to first putting the persons and the ships papers out of any danger.[92] 'If this is not feasible', opines Heintschel von Heinegg, 'destruction is illegal'.[93]

10.7 Human Rights Law and the Law of Naval Warfare

The preceding paragraphs have noted that during international armed conflict force can be used against vessels that are considered to be military objectives. These can be, for example, either vessels that belong to the military opponent of the enemy (enemy warships), but also enemy and neutral merchant vessels that have lost their protection due to hostile activities. A discussion may be raised at this point as to whether human rights law plays a role in this latter situation. If one accepts that human rights law continues to apply during armed conflict, obviously this point of view also applies to armed conflict in the maritime dimension.[94] Both the separate legal regimes of IHRL and the specialized law of naval warfare will co-exist during an international armed conflict. Imagine the following *casus*:

> A neutral merchant container vessel is asked to stop in order to be boarded by a belligerent warship. The commander has reasonable suspicion that the vessel is carrying contraband. After repeatedly hailing the vessel, it still does not comply with the order to stop for inspection. The commander of the belligerent warship decides to administer gradual steps of force; warning-shots across the bow, non-disabling fires and ultimately disabling fire against the vessel if need be or the insertion of a boarding team to take control of the vessel.

---

[91] *Letters to Parliament*, 13 July 2010. Kamerbrief inzake beantwoording vragen van het lid Van Dam over de aanval van Israël op een internationaal hulpkonvooi. At: www.rijksoverheid.nl/documenten-en-publicaties/kamerstukken/2010/07/13/kamerbrief-inzake-beantwoording-vragen-van-het-lid-van-dam-over-de-aanval-van-israel-op-een-internationaal-hulpkonvooi.html.

[92] See rule 2 of the *Submarine Protocol* 1936.

[93] Heinschel von Heinegg 2013, p. 522.

[94] Contrary views also exist, namely the separatist-approach. This approach contains the view that LOAC applies during armed conflict and IHRL applies during peacetime circumstances. See Gill 2013.

The 'traditional' way to look at the use force according to the rules of naval warfare in this case, is that the vessel, by its refusal to cooperate, becomes subject to attack. The fate of the persons on board is part of the proportionality considerations inherent to applying force.

If one would accept that also human rights law continues to apply, another scenario becomes possible relating to targeting of merchant vessels. One could to argue that stopping a neutral merchant vessel is in fact something that must not be seen within the context of whether or not a vessel becomes subject to attack. The neutral merchant vessel is not a party to the conflict and the use of force to stop the vessel does, arguably, not directly weaken the enemy military forces. If one would follow this path, force is used against a civilian merchant vessel with civilians on board and with the ultimate aim to bring the vessel to a prize court. If using force in this case is considered as more of an activity that fits better into the law enforcement paradigm, which, as mentioned in Chap. 2, refers to the exercise by state agents (such as naval forces) of police powers to maintain public security, law and order, it would lead into the direction that the force applied is within the legal regime of human rights. In this perspective, visit and search is approached from the idea that the activity is *de facto* a policing action against civilians. The prevailing view, however, still is that taking measures against resistance to visit and search must be viewed within the context of an act of hostility and therefore under the rules of naval warfare.

Firstly, there exists a set of rules that especially deals with the particular situation. Secondly, the belligerent act of visiting and searching a vessel is not focused on policing, or maintaining public security and law and order at sea, but aims at depriving the enemy of continuing its war effort, for which certain legal instruments exist. It aims, therefore and albeit indirectly, at weakening the enemy armed forces. Supporting this will make the vessel lose its protection. Let us now develop the *casus* a bit further.

> After several warning-shots the vessel has stopped and the boarding team is put on board by helicopter to take control of the vessel. Once on board the target vessel, the crew and passengers appear to be hostile and act through armed resistance against the boarding-team. Some passengers appear to have nothing to do with the resistance against the boarding team and try to stay clear from any violence.

What force can be used against the persons on board? At this stage of the casus, one might again argue that both LOAC and IHRL coexist together. A first view is that by armed resistance the civilians have now lost their protection under LOAC and can be targeted because they are considered to take direct part in hostilities. A second view is that the resistance cannot be brought under the umbrella of taking direct part in hostilities, in which case the persons are still seen as civilians under LOAC protection. This still leaves room for personal self-defence to use force against the persons that may be an imminent threat to the boarding team. Coercive action to control the persons on board in order to ultimately search the vessel, should than be seen to better fit the law enforcement paradigm. In this latter view, force against the persons is regulated by human rights law. Although both views are arguable positions, when seen in the context of the preceded refusal to stop in order for the vessel to be visited and searched which made the vessel subject to attack, subsequent armed resistance by the crew might well be taken as taking up arms against a Party to a conflict aimed at directly causing harm to that Party.

What can be distilled from this small *casus* is that human rights in the context of enforcing belligerent rights against civilian merchant vessels does rise to the foreground and may co-exist as a legal regime next to the law of naval warfare. Once on board and when directly dealing with individuals, there is ground to argue that human rights law plays a role during the conduct of authorities that are based on the law of naval warfare. The *Mavi Marmara* incident shows that opposed boardings are not theoretical and that there might indeed be a mixture of persons on board of persons taking part in hostilities and persons that are not, but under the circumstances may still be threatening to the boarding team. Beyond solely the use of force, the possibility of operational (security) detention also belongs in this discussion. This, also in the context of the *Mavi Marmara* incident, will be touched upon in Chap. 11.

10.8 Use of Force in UN-Mandated Interception Operations

UN-mandated interception operations may range from peacekeeping to peace-enforcement operations in support of or against a target State. Chapter 5 has already commented on the debate on whether a maritime embargo operation can be classified under either Articles 41, 42 or somewhere in between. It was submitted there that explicit maritime embargo operations may well be within the realm of Article 42 of the UN Charter. In such cases, and in the cases where a resolution authorises *all necessary measures*, or similar words, it implies that necessary and proportional force can be used to fulfil the mandate.[95] The phrase does not, however, further clarify within which legal regime force may be applied. The question of how force is applied in a UN-mandated maritime interception operation relates to the question whether the threshold of LOAC is met and whether human rights law applies. The circumstances of the case will drive whether LOAC or human rights law standards apply to force used in a UN-mandated MIO.

---

[95] Interestingly, the first time that the 'all necessary measures' wording was used, was in the context of the Iraqi maritime interception operations in SC Res. 665 (1990), which at that time caused considerable discussions on whether the phrase indicated to authorization for the use of military force. Its exact phrase, however, was not 'all necessary means', but to 'use such measures commensurate to the specific circumstances as may be necessary'. From then on, the precedent of using such wording and especially its meaning was set ever since. See *Security Council Report, 2008 no 1. Security Council actions under Chapter 7; Myths and realities.*

As mentioned above, for LOAC to apply the threshold of armed conflict must be met. The Council's authorization of a maritime embargo operation by itself does not trigger LOAC. The application of LOAC in a UN-mandated MIO does not occur often, especially not in the context of maritime embargo operations. Although the UN measures are on a political level taken against the target State, operationally, the measures taken are directed against the maritime traffic sailing through the embargoed area of operation. The nature of the task and the actual circumstances of how a maritime embargo operation is conducted does not point in the direction that there is an actual armed hostility against the State under sanctions, or a situation in which the embargo-enforcing States by enforcing the embargo have come into a situation of armed conflict with non-state actors. Practice indicates that the authority derived from the laws of naval warfare have not been used in any of the UN-mandated maritime embargo operations. Furthermore, the application of the law of naval warfare is limited to international armed conflicts, which will further limit the scope of application of that part of LOAC in maritime embargo operations.

International armed conflicts that existed while enforcing a UN mandate and which also had a MIO-component were Korea (1950–1953), Iraq (1990) and Libya (2011). Belligerent rights during the MIO were only used in the first two, and not in the case of Libya. In the latter case, as McLaughlin notes (although referring to Iraq operations of 2003, rather than 1990), 'There was no LOAC based notice to mariners or special warning of a nature similar to that promulgated in relations to that of Iraq in 2003'.[96] The difference between Libya and the large-scale operations of Iraq and Korea is that the latter were not specifically implementing economic sanctions, but used the law of naval warfare to fulfil the mandate in a factual situation that amounted to an international armed conflict. The Libya case is unique in the sense that UNSC explicitly authorized a maritime embargo, which was conducted amidst an overall international armed conflict between the NATO-led States and Libya. Once it became clear that the air campaign could be characterised as an armed conflict, what NATO did not do, was adapting the existing authority for maritime embargo force to authority based on the law of naval warfare.

The Libya situation points in the direction that whereas embargo operations may not amount to a situation of armed conflict by itself, the law of naval warfare could more quickly apply when the maritime embargo operations are looked at from a broader campaign perspective in which the maritime embargo is an integrated part of the wider military campaign that based on the factual circumstances of the case could be considered as an international armed conflict against a targeted State, and in which warships participating in the embargo also have a war-fighting task in the wider campaign. A similar argument, although not in the context of enforcing a UN embargo, was used by The Netherlands to apply the law of naval warfare to warships participating in OEF, which on land was considered for a period an international armed conflict. The Netherlands did not divide between the land and

[96] McLaughlin 2015, p. 268. That the law of naval warfare was not applied during the naval operations with regard to Libya has also been my experience, having taken part in OUP.

maritime dimension, even though at sea there was no ongoing factual situation of armed conflict. Going back to the Libya case, from the campaign perspective it could have been argued that also the embargo was integral part of the international armed conflict, a situation derived from the air campaign. Arguably, however, the mandate itself in connection with the phrase *all necessary means* may play a role as a limiting factor as to whether it is actually needed to base the authorities of the embargo on the law of naval warfare. As these authorities are not obligations, they may apply, but at the same time may not sit very comfortable with the overall purpose of the mandate and the political background of why an embargo—as opposed to a belligerent blockade—against specific items was established by the Council in the first place. Therefore, the UN mandate itself may have a limiting effect on the actual use of the law of naval warfare. As McLaughlin concludes; 'In most cases, the UNSC's clear preference is to employ a MEZ [maritime exclusion zone, MDF] of varying scope via the mechanism of non-LOAC based sanctions-enforcement regimes.'[97]

This practice underlines that an embargo that is conducted in the context of an armed conflict could be governed by LOAC, if the States that are conducting the maritime embargo were parties to the armed conflict. This was clearly the case in Korea. In the cases of Iraq (1990–1991) and Libya (2011) this is less straightforward. Some States were and others were not. France, for instance, was engaged in hostilities in both conflicts, whereas the Netherlands was not in either situation. Therefore, the operations involving the use of force by naval forces of the Netherlands conducting the embargo were not governed by LOAC, but by human rights law standards.

Today, there is no doubt that human rights continue to apply in military operations that are based on Chapter VII of the UN Charter. In the *Al Jedda* case the European Court of Human Rights opined that human rights law does not apply only in situations where the UNSC has explicitly stated that it does not.[98] In practice, none of the UN resolutions that have formed the basis for MIO have explicitly mentioned that IHRL does not apply. On the contrary, human rights are mentioned specifically in certain resolutions that are connected to MIO. The UN resolutions

[97] McLaughlin 2015, p. 269.

[98] *Al Jedda*. The Court stated in para 102 that:

> Against this background, the Court considers that, in interpreting its resolutions, there must be a presumption that the Security Council does not intend to impose any obligation on Member States to breach fundamental principles of human rights. In the event of any ambiguity in the terms of a Security Council Resolution, the Court must therefore choose the interpretation which is most in harmony with the requirements of the Convention and which avoids any conflict of obligations. In the light of the United Nations' important role in promoting and encouraging respect for human rights, it is to be expected that clear and explicit language would be used were the Security Council to intend States to take particular measures which would conflict with their obligations under international human rights law.

with regard to piracy have consistently underlined that the fight against piracy must be in accordance with human rights.[99] SC Res. 2020 (2011) noted in several paragraphs that action taken against possible pirates must be in accordance with relevant human rights law. The Netherlands district courts, before which several piracy cases were brought, never doubted that human rights law applies in the cases of pirates captured within the context of the counter-piracy operations off the coast of Somalia and in the context of the UN resolutions. As such, with regard to counter-piracy operations off the coast of Somalia no tension arises between Article 103 UN Charter and the applicability of IHRL.[100] Another example is SC Res. 2146 (2014) with regard to Libya. In this resolution the Council explicitly stated that authority to board and inspect and to use all measures commensurate to the specific circumstances must be in compliance with international humanitarian law and human rights law, as may be applicable.[101]

Secondly, in terms of attribution, in principle human rights violations can be attributed to States even if the State conducts the operation under Chapter VII of the UN Charter. This would not be the case where a maritime interception operation is UN-controlled and actions can be attributed to the UN rather than to the participating State. The only MIO that falls under this situation is MTF UNIFIL. Taking the view that maritime embargo operations do usually not amount to an armed conflict, force used is regulated by human rights law. Force against the vessel, for instance to stop it, must be in line with the *Saiga*-criteria, where after appropriate warnings, reasonable and necessary force as a last resort[102] and where the lives of the persons are not endangered is possible. Once on board the suspect vessel, force used against persons is regulated by human rights law standards.

10.9 Use of Self-Defence Interception Operations

The use of force in self-defence naval operations in the traditional sense will usually trigger the conditions of an international armed conflict to which LOAC applies. In terms of the use of force against the opponent, in general, there is no difference between an IAC and a NIAC. In terms of the application of the law of naval warfare, however, there is a difference as this part of LOAC is considered not to be applicable in a NIAC. The non-applicability of the law of naval warfare in this situation has consequences. As noted above, the rules on prize give the authority to use force against merchant vessels. In a NIAC situation, these authorities cannot be

[99] E.g. 1816, para 11; 1846, para 14; 1851, para 6.

[100] See also Guilfoyle 2010a, p. 152.

[101] SC Res. 2146 (2014), para 5.

[102] The ROE practice is that the more force is applied, the higher the authority must be to apply force. Captain (Royal Navy) Shaun Lyons mentions on the 1990 Iraq mission that in close consultation with the Ministry of Defence, the ROE permitted firing shells across the bow of the ship. Lyons 1993, p. 163.

applied. The result is an unfavourable situation that in a self-defence operation that has the character of a NIAC there are no legal instruments that can be used against non-state actors on board a foreign-flagged vessel. A belligerent right of visit and search does not exist. As mentioned in Chap. 9, one possibility would be to apply self-defence in the manner to provide a legal basis when it is 'harboring' non-state actors and the flag State is unable and or unwilling to act, or when the vessel is completely under the control of the non-state actor and has become a military objective. Although the individuals themselves on board may be directly targeted, from a practical perspective the boarding of the vessel will most probably be one of the prerequisites to get close enough to the individual. Instead of boarding the vessel, directly targeting persons through other, for instance more technical means such as armed UAVs, is possible but would still run against the issue of flag state jurisdiction.

As Chap. 6 has outlined, self-defence is also viewed to be a direct legal ground in cases where the cargo of a vessel is so imminently threatening that it triggers the right of self-defence. In cases where the armed conflict threshold is not passed, it seems obvious that the use of force is regulated by human rights law. Chapter 9 has, however, also noted the existence of a view that is called the "third rail" by Geoffrey Corn,[103] in which the law of self-defence provides both a basis *and* a legal regime for and during military operations. The law of self-defence is not only used to determine whether force *can* be used, but also provides the legal regime in which force *is* used, based on the conditions for the application of military force under the law of self-defence (proportionality, necessity, immediacy). The third rail is argued in cases where the legal basis is self-defence, but where the situation may not be considered as an armed conflict. Corn has correctly noted that his approach completely blurs the distinction between the *ius ad bellum* and the *ius in bello*, as self-defence is not meant to provide also a legal regime on the use of force. It furthermore blurs the divide between the use of force based on the law of armed conflict and human rights law.

10.10 Final Remarks

In order to successfully conduct maritime interception operations it may be necessary that force is used. The legal regimes that regulate the application of force are human rights law and the law of armed conflict. Although the discussion on the application of force in the maritime dimension has traditionally been approached through the law of the sea, it has been submitted in this chapter that human rights law standards have been applied to the maritime dimension, as there are no explicit rules on the application of force available in the framework of the law of the sea. The evolution within human rights of extraterritorial applicability of human rights

[103] Corn 2012.

law allows accepting more readily that the force against vessels and persons at sea can be considered through human rights law standards.

Where maritime interception operations are conducted in the context of an international armed conflict, the law of armed conflict, and in particular the law of naval warfare, applies. This subset of the law of armed conflict has specific rules that regulate force in the maritime dimension during an international armed conflict. This regime does, however, not apply during non-international armed conflicts. As human rights law standards can also apply to MIO during armed conflict, in terms of the application of force human rights law and the law of naval warfare can co-exist. The *Mavi Marmara* incident has shown that the questions on this relationship are not wholly theoretical. There is, however, as of yet not much thought on how these two frameworks interrelate.

References

Allen C (2006) Limits to the use of force in maritime operations in support of WMD counter-proliferation initiatives. In: Sparks T, Sulmasy G (eds) International Law Studies 81. Naval War College, Newport RI, pp. 77–139

Arbitral Tribunal constituted pursuant to Article 287. Guyana vs. Suriname, Award of the Arbitral Tribunal constituted pursuant to Article 287, and in accordance with annex vii, of the United Nations Convention on the Law of the Sea, 17 September 2007

Bartels R (2008) Gewapend conflict is geen eenduidig begrip. Internationaal recht in de kijker. Belgian Red Cross, pp. 69–81

Benbow T (1999) Maritime Power in the 1990–91 Gulf War and the Conflict in the Former Yugoslavia. In: Dorman A, Lawrence Smith M, Uttley M (eds) The changing face of maritime power. Macmillan Press Ltd, London, pp. 107–125

Blank L (2013) Rules of engagement and legal frameworks for multinational counter-piracy operations. Case Western Reserve Journal of International Law 46, pp. 397–409

Cacciaguidi-Fahy S (2007) The law of the sea and human rights. Panoptica Vitoria 1:9, pp. 1–21

Churchill W (1927) The World Crisis, 1916–1918, Part II. Thornton, Butterworth Ltd., London

Corn G (2012) Self-defense targeting: blurring the line between the ius ad bellum and the ius in bello. Watkin K, Norris A (eds) International Law Studies 88. Naval War College, Newport RI, pp. 57–92

den Heijer M (2011) Europe and extraterritorial asylum. Dissertation, Amsterdam

Dinstein Y (2005) The conduct of hostilities under the law of international armed conflict. Cambridge University Press, Cambridge

District Court of Rotterdam, The Netherlands, Al Feddah, 12 October 2012

Doswald-Beck L (2011) Human rights in times of conflict and terrorism. Oxford University Press, New York

Droege C (2008) Elective Affinities? Human rights and humanitarian law. International Review of the Red Cross 90:871, pp. 501–548

ECtHR, Rigoupolos v. Spain, (appl. no. 37388/97), Decision, 12 January 1999

ECtHR, Medvedyev and others v. France, application no. 3394/03. Judgment 29 March 2010

ECtHR, Loizidou v. Turkey, application no. 40/1993/435/514, (Preliminary objections), 23 March 1995

ECtHR, Al-Skeini and others v. The United Kingdom (application no. 55721/07,) Judgment, 7 July 2011

ECtHR, Hirsii Jamaa and others. v. Italy, (appl. no. 27765/09), Judgment, 23 February 2012

ECtHR, Xhavara and others v. Italy and Albania, (appl. no 39473/98), 11 January 2011
ECtHR, Women on Waves and others v. Portugal, (appl. no. 31276/05), 3 February 2009
ECtHR, Bankovic vs Belgium et al., appl. No. 52207/09, Decision Grand Chamber, 21 December 2001
EU Council joint action 2008/851/CFSP, 10 November 2008
Fenrick W (1991) The merchant vessel as legitimate target in the law of naval warfare. In: Delissen A, Tanja G (eds) Humanitarian law of armed conflict challenges ahead. Essays in honour of Frits Kalshoven. Martinus Nijhoff publishers, Dordrecht, pp. 425–443
Gill T (2014) Some thoughts on the relationship between international humanitarian law and international human rights law: A plea for mutual respect and a common sense approach. In: Haek Y, McGonigle Leyh B, Burbano-Herrera C, Contreras-Garduño D (eds) The realisation of human rights: When theory meets practice: Studies in honour of Leo Zwaak. Cambridge, Intersentia, Portland, OR, pp. 335–350
Gill T (2015) Some thoughts on the relationship between international humanitarian law and international human rights law: A plea for mutual respect and a common-sense approach. Yearbook of International Humanitarian Law, pp. 251–266
Gosalbo-Bono R, Boelaert S (2014) The European Union's comprehensive approach to combating piracy at sea: Legal aspects. In: Koutrakos P, Skordas A (eds) The law and practice of piracy at sea: European and international perspectives. Hart Publishing, Oxford/Portland, OR, pp. 81–167
Guilfoyle D (2009) Shipping interdiction and the law of the sea. Cambridge University Press, New York
Guilfoyle D (2010a) Counter-piracy law enforcement and human rights. International & Comparative Law Quarterly 59, pp. 141–169
Guilfoyle D (2010b) The laws of war and the fight against Somali piracy: Combatants or criminals. Melbourne Journal of International Law 11, pp. 1–13
Guilfoyle D (2015) The use of force against pirates. In: Weller M (ed) The Oxford Handbook of the Use of Force in International Law. Oxford University Press, New York, pp. 1057–1076
Heintschel von Heinegg W (2010) Maritime interception/interdiction operations. In: Gill T, Fleck D (eds) The Handbook of the International Law of Military Operations, 2nd edn. Oxford University Press, New York, pp. 375–393
Heintschel von Heinegg W (2013) The law of armed conflict at sea. In: Fleck D (ed) The Handbook of International Humanitarian Law, 3rd edn. Oxford University Press, New York, pp. 486–498
Heintschel von Heinegg W (2014) Maritime warfare. In: Clapham A, Gaeta P (eds) The Oxford Handbook of International Law in Armed Conflict. Oxford University Press, New York, pp. 145–181
ICTY, Prosecutor v. Dusko Tadic, IT-94-1, 2 October 1995
ICTY, Prosecutor v. Haradinaj, Trial Chamber, judgment, 3 April 2008
ITLOS, MV Saiga no. 2, Saint Vincent and the Grenadines vs. Guinea, judgment 1 July 1999
Klein N (2011) Maritime security and the law of the sea. Oxford University Press, New York
Klein N (2014) A case for harmonizing laws on maritime interception of irregular migrants. International & Comparative Law Quarterly 63 pp. 787–814
LA Times (26 December 1990) Gulf 'Peace Ship' Stormed: U.S. Sailors Tussle With Crew, Women on Iraq-Bound Ship. http://articles.latimes.com/1990-12-26/news/mn-6714_1_peace-ship. Accessed 17 February 2017
Letters to Parliament, 13 July 2010. Kamerbrief inzake beantwoording vragen van het lid Van Dam over de aanval van Israël op een internationaal hulpkonvooi (parliamentary questions on the attack of Israel on an international aid convoy)
Lyons S (1993) Naval operations in the Gulf. In: Rowe P (ed) The Gulf war 1990–91 in international and English law. Routledge/Sweet and Maxwell, London/New York
McLaughlin R (2009) United Nations Naval Peace Operations in the Territorial Sea. Martinus Nijhoff Publishers, Leiden

McLaughlin R (2015) United Nations Security Council Practice in relation to the use of force in no-fly zones and maritime exclusion zones. In: Weller M (ed) The Oxford Handbook of the Use of Force in International Law. Oxford University Press, New York, pp. 251–271

Melzer N (2006) Targeted killings in international law. Oxford University Press, New York

Milanovic M (2012) Al Skeini and Al-Jedda in Strasbourg. European Journal of International Law 23:1, pp. 121–139

Nevill P (2015) Military sanctions enforcement in the absence of express authorization. In: Weller M (ed) The Oxford Handbook of the Use of Force in International Law. Oxford University Press, New York, pp. 272–292

Papastavridis E (2010) European court of human rights Medvedyev et al v France (Grand Chamber, application no 3394/03) Judgment of 29 March 2010. International Comparative Law Quarterly 59:03, pp. 867–882

Papastavridis E (2013) The interception of vessels on the high seas. Hart Publishing, Oxford/ Portland, OR

Petrig A (2013) Human rights in counter-piracy operations: No legal vacuum but legal uncertainty. In: Mejia M jr et al (eds) Piracy at sea. WMU Studies in Maritime Affairs 2, Heidelberg, pp. 31–45

Petrig A (2014) Human Rights and Law Enforcement at Sea: Arrest, Detention and Transfer of piracy suspects. Brill Martinus Nijhoff Publishers, Leiden

Pokrant M (1999) Desert Shield at Sea. What the Navy really did. Greenwood Press, Westport, Connecticut/London

Politakis G (1997) Modern aspects of the law of naval warfare and maritime neutrality. Kegan Paul International, London/New York

Pouw E (2013) International human rights law and the law of armed conflict in the context of counterinsurgency. Netherlands Defence Academy, Dissertation, NLDA printing office, Breda

Rothwell D, Stephens T (2010) The International Law of the Sea. Hart Publishing, Oxford/ Portland, OR

Smith H (1950) The law and custom of the sea. 2nd edn. Stevens & Sons limited, London

Stephens D (1999) The impact of the 1982 Law of the Sea Convention on the conduct of peacetime naval/military operations. California Western International Law Journal 29:2, pp. 283–311

The Guardian (2008) British Commando kill two pirates in stand-off. 13 November 2008. www.theguardian.com/world/2008/nov/13/pirates-killed-gulf-aden. Accessed 17 February 2017

Treves T (2009) Piracy, laws of the sea, and use of force: Developments off the coast of Somalia. European Journal of International Law 20:2, pp. 399–408

Treves T (2010) Human Rights and the Law of the Sea. Berkeley Journal of International Law 28:1, pp. 1–13

UN Security Council (2008) Security Council Report, 2008 no 1. Security Council actions under Chapter VII; Myths and realities

Zwanenburg M (2014) Enkele juridische aspecten van militaire beveiligingsteams aan boord van koopvaardijschepen (Vessel Protection Detachments). Militair Rechtelijk Tijdschrift 107:6, pp. 205–218

Chapter 11
Detention and Maritime Interception

The practitioner should be cautioned that authority to intercept a vessel does not always equate to authority to detain the vessel, its contents or its crew.
—Winston G. McMillan, Major United States Marine Corps

Contents

Abstract Detention at sea during maritime interception operations differs somewhat with detention during military operation on land. Whereas generally the same legal regime for operational detention applies in both dimensions, there are some differences. On the on hand, certain legal grounds to detain do not apply at sea, which means that fewer grounds to detain individuals at sea exist. On the other hand, the legal regime for detention at sea has particular rules with regard to certain specific individuals, such as members of an enemy merchant fleet and passengers on board a captured vessel. Lastly, the maritime environment itself may have its effects on the manner in which way legal safeguards are implemented.

Keywords Operational detention · security detainees · criminal detainees · passengers · prisoners of war at sea · *Mavi Marmara* incident · *Freedom Flotilla*

M. Fink, *Maritime Interception and the Law of Naval Operations*,
https://doi.org/10.1007/978-94-6265-249-1_11

11.1 Introduction

In the maritime dimension,[1] there is a more or less traditional view that maritime interception operations have primarily been cargo and vessel-focused, rather than person-focused.[2] UN-mandated maritime embargo operations are generally concerned with prohibited items, which are dealt with by either seizing the goods or diverting the vessels. During international armed conflict, and apart from taking prisoners of war, the law of naval warfare is mainly concerned with contraband goods or the capture of vessels breaching blockades. Also prize courts have no legal interest in persons. It is not its function to punish persons carrying contraband. Detention at sea of persons has, therefore, been a somewhat exceptional activity. This is, however, a view that needs to be left behind. Today's maritime security operations have put a focus on the fact that the military at sea may encounter persons that may, for some reason, need to be detained. For example, because the person is a criminal suspect or is part of an organized armed group. Counter-piracy operations are obviously a clear example and have done much also to surface the challenges that come with detention of persons at sea. During the Libya operation in 2011, the Security Council authorized measures to stop mercenaries, next to arms related materiel. This was a first step away from prohibiting only products. Operation *Enduring Freedom* has searched for terrorists and, interestingly, within the context of armed conflict, the Israeli blockade operations have brought the fate of persons on board vessels under greater and even primary attention, whereas no or hardly any publication on the law of blockade have spoken about the fate of the persons on board before. A general outcry by States was heard to release the persons on board the *Mavi Marmara*, rapidly followed by a request of the Council to release the detained persons that where on the vessels that attempted to breach the blockade. These examples and the awareness that persons may be the subject of maritime interception operations have even prompted a change to the definition of MIO as mentioned in Chap. 1 to include persons next to objects. In sum, situations may exist during maritime interception operations where persons at sea may be deprived of their liberty. This chapter reflects on detention in the context of maritime interception operations. It will briefly introduce the notion of operational detention and will then discuss some particularities of detention in the maritime dimension.

---

[1] McMillan 2011.

[2] This is, however, not to say that at sea in general there has never been any attention to human beings. Obviously, within the context of maritime law enforcement, such as drug- or human trafficking, there is clear attention to human beings at sea. But within the context of conducting naval operations, persons at sea played a secondary role of importance to vessels and cargo.

11.2 Operational Detention

The term *operational detention* is now often used to describe detention in military operations. Kleffner has defined operational detention as: 'the deprivation of physical liberty of a person in the context of a military operation, whether for reasons of security or law enforcement purposes.'[3] He states that this definition of deprivation of physical liberty is intentionally broad, 'to capture military operations in their entire variety'.[4] Within the term operational detention, a threefold distinction is made in persons that can be detained, either for reasons of security (security detainees or administrative detainees), persons that are suspected of criminal offenses (criminal detainees) and persons that can be detained because they fall within the category of prisoners of war (PW). Certain features separate security detainees from criminal detainees, which is important to give some attention to at this stage. First, security detainees are detained for reasons of a possible *future* threat (although that can be based on possible past conduct), while criminal detainees are detained because of a suspected (criminal) action that has already taken place. A second difference concerns the authority to detain. Security detention is ordered by the executive branch (in this case the military) while criminal detention is ordered by the judicial branch. A third difference is that security detention is usually aimed at enhancing the security of the military force, or the persons that are entitled to protection. Criminal detention takes place because a certain act may be punishable under criminal law. Detention in this case is, therefore, not because the person threatens the military itself. Security detention can, therefore, also be considered as defensive measures, whereas criminal detention is more of an active engagement towards suspected criminals.

Next to the three different categories of detainees, one can also distinguish between legal grounds[5] for detention and safeguard and treatment for detention. The first relates to the legal ground upon which a person can be detained. It is underlined here that at all times, as a fundamental requirement for detention, a legal ground must exist, implied or explicit, for the detention of persons. The general challenge in modern conflict within extraterritorial non-international armed conflicts is that not under all circumstances a specific legal ground may exist in situations that operationally a detention is needed, but is argued through interpretation of other provisions. The second, safeguards and treatment for detention, relates to the wellbeing of the detained individual. This point is subdivided in a substantive (treatment) and procedural part (safeguards). For example, treatment relates to how detained persons must be physically treated. Safeguards relate to the individuals rights during detention in terms of legal process, such as to be brought promptly before a judge (Fig. 11.1).

---

[3] Kleffner 2010, p. 465.

[4] Kleffner 2010, p. 465.

[5] I am using the term legal *ground* as oppose to legal basis, to distinguish between the legal bases in general for maritime interception operations and the legal ground for detention in particular.

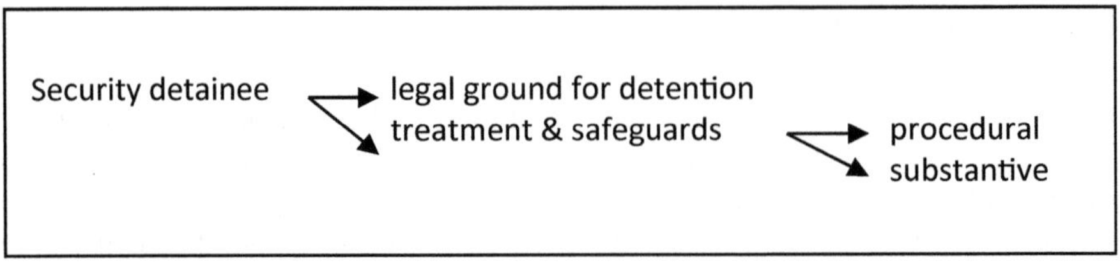

Fig. 11.1 How operational detention can be subdivided; example of a security detainee (*Source* M. Fink)

11.3 What Constitutes Detention During Maritime Interception Operations

In the broadest sense, detention is the deprivation of liberty. On the one hand, this goes beyond the classic detention situation after an arrest. On the other, a detention must also be sufficiently serious not to be merely a temporary restriction of movement. The obvious examples are persons that are being detained on board because they are suspected of having committed a crime or persons that are captured as enemy combatants. There may also be situations in which the answer to the question whether a person is in fact detained, is not so entirely obvious. Three examples to illustrate:

> *Example 1: small boat search*
>
> A boarding team comes on board a small -dhow-type- vessel for a search of the cargo. They tell the persons on board to stay on one side of the vessel until the vessel is searched and the boarding team has left the vessel. If the crew is not cooperating, they can also be forced to do what is ordered. The boarding team is carrying arms and the supporting warship has an armed over-watch on the small vessel and the team. When the vessel is cleared and the boarding team has left, the crew is free to move over the vessel again.
>
> *Example 2: transit of a captured blockade runner*
>
> A vessel is captured because it has tried to breach a blockade. The captured vessel is being escorted into port. During the transit to port the vessel is under military control by an escorting warship and a security team is on board the vessel itself. The captured vessel is still navigated by the original crew. The captain and crew of the vessel will have to stay on board until the vessel is anchored in port. In port, a further decision awaits to possibly keep the captain and relevant crew available during the prize court procedures, or whether they are free to leave.
>
> *Example 3: diversion of a suspected vessel to inspection port*
>
> A large container-vessel is searched during a UN-mandated maritime embargo operation. During the search, the crew not essentially needed for navigating the vessel or assisting the search is asked to gather and stay in one room which is under the control of a security team from the warship that is conducting the boarding. During the inspection the boarding team has gained a reasonable suspicion that there may be forbidden items on board. The MIO commander has therefore decided to divert the vessel to a port for a further and more thorough inspection. The inspection teams leave the vessel. Under convoy of a warship the vessel is ordered to navigate into port X for further inspection.

These three examples give rise to the question of when one can actually speak of detention of person on board a vessel that is under different levels of control by the visiting warship. Doswald-Beck offers that detention exists when persons are restricted to a place and cannot leave when he or she wishes to leave.[6] The European Court's guide on Article 5 ECHR mentions that: 'Relevant objective factors to be considered include the possibility to leave the restricted area, the degree of supervision and control over the person's movements, the extent of isolation and the availability of social contacts'.[7] In the small boat example, there may be good reasons to argue that these persons are deprived of their liberty because during the search of the vessel they are not allowed to move and can be forced to stay at their appointed place, under threat of force. These persons are under control of the boarding party. It is, however, different when the boarding party is on board the small boat during a so-called 'friendly approach'-activity, and no one is restrained in their movements, nor is there any change that coercive force will be used. In the blockade-runner example, the capture is focused on the vessel and not intended to detain the persons. As will be discussed in later sections of this chapter, the crew and passengers are not considered prisoners of war. The persons on board are not physically detained and are free to move on the ship in order to operate it, but they are still forced to navigate it into an assigned port, while under military control. The third example is slightly different in the sense that although the crew is not physically detained and there is also no military control on board the vessel, still the vessel is asked to follow orders to be diverted to an inspection port. Their limitation in liberty is that they cannot sail the vessel elsewhere than ordered by warships enforcing a UN mandate. One could argue that the situation of persons on board a captured *vessel* is in fact merely a practical or logistical one, in which the persons are not deprived of their liberty, but where there is simply no other possibility to let them leave until a port is reached. Persons on board are not held for reasons of security or because of criminal detention, but because they practically cannot leave the vessel and are usually needed to sail the vessel into a port.[8] Could, theoretically, the crew and passengers be transferred at an earlier stage at sea to another vessel, they will be at liberty to do so when the possibility occurs. It has also never been argued that persons limited in their liberty through the execution of rules of the law of naval warfare, because their vessel was captured or diverted, were also automatically detained. The vessel and goods will be brought before a prize court, but no juridical procedures are instigated against the persons on board that vessel. Persons on board a captured vessel can be released as soon as they reach the port. When it is expected that the persons will have to testify in court proceedings, it is more likely that they will be summoned by court order and may, for the purpose of ensuring they will testify, be detained. But all this will happen under

[6] Doswald-Beck 2011, p. 254.

[7] *ECtHR Guide on Article 5 of the Convention Right to liberty and security* (2014), para 8.

[8] The alternative is to bring in a so-called prize crew, which is a military crew that will take over the vessel.

lawful court orders. In sum, the law of naval warfare takes the view that when capturing vessels, the persons are not also automatically detained. It is thus submitted here that the capture or visit of a vessel does not mean that persons on board are thereby automatically detained. The same can apply to a diversion to a port based on the need for further inspection of a vessel for sanctioned goods during a UN-mandated maritime embargo operation: No detention of the persons on board takes place in principle, unless the actual situation on board considered through objective factors lead must lead to the conclusion that persons are in fact detained. For instance, when during the transfer of the vessel persons are physically held on board, confined to a quarter under surveillance of an armed guard for reasons of security of the boarding crew.

11.4 Prisoners of War at Sea and Crews of Enemy and Neutral Merchant Vessels

The first category of operational detainees is prisoners of war (PW). This category exists when there is an existence of an international armed conflict. Article 4 GC III and Articles 43 and 44 API define who can be considered as prisoners of war. The interesting point to note with regard to PWs at sea is that in Article 4 GC III, next to the regular combatants and all who fall within the scope of combatants, subparagraph 5 also includes members of crews, including masters, pilots and apprentices, of the merchant marine of the parties to the conflict. This Article, therefore, opens the possibility that civilians on board enemy merchant vessels (as opposed to neutral merchant vessels) may be considered as prisoners of war. This provision must be read in conjunction with Articles 5–8 of the *Hague Convention XI Relative to certain Restrictions with regard to the Exercise of the Right of Capture in Naval War* (HC XI) that deal with the status of persons on board an enemy merchant vessel. This group of provisions is, basically, grounded in three principles. First is that enemy merchant vessels are liable to capture. Second is that persons on board enemy merchant vessels are not to be made prisoners of war, *if* they formally promise not to take service on an enemy merchant vessel or take part in operations of war.[9] And the third principle is that when the vessel otherwise engages in acts rendering the vessel a military objective,[10] the second principle does not apply.[11] Consequently, they will be made prisoner of war.[12]

---

[9] Articles 5–7 HC XI.

[10] See Section 60 SRM.

[11] Article 8 HC XI.

[12] Tucker (1955, pp. 111–112) opines that the practice in the Second World War has led to the obsoleteness of releasing enemy merchant crews by written promise of not returning to operations of war. The practice during the Second World War, however, must be seen in the context that merchant vessels and crews were effectively integrated in the warfighting capacity of the belligerents and structurally constituted military objectives.

Unlike crews of enemy merchant vessels, Article 4 GC III does not contain grounds to detain a crew of a neutral merchant vessel under PW status. The *US Commander's Handbook on the law of naval operations* notes in this regard that: 'The officers and crews of captured neutral vessels who are nationals of a neutral nation do not become prisoners of war and must be repatriated as soon as circumstances permit'.[13] The logic behind capturing the vessel and not the crew may be that the crew only sails the ship and is not automatically connected to the contraband they are carrying. Although it is not unthinkable that it might be otherwise, captains and crews of, for example, huge container vessels that solely serve as transporters of containers will in principle not be connected to the cargo the vessel is carrying.

11.4.1 Passengers

Passengers are a separate category of persons that can be on board a vessel. With passengers are meant civilian passengers. The fact that a vessel is considered an enemy vessel does not also presuppose that the passengers on board should be considered as enemy, which can be detained under PW status. The distinction is important because, firstly, Article 8 HC XI refers to *ships* taking part in hostilities, not persons. Secondly, the point of view that passengers are not crew or combatants matters in the proportionality consideration when a warship comes in the position that it has to use force against a merchant vessel. Passengers who are not part of the crew must be dealt with on their own individual merits. In line with this approach Heintschel von Heinegg mentions that: 'Passengers who are nationals of a neutral State will be released unless they have directly taken part in hostilities.'[14] As a point of departure, therefore, passengers cannot be detained, but their activity on board will determine whether there are grounds to detain them. A passenger can either be a security threat or directly take part in hostilities.[15] In the latter case, passengers will lose their protection as a civilian.

---

[13] *US Commander's Handbook*, para 7.10.2.

[14] Heintschel von Heinegg 2014, p. 171.

[15] Historical cases exist in which passengers on board neutral vessels were deemed to be combatants by the visiting belligerent forces, such as the *Asama Maru* case in 1940. In 1940 *HMS Liverpool* received the order to board a Japanese-flagged merchant vessel *Asama Maru.* The vessel was suspected of having German passengers on board the vessel, which they had. The Germans were taken as prisoners of war on the basis that these Germans were, although not in the military service, military aged men that could ultimately take service against England. Japan protested against this action. Later, it appeared that several of the captured men were 'relatively unsuitable for military service'. See Dunham 1997; *The Canberra Times*, 8 February 1940, p. 4: 'Settlement of Asama Maru controversy. Anglo-Japanese understanding. Britain offers release of nine men'.

11.5 Security Detainees at Sea

Security detainees are persons that are detained for reasons of security. A core characteristic is that security detainees are civilians. This category is not limited to situations of armed conflict alone, but occurs also in situations outside such circumstances. The necessity to detain persons for reasons of security may exist within the whole range of military operations, from low to full-scale naval operations, from international to non-international armed conflicts to outside armed conflict. Consequently, this means that both IHRL and LOAC might be applicable to security detention.

11.5.1 Security Detention Under LOAC

Security detention under LOAC during an international armed conflict is based on Articles 42[16] and 78[17] of GC IV, in which possibilities exist to detain civilians for imperative reasons of security. What imperative reasons of security means, is not further defined,[18] but it does signal that security detention must be seen as an exceptional authority. Because GC IV applies in occupied territory, it poses a problem for the applicability of these articles to a vessel on the high seas. There are no equivalent provisions of Articles 42 and 78 GC IV for a maritime situation to

[16] Article 42 GC IV reads:

> The internment or placing in assigned residence of protected persons may be ordered only if the security of the Detaining Power makes it absolutely necessary.
> If any person, acting through the representatives of the Protecting Power, voluntarily demands internment and if his situation renders this step necessary, he shall be interned by the Power in whose hands he may be.

[17] Article 78 GC IV reads:

> If the Occupying Power considers it necessary, for imperative reasons of security, to take safety measures concerning protected persons, it may, at the most, subject them to assigned residence or to internment.
> Decisions regarding such assigned residence or internment shall be made according to a regular procedure to be prescribed by the Occupying Power in accordance with the provisions of the present Convention. This procedure shall include the right of appeal for the parties concerned. Appeals shall be decided with the least possible delay. In the event of the decision being upheld, it shall be subject to periodical review, if possible every six months, by a competent body set up by the said Power.
> Protected persons made subject to assigned residence and thus required to leave their homes shall enjoy the full benefit of Article 39 of the present Convention.

[18] See on the discussion what 'security' could mean Pouw 2013, pp. 391–393.

board a vessel on the high seas. If a vessel is captured on the high seas, there will not be a situation of an occupied *territory*. One could argue that a captured enemy vessel under the control of a belligerent State can be *de facto* occupied 'territory'. This does, however, not sit well with the point of view that a vessel is legally not a territory. Taking the legal fiction of the occupied territory-argument just a bit further, one could also argue that the belligerent State that is an occupying power elsewhere on land can extend their occupying powers to vessels from the occupied State. This fictional occupied territory-theory only applies, however, to enemy merchant vessels and not to neutral merchant vessels.

Another argument could be that an implied authority for belligerent naval forces may exist in order to be able to ascertain rights under the law of naval warfare. There may be many different reasons why persons want to breach a blockade, ranging from economic reasons of not wanting to be stuck at a blockaded port, to acts that deliberately are challenging the blockading State. The *Freedom Flotilla* incident is a good example of the latter. Although it may be argued that some persons can be detained on the basis of the fact that they have taken direct part in hostilities or acted in a criminal manner against the boarding team, there may be a need for others that did not take up arms against the boarding to be detained for reasons of security, so that the capturing power can get the vessel safely to port. This argument may be the maritime translation of the view that was submitted by the ICRC: 'It flows from the practice of armed conflict and the logic of IHL that parties to a conflict may capture persons deemed to pose a serious security threat and that such persons may be interned as long as they continue to pose a threat'.[19] Although this view was expressed in the context of implied powers to detain in the context of a NIAC, its core underlines a view that implied authority can exist in LOAC to detain persons. The view is also found in the Turkel Report, which states in para 231: 'Inherent in the authority to use force under international humanitarian law is the power to detain someone who poses a threat to the safety of military personnel or who is interfering with the conduct of a mission'. This argument, although fiercely debated,[20] is, as said, used also to find a legal basis for detention in extraterritorial non-international armed conflict. The issue has surfaced because in the 'traditional' NIACs fought on one's own territory detention can be based on domestic laws, but in an extraterritorial NIAC domestic laws cannot support the original set-up of the NIAC framework. Although no explicit grounds for detention exists, proponents argue it implicitly, for instance through Common Article 3 of the Geneva Conventions, as a result of the principle of military necessity, or as a 'lesser means authority' derived from the authority to kill. The idea is that if one can lawfully kill the opponent, the lesser means (to detain) is also lawful.[21] This view does, however, exclude security detention of persons that cannot be killed in first instance, which still leaves a gap of

[19] Debuf 2009, p. 863.

[20] See e.g. Aughey and Sari 2015a, b and the resulting debate on *EJIL TALK!* At: http://www.ejiltalk.org/ihl-does-authorize-detention-in-niac-a-rejoinder-to-rogier-bartels/; Rona 2015.

[21] Aughey and Sari 2015a, pp. 103–104.

an authority to detain. Yet others remain reluctant to accept such a right, either dismissing such right or staying in the middle by stating that it is not explicitly regulated. From a maritime perspective, security detention based on the domestic laws can only exist when the detention is within the sovereign waters of a coastal State, or when the vessel flies the same flag as the boarding belligerent warship, or when the persons are on board the belligerent warship.

11.5.2 Security Detention Under Human Rights Law

Article 5 para 1, a to f ECHR, states the legal exceptions to the liberty of persons. It is generally accepted that none of the exceptions expressly allow for security detention.[22] The commonly used argument in which way this challenge is circumvented, is that a State derogates from its obligations, in the case of the European Convention, under Article 5 ECHR.[23] Derogation would suspend the obligations of the detaining power. For derogation to be possible Article 15(1) ECHR states that:

> 1. In time of war or other public emergency threatening the life of the nation any High Contracting Party may take measures derogating from its obligations under this Convention to the extent strictly required by the exigencies of the situation, provided that such measures are not inconsistent with its other obligations under international law.

Firstly, there needs to be a time of war or other public emergency threatening the life of the nation. And secondly, a State can do so to the extent strictly required by the exigencies of the situation. Obviously, the Article was not set-up to fit situations on board foreign-flagged vessels. Although, arguably, the capture of the vessel may be regarded as being during a time of war when it is captured during an international armed conflict, but whether the argument can be made that the situation at sea is such that it is required by the exigencies of the situation to derogate is yet another hurdle to take. Be that as it may, what it requires of a State, also in situations of extraterritorial application of human rights, is to derogate from Article 5 ECHR.

In sum, both LOAC and human rights law do not give an explicit right for security detention in the situation of security detention on board a captured foreign-flagged vessel. A solution to circumvent human rights law obligations is to derogate from it, which is an exception with stringent conditions attached to it. Possible implied grounds for security detention might be argued through customary LOAC, only if one accepts that detention of persons during an armed conflict is inherent to conflict and is done to ascertain one's right under the law of armed conflict. Another argument, albeit restricted to enemy merchant vessels, would be to apply the fiction of occupied territory to enemy merchant vessels. Faced by operational necessity in modern military operations, there is a strong feeling to accept that persons can be detained for security reasons. Although seen against the

[22] E.g. Doswald-Beck 2011, p. 263; Pouw 2013, pp. 370–371.

[23] Doswald-Beck 2011, p. 263; Debuf 2009, p. 867.

background of the environment in which naval forces operate, the need for security detention is, arguably, less than in land operations. Situations may still exist where security detention is also needed during the interception of a foreign-flagged vessel. In this sense, it is submitted here that in the absence of an explicit ground, the implied grounds of detention inherent to conflict and the occupied territory fiction could serve as a legal basis.

11.6 Criminal Detention

The third category of detainees is the persons that are detained because they are suspected of criminal offenses (criminal detainees). LOAC provides the possibility for an occupying Power to conduct criminal detentions. Article 43 of the annex to HC IV[24] (Hague Regulations) provides a legal authorization for an occupying Power to restore and ensure public order, which includes arresting persons for criminal acts.[25] Article 43 of the Hague Regulations reads:

> The authority of the legitimate power having in fact passed into the hands of the occupant, the latter shall take all the measures in his power to restore, and ensure, as far as possible, public order and safety, while respecting, unless absolutely prevented, the laws in force in the country.

Whereas Article 43 allows an occupying Power to administer an arrest, the legal ground to arrest is based on the laws in force on the occupied territory, which may be altered if strictly necessary by regulations of the occupying Power. Here, again, the challenge is that the Hague Convention IV and its regulations do not apply on the high seas. No equivalent of Article 43 exists in the law of naval warfare. On the high seas there is no legal ground, therefore, for criminal detention based on LOAC if no form of jurisdiction by the belligerent can be established on board a vessel. As domestic criminal law will apply on the vessels of the occupied State outside the sovereign waters of that State, arguably Article 43 will apply on those vessels. The occupying Power can also amend the legislation in occupied territory to have its effect on the vessels of that State to allow enforcement jurisdiction to restore and ensure public order on board vessels of the occupied State. This still leaves neutral merchant vessels outside the scope of the possibility. Additionally, but outside the realm of LOAC, if a criminal act is committed against a service member of the boarding team, jurisdiction may be derived from the passive nationality principle. But over a fatal fight between two crew members on the vessel, the boarding party of the belligerent warship would not have the authority to detain them within the perspective of criminal detention.

---

[24] *Convention (IV) respecting the Laws and Customs of War on Land and its annex: Regulations concerning the Laws and Customs of War on Land.* The Hague, 18 October 1907.

[25] Pouw 2013, p. 395.

Although no direct legal ground for criminal detention based on LOAC appears to exist on the high seas, outside the situation of armed conflict criminal detention can be based on domestic criminal law and international agreements. Exemplary of the latter category are persons detained for piracy, drugs or terrorist offences. The SUA Convention does not allow a State to arrest persons suspected of SUA crimes. Instead, it poses an obligation for State parties to make punishable in national law those crimes that are listed in SUA. This would mean that enforcement jurisdiction exists, but it is still with the flag State to arrest and punish such persons, unless it agrees otherwise with the boarding State. Obviously, in the recent counter-piracy operations criminal detention of pirate-suspects has been under attention. The starting point for arresting pirates on board foreign-flagged vessels is found in Article 105 UNCLOS. It reads:

> On the high seas, or in any other place outside the jurisdiction of any State, every State may seize a pirate ship or aircraft, or a ship or aircraft taken by piracy and under the control of pirates, and arrest the persons and seize the property on board. The courts of the State which carried out the seizure may decide upon the penalties to be imposed, and may also determine the action to be taken with regard to the ships, aircraft or property, subject to the rights of third parties acting in good faith.

This Article allows every State to arrest suspected pirates on board foreign-flagged vessels. The challenge of Article 105 is that it establishes (or codifies the customary law of) universal jurisdiction over the crime of piracy, which allows States to impose the boarding State's jurisdiction onto the vessel and its individuals. But in order for universal jurisdiction to be effective, it still needs domestic laws for States to be able to prosecute suspected pirates, for instance making the crime of piracy punishable under domestic laws (UNCLOS does provide that piracy is an internationally punishable act) and allowing warship commanders to legally act against pirates. A further legal basis therefore must be sought within domestic legal frameworks that will authorize a State to make use of the legal opportunity that is given by Article 105 UNCLOS. Quite logically, as Article 105 leaves the actual execution phase of apprehending pirates to States, UNCLOS also does not contain any provisions on the treatment of suspected pirates. This is within the realm of domestic criminal law and will be subject to international human rights law. The UNSG report on piracy (2013) reiterates that:

> 43. National authorities and courts should comply with international human rights obligations in all phases of counter-piracy operations, including apprehension, detention, prosecution, trial and transfer of suspected pirates and imprisonment of convicted pirates.[26]

[26] S/2013/21, October 2013, para 43.

11.7 Safeguards and Treatment at Sea

Having touched upon the legal grounds for the three forms of detention at sea, a short remark is made here on safeguards and treatment. Safeguards and treatment of detainees at sea are in either regime as a matter of applicable rules no different than as they would be on land. Two points, however, can still be made.

First is to note the special regulations in GC III in case persons are detained at sea. Article 22 GCIII indicates that prisoners of war taken at sea should be put on land as soon as possible. The idea behind this article, besides the fact that prisoners should not be exposed to hostilities, comes from the circumstances in which prisoners during World War II aboard Japanese vessels suffered severely.[27] Today, however, with modern warships with fairly good conditions, this idea does not per se need to apply to modern warships. Rather, it is sometimes argued that placing prisoners temporarily on board a warship might be a better place for the care and protection of prisoner of war than on land.[28] The essence regarding prisoners of war seems rather to have moved to Article 19 GCIII, indicating that prisoner of war within the shortest possible time after their capture, are transported to camps, far enough out of the combat zone to be out of danger.[29] Nevertheless, the rule remains that prisoner of war should be held on land, unless circumstances necessitate a different decision. Practice also exists. Both in the Falklands as the Iraq War of 2003, prisoners of war were temporarily held on board ships instead of on land.[30] During Operation *Iraqi Freedom* prisoners of war made by the United States were brought aboard US warships in the Persian Gulf. The American warship *USS Dubuque* served as a PW camp until the PW camps were ready to be used on land.[31]

Second is the issue of promptness within the context of human rights law and detention. With regard to safeguards and treatment within the context of human

---

[27] The so-called 'hell ships'.

[28] This thought is also articulated by the ICRC, including in Frederic de Mulinen's *Handbook on the law of war for armed forces*, which states that: Prisoner of war camps shall be located on land except where clause there are better temporary conditions elsewhere (e.g. an advanced camp on heated ship rather than open tents on land unusually cold climate). De Mulinen 1987, no. 674.

[29] Article 19 GC III reads:

> Prisoners of war shall be evacuated, as soon as possible after their capture, to camps situated in an area far enough from the combat zone for them to be out of danger.
> Only those prisoners of war who, owing to wounds or sickness, would run greater risks by being evacuated than by remaining where they are, may be temporarily kept back in a danger zone. Prisoners of war shall not be unnecessarily exposed to danger while awaiting evacuation from a fighting zone.

[30] Noone 2004; Mordarai et al. 2013.

[31] See: http://www.history.navy.mil/content/dam/nhhc/research/archives/command-operation-reports/ship-command-operation-reports/d/dubuque-lpd-8/pdfs/2003.pdf.

rights law, there are no specific differences between the application on land or at sea. In terms of treatment, Pouw mentions a number of subjects to be dealt with within the context of human rights law when a person is detained, such as physical and mental integrity, dignity and respect, food and drinking water, hygiene and clothing, medical care, religion, personal belongings, public curiosity, and torture, cruel or degrading treatment or punishment.[32] With regard to safeguards Pouw mentions that detainees must not be held secretly, must be granted access to communicate with the outside world, must be notified on the reason for detention, must be compensated for unlawful detention, and additionally for criminal detainees, must be brought promptly before a judge.[33] Although these conditions for treatment and safeguards apply equally at sea, what differs is that the specific maritime dimension has its effects on the way how safeguards are fulfilled in practice. In this context, it is worth mentioning the safeguard of promptness in connection to maritime interception. With regard to promptness, Article 5(3) ECHR states that:

> 3. Everyone arrested or detained in accordance with the provisions of paragraph 1 (c) of this Article shall be brought promptly before a judge or other officer authorised by law to exercise judicial power and shall be entitled to trial within a reasonable time or to release pending trial. Release may be conditioned by guarantees to appear for trial.

The ECtHR has judged several times on the issue of promptness at sea (*Rigopoulos, Medvedyev*),[34] twice particularly with regard to piracy, in *Hassan* and *Ali Samatar*. With regard to the requirement that detained persons should be brought promptly before a judge the practical fact is that it can take time to bring a person before a judge when a person is detained somewhere on the high seas, where it could take days to sail into a port, to fly in an investigating judge, or where the technological means are sufficient enough to allow for a meeting in a digital manner. In different court cases the ECtHR has developed a "wholly exceptional circumstances"-view. In the *Rigopoulos* case the Court stated that:

> The Court nevertheless considers that a period of sixteen days does not at first sight appear to be compatible with the concept of "brought promptly" laid down in Article 5 § 3 of the Convention. Accordingly, only wholly exceptional circumstances could justify such a period. It must therefore examine whether there were such exceptional circumstances in the instant case.[35]

The judgment provides a guideline with regard to promptness in the context of maritime operations. As a key point 'wholly exceptional circumstances' must exist that necessitates to prolong appearance before a judge. Therefore, there is no use in identifying a maximum of days covering the term promptness, but rather specific

[32] Pouw 2013, p. 381.

[33] Pouw 2013, pp. 373–377.

[34] In these cases persons where held for 16 (*Rigopoulos*) and 13 (*Medvedyev*) days on board the vessel.

[35] *Rigopoulos*, in "The law"-section.

and exceptional circumstances must exist which makes it impossible to bring an individual before a judge. Case law suggests that factors as place of detention (far away from the territory of a detaining State),[36] weather conditions, the State and capabilities of the vessel all play a role whether exceptional circumstances exist. From *Medvedyev* another guideline can be found in which the Court stated that it could not find indications that France did anything that would unnecessarily take more time than needed. Interestingly, the Court also indicated in *Medvedyev* that it was not for the Court to assess whether France had other means to make the process go faster. Bodini concludes from this there is no *obligation* rising out of case law to transfer pirate suspect to other faster vessels or to airplanes in order to get the individuals before a judge.[37] In assessing promptness, the Court seems to make a separation between the situations at sea and the moment individuals arrive on the territory of the detaining State. At sea it seems to except the circumstances and limitations of the capabilities at hand (e.g. a vessel that needs to sail 500 miles to Spanish territory), whereas at the moment the detainee arrives on the territory of the State itself, the Court does not accept any excuses and orders nothing else than immediately, without any delay, taking into account that he individuals have already been detained for a significant period while at sea.[38] As happened in the *Hassan* case, therefore, a two days period[39] to get Hassan and others from the plane in France before a judge without any justification proved to be a violation of the obligation of promptness in Article 5(3) ECHR.

In other instances during counter-piracy operations off the coast of Somalia the issue of promptness has led to the decision to release pirate suspects. In recent multinational counter-piracy operations the legal challenges start with the inability to find a State that would want to prosecute pirate-suspects. More political considerations, such as that pirate suspects should be tried regionally or that a State has a policy to only prosecute a pirate when there are national interests at stake (for instance that there were nationals on board or the vessel belonged to a certain State), hampers prompt criminal prosecution. But also legally, as the former NATO legal advisor Peter Olson mentions; 'The reluctance for States in Ocean Shield to try persons for piracy…[…]…derives largely from the perceived risk that prosecution will fail due to procedural or evidentiary failures following from the operational circumstances in which they were detained'.[40] The EU Council Joint Action (CJA) 2008/851/CFSP, in Article 12 states that:

> …persons having committed, or suspected of having committed, acts of piracy or armed robbery in Somali territorial waters or on the high seas, who are arrested and detained, with a view to their prosecution, and property used to carry out such acts, shall be transferred:

[36] E.g. *Hassan*, para 97.
[37] Bodini 2011, p. 833.
[38] *Hassan*, para 104.
[39] From 23 September to 25 September 2008.
[40] Olson 2014, p. 189.

— to the competent authorities of the flag Member State or of the third State participating in the operation, which took them captive, or
— if this State cannot, or does not wish to, exercise its jurisdiction, to a Member States or any third State which wishes to exercise its jurisdiction over the aforementioned persons and property.[41]

The process to find a State that wants to prosecute takes time. And if it takes too long, human rights law safeguards will necessitate releasing the detained persons. One such example is the *BBC Togo* incident in 2009, where the captured pirate-suspects were held on board the Netherlands warship *Hr. Ms. Evertsen* during participation in Operation *Atalanta.* Thirteen persons suspected of attacking the Antigua and Barbados-flagged *BBC Togo* and a Yemeni dhow were captured some 150 nautical miles from the coast of Oman. The Dutch prosecuting office decided not to prosecute because of a lack of Dutch interests, after which the EU took over the efforts to find a State that would prosecute. Ultimately, after about two weeks in which several States were approached, the persons were released as no State was willing to take up prosecution in a national court.[42]

11.8 Detention in UN-Mandated Maritime Interception Operations

The fact that a maritime interception operation is mandated by the UN Security Council does not automatically also create a ground for detention. Operational detention within UN-mandated MIO must be viewed along the lines of the applicable legal regime as elaborated upon in this chapter. In maritime embargo operations the main focus has always been with prohibited items. Detention of persons has never been much on the foreground of attention. Only in SC Res. 1973 with regard to Libya did the Council state that mercenaries could be halted,[43] which was the first time that individuals were explicitly subject to an embargo operation. This implies that in order to enforce such an authority a person may be detained. More often, however, during embargo operations, persons are only seen in the context of a possible threat to the boarding team. As mentioned above, whether one can actually speak of detention or whether the crew of the vessel is temporarily restricted in movement depends on factors such as duration, manner, effects and consent. Typical ROE in UN-mandated maritime embargo operations to enforce UN sanctions do not per definition also include detention ROE. Rather, it focuses on the vessel and its goods and authorizes for instance seizure of the goods or diversion of the vessel. Even so, one of the procedures of a boarding team to make

[41] EU Council. Joint Action (CJA) 2008/851/CFSP.

[42] See more elaborately on this case (in Dutch) Verkroost and Fink 2011.

[43] SC Res. 1973 (2011), para 13.

sure that the crew of the vessel does not hamper or endanger the inspections and to ensure a level of control, crew and passengers that are not essential to operate the vessel are assembled as much as possible to an area during the search for a better control and observance of the crew and passengers.[44] Interestingly, the NATO tactical doctrine on MIO, ATP 71 (2005), has nothing specific on detention of persons. It did, however, recognize in its rephrased definition of MIO (see Chap. 1) that persons can be the focus of MIO. Other than that UN-mandated maritime embargo operations can be considered as part of an international armed conflict between the enforcing State and the targeted State, which opens the door to PW status, the activities of an embargo operation by itself will usually not pass the threshold of an armed conflict.

One particular point to note in the context of detention during UN-mandated MIO is the phrase *all necessary means*. Arguably, such wording in the resolution provides an implied legal ground to detain for security reasons. Practice to that effect is found in the ISAF operation in Afghanistan, it was argued as a legal ground for detention during NATO operations in Kosovo (KFOR)[45] and is also argued as an implied ground for detention during counter-piracy operations. ICJ Judge Greenwood is quoted in the *Serdar Mohammed v. Ministry of Defence* case[46] to have said in this context:

> That (or very similar) language has been employed by the UNSC when it wished to authorise the use of force and it was plainly intended to carry such a connotation in Afghanistan. It would be wholly illogical for the authorisation to extend to the use of lethal force against persons but not to include their detention.[47]

Others point out that in order for *all necessary means* to be a legal ground for detention, it must adhere to the principle of legal certainty. The ECtHR stated on this principle in the *Medvedyev* case:

> 80. The Court stresses that where deprivation of liberty is concerned it is particularly important that the general principle of legal certainty be satisfied. It is therefore essential that the conditions for deprivation of liberty under domestic and/or international law be clearly defined and that the law itself be foreseeable in its application, so that it meets the standard of "lawfulness" set by the Convention, a standard which requires that all law be sufficiently precise to avoid all risk of arbitrariness and to allow the citizen – if need be, with appropriate advice – to foresee, to a degree that is reasonable in the circumstances of the case, the consequences which a given action may entail.[48]

---

[44] See for example the practical 'to do'-list of the boarding team in *ATP* 71, p. 5-15. (e) Place a security team member in position above the assembled crew/passengers to observe the entire group, if possible. Furthermore, the ATP 71 notes that one of the principles of crew control is to 'keep the crew together'.

[45] See e.g. Davidson and Gibson 2008.

[46] High Court of Justice, Queen's Bench Division, *Serdar Mohammed v. Ministry of Defence*, 2 May 2014.

[47] *Serdar Mohammed*, para 218.

[48] *Medvedyev*, para 80.

The qualitative and procedural requirements of detention must therefore be sufficiently defined, which in an *all necessary means* mandate that details nothing more is a challenge. Within the context of MIO, multinational counter-piracy operations off the coast of Somalia may serve as an example. The counter-piracy operations are based on a combination of UNCLOS, domestic laws and UN resolutions. Petrig mentions that with regard to detention a number of States[49] within the EU Operation *Atalanta* have two different moments in time which are separated. The first moment is the capture and detention of individuals and the second is the decision of a prosecutor to start criminal proceedings.[50] This separation, Petrig argues, is needed in some States because the military are not authorized under the national criminal procedural codes to act against criminal acts. The legal basis for the first moment of detention is sought in Article 105 UNCLOS and the applicable resolution itself, which includes the *all necessary means* phrase.[51] As Article 105 UNCLOS does not apply in the territorial waters of Somalia, the only legal basis for that area is the extant resolution. Once a prosecutor decides to prosecute the detained persons, they will come under the domestic criminal law and thus also under the safeguard and treatment of domestic laws. Petrig has cast some doubt on the question whether the *all necessary means* phrase by itself is sufficiently clear to meet the qualitative and procedural requirements of Article 5 ECHR. The rule must be sufficiently clear on what will happen after the moment of detention. As Article 105 UNCLOS has no procedural content and *all necessary means* is substantively not sufficiently clear on rules and procedures of detention either, she argues that both cannot hold as a sufficient legal ground for detention.[52] This is not a wholly illogical view in light of the *Medvedyev* case in which the diplomatic note was not sufficiently clear ("take legal action") to contain a sufficiently clear legal ground for detention and its subsequent procedures.[53] With regard to Article 105 UNCLOS this view is shared by Pierini, who states:

> In my view, Article 105 of UNCLOS and the provision that the apprehending State "may" apply its laws, though not obliged to do so, represents an intrinsically contradictory element, weakening the assertion that article 105 provides itself legal certainty as to the existence of a cause for detention. The authorization vis-à-vis other States to capture pirate vessels and its crew and to apply its own criminal laws needs to be supported by proper and adequate provisions under domestic law in order to grant legal certainty.[54]

Article 105 UNCLOS may be sufficient enough because it explicitly mentions the possibility of arrest and the system that Article 105 foresees is that the details of the arrest and detention are meant to be filled by domestic legislation, and not dealt

[49] Petrig 2014 has studied the cases of Denmark and Germany, but also The Netherlands appears to have this view. See Verkroost and Fink 2011, pp. 21–22.

[50] Petrig 2014.

[51] See e.g. SC Res. 1846 (2008).

[52] Petrig 2014, pp. 228–230.

[53] *Medvedyev*, para 99. See also on this point Guilfoyle 2010b, pp. 437–442.

[54] Pierini 2011, p. 8.

with on the level of international law. It does imply, however, that a State should have such legislation for it to be a sufficient legal ground. Interestingly, in December 2014, the ECtHR in the *Hassan* case viewed that SC Res. 1816 that included the *all necessary means* phrase viewed that this phrase under the circumstances might be construed as the legal basis for detention, but (at that time) lacked rules with regard to the conditions of deprivation of liberty imposed on the captured persons pending appearance before a court.[55] It, therefore, did not meet the qualitative requirement for a sufficient legal basis. Arguably, if there are underlying documents that will sufficiently detail the possibility of detention including its qualitative and procedural requirements, it could hold as a legal ground for detention. As the resolution also explicitly emphasized the application of human rights, an *all necessary means* mandate cannot be used to sidestep human rights obligations based on Article 103 UN Charter.[56]

11.9 The *Freedom Flotilla* Incident

The *Mavi Marmara* incident of May 2010 is interesting to note in the context of detention. The incident contains some interesting points with regard to the relationship between human rights law at sea and the law of naval warfare. This relationship is still quite unchartered waters. As Eliav Lieblich has noted: ‘It is common knowledge, among those dealing with the nitty-gritty of IHL, that the process known as the “humanization of international humanitarian law” – as famously put by Theodor Meron – has generally not trickled to the law on maritime warfare. Prize law is perhaps a key example for this phenomenon’.[57] Interestingly, in this incident the issues went beyond capturing ships during a blockade and also dealt with the individuals on board during a boarding. The incident is interesting because apart from being recent practice it was subject to several investigative reports. The three main reports[58] are the report from the Human Rights Council (HRC),[59] the report from the Israeli committee (Turkel Report)[60] and the report written on assignment of the UN Secretary-General (Palmer Report).[61] All three reports noted the application of both the law of naval warfare and human rights law

[55] *Hassan*, para 69.

[56] See also Guilfoyle 2010a, p. 152.

[57] Lieblich 2014.

[58] Another report was written by the Turkish national authorities.

[59] A/HRC/51/21.

[60] *The Public Commission to Examine the Maritime Incident of 31 May 2010* (Turkel Commission). The Turkel Commission in fact produced also a second report. This second report (Part II) relates to *Israel's Mechanisms for Examining and Investigating Complaints and Claims of Violations of the Laws of Armed Conflict According to International Law* (February 2013).

[61] *Report of the Secretary-General's Panel of inquiry on the 31 May 2010 Flotilla incident* (September 2011).

and all have taken an interest in the detention issue that emerged from the capturing the vessels. In short, the *Freedom Flotilla* incident involved the following situation:

> While in international waters, the six vessels of the so-called *Freedom Flotilla* were hailed and warned by the Israeli Defence Forces (IDF) not to sail any further as they would be breaching the Israeli blockade of Gaza. When the vessels did proceed, the IDF boarded the vessels in order to take control over them. During the boarding of the vessels, one of which was the *Mavi Marmara*, they were met with resistance by the persons on board. The subsequent struggle on board between the IDF and the persons on board resulted in nine dead passengers and a number of wounded persons. The struggle ended in the IDF gaining control over the vessel and persons. Captured vessels and the persons on board were taken to the Israeli port of Ashdod. The HRC report mentions that during this phase approximately 700 persons, passengers and crew from six vessels altogether, were detained, up to 12 hours, and a number of persons were handcuffed.[62] In Israel the persons were transferred to a detention facility.[63] Immediately after the capture of the *Freedom Flotilla*, the UN Security Council requested the release of the vessels and persons on board the *Freedom Flotilla* vessels.[64] Several States called for the same through national statements. The persons that were on board were ultimately released.

The three reports note several points on the detention of persons. The Palmer report discusses the treatment of detained persons on board and during their stay in detention on land.[65] It also discusses the general legal framework to include both LOAC, and the law of naval warfare in particular, and human rights law. According to the Panel of Inquiry the latter regime applied, 'once the enforcing State of a blockade asserts physical control over the vessels and its passengers, regardless of the ship's position on the high seas'.[66] Here, the report accepts that during the blockade both the law of naval warfare and human rights law co-existed. The report does, however, not link this to the issue of detention and whether grounds for any kind of detention on board could be found in either LOAC or human rights law. The Palmer Report, therefore, stays in the dark on the exact legal grounds for detention of the civilians on board.

The HRC report takes the view that the conduct on board the *Mavi Marmara* is in general subject to human rights law during the blockade operations.[67] In concluding that the blockade is unlawful, because in the view of the HRC it inflicts disproportionate damage on the civilian population,[68] the HRC report states the following on the legal basis for detention:

---

[62] HRC, para 176. Turkel (para 164) mentions the same the number of persons.

[63] HRC, paras 195–196.

[64] S/PRST/2010/9.

[65] Palmer, paras 135–145.

[66] Palmer, conclusion para 69.

[67] HRC, para 70.

[68] HRC, paras 52–56. Interestingly, the HRC applies Section 102(b) of the *San Remo Manual*. While the HRC is satisfied that the blockade impacts in a disproportionate manner on the civilian population, the Turkel Report finds it hard to conclude whether or not this is actually the case, also in light of the land-crossings policy imposed on the Gaza. In fact it concludes that the blockade

> 215. As stated above, Article 9, paragraph 1, of the International Covenant on Civil and Political Rights guards against arbitrary arrest or detention. Since the Israeli interception of the flotilla was unlawful, the detention of the passengers and crew from the seven vessels at Ashdod was also prima facie unlawful since there was no legal basis for the Israeli authorities to have detained and transported these people to Israel. The passengers found themselves in Israel on the basis of an unlawful act by the State of Israel. The Israeli authorities were therefore under an obligation to deal with these people in accordance with their international human rights obligations.[69]

Different than the Palmer Report, the HRC report takes the view that the blockade itself was unlawful and concludes that firstly that no legal ground existed for detention based on the law of naval warfare. Secondly, any detention and treatment of persons must be viewed within the context of human rights law. Thirdly, it goes on to conclude that the detention within the context of human rights law was unlawful since there was no legal basis.

The Turkel Commission first takes the approach that the blockade was lawfully established.[70] Secondly, in discussing the applicability of human rights law, it concludes that, although it might be the case, the *lex specialis* of the law of armed conflict applied in this particular circumstance.[71] It also questions whether the IDF had effective control over the vessels before they had control over the bridge and subsequent cessation of resistance.[72] Turkel, therefore, accepts co-existence of both legal regimes and in this particular case LOAC as the *lex specialis* applied and persons on board should be regarded within the context of the law of armed conflict. The report has categorized the passengers, who are in essence civilians, in those who took direct part in hostilities (DPH) and those did not.[73] The report mentions that force used against the latter group of persons was based on the human rights law standards of necessity and proportionality.[74] It appears to conclude that using force against the civilians on board that did not rise against the military boarding team must not be considered as hostilities, but as an action of law enforcement. Furthermore, the report notes that: 'some of the flotilla participants were handcuffed, mainly young men who the forces were concerned would try to attack them or to cause a disturbance.'[75] It also states that: '195 passengers were under the supervision of members of this unit and were not handcuffed, and that only the 'people with fighting potential' were handcuffed'.[76] This would signify that persons were detained for security purposes. When arrived in Ashdod port the

---

was in compliance with the proportionality requirement as it is set out in the San Remo Manual. Turkel, paras 62 and 97.

69 HRC, para 215.

70 Turkel, para 112.

71 Turkel, para 99.

72 Turkel, para 186.

73 Turkel, para 190.

74 Turkel, para 191.

75 Turkel, p. 177.

76 Turkel, para 144.

report does not make any difference in processing the persons, whether DPH or security detainee. Each participant of the flotilla underwent the same process and arrest warrants were issued to each participant.[77] After the process, the report states that:

> Forty-five flotilla participants requested immediate deportation from the territory of the State of Israel, and thus they were escorted directly from the Ashdod port to Ben-Gurion airport by the Nachshon unit of the Prison Service, those persons that represented a potential security threat and others.[78]

Others, who rose against the military, were put under criminal investigation, until diplomatic pressure caused the release of these persons. After the request of the UNSC, to avoid any more diplomatic issues, the Israeli Attorney-General recommended to stop any legal proceedings against participants who had acted against the Israeli military, who subsequently decided to release those participants.

What can be concluded from the reports is the notion that the law of naval warfare and human rights law can co-exist during and armed conflict. It can also be concluded that there may be situations were belligerents are ascertaining their rights under the law of naval warfare and where human rights law may play a role simultaneously. Interesting is also that different investigative bodies arrive at different conclusions. The Turkel Report is the most detailed and submits that some persons were detained based on LOAC and others were dealt with through human rights standards. The incident with the *Freedom Flotilla* is a good example where circumstances may arise that persons must be detained for security reasons. As noted in this chapter, on the high seas there is neither an explicit ground for security detention in LOAC nor in human rights law. As the vessels belonged to neutral States, the only implied legal ground left would have been to accept that the law of naval warfare in ascertaining these rights implies also an authority to detain.

11.10 Final Remarks

As the introduction of this chapter noted, individuals are today more at the centre of attention in the maritime dimension. It has been submitted that the capture of a vessel does not, in principle, mean that the persons on board are automatically detained. Whether persons are detained will still depend on the specific circumstances of the case. In terms of legal grounds for detention at sea, it appears that there are fewer explicit grounds to detain on the high seas, as GCIV does not apply to the high seas. Applying the rules of occupation law to vessels on the high seas may partly close this gap, but only for vessels that fly the flag of the occupied territory. Furthermore, the same challenge of (a lack of) an existing legal ground for security detention in an extraterritorial NIAC applies at sea. An *all necessary means*

[77] Turkel, p. 187.

[78] Turkel, para 153.

mandate may provide a legal basis for detention during MIO, but needs to meet the principle of legal certainty. Qualitative and procedural requirements of a sufficient legal basis must be fulfilled. Some authors have argued that an *all necessary means* mandate, therefore, may not be sufficient to provide such legal basis for detention. Finally, the *Freedom Flotilla* incident is a good example of the complexity of operational detention on the high seas. The incident, underlines that that although the law of naval warfare does not concern itself with individuals on board, it may be necessary to look beyond the hull of the vessel and deal separately with individuals on board. It furthermore, underlines that discussion on co-existing legal regimes can arise also in the maritime dimension. And lastly, it underlines that the need for security detention exists also on the high seas, during maritime interception operations.

References

Aughey S, Sari A (2015a) Targeting and Detention in Non-International Armed Conflict: Serdar Mohammed and the Limits of Human Rights Convergence. International Law Studies 91. Naval War College, Newport RI pp. 60–118

Aughey S, Sari A (2015b) IHL does authorize detention in NIAC: A rejoinder to Rogier Bartels. EJIL-talk. http://www.ejiltalk.org/ihl-does-authorize-detention-in-niac-a-rejoinder-to-rogier-bartels. Accessed 12 February 2017

Bodini S (2011) Fighting piracy under the European Convention on Human Rights. European Journal of International Law 22:3, pp. 829–848

Davidson T, Gibson K (2008) Experts meeting on security detention report. Case Western Reserve University School of Law 40, pp. 323–380

De Mulinen F (1987) Handbook on the law of war for armed forces. ICRC, Geneva

Debuf E (2009) Expert meeting on procedural safeguards for security detention in non-international armed conflict. International Review of the Red Cross 91:876, pp. 859–881

Doswald-Beck L (2011) Human rights in times of conflict and terrorism. Oxford University Press, New York

Dunham C (1997) The Asama Maru Incident of January 21, 1940. Paper prepared for presentation at the Thirteenth Annual Ohio Valley History Conference

ECtHR, Rigoupolos v. Spain, (appl. no. 37388/97), Decision 12 January 1999

ECtHR, Medvedyev and others v. France, application no. 3394/03, Judgment 29 March 2010

ECtHR, Hassan and others vs. France (appl. nos. 46695/10 and 54588/10), 4 December 2014

ECtHR (2014) Guide on Article 5 of the Convention Right to liberty and security EU Council. Joint Action (CJA) 2008/851/CFSP

Guilfoyle D (2010a) Counter-piracy law enforcement and human rights. International and Comparative Law Quarterly 59, pp. 141–169

Guilfoyle D (2010b) Current Legal Developments European Court of Human Rights. Medvedyev and Others v. France, European Court of Human Rights. The International Journal of Marine and Coastal Law 25, pp. 437–442

Heintschel von Heinegg W (2014) Maritime warfare. In: Clapham A, Gaeta P (eds) The Oxford Handbook of International Law in Armed Conflict. Oxford University Press, New York, pp. 145–181

High Court of Justice (UK), Queen's Bench Division Serdar Mohammed v. Ministry of Defence, 2 May 2014

Kleffner J (2010) Operational detention and treatment of detainees. In: Gill T, Fleck D (eds) The Handbook of International Law of Military Operations. Oxford University Press, New York, pp. 465–480

Lieblich E (2014) Yet Another Front in Israeli/Palestinian Lawfare – International Prize Law. Opinio Juris, 13 January 2014. http://opiniojuris.org/2014/01/13/lieblich-guest-post-yet-another-front-israelipalestinian-lawfare-international-prize-law/. Accessed 17 February 2017

McMillan W (2011) Something more than a three hour tour: rules for detention and treatment of persons at sea on U.S. naval warships. The Army Lawyer 31, February 2011, pp. 31–45

Mordarai G, O'Connell D, Kelly T, Farrant J (2013) The seizure of Abu Anas Al-Libi: An international law assessment. International Law Studies 89. Naval War College, Newport RI, pp. 817–839

NATO. Allied tactical publication (ATP) 71. Allied maritime interdiction operations (2013)

Noone G (2004) Prisoners of War in the 21st Century: Issues in Modern Warfare. Naval Law Review 1:50, pp. 1–56

Olson P (2014) Countering piracy off the coast of Somalia: A NATO perspective. In: Koutrakos P, Skordas A (eds) The law and practice of piracy at sea: European and international perspectives. Hart Publishing, Oxford/Portland, OR, pp. 183–194

Petrig A (2014) Human Rights and Law Enforcement at Sea: Arrest, Detention and Transfer of piracy suspects. Brill Martinus Nijhoff Publishers, Leiden

Pierini J (2011) Apprehension, arrest, detention and transfer of suspected pirates and armed robbers within the legal framework of the European Security and Defence Policy (ESDP): The "mantra" of the existence of a proper legal base. I Quaderni Europei, March 2011, 1–10

Pouw E (2013) International human rights law and the law of armed conflict in the context of counterinsurgency. Netherlands Defence Academy, Dissertation, NLDA printing office, Breda

Rona G (2015) Is there a way out of the non-International armed conflict detention dilemma? International Law Studies 91. Naval War College, Newport RI, pp. 32–59

The Canberra Times (1940) Settlement of Asama Maru controversy. Anglo-Japanese understanding. Britain offers release of nine men. p. 4, 8 February 1940

Tucker R (1955) The law of war and neutrality at sea. NAVPERS 15031, Government Printing Office, Washington

Turkel Report I. The Public Commission to Examine the Maritime Incident of 31 May 2010

Turkel Report II. Israel's Mechanisms for Examining and Investigating Complaints and Claims of Violations of the Laws of Armed Conflict According to International Law (February 2013)

UN General Assembly. A/HRC/15/21, 27 September 2010

UN Security Council. S/PRST/2010/9

UN Security Council. Report of the Secretary-General's Panel of inquiry on the 31 May 2010 Flotilla incident, September 2011

UN Security Council. S/2013/21, Report of the Secretary-General on the situation with respect to piracy and armed robbery at sea off the coast of Somalia, October 2013

US Department of the Navy. 3 August 2004. USS Dubuque. www.history.navy.mil/content/dam/nhhc/research/archives/command-operation-reports/ship-command-operation-reports/d/dubuque-lpd-8/pdfs/2003.pdf. Accessed 17 February 2017

Verkroost P, Fink M (2011) Juridische aspecten van de Nederlandse deelname aan anti-piraterij operaties rondom de Hoorn van Afrika. Militair Rechtelijk Tijdschrift 104:1, pp. 9–26

Part IV
Conclusions

Chapter 12
Conclusions

> *States may use their navies to demonstrate and enforce their perception of the proper law of the sea. If such naval operations are consistent, effective and accepted, customary international law of the sea may develop. But if such naval operations are inconsistent, ineffective, or resisted, chaos may result.*
>
> —Mark W. Janis—Sea Power and the Law of the Sea

Contents

12.1 Introduction

I used Mark Janis'[1] quote already in the introduction of this book to underline the quest I was embarking on to explore the legal aspects of maritime interception operations. The central focus of this study has been to examine the scope and content of international legal frameworks applicable to naval operations conducting a maritime interception role outside the sovereign jurisdiction of States and in the context of international peace and security.

Maritime interception operations are a well-known, much exercised and often used tasking in the naval community. Through operational experience and academic thought over the past twenty-five years it can be concluded that a relatively clear structure has emerged with regard to the legal bases and legal regimes for MIO. These legal bases and regimes are now generally accepted and used by States and academics, and are also familiar to military operators. The view that the term

[1] Janis 1976, p. 75.

M. Fink, *Maritime Interception and the Law of Naval Operations*,
https://doi.org/10.1007/978-94-6265-249-1_12

MIO is only strictly limited to UN-mandated maritime embargo operations is clearly behind us. On an operational level it is also understood that in the practical sense maritime interception operations are generally conducted much in the same way, but due to the existence of different legal bases and regimes its exact parameters will differ. Although the structure is clear and accepted, points of contention related to these bases have raised discussions on the exact scope over the years. Examples discussed in this study are the issue of master and flag State consent and the question of when the UNSC has authorized maritime enforcement measures. Furthermore, using the term MIO to include interceptions based on the law of armed conflict is also not an entirely accepted way forward yet. While these issues have emerged and indeed new issues have been added throughout the years, such as the issue of how self-defence might serve as a legal basis for conducting MIO against WMD, interestingly, the evolution of maritime strategy during those same years has also given direction to the acceptability of some issues. A changing maritime strategy during the last ten years that has focused on enhancing maritime security has shed new light on the acceptability to board under master's consent authority as a concept that makes operating at sea more workable. It has for instance opened the door to make *modus operandi* like approach and assist visits or friendly approaches more palpable for States. And obviously counter-piracy operations have brought the issue of 'the legal finish' and the relationship between human rights law and the law of the sea more to the foreground.

The fact that current conflicts can often be characterized as non-international armed conflicts has not left the maritime dimension untouched. One challenge in this respect is that the authorities derived from the law of naval warfare, such as the belligerent right of visit and search, do not apply in non-international armed conflict. Modern conflict at sea, therefore, appears to have a legal gap. As a result, maritime interception operations that are conducted during non-international armed conflict and against non-state actors do not stand out with much legal clarity and have also given rise to activities or theoretical argumentation that may be debatable. Three examples are the practice of friendly approaches, boarding foreign-flagged vessels suspected of carrying WMD based on self-defence, and the use of statelessness to intervene on foreign-flagged vessels. In the context of modern conflict at sea that also needs to deal with non-international armed conflicts it would perhaps also be necessary to look into future ideas that today may still be considered too far-reaching, such as a NIAC right of visit that has been touched upon as a first thought.

One other point that clearly stands out from twenty-five years of evolution of maritime interception operations is the expanding focus on individuals, besides vessels and goods. One reason is the focus on enhancing maritime security, which puts the human being central during maritime interceptions operations. Another important reason is the greater acceptance of extraterritorial applicability of human rights law, and its subsequent practice in, for instance, counter-piracy operations. The focus on human beings and the broader scope of application of human rights law has firmly introduced human rights law within the realm of maritime interception operations. This focus and also regular maritime deployments in situations that do not amount to an armed conflict, has put more attention to analyse *modus operandi* of warships from a law enforcement perspective, and the use of force and detention in particular. If one would accept the extraterritorial application of human rights law to situations at sea, it may also mean that one could accept that the use of force standard that has crystallized over the years and through law of the sea jurisprudence and international agreements related to the sea is in fact the application of human rights law standards at sea. One particular area where academic thought and practice is extremely meagre is the question how co-existing legal regimes would relate in situations where both the law of naval warfare and human rights law exist. Be that as it may, today it is clear that human rights law also has a role to play in maritime interception operations.

In sum, maritime interception operations cannot be approached anymore solely from the traditional law of the sea perspective or from the vantage point of the UN collective security system. It is generally accepted that the legal bases and regimes applicable to MIO now encompass the whole spectrum of international legal frameworks—bases and regimes—applicable to military operations. The international law that relates to maritime interception operations has over the last twenty-five years matured by embracing the whole spectrum of general international law as applicable to military operations in the maritime dimension. Where it necessitated more in-depth legal nuances have emerged to better apply the law into the specific maritime dimension.

12.2 Legal Bases for MIO

Part II has analysed the legal bases that are generally accepted to serve as a legal ground for maritime interception operations. With regard to legal bases for MIO, it may be concluded that an evolution has taken place in which at the start of the use of the term the legal basis was very much connected with the UN collective security system. Gradually, MIO has evolved into an operational term to define an activity at sea which can be based on different legal bases. Practice and theory have generally accepted that MIO can be based on the UN collective security system, self-defence and consent, either *ad hoc* or through international agreements. Basically, these legal bases follow the general international law of accepted legal bases for the use of military force. While these legal bases for MIO are not contested, the scopes in which the legal bases are applied do have several points of discussion.

With regard to the legal basis of the UN collective security system it can be said that the practice of UN-mandated maritime interception operations has evolved into a fully accepted notion that the UNSC can authorize military enforcement measures at sea to enforce sanctions. Over the last twenty-five years, the UNSC has made use of this authority which on the one hand has crystallized into typical wording that signals the authority to enforce sanctions at sea, but on the other hand also created embargo operations through other kind of language, more specifically tailored to the conflict and situation at hand, such as in the cases of Lebanon and Libya.

Whereas the heart of the UNSC decision to authorize naval assets to implement economic sanctions at sea lies with Article 41 of the UN Charter, the justification and authority to act with military means to enforce implemented sanctions is more closely related to Article 42 of the Charter.

Self-defence can also be a ground for MIO. Firstly, invoking self-defence can be the start of a situation of an international armed conflict during which boarding operations may take place based on the legal regime of the law of armed conflict, the law of naval warfare in particular. Secondly, self-defence is also argued against single actions threats, such as seaborne WMD, and non-state actors. With regard to WMD, self-defence is argued in an anticipatory manner, in which the requirement of immediacy is interpreted in such a way that it primarily focuses on the gravity of the possible act. The key difference is that in the traditional approach self-defence is a condition that allows for the application of the law of armed conflict. LOAC—*ius in bello*—then provides the right to board vessels, albeit limited to international armed conflicts. In the other approach, related to NSA and WMD, the right to board a foreign-flagged vessel is derived from the *ius ad bellum* itself, which brings unique argumentation into play, such as the argument that the use of self-defence is not dependent on other States, which, connected to the debate on the conditions to cross borders in a NIAC, leads to the view that non-state actors can, under certain conditions, be attacked beyond the attacked State's borders in other States, and thus on foreign-flagged vessels in the maritime dimension. With regard to non-state actors, self-defence is argued to circumvent the legal challenge that no belligerent right of visit is currently generally accepted in non-international armed conflict. In this view, the right of self-defence and the view that it is not dependent of the will of other States is balanced against the situation in which States are unable or unwilling to act against non-state actors.

The central point of discussion related to the basis of *ad hoc* consent is the master or flag state consent issue. This study submits that the answer to the issue very much depends on two key considerations. The first is the position the flag State takes with regard to boarding its flagged vessels. The second is the actual activities that a boarding team will conduct once they are aboard the vessel. The second consideration, therefore, does not completely discharge the possibility that there are situations that foreign-flagged vessels can be visited by a warship based on master's consent. At this point a very thin line exists between activities that may be regarded as enforcing State authority through its military, which lies with the flag State, or whether it does not pass this threshold. In this perspective, a boarding at the invitation of the master would be allowable, but once the boarding team conducts any activity that may be deemed as a law enforcement activity it has surpassed its authority. The practice of friendly approaches or AAV visits to communicate with and help the fellow mariners at sea adds to the view that master's consent is gaining more support in the operational arena.

As a last, the instrument of international agreements as a legal basis for MIO has since 9/11 also been more often used as a tool to enhance the possibility to use maritime interception. In particular, the 2005 SUA Protocol and the bilateral agreements between the US and other States are of note. Although debates are raised, mainly to underline that the traditional freedom of navigation is eroded by these agreements, it is generally accepted that international agreements can serve as a basis for MIO. When one considers the content of the agreements, exclusive jurisdiction of a flag State over its flagged vessel still stands, however, as the legal point of departure. The authorities of the boarding State are strict and limited and mainly focused on procedural authorities that ensure timely reaction to a threat on board another vessel. In other words, the flag State has not lost jurisdictional grip on its vessels and persons on board once it explicitly, or implicitly by the passing of time, approves a boarding.

It is possible that maritime interception operations are based on more than one legal basis. Counter-piracy operations off the coast of Somalia are framed both in UN resolutions to the extent that it concerns operating in the territorial waters of Somalia, in consent from the (Somali) authorities to operate within the territorial sea of Somalia, and in the law of piracy that is codified in UNCLOS. Another example is the maritime embargo operations off the coast of Lebanon conducted by MTF UNIFIL, which is set-up through a combination of a UN resolution and consent by the Lebanon authorities.

12.3 Legal Regimes in MIO

Part III has studied three specific activities central to maritime interception operations in the context of applicable legal regimes: the right of visit, the use of force during MIO and detention at sea. A general conclusion that can be drawn is that through both the current focus on enhancing maritime security and the acceptance of extraterritorial applicability, human rights law has firmly introduced itself within the realm of maritime interception operations. This conclusion might be an open door at this stage of the debate on legal aspects of MIO, but it certainly was not the case when MIO first emerged as means to deal with international peace and security. The obvious consequence is that the relationship between human rights law, LOAC and the law of the sea becomes an important issue in establishing what authority the military may have during maritime interception operations. Especially on the subjects of the use of force and detention at sea the legal parameters during MIO are very much affected by human rights law. The manner in which way force can be applied depends on the applicable legal regime, human rights law or LOAC. Both legal regimes have their own conditions for application, which also means that the question of whether human rights law or LOAC applies is a separate consideration. Whereas the law of the sea and the law of naval warfare mainly focus on vessels and goods, the attention of human rights urges to look beyond the hull of the ship and get more concerned with the persons on board. Guilfoyle commented with regard to legal grounds for detention in the *Medvedyev* case that, 'One might wonder how it is possible that the note granted authority to detain a vessel on the high seas, but not those aboard it'.[2] This is exactly the thinking-gap that lies between the vessel-focused law of the sea and the person-focused human rights law.

A second general conclusion that can be drawn from Part III is that non-international armed conflicts at sea have particular impact on the right of visit. Chapter 9 has underlined firstly that there are more manifestations of the right of visit than the traditional peacetime and belligerent right of visit when one approaches this subject from general international law. The scope, purpose and content differ per right of visit. Some of the rights are detailed as they are part of either international agreements or its details have been widely accepted in customary international law, such as the belligerent right of visit and search. Others are less clear and must either be detailed in the State's consent that waivers the flag State authority, or must be interpreted through actual texts of UN resolutions. A further challenge with regard to visits during non-international armed conflicts is that whereas LOAC in international armed conflicts provide a detailed right of visit and search, it is still viewed that this does not apply in NIAC situations. It is quite imaginable that it is operationally unsatisfying that existing naval rules to conflict do not fit current conflict in the sense that this tool is not available to effectively act against non-state actors at sea. Legal solutions to what seems to be a gap have been suggested. The challenge that non-international armed conflicts or non-state actors pose to MIO has developed into creative thoughts to fill the gap made by the fact that traditional rights of visit do not suffice in NIAC situations at sea. There may a view which can be called 'self-defence right of visit' or a 'NIAC right of visit'. In this view the right to board and undertake subsequent actions on board are brought within the context of the *ius ad bellum* in competition with sovereignty, rather than that it is derived from the *ius in bello*, the law of naval warfare in particular. This development of thought, however, does not do justice to the basic framework of international law that starts with keeping basis and regime apart.

Detention has become much more important in maritime interception operations than during the days when MIO where only considered to be UN-mandated maritime embargo operations to enforce UN sanctions at sea. Academic literature of how operational detention is applied in the maritime dimension has only emerged in the last few years, mainly as a result of counter-piracy operations. In terms of legal grounds for detention at sea, it appears that there are lesser explicit grounds to detain on the high seas, as GCIV does not directly apply to the maritime environment. Applying the rules of occupation law to vessels on the high seas may partly close this gap, but only for vessels that fly the flag of the occupied territory. The same challenge of (a lack of) an existing legal ground for security detention in an extraterritorial NIAC applies at sea. An all necessary means-mandate may provide a legal basis for detention during MIO, but needs to meet the principle of legal certainty. Qualitative and procedural requirements of a sufficient legal basis must however be fulfilled. Some authors have argued that an all necessary means-mandate, therefore, may not be sufficient to provide such legal basis for detention.

[2] Guilfoyle 2010, p. 440.

As a last, the *Freedom Flotilla* incident is a good example of the complexity of operational detention on the high seas. The incident underlines that although the law of naval warfare does not concern itself with individuals on board, it may be necessary to look beyond the hull of the vessel and deal separately with individuals on board. It furthermore underlines that discussion on co-existing legal regimes can arise also in the maritime dimension. And lastly, it underlines that the need for security detention during maritime interception operations also exists on the high seas.

12.4 Final Remarks

The laws applicable to naval operations have always been regarded as a sort of a special thing in international law, with specialized lawyers speaking the secret language of the international law of the sea, and sometimes even its highly incomprehensible dialect of the law of naval warfare. There is nothing, however, that suggests that the law applicable to the maritime dimension can close its eyes to the developments and discussions that are raging on the mainland with regard to the application of more fields of international law to conflict, their interrelationships and the character of conflict. The maritime dimension of military operations must, in a similar fashion, be eager to embrace those debates on how the developments in the laws applicable to military operations in general, apply at sea. The question of what non-international armed conflict does to naval operations in the legal context and the more and more accepted application of human rights law at sea will remain a legal focus point in the development of the law of naval operations.

Glancing at the matrix that I mentioned in the first sentence of the introduction, on board *Hr. Ms. De Zeven Provinciën*, and looking both back and forward, undoubtedly, the various rules applicable to naval operations will certainly not make operating for military operators much easier. After a study of the scope and content of the international law applicable to maritime interception operations, one can at least conclude that these frameworks have grown and their interaction has become more complex. Having that in mind, I would like to end with a quote from the Commander-in-Chief of the Netherlands Naval Forces during the Second World War, Admiral J. Th. Furstner, who at the outbreak of the war commented on the distinction that must be made with regard to the law of naval warfare at sea and in the courtroom. He stated:

> De prijsrechter zelf blijft uiteraard steeds de instantie, die eventueel noodzakelijke correcties op de maatregelen der Commandanten aanbrengt. Het is echter van het grootste belang de procedure in open zee zoo eenvoudig mogelijk te maken.[3]

---

[3] Letter of the Netherlands Commander of the Naval Forces, J. Th. Furstner to the Minister of Defence, London 17 September 1940, no. S. 200/27/3. *National Archives, Londense Archief*, GA/JUZA, no. 1328.

This quote can be translated as: 'Obviously, the prize judge will remain the one who, if need be, will correct the measures taken by commanders. It is, however, of the greatest importance that procedures at sea stay as simple as they possibly can.' I take from his opinion that the law applicable to naval operations must be *workable* for naval operators at sea. Now, 75 years later, the challenge put to naval officers to adhere to, understand, and work with the law applicable to naval operations has not become easier. Quite the contrary. I sincerely hope that some of what I have written here on the one hand provides something of a feeling to the academic arena of how challenging the task at sea can be, but will also help practitioners during their, at times, daunting task to find their way through the legal battle which may come upon their path, whilst being confronted with the many, many other challenges the members of the Armed Forces need to endure in military operations.

References

Guilfoyle D (2010) Current legal developments European Court of Human Rights. The International Journal of Marine and Coastal Law 25, pp. 437–442

Janis M (1976) Sea power and the law of the sea. Lexington Books, Massachusetts/Toronto

National Archives, Londense Archief, GA/JUZA, no. 1328. Letter of the Netherlands Commander of the Naval Forces, J. Th. Furstner to the Minister of Defence, London 17 September 1940, no. S. 200/27/3

Annex A
List of Vessels

Vessel name	Date	Flag State	Boarded by	Action
Achille Lauro	1985	Italy	PLO	Sailed to Egypt
Al Feddah	2010	Unknown	The Netherlands	Pirates detained and tried
Arctic Sunrise	2013	The Netherlands	Russia	Vessel and persons detained
Asama Maru	1940	Japan	UK	21 Germans taken off board
Barber Perseus	1986	UK	Iran	Released after inspection
BBC China	2003	Germany	–	Diverted to Italy
BBC Togo	2009	Antigua and Barbados	Pirates	Pirates released after capture
Borndiep	2004	The Netherlands	–	Denied access to Portugal
Bozkourt	1926	Turkey	–	Collided with SS Lotus
Caroline	1834	United States	UK/Canada	Burned vessel, killed 2
Estelle	2012	Finland	Israel	Captured, to prize court
Francop	2009	Antigua and Barbados	Israel	Detained vessel and cargo
Heng Chung Hai	1990	China	US	Released after inspection
Ibn Khaldoon	1991	Iraq	US	Diverted after boarding
I'm Alone	1929	Canada	–	Intentionally sunk by USCG
Joanna V	1966	Greece	UK	Refused to divert after boarding
Kater I Rades	1997	Albania	Italy	Sunk after collision with Italian vessel

(continued)

M. Fink, *Maritime Interception and the Law of Naval Operations*,
https://doi.org/10.1007/978-94-6265-249-1

(continued)

Vessel name	Date	Flag State	Boarded by	Action
Klos C	2014	Panama	Israel	Captured brought into ISR port
Lido II	1994	Malta	The Netherlands	Diverted to Brindisi, Italy
Light	2011	Belize	–	Turned back to North Korea
Limburg	2000	France	–	Attacked by small boat
Lotus	1926	France	–	Collided with Bozkourt
Karine-A	2002	Tonga	Israel	Detained vessel and cargo
Maersk Alabama	2009	US	US	Pirate detained, tried in US
Mavi Marmara	2010	Comoros	Israel	Captured vessels
Morning Glory	2014	Stateless	US	Stopped and returned to Libya
Ponant	2007	France	Somali pirates	Pirates captured on land
Red Crusader	1961	British	Denmark	Fired upon by *Niels Ebbesen*
Saiga	1997	St. Vincent and Grenadines Guinea		Vessel and crew detained
Samanyolu	2009	NL Antilles	Denmark	Detained pirates, tried in NL
Santa Catharina	1603	Portuguese	The Netherlands	Captured vessel and cargo
Sea Isle City	1987	US reflagged	–	Damaged by missile attack
So San	2001	Cambodia	Spain	US released after inspection
Taipan	2010	Germany	The Netherlands	Pirates detained, tried in Germany
USS Cole	2000	US	–	Small boat attack
USS Samuel B. Roberts	1988	US	–	Struck by mines
Winner	2002	Cambodia	France	Detained vessel and persons

Annex B
List of Incidents

For ease of reference, this annex contains an alphabetical (by ship's name) list of the most important incidents used throughout the book with a short description of the incident.

Achille Lauro
In October 1985, the Italian-flagged *Achille Lauro* was hijacked by Palestinians off the coast of Egypt. They demanded the release of 50 Palestine prisoners. The hijackers were given safe passage to Egypt and allowed to board an airplane to fly to Tunisia. US fighters forced the plane to divert and land in Italy. The case prompted discussion on the legal possibilities to intervene on foreign-flagged vessels in case of terrorist actions on board the vessel. As a result, the SUA Convention was drafted.

Al Feddah
In 2009, Netherlands Royal Marines from *Hr. Ms. Tromp* in a Rhib were fired upon when approaching a dhow that also held Iranian hostages. Their reaction led to the death of two hostage takers and the capture of pirates that were subsequently tried and sentenced in the Netherlands. The case went all the way up to the Supreme Court of the Netherlands (Hoge Raad der Nederlanden), which in 2015 judged that the commander of the warship *Hr. Ms. Tromp* had a legal ground to arrest the pirates and the Netherlands did not breach Article 5 ECHR.

Arctic Sunrise
In 2013, The Netherlands-flagged vessel *Arctic Sunrise* was used by Greenpeace as a mothership, which sent its Rhibs to demonstrate on the Russian oil platform Prirazlomnaya, in the Russian EEZ. The ship was captured by the Russian authorities and taken with its crew to Russia to stand trial. The Netherlands argued before the ITLOS and the PCA that the boarding of the vessel was unlawful. The PCA considered that the boarding was indeed unlawful as the boarding did not comply with all the elements of hot pursuit.

M. Fink, *Maritime Interception and the Law of Naval Operations*,
https://doi.org/10.1007/978-94-6265-249-1

Barber Perseus
In January 1986, during the Iran-Iraq War, the UK-flagged vessel *Barber Perseus* was boarded by Iranian warships some miles outside the Iranian territorial waters. It caused a discussion in the UK parliament on the right of self-defence and the belligerent right of visit.

BBC China
In 2003, The German-flagged vessel *BBC China* carried centrifuge parts for the Libyan nuclear program. The vessel was ordered by Germany to divert to the Italian port Taranto in Southern Italy, where it was boarded and searched.

BBC Togo
In 2009, the Netherlands warship *Hr. Ms. Evertsen* during participation in Operation *Atalanta* captured 13 pirate-suspects who were held on board the warship. They were suspected of attacking the Antigua and Barbados-flagged *BBC Togo* and a Yemeni dhow and were captured some 150 nautical miles from the coast of Oman. The Dutch prosecuting office decided not to prosecute because of a lack of Dutch interests, after which the EU took over the efforts to find a State that would prosecute. Ultimately, after about two weeks in which several States were approached, the persons were released as no State was willing to take up prosecution in a national court.

Borndiep
In 2004, the Netherlands-flagged *Borndiep*, a floating medical facility from the *Women on Waves* organization aimed at undertaking abortions, was not allowed into Portuguese territorial waters. Warships obstructed the passage into the territorial waters of Portugal. The issue came before the ECHR.

C. E. Thornton
In 2000, Suriname threatened to use force by means of two gunboats of the Suriname Navy to expel the vessel *C. E. Thornton,* which was in the service of Guyana, and operated in a disputed area between both States (Guyana vs. Suriname, Award of the Arbitral Tribunal constituted pursuant to Article 287, and in accordance with annex vii of the United Nations Convention on the Law of the Sea, 17 September 2007).

Estelle
In 2012, the Finnish vessel Estelle tried to run the Gaza blockade established by Israel. It was captured by Israel and was brought before an Israeli prize court.

Francop
On 3 November 2009, Israel boarded the *MV Francop*, which sailed under the flag of Antigua and Barbuda. It found more than 300 tons of weapons on board, according to Israel said to be meant for Hezbollah. The vessel was directed to Ashdod Port for further examination. The weapons shipment was said to originate from Iran. In a letter to the UNSG Israel stated that the shipment constituted a

breach of SC Res. 1747 and because of 'The intended route of the Francop - coupled with the types of weaponry found on board - raise serious concerns that this incident also constitutes a violation of UN Security Council Resolution 1701 and 1373.'

Ibn Khaldoon
The *Ibn Khaldoon* was a merchant vessel, dubbed the 'peace-ship' that sailed in 1990 from Algeria to Iraq, during the MIF-period. The *Khaldoon*, similarly to the *Mavi Marmara*, had protestors, congressmen and women on board and purposely attracted a lot of media attention. After the helicopter insertion of the US boarding team, passive resistance occurred by the passengers to try to stop the boarding team from taking control of the vessel. The boarding team used smoke grenades to control the vessel. After the boarding team discovered prohibited items on board a port needed to be found to offload the prohibited cargo. Ultimately, the cargo was offloaded in Oman.

I'm Alone
The Canadian-flagged vessel *I'm Alone* was sunk in March 1929 by the US coast guard cutter *Dexter* during a hot pursuit on the high seas in the Gulf of Mexico. The vessel was engaged in prohibited liquor trafficking.

Joanna V
The Greek tanker *Joanna V* was boarded by the UK warship *HMS Berwick* on 4 April 1966, after which it refused to divert from the port of Beira, without the UK being able to do anything about it. After the incident the UNSC took measures that involved the authority to arrest the *Joanna V* upon departure and to stop vessels breaching the embargo going into Beira.

Karin-A
In 2002, the Israeli Defense Force boarded the Tonga-flagged vessel *Karin-A* in the Red Sea. The vessel carried 50 tons of weapons, suspected to be for the Palestinian authority.

Kater-I-rader
The Albanian-flagged *Kater-I-rader* was carrying Albanian refugees when it was pursued by the Italian warship *Sibilia*. The ships collided and caused the Albanian vessel to sink. The case was put before the ECtHR, but was considered to be inadmissible.

Klos-C
In March 2014, Israel boarded the Panama-flagged *Klos-C* on suspicion of carrying a large bulk of weapons (surface-to-surface rockets) in the Red Sea on its way to Sudan, ultimately destined for the Gaza in an operation codenamed Operation *Full Disclosure*. According to the foreign minister of Israel, it had obtained permission from Panama to board the vessel. The vessel was diverted to Eilat and the crew

members, according to an Israeli spokesman, who were probably not aware of the cargo, were released.

Lido II

In 1994, the Maltese-flagged vessel *Lido II* left Tunisia to sail for Croatia, with mainly petroleum products as its cargo. After a first inspection by NATO/WEU forces while entering the Adriatic, it proceeded on its way to Croatia. The *Lido II* however changed course to the Albanian port of Durazzo, while repeating requests for assistance as the vessel started to take water into the engine room. The master then changed course again towards Montenegro, which was off limits under the SC Res. 820 mandate. Dutch forces were inserted by helicopter to take over the vessel before it entered the territorial waters of Montenegro. The *Lido II* was towed to Brindisi, Italy, to be dealt with by the Italian authorities.

MV Light

The Belize-flagged vessel *MV Light* from North Korea on its way to Myanmar and suspected of carrying missile parts was forced to turn back by the US who dispatched the *USS McCampbell* to intercept the *M/V Light*. Although authority to board was given by Belize, based on the US-Belize shipboarding agreement the master refused. Instead it finally turned back to North Korea.

SS Lotus (Bozkourt)

The Turkish vessel *Bozkourt* and the French-flagged mail boat *SS Lotus* collided on 2 August 1926 on the high seas. Eight persons on board the *Bozkourt* died because of the collision. The Turkish Government prosecuted the French first officer Demons of the *Lotus* for his part in the incident. The question whether Turkey could have jurisdiction over Demons was put before the PICJ. The Court ruled that there was no rule in international law that prohibited Turkey from prosecuting the French lieutenant.

MV Maersk Alabama

In April 2009, the United States boarded the US-flagged vessel *Maersk Alabama*. The vessel was hijacked by pirates. The pirates were tried in the US. The story of the captain (Philips) of the *Maersk Alabama* was made into a movie.

Mavi Marmara

In May 2010, Israel boarded the *Mavi Marmara* and six other vessels that were part of the so-called *Freedom Flotilla*, which attempted to breach the blockade off the coast of the Gaza. The IDF boarded the vessels. The boarding turned into an opposed boarding situation and the subsequent fight between the boarding party and the attackers resulted in nine dead persons and a number of wounded. The vessels and persons on board were taken to Israel, after which, ultimately, the persons were released. The incident led several national and international committees to examine the incident.

Morning Glory
On 17 March 2014, US Navy Seals operating from *USS Roosevelt* stopped and boarded the *Morning Glory* in international waters in the vicinity of Cyprus. The vessel was said to be stateless and tried to sell crude oil with a tanker that was stolen earlier. The vessel was escorted back by *USS Stout* to the Libyan port of Es Sidra.

Ponant
In 2007, the French-flagged vessel *Ponant* was hijacked by Somali pirates. The French authorities pursued and arrested the pirates on Somali territory. The incident came before the ECtHR in 2014 (Samatar vs. France).

Red Crusader
In 1961 the Danish fisheries inspection vessel *Niels Ebbessen* boarded the British-flagged vessel *Red Crusader* and arrested the crew on suspicion of fishing within a prohibited area. After initially cooperating to follow the *Niels Ebbessen* to the Faroe Islands, it stopped cooperating to follow the *Ebbessen*. The *Ebbessen* first fired warning shots upon the *Red Crusader*, hailed it to stop and then proceeded to aim at the *Red Crusader*. The commission of inquiry concluded that firing upon the *Red Crusader* was not justified and that other means should have been sought to pursue arrest. (Permanent Court of Arbitration (PCA), 23 March 1962.)

MV Saiga
The oil tanker *MV Saiga* was attacked and boarded by Guinean officials in 1997. The vessel and persons were brought to Conakry and placed under arrest. The ITLOS found that Guinea, under the specific circumstances of the case, used excessive force against the vessel, which was fully loaded with fuel, unarmed and travelling at a speed of 10 knots. (MV Saiga no. 2, Saint Vincent and the Grenadines vs. Guinea, ITLOS Judgment 1 July 1999.)

Samanyolu
In January 2009, The Netherlands-Antilles-flagged *Samanyulo* was hijacked by pirates. The Danish warship *Absalon* boarded and freed the vessel. The pirates were ultimately handed over to the Netherlands and were tried before the district court of Rotterdam, The Netherlands.

So San
In December 2002, the vessel *So San* was suspected of carrying scud missiles from North Korea to Yemen. After the boarding by Spanish forces from the Spanish warship *Navarra* upon request of the US this suspicion proved to be true. The name *So San* was freshly painted on the stern while no vessel was registered under that name in North Korea. According to Roach after being queried, the master of the vessel replied that it was registered in Cambodia. The Cambodian authorities appeared to have confirmed that a vessel meeting the description was registered in Cambodia, but under the name of *Pan Hope* instead of *So San*. No legal ground was, however, found to seize the scuds. Nothing prohibited North Korea from

shipping scuds to Yemen. The *So San* was released to proceed to Yemen with its original cargo still aboard.

Taipan
On 19 October 2012, the District Court in Hamburg sentenced ten Somali pirates that had hijacked the German-flagged vessel *Taipan*. The pirates were detained after a Netherlands boarding team from *Hr. Ms. Tromp* boarded the vessel by fast-roping from a helicopter in 2010 and detained the pirates.

Winner
In early June 2002, the French authorities requested Cambodia to intercept the Cambodian-flagged vessel *Winner* that was suspected of carrying large quantities of drugs. France requested and got the authority via a diplomatic note exchange between France and Cambodia. The French warship *Lieutenant de vaisseau Le Henaff* was instructed to intercept the *Winner* and intercepted the *Winner* near the Cape Verde Islands.

Annex C
List of Naval Operations

Name	Date	State/Org	Legal basis
Active Endeavour	2001–2016	NATO	Self-defence
Allied Force	1999	NATO	Humanitarian intervention
Allied Protector I (Provider)	2008	NATO	UN mandate/UNCLOS
Allied Protector II	2009	NATO	UN mandate/UNCLOS
Atalanta (EUNAVFOR)	2009–present	EU	UN mandate/UNCLOS
Beira Patrol	1966–1975	UK	UN mandate
Cast Lead	2009–present	Israel	Self-defence
Change of Direction	2006	Israel	Self-defence
Desert Shield	1990	Coalition	UN mandate
Desert Storm	1990	Coalition	UN mandate
Enduring Freedom	2001–present	Coalition	Self-defence
Full Disclosure	2014	Israel	(ad hoc) Consent
Iraqi Freedom	2003	Coalition	UN mandate (disputed)
Maritime Interception Force	1990–2003	Coalition	UN mandate
Maritime Guard	1992–1993	NATO	(NAC decision)
Maritime Monitor	1992	NATO	(NAC decision)
Maritime Taskforce UNIFIL	2006–present	UN	UN mandate
Ocean Shield	2009–present	NATO	UN mandate/UNCLOS
Odyssey Dawn	2011	Coalition	UN mandate
Sea Guardian	2016	NATO	(NAC decision)
Sharp Fence	1992–1993	WEU	–
Sharp Guard	1993–1996	NATO/WEU	UN mandate
Sharp Vigilance	1992–1992	WEU	–
Unified Protector	2011	NATO	UN mandate
United Nations Korea	1950–1953	Coalition	UN mandate

M. Fink, *Maritime Interception and the Law of Naval Operations*,
https://doi.org/10.1007/978-94-6265-249-1

Annex D
Table of UN-Mandated Maritime Embargo Operations

	Conflict	Operation alias	Duration of operation	Organization	Resolutions
1	Southern Rhodesia	Operation London (Beira Patrol)	1966–1975	UK	217 (1965) 221 (1966) 232 (1966)
2	Iraq	Multinational interception Force (MIF)	25 August 1990–2003	Coalition	661 (1990) 665 (1990)
3	Former Yugoslavia	Maritime Monitor	16 July–22 November 1992	NATO	713 (1991) 757 (1992)
		Maritime Guard	22 November 1992–15 June 1993	NATO	787 (1992)
		Sharp Guard	15 June 1993–1 October 1996	NATO/WEU	787 (1992) 820 (1993)
		Sharp Vigilance	July 1992–November 1992	WEU	713 (1991) 757 (1992)
		Sharp Fence	November 1992–June 1993	WEU	787 (1992)
4	Lebanon	Maritime Taskforce UNIFIL	August 2006–present	UN	1701 (2006)
5	Haiti	Restore/uphold democracy	1995–1995	(US-led) coalition	875 (1993) 940 (1994)
6	Sierra Leone	–	October 1997–2010	ECOMOG	1132 (1997)
7	Libya	Unified Protector (OUP)	March 2011–October 2011	NATO	1970 (2011) 1973 (2011) 2009 (2011)
		No alias	March 2014–present	UN Member States	2146 (2014)

M. Fink, *Maritime Interception and the Law of Naval Operations*,
https://doi.org/10.1007/978-94-6265-249-1

Table of Cases

European Court of Human Rights (ECtHR)

2014 *Hassan and others vs. France* (appl. no's 46695/10 and 54588/10), 4 December 2014
2014 *Ali Samatar and other vs. France* (appl. no's 17110/10 and 17301/10), 4 December 2014
2012 *Hirsii Jamaa and others v. Italy*, (appl. no. 27765/09), Judgment, 23 February 2012
2011 *Al-Skeini and others v. The United Kingdom* (application no. 55721/07), Judgment, 7 July 2011
2011 *Al Jedda v. United Kingdom*, appl. no. 27021/08, Judgment, 7 July 2011
2011 *Xhavara and others v. Italy and Albania*, (appl. no 39473*/98),* 11 January 2011
2010 *Medvedyev and others vs. France*, (appl. no. 3394/03), Judgment 29 March 2010
2009 *Women on Waves and others v. Portugal*, (appl. no. 31276/05), 3 February 2009
2001 *Bankovic v. Belgium* et al. (appl. No. 52207/09), Decision Grand Chamber, 21 December 2001
1999 *Rigoupolos v. Spain,* (appl. no. 37388/97), Decision, 12 January 1999
1995 *Loizidou v. Turkey, (*appl. no. 40/1993/435/514) (Preliminary objections), 23 March 1995

European Court of Justice

1997 *Lido II, ECJ,* case no. C-177/95, 27 February 1997

Gerechtshof Den Haag (Appeals Court The Hague)

2012 Gerechtshof Den Haag, ECLI:NL:GHSGR:2012:BY6945 (Choizil)

M. Fink, *Maritime Interception and the Law of Naval Operations*,
https://doi.org/10.1007/978-94-6265-249-1

Rechtbank Rotterdam (District Court of Rotterdam)

2014 Rechtbank Rotterdam, ECLI:NL:RBROT:2014:119 (Mohsen)
2012 Rechtbank Rotterdam, LJN BX9986, 12 October 2012 (Fedda)
2011 Rechtbank Rotterdam, LJN BR4930, 12 August 2011 (Choizil)
2010 Rechtbank Rotterdam, LJN: BM116, 17 June 2010 (Samanyolu)

International Court of Justice (ICJ)

2003 *Oil Platforms Case* (Islamic Republic of Iran v. United States of America), Judgment, I.C.J. Reports, 2003
1949 *Corfu Channel Case,* 9 April 1949
1927 *SS Lotus Case*, PICJ, Series A, No. 10, 7 September 1927

International Tribunal for the Former Yugoslavia (ICTY)

2008 *Prosecutor v. Ramush Haradinaj, Idriz Balaj, Lahi Brahimaj,* judgment Trial Chamber, 3 April 2008
1995 *Prosecutor v. Dusko Tadic*, IT-94-1, 2 October 1995

International Tribunal of the Law of the Sea (ITLOS)

2013 Case no. 22. *Arctic Sunrise*, order of 22 November 2013
1999 Case no. 2, The M/V "Saiga", Saint Vincent and Grenadines v. Guinea, Judgment 1 July 1999

Permanent Court of Arbitration (PCA)

1962 *Red Crusader* incident (Great Britain Denmark). Fact-finding commission of inquiry, 23 March 1962

Arbitral Tribunal constituted pursuant to Article 287 UNCLOS

2007 *Guyana vs. Suriname*, Award of the Arbitral Tribunal constituted pursuant to Article 287, and in accordance with annex vii of the United Nations Convention on the Law of the Sea, 17 September 2007

High Court of Justice (UK)

2014 *Serdar Mohammed v. Ministry of Defence*, High Court of Justice, Queen's Bench Division, 2 May 2014

Literature

Adebajo, A.

2007 Sierra Leone. In: Berdal M, Economides S (eds) United Nations Interventionism, 1991–2004. Cambridge University Press, New York, pp. 246–273

Ahmed, D.

2013 Defending Weak States Against the "Unwilling or Unable" Doctrine of Self-Defense. Journal of International Law and International Relations 9, pp. 1–37

Akande, D., T. Liefländer

2013 Clarifying necessity, imminence, and proportionality in the law of self-defense. American Journal of International Law 107, pp. 364–570

Allen, C. H.

2014 International law for seagoing officers, 6th edn. Naval Institute Press, Annapolis Maryland

2010 Cargoes of doom: National and multilateral strategies to combat the illicit transport of weapons of mass destruction by sea. In: Caron D, Scheiber H (eds) The Oceans in the Nuclear Age: Legacies and Risks. Martinus Nijhoff, Leiden/Boston, pp. 295–336

2008 The influence on Sea Power Doctrines: The new maritime strategy and the future of the global legal order. Carsten M (ed) International Law Studies 84. Naval War College, Newport RI, pp. 3–32

2007 A Primer on the non-proliferation regime for maritime security operation forces. Naval Law Review 54, pp. 1–28

2007 Maritime Counter-Proliferation Operations and the Rule of Law. Praeger Security International, Westport, CT

M. Fink, *Maritime Interception and the Law of Naval Operations*,
https://doi.org/10.1007/978-94-6265-249-1

2006 Limits to the use of force in maritime operations in support of WMD counter-proliferation initiatives. In: Sparks T, Sulmasy G (eds) International Law Studies 81. Naval War College, Newport RI, pp. 77–139

Ashley-Roach, R.

2012 Global Conventions on piracy, ship hijacking, hostage taking and maritime terrorism. In: Beckmann R, Ashley-Roach R (eds) Piracy and international maritime crimes in ASEAN. Prospects for cooperation. NUS center for international law, pp. 38–61

1993 Developments in the Law of Naval Operations. In: Lefeber R (ed) Contemporary International Law Issues: Opportunities at a Time of Momentous Change. Martinus Nijhoff Publishers, Dordrecht

Asmussen, J.

2008 Diplomacy and conflict during the 1974 crisis. Cyprus at war. I.B. Tauris, London/New York

Aughey, A.

2015 Targeting and Detention in Non-International Armed Conflict: Serdar Mohammed and the Limits of Human Rights Convergence. International Law Studies 91. Naval War College, Newport RI, pp. 60–118

2015 IHL does authorize detention in NIAC: A rejoinder to Rogier Bartels. EJIL-talk. http://www.ejiltalk.org/ihl-does-authorize-detention-in-niac-a-rejoinder-to-rogier-bartels. Accessed 12 February 2017

Baer, G. W.

1993 One hundred years of seapower. The U.S. Navy 1890–1990. Stanford University Press, Stanford CA

Ballard, J. R.

1998 Upholding Democracy. The United States military campaign in Haiti 1994–1997. Praeger Publishers, Westport CT

Bannelier, K.

2013 Under the UN Security Council's watchful eyes: Military intervention by invitation in the Malian Conflict. Leiden Journal of International Law 26, pp. 855–874

Bartels, R.

2008 Gewapend conflict is geen eenduidig begrip. Internationaal recht in de kijker, Belgian Red Cross, pp. 69–81

Bateman, S.

2014 Piracy and armed robbery against ships in the South China Sea – Possible causes and solutions. In: Wu S, Zou K (eds) Non-Traditional Security Issues and the South China Sea. Routledge, Oxford, pp. 133–144

Becker, M.

2005 Shifting public order of the oceans. Harvard International Law Journal 46:1, pp. 131–230

Becker-Weinberg, V.

2015 Proliferation of weapons of mass destruction and shipping interdiction. In: Weller M (ed) The Oxford Handbook of the Use of Force in International Law. Oxford University Press, New York, pp. 1017–1033

Beckman, R. C.

2002 Combating piracy and armed robbery against ships in Southeast Asia: The way forward. Ocean Development and International Law 33, pp. 317–341

Bellairs, C.

1919 The battle of Jutland. The sowing and the reaping. Hodder & Stoughton, London

Benbow, T.

1999 Maritime Power in the 1990–91 Gulf War and the Conflict in the Former Yugoslavia. In: Dorman A, Lawrence Smith M, Uttley M (eds) The Changing Face of Maritime Power. Macmillan Press Ltd, London, pp. 107–125

Bergen, P. L.

2011 The Longest War. The Enduring Conflict between America and Al-Qaeda. Free Press, New York/London/Toronto/Sydney

Bethlehem, D.

2012 Self-defense against an imminent or actual armed attack by non-state actors. American Journal of International Law 106, pp. 769–777

Blank, L. R.

2013 Rules of engagement and legal frameworks for multinational counter-piracy operations. Case Western Reserve Journal of International Law 46, pp. 397–409

Blokker, N.

2005 The Security Council and the use of force – one recent practice. In: Blokker N, Schrijver N (eds) The Security Council and the use of force. Theory and reality - A need for a change. Martinus Nijhoff Publishers, Leiden/Boston, pp. 1–30

2000 Is the Authorization Authorized? Powers and Practice of the Security Council Resolution to Authorize the Use of Force by “Coalitions of the Able and Willing”. European Journal of International Law 11, pp. 541–568

de Boer, T.

2014 Closing Legal Black Holes: The Role of Extraterritorial Jurisdiction in Refugee Rights Protection. Journal of Refugee Studies (2014), 2–17

Boddens Hosang, J. F. R.

2017 Rules of Engagement. Rules on the use of force as linchpin or the international law of military operations. Dissertation, University of Amsterdam, Amsterdam

Bodini, S. P.

2011 Fighting piracy under the European Convention on Human Rights. European Journal of International Law 22:3, pp. 829–848

Boelaert, S.

2014 The European Union’s comprehensive approach to combating piracy at sea: Legal aspects. In: Koutrakos P, Skordas A (eds) The law and practice of piracy at sea: European and international perspectives. Hart Publishing, Oxford/Portland OR, pp. 81–167

Booth, K.

1985 Law, force and diplomacy at sea. George Allen and Unwin, London/Boston/Sydney

Bono, G.

2003 NATO's 'peace enforcement' tasks and 'policy community': 1990–1999. Routledge, London

Boraz, S. C.

2009 Maritime domain awareness. Myth and realities. Naval War College Review 62:3, pp. 137–146

Both, S. J. J.

2010 Combined Maritime Forces. Het belang van deelname in een unieke maritieme coalitie. Militaire Spectator, pp. 600–617

Bradford, E.

1972 The Shield and the Sword. The Knights of St John. Penguin Classic, London

Brown, N.

2015 Jurisdictional Problems Relating to Non-Flag State Boarding of Suspect Ships in International Waters: A Practitioner's Observations. In: Ringbom R (ed) Jurisdiction over ships. Brill, Dordrecht, pp. 69–82

2010 Legal Considerations in Relation to Maritime Operations against Iraq. In: Pedrozo R (ed) International Law studies 86. Naval War College, Newport RI, pp. 127–137

2003 Panel III, Commentary – Maritime and coalition operation. In: Borch F, Wilson P (eds) International Law Studies 79. Naval War College, Newport RI, pp. 303–307

Brown, T. M.

2010 For the "Round and Top of Sovereignty": Boarding Foreign Vessels at Sea on Terror-related Intelligence Tips. Naval Law Review 59, pp. 63–104

Bryant, D. L.

2004 Historical and Legal Aspects of Maritime Security. University of San Francisco Maritime Law Journal 1:3–4, pp. 1–27

Buchan, R. J.

2012 Determining the legality of Israel's interception of the peace flotilla on May 31 2010. International and Comparative Law Quarterly 61:1, pp. 264–273

Burke, W. T.

1962 The public order of the oceans. A contemporary International law of the Sea. Yale University Press, New Haven/London

Cacciaguidi-Fahy, S.

2007 The law of the sea and human rights. Panoptica Vitoria 1:9, pp. 1–21

Campbell, P.

2009 Task Group Command Legal Officer SLIPPER Four, BASTILLE & FALCONER. In: Mortimer J, Stevens D (eds) Presence, Power Projection and Sea Control. The RAN in the Gulf 1990–2009, pp. 257–265

Carr, A.

2002 Maritime interdiction operations in support of the counter-terrorism war. Naval War College paper

Carvalho de Oliviera, G.

2012 Naval peacekeeping and piracy: Time for a critical debate. International Peacekeeping, 19:1, pp. 48–61

Cassese, A.

1989 Terrorism, politics and law. The Achille Lauro affair. Polity Press, Oxford

Cesaretti, R.

2005 Combating terrorism in the Mediterranean. NATO Review, Autumn 2005

Chan, J.

2014 Piracy and armed robbery against ships in the South China Sea – Possible causes and solutions. In: Wu S, Zou K (eds) Non-Traditional Security Issues and the South China Sea. Routledge, Oxford, pp. 133–144

Charron, A.

2011 UN Sanctions and conflict. Responding to peace and security threats, Routledge, London

Christakis, T.

2013 Under the UN Security Council's watchful eyes: Military intervention by invitation in the Malian Conflict. Leiden Journal of International Law 26, pp. 855–874

Churchill, R. R.

2008 UN Security Council resolutions and 1982 LOS Convention. Carsten M (ed) International Law Studies 84. Naval War College, Newport RI, pp. 143–157

1999 The Law of the Sea. Manchester University Press, Manchester

Churchill, W. S.

1927 The World Crisis, 1916–1918, Part II. Thornton, Butterworth Ltd., London

Colombos, C. J.

1962 The International Law of the Sea, 5th edn. Longmans Green, London

Conforti, B.

1991 Non-coercive Sanctions in the United Nations Charter: Some Lessons from the Gulf War. European Journal of International Law 2, pp. 110–113

Corn, G.

2012 Self-defense targeting: Blurring the line between the ius ad bellum and the ius in bello. In: Watkin K, Norris R (eds) International Law Studies 88. Naval War College, Newport RI, pp. 57–92

Cortright, D.

2000 The Sanctions decade. Assessing UN strategies in the 1990s. Lynne Rienner Publishers Inc., Boulder CO

Crawford, J.

2002 ILC Draft Articles on State Responsibility: Articles and commentaries

Crist, D. B.

2008 The formation of a coalition of the willing and Operation Iraqi Freedom. In: Elleman B, Paine S (eds) Naval coalition warfare. From the Napoleonic War to Operation Iraqi Freedom. Routledge, London, pp. 208–217

Dafrancia, C.

2012 Enforcing the Nuclear Non-proliferation Regime: The Legality of Preventive Measures. Vanderbilt Journal of Transnational Law 45:705, pp. 705–783

Davidson, B.

2009 Modern naval diplomacy - a practitioner's view. Journal of Military and Strategic Studies 11:1–2, pp. 1–47

Davidson, T.

2008 Experts meeting on security detention report. Case Western Reserve University School of Law 40, pp. 323–380

Davis, I.

2013 The Proliferation Security Initiative. Effective multilateralism or "smoke and mirrors"? In: Meier O, Daase C (eds) Arms Control in the 21st Century. Routledge, London, pp. 146–166

De Jonge Oudraat, C.

2000 Making Sanctions Work. Survival 42, pp. 105–127

De Mulinen, F.

1987 Handbook on the law of war for armed forces. ICRC, Geneva

Debuf, E.

2009 Expert meeting on procedural safeguards for security detention in non-international armed conflict. International Review of the Red Cross 91:876, pp. 859–881

den Heijer, M.

2011 Europe and extraterritorial asylum. Dissertation, Amsterdam

Dinstein, Y.

2005 The conduct of hostilities under the law of international armed conflict. Cambridge University Press, Cambridge

2003 War, Aggression and Self-Defence, Cambridge University Press, Cambridge

Doolin, J. A.

2006 The Proliferation Security Initiative. Cornerstone of a new international norm. Naval War College Review 59:2, pp. 29–57

Doswald-Beck, L.

2011 Human rights in times of conflict and terrorism. Oxford University Press, New York

2005 Customary International Humanitarian Law, volume 1. Rules. Cambridge University Press, Cambridge

1995 San Remo Manual on International Law Applicable to Armed Conflicts at Sea. Grotius Publications, Cambridge University Press, Cambridge

Droege, C.

2008 Elective Affinities? Human rights and humanitarian law. International Review of the Red Cross 90:871, pp. 501–548

Ducheine, P. A. L.

2009 Operation Change of Direction: A short survey on the legal basis and applicable legal regimes. NL ARMS, Netherlands Defence Academy, Breda, pp. 51–96

Duncan, J. C.

1999 Annotated Supplement to the Commander's Handbook on the Law of Naval Operations. International Law Studies 73, Naval War College, Newport RI

Dunham, C. G.

1997 The Asama Maru incident of January 21, 1940. Paper prepared for the Thirteenth Annual Ohio Valley History Conference, October 1997

Dupont, P. E.

2012 Countermeasures and Collective Security: The Case of the EU Sanctions against Iran. Journal of Conflict and Security Law 17, pp. 301–336

von Eindsiedel, S.

2007 Haiti. In: Berdal M, Economides S (eds) United Nations Interventionism, 1991–2004. Cambridge University Press, New York, pp. 168–191

Farhang, C.

2014 The notion of consent in part of the draft articles on State responsibility. Leiden Journal of International Law 27, pp. 55–73

Farrant, J.

2013 The Gaza Blockade incident and the modern law of blockade. Naval War College Review 66:3, pp. 81–98

Fenwick, W. J.

1991 The merchant vessel as legitimate target in the law of naval warfare. In: Delissen A, Tanja G (eds) Humanitarian law of armed conflict challenges ahead. Essays in honour of Frits Kalshoven. Martinus Nijhoff publishers, Dordrecht, pp. 425–443

Fielding, L. E.

1997 Maritime interception and U.N. Sanctions. Austin & Winfield, San Francisco/London/Bethesda

1993 Maritime Interception: Centrepiece of Economic Sanctions in the New World Order. Louisiana Law Review 53, pp. 1191–1241

Fink, M. D.

2013(a) Toute prise doit être jugée. Opmerkingen over het Nederlandse prijs (proces)recht. Militair Rechtelijk Tijdschrift vol. 106, no. 6, pp. 211–219

2013(b) De status van militaire Vessel Protection Detachments. Militair Rechtelijk Tijdschrift, vol. 106, pp. 41–53

2013(c) Maritime embargo operations: naval implementation of UN sanctions at sea under Articles 41 and 42 of the UN-Charter. Netherland International Law Review, 60:1, pp. 73–92

2012 De ontwikkeling van de strafrechtelijke rechtsmacht over het personeel van de NAVO-trainingsmissie in Irak (NTM-I). Militair Rechtelijk Tijdschrift 6, pp. 261–264

2011(a) UN-mandated maritime arms embargo operations in Operation Unified Protector. Revue de Droit Militaire et Droit de la Guerre 1:2, pp. 237–260

2011(b) Contemporary views on the lawfulness of naval blockades. Aegean Review of the Law of the Sea and Maritime Law 1:2, pp. 191–215

2011(c) Juridische aspecten van de Nederlandse deelname aan anti-piraterij operaties rondom de Hoorn van Afrika. Militair Rechtelijk Tijdschrift vol. 104, no. 1, pp. 9–26

2008 De maritieme taakgroep UNIFIL. Militair Rechtelijk Tijdschrift 4, pp. 103–112

2006 Zeeroof. Militair Rechtelijk Tijdschrift, pp. 225–233

Fitzgerald, M. A.

2008 Seizing weapons of mass destruction from foreign flagged ships on the high seas under article 51 of the UN Charter. Virginia Journal of International Law 49:2, pp. 473–506

Franck, T. M.

2006 Iraq and the law of armed conflict. Jacques R (ed) International Law Studies 80. Naval War College, Newport RI, pp. 15–20

Freedman, L.

1993 The Gulf Conflict 1990–1991. Diplomacy and War in the New World Order. Faber & Faber, London

Fye, R.

2004 Coast Guard Operations during Operation Iraqi Freedom. Center for Naval Analysis

Garmon, T.

2002 International law of the seas: Reconciling the law of piracy and terrorism in the wake of September 12. Tulane Maritime Law Journal 27, pp. 257–275

Garvey, J. I.

2005 The international institution imperative for countering the spread of weapons of mass destruction: Assessing the Proliferation Security Initiative. Journal of Conflict and Security Law 10:2, pp. 125–147

Gavouneli, M.

2007 Functional jurisdiction in the Law of the Sea. Brill/Martinus Nijhoff Publishers, Dordrecht

Gazzini, T.

2005 The Changing Rules on the Use of Force in International Law. Manchester University Press, Manchester

Geiss, R.

2015 Non-Flag States as Guardians of the Maritime Order: Creeping Jurisdiction of a Different Kind? In: Ringbom H (ed) Jurisdiction over ships, Brill, Dordrecht, pp. 19–49

Gibson, K.

2008 Experts meeting on security detention report. Case Western Reserve University School of Law 40, pp. 323–380

Gill, T. D.

2015 Some considerations concerning the role of ius ad bellum in targeting. In: Ducheine P, Schmitt MN, Osinga F (eds) Targeting. The challenges of modern warfare. T.M.C. Asser Press, The Hague, pp. 101–120

2015 Concept and sources of the international law on military operations. In: Gill T, Fleck D (eds) The Handbook of the International Law of Military Operations, 2nd edn. Oxford University Press, New York

2015 When does self-defence end? In: Weller M (ed) The Oxford Handbook of the Use of Force in International Law. Oxford University Press, New York, pp. 737–751

2015 Some thoughts on the relationship between international humanitarian law and international human rights law: A plea for mutual respect and a common-sense approach. Yearbook of International Humanitarian Law, pp. 251–266

2014 Some thoughts on the relationship between international humanitarian law and international human rights law: A plea for mutual respect and a common sense approach. In: Haek Y, McGonigle Leyh B, Burbano-Herrera C, Contreras-Garduño D (eds) The realisation of human rights: When theory meets practice: Studies in honour of Leo Zwaak. Cambridge/Intersentia, Portland OR, pp. 335–350

2010(a) Peace Operations. In: Gill T, Fleck D (eds) The Handbook of the International Law of Military Operations. Oxford University Press, New York, pp. 135–142

2010(c) Military intervention at the invitation of the government. In: Gill T Fleck D (eds) The Handbook of the International Law of Military Operations. Oxford University Press, New York, pp. 229–234

2007 The Temporal Dimension of Self-Defence: Anticipation, Pre-Emption, Prevention and Immediacy. In: Schmitt M, Pejic J (eds) International Law and Armed Conflict: Exploring the faultlines - Essays in honour of Yoram Dinstein. Martinus Nijhoff Publishing, Leiden, pp. 113–157

2003 The Eleventh of September and the Right of Self-Defense. In: Heere W (ed) Terrorism and the military: international legal implications. T.M.C. Asser Press, The Hague, pp. 23–37

2002 The 11th of September and the International Law of Military Operations. Vossiuspers, UVA, Amsterdam

1990 De Golf crisis. De volkenrechtelijke regels inzake het gebruik van militair geweld. Nederlands Juristenblad 38, pp. 1475–1487

Gioia, A.

1992 The law of neutrality: Third states' commercial rights and duties. In: Dekker I, Post H (eds) The Gulf War of 1980–1988. Martinus Nijhoff Publishers, Dordrecht, pp. 221–242

Goldrick, J.

2006 Maritime Sanctions Enforcement against Iraq, 1990–2003. In: Elleman B, Paine S (eds) Naval Blockades and Seapower. Strategies and Counter-strategies, 1805–2005. Routledge, London, pp. 201–214

Goldsworthy, A.

2006 Caesar. Life of a colossus. Yale University Press, New Haven/London

Gordon, P. H.

2002 NATO after 11 September. Survival 43:4, pp. 1–18

Gosalbo-Bono, R.

2014 The European Union's comprehensive approach to combating piracy at sea: Legal aspects. In: Koutrakos P, Skordas A (eds) The law and practice of piracy at sea: European and international perspectives. Hart Publishing, Oxford/Portland OR, pp. 81–167

Gowland-Debbas, V.

2004 Sanctions regimes under Article 41 of the UN Charter. In: Gowland-Debbas V (ed) National implementation of UN Sanctions. Kluwer Law International, The Hague/London/Boston, pp. 3–31

Graham, E.

2011 Maritime Counter-Proliferation: The Case of MV LIGHT. RSIS Commentaries, no. 96/2011, 29 June 2011

Graham-Brown, S.

1999 Sanctioning Saddam. The Politics of Intervention in Iraq. London/New York

Gray, C.

2008 International Law and the Use of Force. Oxford University Press, New York

1988 The British position in regard to the Gulf Conflict. International Law and Comparative Law Quarterly 37, pp. 420–428

Gregory, F.

1994 Maritime constabulary roles for non-military security. In: Pugh M (ed) Maritime security and peacekeeping. A framework for United Nations operations. Manchester University Press, Manchester/New York

Guilfoyle, D.

2015 The use of force against pirates. In: Weller M (ed) The Oxford Handbook of the Use of Force in International Law. Oxford University Press, New York, pp. 1057–1076

2014 Piracy and terrorism. In: Koutrakos P, Skordas A (eds) The law and practice of piracy at sea: European and international perspectives. Hart Publishing, Oxford/Portland OR, pp. 33–52

2012 Somali pirates as agents of change in international law making and organization. Cambridge Journal of International and Comparative Law 1:3, pp. 81–106

2011 Guilfoyle D (2011) Human Rights Issues and Non-Flag State Boarding of Suspect Ships in International Waters. In: Symmons C (ed) Selected Contemporary Issues in the Law of the Sea. Brill Nijhoff, Dordrecht, pp. 83–104

2010(a) Counter-piracy law enforcement and human rights. International & Comparative Law Quarterly 59 pp. 141–169

2010(b) The Mavi Marmara incident and blockade in armed conflict. British Yearbook of International Law 81, pp. 171–213

2010(c) The laws of war and the fight against Somali piracy: Combatants or criminals. Melbourne Journal of International Law 11, pp. 1–13

2010(d) Current Legal Developments European Court of Human Rights. Medvedyev and Others v. France, European Court of Human Rights. The International Journal of Marine and Coastal Law 25, pp. 437–442

2009 Shipping interdiction and the law of the sea. Cambridge University Press, New York

2005 The Proliferation Security Initiative: Interdiction vessels in international waters to prevent the spread of weapons of mass destruction. Melbourne University Law Review 29, pp. 733–764

Hammicks, D.

2007 Navies Endeavour to police the Mediterranean Sea. Jane's Navy International, July/August 2007, pp. 28–36

Haussler, U.

2011 Crisis response operation in maritime environments. In: Odello M, Piotrowicz R (eds) International Military Missions and International Law, Brill Nijhoff, Dordrecht, pp. 161–21

Heintschel von Heinegg, W.

2015 Maritime interception/interdiction operations. In: Gill T, Fleck D (eds) The Handbook of the International Law of Military Operations, 2nd edn. Oxford University Press, New York, pp. 375–393

2015 Blockades and interdictions. In: Weller M (ed) The Oxford Handbook of the Use of Force in International Law. Oxford University Press, Oxford, pp. 925–946.

2014 Maritime warfare. In: Clapham A, Gaeta P (eds) The Oxford Handbook of International Law in Armed Conflict. Oxford University Press, New York, pp. 145–181

2013 The law of armed conflict at sea. In: Fleck D (ed) The Handbook of International Humanitarian Law, 3rd edn. Oxford University Press, New York, pp. 486–498

2012 Naval blockade. In: Schmitt M, Heintschel von Heinegg W (eds) The conduct of hostilities in International Humanitarian Law 1. Ashgate, Farnham, Burlington, pp. 203–228

2011 Methods and means of naval warfare in non-international armed conflicts. In: Watkin K, Norris A (eds) International Law Studies 88. Naval War College Newport RI, pp. 211–236

2007 "Benevolent" third states in international armed conflicts: The myth of the irrelevance of the law of neutrality. In: Schmitt M, Pejic J (eds) International law and armed conflict: Exploring the faultlines. Martinus Nijhoff Publisher, Leiden, pp. 543–568

2004 Current legal issues in maritime operations: Maritime interception operations in the global war on terrorism, exclusion zones, hospital ships and maritime neutrality. Israel Yearbook of International Law 34, pp. 151–178

2003 The protection of navigation in case of armed conflict. The International Journal of Marine and Coastal Law 18:3, pp. 401–422

1995 VisitCapture, search and capture – conditions for applicability. In: Heintschel von Heinegg W (ed) Reports and Commentaries of the Round-Table of experts on international humanitarian law applicable of armed conflicts at sea. Bochumer Schriften zur Friedessicherung und zum Humanitarischen Volkerrecht 24. Berliner Wissenschafts-Verlag GmbH, Berlin, pp. 1–92

1994 The current state of international prize law. In: Post H (ed) International Economic Law and Armed conflict. Martinus Nijhoff Publishers, the Netherlands, pp. 5–34

1991 Visit, search and capture in naval warfare. Part 1: The traditional law. CYIL (1991), pp. 283–329

Henckaerts, J. M.

2005 Customary International Humanitarian Law, volume 1. Rules. Cambridge University Press, Cambridge

Higgins, A. P.

1926 Visit, Search and Detention. British Yearbook of International Law 43, pp. 43–53

Hirsch, J.

2004 Sierra Leone. In: Malone D (ed) The UN Security Council. From the Cold War to the 21st Century. Lynne Rienner Publishers, London, pp. 521–536

Hodgkinson, S. L.

2007 Challenges to Maritime Interception Operations in the War on Terror: Bridging the Gap. American University International Law Review 22:4, pp. 853–671

Houben, M.

2008 Food for Life. De inzet van Hr. Ms. Evertsen ter ondersteuning van het VN Wereldvoedselprogramma. Working Paper Maritiem optreden nr. 1, Maritieme Doctrine en Tactieken Centrum, Den Helder

2007 Making Waves and Building Bridges: Dutch Experiences in the Arabian Sea. RUSI Defence system, June 2007, pp. 82–85

Janis, M. W.

1976 Sea power and the law of the sea. Lexington Books, Massachusetts/Toronto

Jose Luis Jesus, H. E.

2003 Protection of foreign ships against piracy and terrorism at sea: legal aspects. The International Journal of Marine and Coastal Law 18:3, pp. 363–400

Joyner, D. H.

2015 The implications of the proliferation of Weapons of mass destruction for the prohibition of the use of force. In: Weller M (ed) The Oxford Handbook of the Use of Force in International Law. Oxford University Press, New York, pp. 1034–1056

Karsh, E.

1993 The Gulf conflict 1990–1991. Diplomacy and war in the New World Order. Faber & Faber, London

Kidd, J.

2004 Campaign analysis: Maritime forces. In: Cornish P (ed) The conflict in Iraq, 2003. Palgrave Macmillan, pp. 134–144

Kizanis, I.

2008 'Probable cause' for maritime interdictions involving illicit radioactive materials. Thesis for the Naval Postgraduate School, California

Kleffner, J. K.

2010 Operational detention and treatment of detainees. In: Gill T, Fleck D (eds) The Handbook of International Law of Military Operations. Oxford University Press, New York, pp. 465–480

Klein, N.

2014 A case for harmonizing laws on maritime interception of irregular migrants. International and Comparative Law Quarterly 63, pp. 787–814

2011 Maritime Security and the Law of the Sea. Oxford University Press, New York

2010 Intelligence gathering and information sharing for maritime security purposes under international law. In: Klein N, Mossop J, Rothwell D (eds) Maritime security. International law and policy perspectives from Australia and New Zealand. Routledge, London/New York, pp. 224–241

2005 The right of visit and the 2005 Protocol on the suppression of unlawful acts against the safety of maritime navigation. Denver Journal of International Law and Policy 35:2, pp. 287–332

Kontorovich, E.

2009 "A Guantanamo on the sea". The difficulties of prosecuting pirates and terrorists. Northwestern University of Law, Public Law and Legal Theory, series 09-10

Krajewski, J. M.

2008 Out of Sight, Out of Mind? A Case for Long Range Identification and Tracking of Vessels on the High Seas. Naval Law Review 56, pp. 219–250

Kraska, J.

2013 International Maritime Security Law. Martinus Nijhoff Publishers, Leiden/Boston

2010(a) Rule selection in the case of Israel's naval blockade of Gaza: law of naval warfare or the law of the sea? In: Schmitt MN (ed) Yearbook of humanitarian International Law 13. T.M.C Asser Press, The Hague, pp. 367–395

2010(b) Broken taillight at sea: The peacetime international law of visit, board, search and seizure. Ocean and Coastal Law Journal 16:1, pp. 1–46

2009 Grasping the influence of law on sea power. Naval War College Review 62:3, pp. 113–135

2004 Maritime power and the law of the sea. Oxford University Press, New York

Kreps, S.

2007 The 1994 Haiti intervention: A unilateral operation in multilateral clothes. The Journal of Strategic Studies 30:3, pp. 449–474

Kreß, C.

2010 Some reflections on the international legal framework governing transnational armed conflicts. Journal of Conflict and Security Law 15:2, pp. 245–274

Kretzmer, D.

2013 The inherent right to self-defence and proportionality in ius ad bellum. European Journal of International Law 24, pp. 235–282

van der Kruit, P. J.

2007 Maritime drug interdiction in international law. Dissertation, Den Helder

Kuijper, D. J.

2010 Combined Maritime Forces. Het belang van deelname in een unieke maritieme coalitie. In Militaire Spectator, pp. 600–617

Leijnse, M.

2002 De bijdrage van de Koninklijke Marine aan de strijd tegen het terrorisme. Marineblad, May 2002, pp. 149–154

Letts, D.

2005 Recent Australian Experience of the Law of the Sea and Military Operations. Australian Yearbook on International Law 24

Leurdijk, D. L.

1996 The United Nations and NATO in Former Yugoslavia. Partners in International Cooperation. Netherlands Institute of International Relations 'Clingendael', The Hague

Lieblich, E.

2014 Yet Another Front in Israeli/Palestinian Lawfare–International Prize Law. Opinio Iuris. http://opiniojuris.org/2014/01/13/lieblich-guest-post-yet-another-front-israelipalestinian-lawfare-international-prize-law/. Accessed 18 February 2017

Lieflânder, T.

2013 Clarifying necessity, imminence, and proportionality in the law of self-defense. American Journal of International Law 107, pp. 364–570

Lopaz, D. A.

2000 The Sanctions Decade. Assessing UN strategies in the 1990s. Lynne Rienner Publishers Inc., Boulder CO

Lowe, A. V.

1999 The Law of the Sea, Manchester University Press, Manchester

Luke, I. T.

2013 Naval operations in peacetime. Not just "warfare lite". Naval War College Review 66–2:11–26

Lyons, S.

1993 Naval operations in the Gulf. In: Rowe P (ed) The Gulf war 1990–91 in international and English law. Routledge, Sweet and Maxwell, London/New York

van Maanen, M. A.

1994 Embargo operaties in de Adriatische zee. Militair Rechtelijk Tijdschrift, pp. 15–18

MacCartney, A.

1925 Shepard, Sea power in ancient history. William Heinemann LTD, London

MacAskill, E.

2011 Libya: NATO defence ministers agree on minimal intervention. Victory for US as agreement to move warships closer to Libya falls far short of measures called for by Britain and France. The Guardian, 10 March 2011. www.guardian.co.uk/world/2011/mar/10/libya-gaddafi-nato-us-minimal-intervention. Accessed 17 February 2017

MacDonald, S. D.

2013 The SUA 2005 Protocol: A critical reflection. The International Journal of Marine and Coastal Law 28, pp. 485–516

Malone, D. M.

2007 Haiti. In: Berdal M, Economides S (eds) United Nations Interventionism, 1991–2004. Cambridge University Press, New York, pp. 168–191

1998 Decision-Making in the UN Security Council. The case of Haiti, 1990–1997. Clarendon Press, Oxford

Marolda, E. J.

2001 Shield and Sword. The United States Navy and the Persian Gulf War. Naval Institute Press, Annapolis MD

McDougal, M. S.

1962 The public order of the oceans. A contemporary International law of the Sea, Yale University Press, New Haven/London

McLaughlin, R.

2015 United Nations Security Council Practice in relation to the use of force in no-fly zones and maritime exclusion zones. In: Weller M (ed) The Oxford Handbook of the Use of Force in International Law. Oxford University Press New York, pp. 251–271

2011 Terrorism as a Central Theme in the Evolution of Maritime Operations Law Since 11 September 2001. Yearbook of International Humanitarian Law 14, pp. 391–409

2009 United Nations Naval Peace Operations in the Territorial Sea. Leiden, Martinus Nijhoff Publishers, Leiden

2007 The Legal Regime Applicable to Use of Lethal Force When Operating under a United Nations Security Council Chapter VII Mandate Authorising "All Necessary Means". Journal of Conflict and Security Law 12, pp. 389–417

2002 United Nations Mandated Naval Interdiction Operations in the Territorial Sea? International and Comparative Law Quarterly 51, pp. 249–278

McMillan, W. G.

2011 Something more than a three hour tour: rules for detention and treatment of persons at sea on U.S. naval warships. The Army Lawyer 31, February 2011, pp. 31–45

McNeill, J. H.

1991 Neutral rights and maritime sanctions: The effects of two Gulf wars. Virginia Journal of International Law 31 pp. 631–43

Mejia jr., M.

2003 Maritime gerrymandering: dilemmas in defining piracy, terrorism and other acts of maritime violence. Journal of International Commercial Law 2:2, pp. 153–175

Melzer, N.

2010 Conceptual distinction and overlaps between law enforcement and the conduct of hostilities. In: Gill T, Fleck D (eds) The Handbook of International Law of Military Operations. Oxford University Press, New York, pp. 33–50

2009 Interpretative guidance on the notion of direct participation of hostilities under international humanitarian law. ICRC

2006 Targeted killings in international law. Oxford University Press, New York

Menefee, S. M.

1999 Foreign naval intervention in cases of piracy: Problems and strategies. The international Journal of Marine and Coastal Law 14:3, pp. 353–370

Meyer, H.

1967 The Nationality of Ships. Martinus Nijhoff, The Hague

Michaelsen, C.

2014 Human rights as limits for the Security Council: A matter of substantive law or defining the application of proportionality. JCSL vol. 19, no. 3 (2014), pp. 451–469

Milanovic, M.

2012 Al Skeini and Al-Jedda in Strasbourg. European Journal of International Law 23:1, pp. 121–139

2009 Norm conflict and international law: Whither human rights? Duke Journal of Comparative and International Law, vol. 20 (2009), pp. 69–131

Mobley, R.

2002 The Beira Patrol. Britain's Broken Blockade. Naval War College Review 55, pp. 64–84

Morabito, R. E.

1991 Morabito R (1991) Maritime interdiction: Evolution of a strategy. Ocean Development and International Law 22, pp. 301–311

Mordarai, G.

2013 The seizure of Abu Anas Al-Libi: An international law assessment. International Law Studies 89, Naval War College, Newport RI, pp. 817–839

Nevill, P.

2015 Military sanctions enforcement in the absence of express authorization. In: Weller M (ed) The Oxford Handbook of the Use of Force in International Law. Oxford University Press, New York, pp. 272–292

Ngantcha, F.

1990 The right of innocent passage and the evolution of the international law of the sea: The current regime of "free" navigation in coastal waters of third states. Pinter Publishers

Nimmich, J.

2007 Maritime Domain Awareness: The Key to Maritime Security. In: Carsten M (ed) International Law Studies 83. Naval War College, Newport RI, pp. 57–65

Nincic, D. J.

2005 The challenge of maritime terrorism: Threat identification, WMD and regime response. The Journal of Strategic Studies 28:4, pp. 619–644

Noone, G. P.

2004 Prisoners of War in the 21st Century: Issues in Modern Warfare. Naval Law Review 1:50, pp. 1–56

O'Connell, D. P.

1975 The influence of law on sea power. Manchester University Press, Manchester

1970 International Law and Contemporary Naval Operations. British Yearbook of International Law 44, pp. 19–68

Olson, J. J.

1993 Naval Interdiction Considerations in the Use of Limited Naval Force short of war. Naval War College Paper, Newport RI

Olson, P. M.

2014 Countering piracy off the coast of Somalia: A NATO perspective. In: Koutrakos P, Skordas A (eds) The law and practice of piracy at sea: European and international perspectives. Hart Publishing, Oxford/Portland OR, pp. 183–194

Oppenheim, L.

1906 International Law. A Treatise vol. II War and Neutrality. Longmans and Green and Co, London/New York/Bombay

Ormerod, H.

1924 Piracy in the ancient world. An essay in Mediterranean history. Hodder & Stoughton Ltd., London

O'Rourke, D.

2009 Navy Role in Irregular Warfare and Counterterrorism: Background and Issues for Congress, Congressional Research Service Report for congress, 4 June 2009

Papastavridis, E.

2013(a) European Convention on Human Rights and the Law of the Sea: The Strasbourg Court in unchartered waters? In: Fitzmaurice M, Merkouris P (eds) The Interpretation and Application of the European Convention of Human Rights: Legal and Practical Implications. Martinus Nijhoff Publishers, Leiden, pp. 117–146

2013 The interception of vessels on the high seas. Hart Publishing, Oxford/Portland OR

2011 The Right of Visit on the High Seas in a Theoretical Perspective: Mare Liberum versus Mare Clausum Revisited. Leiden Journal of international Law 24, pp. 45–69

2010 European Court of Human Rights Medvedyev et al v France (Grand Chamber, application no 3394/03) judgment of 29 March 2010. International Comparative Law Quarterly 59:03, pp. 867–882

2007 Interpretation of Security Council Resolutions under Chapter VII in the Aftermath of the Iraqi Crisis. International and Comparative Law Quarterly 83, pp. 83–118

Paust, J. J.

2010 Self-defense targeting of non-state actors and permissibility of U.S. use of drones in Pakistan. Journal of Transnational Law and Policy 19:2, pp. 237–280

Peace, D. L.

1991 Major maritime events in the Gulf. Virginia Journal of International Law 31, pp. 545–566

Pedrozo, R.

2013 International Maritime Security Law. Martinus Nijhoff Publishers, Leiden/Boston

Pejic, J.

2007 Unlawful/enemy combatants: Interpretations and consequences. In: Schmitt M, Pejic J (eds) International law and armed conflict: exploring the faultlines. Martinus Nijhoff Publishing, Dordrecht, pp. 335–355

Petrig, A.

2014 Human Rights and Law Enforcement at Sea: Arrest, Detention and Transfer of Piracy Suspects. Brill Martinus Nijhoff Publishers, Leiden

2013 Human rights in counter-piracy operations: No legal vacuum but legal uncertainty. In: Mejia, M jr. et al (eds) Piracy at sea. WMU Studies in Maritime Affairs 2, Heidelberg, pp. 31–45

Pierini, J. P.

2011 Apprehension, arrest, detention and transfer of suspected pirates and armed robbers within the legal framework of the European Security and Defence Policy (ESDP): The "mantra" of the existence of a proper legal base'. I Quaderni europei (March 2011), pp. 1–10

Plutarch

1925 Levensbeschrijvingen van Alexander (den Groote) en Cajus (Julius) Caesar. Mendes da Costa M (transl.). Wereldbibliotheek, Amsterdam

Politakis, G. P.

1997 Modern aspects of the law of naval warfare and maritime neutrality. Kegan Paul International, London/New York

1994 UN-Mandated Naval Operations and Notion of Pacific Blockade: Comments on Some Recent Developments. Revue Africaine de Droit International et Comparé 6, pp. 173–208

Pokrant, M.

1999 Desert Shield at Sea. What the Navy Really Did. Greenwood Press, Westport CN/London

Pouw, E. H.

2013 International human rights law and the law of armed conflict in the context of counterinsurgency. Netherlands Defence Academy, Dissertation, NLDA printing office, Breda

2009 Operation Change of Direction: A short survey on the legal basis and applicable legal regimes. NL ARMS, Netherlands Defence Academy, Breda, pp. 51–96

Pugh, M.

1998 Sea power, security and peacekeeping after the Cold War. In: Pugh M (ed) Maritime security and peacekeeping. A framework for United Nations operations. Manchester University Press, Manchester/New York

1994(a) Peacekeeping, Monitoring and Verification. In: Haydon P, Griffiths A (eds) Maritime Security and Conflict Resolution at Sea in the Post-Cold War Era. Centre of Foreign Policy Studies, Halifax, NS, pp. 207–224

1994(b) Maritime constabulary roles for non-military security. In: Pugh M (ed) Maritime security and peacekeeping. A framework for United Nations operations. Manchester University Press, Manchester/New York

Pyke, H. R.

1915 The law of contraband of war. Clarendon Press, Oxford

Roberts, G. B.

2009 Hostis Humani Generis: The threat of WMD terrorism and how NATO is facing the ultimate threat. Defence Against Terrorism Review 2:1, pp. 1–13

Robertson, H. B.

1991 Interdiction of Iraqi Maritime Commerce in the 1990–1991 Persian Gulf conflict. Ocean Development and International Law 22, pp. 289–299

Rogers, F.

2005 The international force in East Timor – legal aspects of maritime operations. UNSW Law Journal 28:2, pp. 566–580

Rona, G.

2015 Is there a way out of the non-International armed conflict detention dilemma? International Law Studies 91. Naval War College, Newport RI, pp. 32–59

Ronzitti, N.

1992 The law of neutrality: Third states' commercial rights and duties. In: Dekker I, Post H (eds) The Gulf War of 1980–1988. Martinus Nijhoff Publishers, Dordrecht, pp. 221–242

Rostow, N.

2006 International Law and the 2003 Campaign against Iraq. Jacques R (ed) International Law Studies 80. Naval War College, Newport RI, pp. 21–42

Roth, B.

2004 Coast Guard Operations during Operation Iraqi Freedom. Center for Naval Analysis

Rothwell, D. R.

2010 The International Law of the Sea. Hart Publishing Oxford/Portland OR

2009 Maritime security and the law of the sea. In: Klein N, Mossop J, Rothwell D (eds) Maritime security. International law and policy perspectives from Australia and New Zealand. Routledge, New York, pp. 22–37

Ruiz Palmer, D. A.

2016 A maritime renaissance. Naval power in NATO's future. In: Krause J, Bruns S (eds) Routledge Handbook on naval strategy and security. Routledge, London, pp. 364–380

2007 New operational horizons: NATO and maritime security. NATO Review. www.nato.int/docu/review/2007/issue4/english/analysis4.html. Accessed 12 February 2017

Ruys, T.

2010 'Armed attack', and Article 51 of the UN Charter. Cambridge University Press, Cambridge

2008 Quo vadit ius ad bellum?: A legal analysis of Turkey's military operations against the PKK in Northern Iraq. Melbourne Journal of International Law, vol. 9 (2008), pp. 334–364

Ryan, M.

2000 Some practical advice for a joint force commander contemplating the use of blockade, visit and search, maritime interception operations, maritime exclusion zones, cordon sanitaire, and maritime warning zones during times of international armed conflict. Paper Naval War College, Newport RI

Sandalli, P.

2010 Maritime task force's role in UNIFIL. Al Janoub, 6 January 2010

Sanger, D.

2011 U.S. Said to Turn Back North Korea Missile Shipment. New York Times, 12 June 2011. www.nytimes.com/2011/06/13/world/asia/13missile.html?_r=0. Accessed 14 June 2012

Sari, A.

2015 Targeting and Detention in Non-International Armed Conflict: Serdar Mohammed and the Limits of Human Rights Convergence. International Law Studies 91. Naval War College, Newport RI, pp. 60–118

2015 IHL does authorize detention in NIAC: A rejoinder to Rogier Bartels. EJIL-talk. http://www.ejiltalk.org/ihl-does-authorize-detention-in-niac-a-rejoinder-to-rogier-bartels. Accessed 12 February 2017

Shaw, M.

2000 International Law, 4th edn. Cambridge University Press, Cambridge

Shaw, T. P.

1999 Arabian Gulf Maritime interception operations: balancing the ends, ways, means and risks. Paper Naval War College, Newport RI

Schmitt, M. N.

2013 Extraterritorial Lethal Targeting: Deconstructing the Logic of International Law. Columbia Journal of Transnational Law 52, pp. 79–114

2008 "Change Direction" 2006: Israeli operations in Lebanon and the International law of self-defense. Michigan Journal of International Law 29:2, pp. 127–164

Schneller, R.

2008 Operation Enduring Freedom. Coalition warfare from the sea and on the sea. In: Elleman B, Paine S (eds) Naval Coalition Warfare. From the Napoleonic war to Operation Iraqi Freedom. Routledge, London, pp. 193–207

2001 Shield and Sword. The United States Navy and the Persian Gulf War. Naval Institute Press, Annapolis MD

Schrijver, N. J.

1994 The Use of Economic Sanctions by the Security Council: An International Law Perspective. In: Post H (ed) International Economic Law and Armed Conflict. Martinus Nijhoff Publishers, Dordrecht, pp. 153–154

Schulman, M. R.

2006 The Proliferation Security Initiative and the evolution of the law on the use of force. Houston Journal of international law, vol. 28 no. 3 (2006), pp. 771–828

Scott, G. M.

2010 Israel's seizure of the Gaza-bound flotilla: applicable laws and legality. Research paper no. 42/2010, Osgoode Hall Law School

Shaw, M. N.

2000 International Law, 4th edn. Cambridge University Press, Cambridge

Smart, S. M.

2015 Maritime interdiction operations. In: Corn G, VanLandingham R, Reeves S, McChrystal S (eds) U.S. Military Operations: Law, Policy, and Practice. Oxford University Pres, New York, pp. 730–777

Smith, H. A.

1950 The law and custom of the sea. 2nd edn. Stevens & Sons Limited, London

Smith-Windsor, B.

2009 Securing the Commons: Towards NATO New Maritime Strategy. Research paper, NATO Defence College 49

Somers, E.

2010 Inleiding tot het internationaal zeerecht. Kluwer, Mechelen

Song, Y.-H.

2007 The U.S.-Led Proliferation Security Initiative and UNCLOS: Legality, implementation, and an assessment. Ocean Development and International Law 38, pp. 101–145

Soons, A. H. A.

2000 A "New" Exception to the Freedom of the High Seas: The Authority of the U.N. Council. In: Gill T, Heere W (eds) Reflections on the Principles and Practice of International Law: Essays in Honour of Leo J. Bouchez. Nijhoff, Dordrecht, pp. 205–211

Staley, R.

1992 The Wave of the Future: The United Nations and naval peacekeeping. International Peace Academy, Occasional Paper series, Boulder CO/London

Stephens, D. G.

2006 Coalition warfare – challenges and opportunities. International Yearbook of Human Rights 36, pp. 17–27

1999 The impact of the 1982 Law of the Sea Convention on the conduct of peacetime naval/military operations. California Western International Law Journal 29:2, pp. 283–311

Stephens, T.

2010 The International Law of the Sea. Hart Publishing Oxford/Portland OR

Stigler, A. L.

2008 Coalition warfare over Kosovo. In: Elleman B, Paine S (eds) Naval coalition warfare. From the Napoleonic War to Operation Iraqi Freedom. Routledge, London, pp. 183–192

Su, J.

2012 The Proliferation Security Initiative (PSI) and Interdiction at Sea: A Chinese Perspective. Ocean Development and International Law 43, pp. 96–118

Suetonius

1957 The twelve Caesars. Graves R (transl.). Penguin Books Inc., Baltimore

Syrigos, A. M.

2006 Development on the interdiction of vessels on the high seas. In: Strati A, Gavouneli M, Skourtos N (eds) Unresolved issues and new challenges to the law of the sea. Time before and time after. Publication on Ocean Development 54, pp. 149–202

Tabori-Szabo, K.

2015 Self-defence and the policy of drone strikes. Journal of Conflict and Security Law 3, pp. 381–413

Tams, C. J.

2015 Non-Flag States as Guardians of the Maritime Order: Creeping Jurisdiction of a Different Kind? In: Ringbom H (ed) Jurisdiction over ships. Brill, Dordrecht, pp. 19–49

Thomas A. R.

1999 Annotated Supplement to the Commander's Handbook on the Law of Naval Operations. International Law Studies 73, Naval War College, Newport RI

Till, G.

2013 Seapower. A guide for the twenty-first century. Routledge, London/ New York

Tondini, M.

2012 The legality of intercepting boat people under search and rescue and border control operations. The Journal of International Maritime Law 12, pp. 59–74

Trapp, K. N.

2015 Can Non-State Actors Mount an Armed Attack? In: Weller M (ed) The Oxford Handbook of the Use of Force in International Law. Oxford University Press, New York, pp. 679–719

Traynor, I.

2011 Libya: NATO defence ministers agree on minimal intervention. Victory for US as agreement to move warships closer to Libya falls far short of measures called for by Britain and France. The Guardian, 10 March 2011. www.guardian.co.uk/world/2011/mar/10/libya-gaddafi-nato-us-minimal-intervention. Accessed 17 February 2017

Treves, T.

2010 Human Rights and the Law of the Sea. Berkeley Journal of International Law 28:1, pp. 1–13

2009 Piracy, laws of the sea, and use of force: Developments off the coast of Somalia. European Journal of International Law 20:2, pp. 399–408

1990 The Rome Convention for the Suppression of Unlawful Acts against the Safety of Maritime Navigation. In: Ronzitti N (ed) Maritime terrorism and international law. Nijhoff, Dordrecht, pp. 69–90

Tripsas, B.

2004 Coast Guard Operations during Operation Iraqi Freedom. Center for Naval Analysis

Tucker, R. W.

1955 The law of war and neutrality at sea. NAVPERS 15031, Government Printing Office, Washington

Van Dyke, J. M.

2004(a) The disappearing right to navigational freedom in the exclusive economic zone. Marine Policy 29, pp. 107–121

2004(b) Balancing Navigational Freedom with Environmental and Security Concerns. Colorado Journal of International Environmental law and Policy 19, pp. 19–28

van Steenberghe, R.

2010 Self-defence in response to attacks by non-state actors in the light of recent state practice: A step forward. Leiden Journal of International Law 23, pp. 183–208

Vego, M. N.

2008 On Naval Power. Joint Force Quarterly 50:3, pp. 8–17

Veridame, G.

2015 Proliferation of weapons of mass destruction and shipping interdiction. In: Weller M (ed) The Oxford Handbook of the Use of Force in International Law. Oxford University Press, New York, pp. 1017–1033

Verkroost, P.

2011 Juridische aspecten van de Nederlandse deelname aan anti-piraterij operaties rondom de Hoorn van Afrika. Militair Rechtelijk Tijdschrift, vol. 104:1, pp. 9–26

Vervliet, J.

2009 General Introduction. In: Grotius H (1609) Mare Liberum. Brill, Leiden/Boston

Voetelink, J. E. D.

2013 De status van militaire Vessel Protection Detachments. Militair Rechtelijk Tijdschrift 106, pp. 41–53

2013 Militair operationeel recht. Wolff Legal Publishers, Oisterwijk

Walker, G. K.

2009 Self-defense, the law of armed conflict and port security. South Carolina Journal of International Law and Business, 5:2, pp. 347–410

Waxman, M. C.

2013 Regulating resort to force: Form and substance of the UN Charter regime. European Journal of International Law 24:1, pp. 151–189

Weijne, J. E.

2002 De bijdrage van de Koninklijke Marine aan de strijd tegen het terrorisme. Marineblad, May 2002, pp. 149–154

Weingarter, J.

2007 Das Unifil-mandat der Bundeswehr – politische und rechtliche Aspekte. Journal of International Law of Peace and Armed Conflict, 20:2, pp. 116–119

Weller, M.

1993 The United Nations and the Ius ad Bellum. In: Rowe P (ed) The Gulf War 1990–1991 in International and English Law. Routledge, London, pp. 29–54

Wendel, P.

2007 State Responsibility for Interferences with the Freedom of Navigation in public international law. Hamburg Studies on Maritime Affairs 11 Springer Berlin/Heidelberg

Westra, J. H.

2007 International Law and the Use of Armed Force. Routledge, London/New York

Williams, D.

2014 Israel seizes arms shipment. www.reuters.com/article/us-israel-gaza-ship-idUSBREA240X720140305. Accessed 22 March 2017

Wilson, B.

2016 The complex nature of today's maritime security issues. Why whole-of-government frameworks matter. In: Krause J, Bruns S (eds) Routledge Handbook on naval strategy and security. Taylor & Francis Group, London/New York, pp. 153–165

Wilson, D. G.

2008 Interdiction on the high seas: The role and authority of a master in the boarding and searching of his ship by foreign warships. Naval Law Review 55, pp. 170–185

Windsor-Smith, B.

2009 Securing the Commons. Towards NATO's New Maritime Strategy. Research paper, NATO Defense College, Rome

Wirtz, J. J.

2009 Introduction. In: Wirtz J, Larsen J (eds) Naval Peacekeeping and humanitarian operations. Stability from the sea. Routledge, London/New York, pp. 1–13

Wright, R.

2004 Ship Incident May Have Swayed Libya. Washington Post, 1 January 2004

Yong-Joong Lee, E.

2007 Legal Analysis of the 2006 U.N. Security Council Resolutions Against North Korea's WMD Development. Fordham International Law Journal 31:1, pp. 1–33

Yoshihara, T.

2016 Chinese views of the U.S.-led maritime order. In: Krause J, Bruns S (eds) Handbook on naval strategy and security. Routledge, New York, pp. 351–363

Zeigler, R. D.

1996 Ubi Sumus? Quo Vadimus? Charting the Course of Maritime Interception Operations. Naval Law Review 43, pp. 1–55

Zheng, H.

2012 Confidence Building Measures and Non-Traditional Security. In: Dutton P, Ross R, Tunsjo O (eds) Twenty-First Century Seapower. Cooperation and Conflict at Sea. Taylor & Francis Group, London/New York, pp. 298–314

Zwanenburg, M. C.

2014 Enkele juridische aspecten van militaire beveiligingsteams aan boord van koopvaardijschepen (Vessel Protection Detachments). Militair Rechtelijk Tijdschrift 107:6, pp. 205–218

(Selected) Other Materials

International Organizations

Combined Maritime Forces

- CMF press release, 24 March 2013, HMS Monmouth conducts Maritime Approach and Assist operations

European Union

- EU Council decision 2008/918/CFSP, 8 December 2008
- EU Council Joint Action (CJA) 2008/851/CFSP
- EU Maritime Strategy (EUMS) (2015)

- JOIN(2014) 9 final, Brussels, 6.3.2014. Joint communication to the European Parliament and the council for an open and secure global maritime domain: elements for a European Union maritime security strategy
- Press release, European Commission, 'Towards an EU integrated approach to global maritime security', Brussels 6 March 2014

NATO

- *NATO* Briefing paper, Active Endeavour, July 2006
- NATO Factsheet (2011), Operation UNIFIED PROTECTOR NATO Arms Embargo against Libya
- NATO Factsheet (October 2011), Operation UNIFIED PROTECTOR NATO-led Arms Embargo against Libya
- Allied joint maritime operations (AJP 3.3)
- Allied tactical publication (ATP) 71. *Allied maritime interdiction operations* (2005)
- Allied tactical publication (ATP) 71. *Allied maritime interdiction operations* (2013)
- Allied Maritime Strategy (2011)
- NATO press release 124, 12 September 2011

United Nations

- A/HRC/3/2, Report of the commission of inquiry on Lebanon pursuant to Human Rights Council resolution S-2/1, 23 November 2006
- A/HRC/51/21, Report of the international fact-finding mission to investigate violations of international law, including international humanitarian and human rights law, resulting from the Israeli attacks on the flotilla of ships carrying humanitarian assistance (27 September 2010)
- Report of the Secretary-General's Panel of inquiry on the 31 May 2010 Flotilla incident (September 2011)
- UN blue book series, volume IX, United Nations and the Iraq-Kuwait Conflict (1990–1996), 1996

National Materials

Israel

The Public Commission to Examine the Maritime Incident of 31 May 2010 (Turkel Commission)

The Netherlands

- *Kamerstukken II*, no. 29 521, 131, 7 January 2010
- Ministerie van Defensie, Eindevaluatie UNIFIL Maritiem, 25 April 2008
- Ministerie van Defensie, Eindevaluatie CTF 150, 18 September 2006

- Ministerie van Defensie, Grondslagen van het maritiem optreden (2014)
- Ministerie van Defensie, Leidraad maritiem optreden (2005)
- National Archives, Londense Archief, GA/JUZA, no. 1328. Letter of the Netherlands Commander of the Naval Forces, J. Th. Furstner to the Minister of Defence, London 17 September 1940, no. S. 200/27/3

United Kingdom

- BR 1806 (2004) British Maritime Doctrine, 3rd edn, The Stationary Office, Norwich
- UK Ministry of Defence. UK Manual on the Law of Armed Conflict (Oxford University Press, New York, 2005)

United States

- Joint Publication 3-03, 14 October 2011
- Joint Publication 3-32, 7 August 2013
- National Strategy for Maritime Security (2005)
- US Department of defense, press release, no. NR-126-14; March 17, 2014, DoD Statement on Boarding of Commercial Tanker Morning Glory
- US Navy press release, Ramage VBSS team conducts 100th Approach and assist visit

Index

M. Fink, *Maritime Interception and the Law of Naval Operations*,
https://doi.org/10.1007/978-94-6265-249-1

MIX
Papier aus verantwortungsvollen Quellen
Paper from responsible sources
FSC® C105338

If you have any concerns about our products,
you can contact us on
ProductSafety@springernature.com

In case Publisher is established outside the EU,
the EU authorized representative is:
Springer Nature Customer Service Center GmbH
Europaplatz 3, 69115 Heidelberg, Germany

Printed by Libri Plureos GmbH
in Hamburg, Germany